MW00979464

The Fortifications of Arkadian City States in the Classical and Hellenistic Periods

MATTHEW P. MAHER

Great Clarendon Street, Oxford, OX2 6DP,
United Kingdom

Oxford University Press is a department of the University of Oxford.
It furthers the University's objective of excellence in research, scholarship,
and education by publishing worldwide. Oxford is a registered trade mark of
Oxford University Press in the UK and in certain other countries

First Edition published in 2017

Impression: 1

Published in the United States of America by Oxford University Press
198 Madison Avenue, New York, NY 10016, United States of America

British Library Cataloguing in Publication Data

Data available

Library of Congress Control Number: 2017932071

ISBN 978–0–19–878659–7

Printed and bound by
CPI Group (UK) Ltd, Croydon, CR0 4YY

Contents

Contents

List of Figures

List of Tables

Introduction

The earliest scholarship on ancient Arkadia, perhaps echoing a view held by the ancient Greeks themselves, focused on the idea of the region as a cultural and political backwater, inhabited by the proverbial 'acorn eaters'.[1] This was certainly the view held in the early twentieth century and one that, despite much recent scholarship, unfortunately persists to some extent into the early twenty-first century present day.[2] Fortunately, beginning in the 1980s, there has been a fundamental evolution in the theoretical assumptions and general disciplinary predispositions that dominated earlier Arkadian scholarship. This evolution is characterized by a move away from traditional stereotypical interpretations of a poor and isolated Arkadia towards a view of a moderately prosperous region whose inhabitants generally followed the same patterns of social, political, and cultural development seen elsewhere in ancient Greece.[3]

Historical and archaeological research focusing specifically on Arkadian issues has received a great deal of scholarly attention in the last three decades. One has only to consider the comprehensive and thorough inventory of Arkadian sanctuaries and religious traditions by Jost,[4] or the attention given to individual temples such as Apollo's at Bassai[5] or Athena Alea's at Tegea,[6] to appreciate the extent of this research. Nor has the study of Arkadian *poleis*,[7] inscriptions, or numismatics[8] been neglected. Archaeological interest in the region has led to scholarly investigations with a focus on topics as diverse and specific as road networks,[9] individual buildings,[10] ceramics,[11] the economy,[12] settlement patterns,[13] and archaeological survey.[14] This short review provides

---

[1] Hdt. 1.66; Nielsen (2002: 11).

[2] e.g., 'Arcadia . . . was marginal in terms of its cultural development and its relative lack of city-states' (Hunt 1998: 197, n. 1).

[3] Nielsen and Roy (1999: 12–13).   [4] Jost (1985, 1994).   [5] Cooper (1996).

[6] Norman (1984); Østby (1994; 2014a; 2014b); Pakkanen (1998, 2005); Tarditi (2005).

[7] Roy (1972, 1996); Jost (1973); Nielsen (1996a, 1996b, 1996c, 2002).

[8] Head (1963: 418, 444–56).   [9] e.g., Pikoulas (1992–3, 1995, 1999a, 1999b).

[10] e.g., Cooper (1972).   [11] e.g., Cracolici (2005);Voyatzis (2005).

[12] e.g., Roy (1999).   [13] e.g., Jost (1999).

[14] e.g., Howell (1970); Forsén and Forsén (2003); Cracolici (2005); Bakke (2010).

an overview, but it must be noted that it does not exhaust the amount of quality research being conducted in Arkadia, much of which will be explored in greater detail in the chapters to follow. There is, however, one area of interest that has not received extensive scholarly attention: the study of Arkadian fortifications. While it is true that the fortifications of some Arkadian settlements have been thoroughly documented and studied (e.g. Gortys,[15] Stymphalos,[16] Theisoa [Lavda],[17] and, most recently, Pheneos[18]), such studies are often undertaken as part of the investigation of a specific site, with little concern for the fortifications in their own right, their relation to the natural topography, or for any interregional comparison. In any case, even these examples are in the minority. What is in the majority are those sites where information is either scant or lacking altogether.[19] In the case of these neglected sites, we often have to rely on a combination of descriptions left to us by Pausanias, early modern travel writers, extremely outdated or merely tentative plans, or descriptions in general reference works. In some cases we must be thankful to have any of these at our disposal, as they remain our only sources of information. The fact remains that there is much room for an updated regional study focusing on Arkadian fortifications.

To the detriment of the discipline, the study of fortifications has been neglected in classical archaeology. There are several oft-cited reasons for this; for example, that fortifications are frustratingly difficult to date; that the often meagre remains have little interest from the art-historical point of view; or that personal observation is a prerequisite for their study.[20] Although the usual repeated reasons are understandable, they are not insurmountable or altogether justified. The lack of a precise date does not completely negate their value as a historic source, and their relative lack of value from the art-historical point of view is irrelevant. Finally, the fact that fieldwork on the ground is an essential component in the study of walls should not deter their study, but encourage it. After all, unlike many other artefacts, 'the provenience of a wall is rarely an issue; they tend to stay where they were put and that immutability makes them unique among Greek artifacts'.[21] While additional reasons are addressed in Chapter 2, there are two primary reasons why fortifications should receive more scholarly attention: not only do they often form the most conspicuous remains surviving on the surface today, but the construction of city walls both reflected and protected a city's autonomy, and as such they are a fundamental characteristic of the *polis* itself.[22]

[15] Martin (1947–8).	[16] Gourley and Williams (2005).	[17] Feije (1994).
[18] Giannakopoulos et al. (2012); Kissas et al. (2014).	[19] Jost (1999: 192).
[20] Winter (1971a: p. ix); Camp (2000: 41).	[21] Camp (2000: 41).
[22] While it is true that a fortification circuit does not equal a *polis* in every case, 'a fortification wall around the urban centre is one of the features commonly connected with the concept of the *polis*' (Hansen 1995: 9). This point is addressed in greater detail in Chapter 1.

AIMS

The overall objective of the following study is a comprehensive and detailed survey of the historical development of Greek military architecture and defensive planning specifically in Arkadia from the Classical period to the Roman arrival in Greece. The word survey here does not denote simply a cataloguing of extant defensive works, although that is an important part of the study.[23] Instead, it is meant to include meaningful archaeological and historical syntheses in which a number of related elements will be addressed.[24] The objectives of the present study were attainable only through the comprehensive understanding of the fortifications of every Arkadian *polis*—an understanding that is, of course, reached through the examination of the city walls at the individual site level. The fortification data collected at individual sites as well as the larger patterns revealed through their comparison are applied to meet five primary objectives. Broadly speaking, these objectives include: (1) an accurate chronology of the walls in question; (2) an understanding of the relationship between the fortifications and the local topography; (3) a detailed catalogue of all the fortified *poleis* of Arkadia; (4) a regional synthesis based on this catalogue; and (5) the probable historical reasons behind the patterns observed through the regional synthesis. In the end, a picture of the different fortifications characteristic of Arkadia from an architectural, topographical, and historical point of view will be truly comprehensive only if all these stated objectives are met. As stated in the introduction of his book *Greek Fortifications*, Winter tells us that he does not expect his work to be revolutionary nor to be necessarily at odds with the prevailing scholarship.[25] I would like to echo such sentiments here. Although the present study comprises an original piece of research in the field of Arkadian archaeology, the primary objective in this regard is to fill in the large gap in our knowledge of Arkadian fortifications.

SOURCES AND EVIDENCE

Although it has been argued that, owing to the increasing interest in Arkadian research, this area now represents a 'well-illuminated region',[26] piecing together a comprehensive understanding of its general history remains a complicated task.[27] For instance, while Callmer's *Studien zur Geschichte Arkadiens bis zur*

---

[23] Detailed information on the fornications of every Arkadian *polis* is presented in Part Two, the Catalogue.

[24] See Chapter 4 for the topographical, architectural, and historical analyses.

[25] Winter (1971a: p. xvii).   [26] Nielsen and Roy (1999: 13).

[27] Jost (1999: 192). What follows is a brief summary of the sources employed in the present study and is not meant to be exhaustive. In the following chapters and then Part Two, the

Gründung des arkadischen Bundes can be said to be the first modern attempt
at a history of Arkadia, it is really concerned only with the period of Spartan
dominance, and, as the title suggests, the work ends before the foundation of
Megalopolis.[28] Roy's *Studies in the History of Arcadia in the Classical and
Hellenistic Periods* picks up the story in the fifth century BC, largely omitting
events of the Archaic period.[29] Even Nielsen's *Arkadia and its Poleis in the
Archaic and Classical Periods* (certainly the most up to date and arguably the
most comprehensive) is selective in its coverage, essentially excluding events
after 323 BC.[30] This short review illustrates the fact that an understanding of
the history of Arkadia cannot be found in a single all-inclusive composition
and, instead, must be sought in a variety of specific studies, aimed at its
constituent parts. Research of the region's fortifications is no different in
this respect and requires the collection and integration of evidence from a
number of different sources. These sources, taken from the spheres of both
history and archaeology, are as extensive and diverse as the evidence itself but
can be broadly categorized here under the headings of ancient literature,
historical scholarship, archaeological scholarship (including topographical
studies and travel writing), scholarship pertaining to ancient Greek fortifications in general, and personal observation.[31]

To meet the objectives of the study, the ancient sources employed are
primarily those by authors who have had occasion to mention specifics
regarding the historical events surrounding the fortified Arkadian *poleis* in
the chronological period under investigation—authors such as Herodotus,
Thucydides, Xenophon, Aeneas Tacticus, Polybius, Strabo, Diodorus, Plutarch,
and Pausanias. Immediately conspicuous by his absence from this list is Philo
of Byzantium. Although his *Poliorketika* is an important primary source for
the study of Greek fortifications, this treatise was written around the middle of
the third century BC, and so falls largely outside the chronological scope of this
study.[32] In any event, this list represents only a selection of the ancient sources
employed and is not intended to be comprehensive.

Archaeological and historical investigations focusing specifically on Arkadian
subject matter have received a great deal of scholarly attention since the 1980s.
Although this literature varies in regards to its immediate relevance to Arkadian
fortifications specifically, it has a significant bearing on the overall history
of Arkadia, and, thus, the contextual history of individual fortification circuits.
In addition to the works of Roy, Nielsen, and Callmer already cited, general

---

Catalogue, the sources and associated evidence are explored in detail on a site per site basis.
A detailed bibliography for each site is presented in the chapters in Part Two.

[28] Callmer (1943).   [29] Roy (1968).   [30] Nielsen (2002).

[31] As well as being a source of evidence for the sites in question, personal observation is
inherently a methodological approach, and is addressed as such below under Methodology.

[32] For an English translation and commentary on the *Poliorketika*, see Lawrence (1979:
69–107).

Arkadian historical scholarship concerning religion, the *polis*, and the economy are also utilized to gain insight into both the contextual history of each site and, by association, its fortifications. While the ancient sources and modern historical analyses are crucial elements, it is the evidence derived from personal observation and archaeological sources that comprises the majority of the data employed in this book. The archaeological evidence is drawn from surveys and excavation reports on individual Arkadian sites (and often their fortifications), the written accounts of early modern travellers in Greece, topographic works, and epigraphic, numismatic, ceramic, and, of course, general fortification scholarship.

PREVIOUS RESEARCH ON GREEK FORTIFICATIONS

Scholarly interest in the fortifications of mainland Greece can be traced in the literature as far back as the early nineteenth century—a time when the sites and antiquities of a newly independent Greece were viewed with a renewed appreciation by West European travellers. While the fortifications of the sites they encountered were admittedly not their primary concern (nor were they Pausanias', in whose footsteps many of them followed), the walls could not be ignored, because they were often the most conspicuous remains on the surface. Thus, even if their classifications of architectural details were imperfect, writers such as Dodwell, Leake, and Gell have left us important observations about the walls of several sites from which we may learn something about the remains at the time.[33] More scientific in its approach was the French *Expédition de Morée*.[34] Again, however, although the publications from this scientific/military expedition contain accurate and detailed measurements of the ruins encountered, the interest was largely in architecture and ancient engineering and not the historical development of Greek fortification circuits.[35] Finally, around the middle of the century there appeared a prodigious output of geographical and historical studies of Greece led largely by German, British, and French travellers and scholars such as Ross, Curtius, Rangabé, Clark, Busian, Wyse, and Welcker.[36] Their works, like those already cited, were not primarily concerned with fortifications specifically, and, when city walls are mentioned, the descriptions generally conform to the early disciplinary tendency regarding the study of Greek fortifications, which stressed observation rather than architectural development or historical contextualization.

---

[33] Dodwell (1819, 1834); Leake (1830); Gell (1831).
[34] On Arkadia, see Boblaye (1836: 137–68).   [35] Winter (1971a: p. xiii).
[36] Ross (1841); Curtius (1851); Rangabé (1857); Clark (1858); Bursian (1862); Wyse (1865); Welcker (1865).

It was not until the late nineteenth and early twentieth century that Greek fortifications received more than passing scholarly interest as a derivative of larger topographic projects and began to mature into an independent field of study. We see arguably the first survey of fortifications focused on the more theoretical aspects concerning form and function with *Principes de la fortification antique* by d'Aiglun, published in 1881. That is not to say, however, that topographical works did not continue to contribute significantly in this regard. In fact, one of the most useful works for the present purposes is Frazer's unparalleled commentary *Pausanias' Description of Greece* published in 1898 in six weighty volumes. Not only did the author cover an incredibly large area, usually providing accurate descriptions of the architecture and of the nature of the terrain traversed by the walls, but he carefully traced as much of a circuit wall as possible, and this perhaps 'made him more aware than others [before him] of strategic considerations'.[37] Another valuable early topographic source for the study of Greek fortifications (especially Arkadian ones) is Hiller von Gaertringen and Lattermann's *Arkadische Forschungen* published in 1911. As well as providing useful plates and measurements of certain Arkadian circuits based on their own observations, the authors, in a move that was indicative of the evolving disciplinary tendency, often attempt to understand the strategic importance of the walls by placing them in their proper historical context.

While scholarship in the first half of the twentieth century continued to emphasize architectural details, including accurate descriptions of masonry styles and their stylistic relationships, the study of Greek fortifications was still plagued by the problem of differing terminology.[38] It was not until 1941, with the appearance of Scranton's *Greek Walls*, that the problem of terminology was 'finally reduced to a reasonably ordered system'.[39] This work is primarily a chronological study with the specific aim of developing a sequence of masonry styles, and little attention is given to larger defensive considerations. Nonetheless, its scope and attention to detail confirm the fact that this work represents more than just an 'introductory phase'[40] of the discipline, as Scranton humbly maintains, but is instead a landmark publication in the study of Greek fortifications—a study that would reach its maturity three decades later.

From Dodwell to Scranton, the first hundred years of the study of Greek fortifications evolved from passing scholarly interest based on observation with minimal description (often indistinguishable from larger topographic

[37] Winter (1971a: pp. xiii–xiv). If this was not enough of a contribution, it is important to note that in many cases Frazer's descriptions of the walls of certain sites remain today the only detailed published account.
[38] Frazer and Dodwell, for example, employed their own different classification systems.
[39] Winter (1971a: p. xv). The traditional styles of masonry have since been refined by others. The problems with using masonry style for dating purposes are addressed in Chapter 2.
[40] Scranton (1941: 5).

studies) to an independent discipline regulated by proper archaeological standards.[41] Yet, all these earlier works tended to concentrate on purely architectural details of the walls in their present fragmentary state, and there seemed to be little interest in the larger picture. It was not until 1971 and the publication of Winter's *Greek Fortifications* that this apparent lack of interest was finally confronted. In his attempt to pull all of the pieces together to form a better understanding of the basic principles of design for a given circuit and ultimately the larger contextual picture, Winter combines the earlier disciplinary tendencies of topographical observation, detailed measurements, and masonry styles with complementary considerations given to choice of site, natural resources, water supply, and historical circumstance. A crucial component of the work deals with the more theoretical and strategic aspects of Greek walls, including the form, function, and placement of their constituent parts. While such considerations may today seem an obvious part of any study concerning military architecture, at the time it represented an innovative approach and one that remains influential.

Although Winter's *Greek Fortifications* remains the seminal work on the subject, the discipline has not been idle in the forty-five years since its publication.[42] Of note is Lawrence's *Greek Aims in Fortification* published in 1979. Like Winter before him, Lawrence explores the development of the different components of city walls across the Greek world, the construction techniques involved in building them, the historical circumstances behind their necessity, and their evolution in response to technological innovation. Furthermore, other now (or soon to be) standard handbooks in the discipline are Adam's *L'Architecture militaire greque* published in 1982, McNicoll's *Hellenistic Fortifications: From the Aegean to the Euphrates* published posthumously in 1997, and, most recently, Frederiksen's *Greek City Walls of the Archaic Period* published in 2011. What all these works hold in common is their general Panhellenic focus. From the Greek mainland to Asia Minor and from Italy to the Near East, until relatively recently, one characteristic of the discipline was an attempt to trace, categorize, and classify Greek military architecture in all its guises throughout the Mediterranean. But perhaps, in Typaldou-Fakiris's *Villes fortifiées de Phocide. Et la 3ᵉ guerre sacrée (356–346 J.C.)* published in 2004, and the 2013 book *Défenses crétoises: Fortifications urbaines et défense du territoire en Crète aux époques classique et hellénistique* by Coutsinas, we are witnessing the continued evolution of the discipline.

---

[41] There are a number of other more modern works that are also the products of first-hand observation, and, although they contribute little to the study of fortifications specifically, are equally valuable for the present study: e.g., Pritchett (1969, 1989), Howell (1970), Jost (1985), and Papachatzis (1994), and all have occasion to mention and describe to some degree the fortifications of various Arkadian *poleis*.

[42] For a detailed summary of the work during the early part of this period, see Winter (1982).

Besides this present work, Typaldou-Fakiris's study of the fortifications of Phokis and Coutsinas's book on Cretan fortifications remain the only studies concerning fortifications in Greece conducted within a regional scope. Such an approach has the potential to shed light on a number of issues. Instead of searching for Panhellenic patterns, perhaps the disciplinary focus should be narrowed to the individual site in a given region. Indeed, in the early 1940s Scranton maintained that 'the most valuable contributions have been made in the form of monographs on individual sites',[43] and, similarly, Winter believes that 'the advantages of studying a single site . . . was demonstrated by Martin's work on the walls of Gortys in Arkadia'.[44] Although the focus of the present research is the region of Arkadia, it is ultimately the study of the individual sites that comprised this area.

ARKADIAN REGIONAL FOCUS

In his landmark study of the walls at Gortys published in the 1940s, Martin wrote that a comprehensive study of a given fortification circuit should consider not only the architecture, history, and historical probability, but also the 'histoire des enceintes de la même région, classées en séries typologiques et chronologiques'.[45] More recently, Camp has echoed this view, writing that, where the study of fortifications is concerned, 'there are instances where . . . we should actually think in terms of regional or local styles of wall-building'.[46] Although it appears that the advantages of studying fortifications on a regional level have long been recognized, little has been done to advance the discipline in this regard. While there are to my knowledge only two other studies concerning fortifications in Greece that have been conducted within a regional scope,[47] an exclusively regional focus has the potential to shed light on a number of issues, not least the possibility of adding support to the identification of local Arkadian fortification patterns. It is a well-established and common practice in archaeology to recognize regional styles, whether they be in ceramics, fine arts, letter-forms, or architecture,[48] and to utilize these styles for chronological purposes or for the identification of imported/exported influences; it follows that the same might hold true of fortifications.[49]

It might be asked, why Arkadia? Ultimately, a regional survey of fortifications in Arkadia will go a long way not only to complement the existing archaeological

---

[43] Scranton (1941: 9).   [44] Winter (1971a: p. xvi).   [45] Martin (1947–8: 120).
[46] Camp (2000: 44).   [47] See Typaldou-Fakiris (2004); Coutsinas (2013).
[48] e.g., Winter (2005) has tentatively demonstrated a regional style for Arkadian Doric temple architecture.
[49] Camp (2000: 44).

data but also to supplement the growing interests in landscape studies both within our discipline and in ancient Arkadia itself. Moreover, a review of the existing literature regarding individual Arkadian *poleis* has demonstrated that, while much proficient but wide-ranging historical scholarship—largely under the auspices of the Copenhagen Polis Centre (CPC)—has appeared relatively recently, there is much work to be done concerning the archaeology on the individual site level. Estimates vary based on the selection criteria used, but there are between thirty-five and forty-five Arkadian sites (most of which could be considered *poleis*) known to have existed between the Archaic and the Hellenistic periods.[50] Only a handful of these sites, however, have received any satisfactory scholarship, and even fewer have received it after the middle of the twentieth century. An understanding of the fortifications on an individual site level is crucial, as it provides the data from which larger regional patterns may be drawn. This book also presents the city walls of every fortified Arkadian *polis* to supplement the continuing collection of Greek mainland comparanda.

The value of the local comparanda that can be obtained in a regional study is a significant point and one that is often overlooked. The comparanda most often employed in the studies of Greek fortifications are dictated both by their preservation and by the relative historical importance of the site. From the Greek mainland, for example, the reader is constantly confronted with comparisons drawn from well-preserved and 'important' fortifications from sites such as Athens, Messene, Tiryns, Mycenae, Corinth, and Eleusis. That this present work presents the detailed analysis of every fortified *polis*—many of which may be relatively unknown outside Arkadian scholarship—is precisely what makes their individual study important. In other words, it is the fortifications of these modest settlements which are representative of the majority, and thus, by default, the average Greek *polis*. For the same reason, the comparanda employed in this survey are limited largely (though not exclusively) to other Arkadian sites, with which they will have more in common than other, more distant sites whose walls are notable only because of their preservation or because the city is historically well known.

CHRONOLOGICAL RANGE

It is important to remember that it is the chronology of the construction of the fortifications specifically and not the date of the foundation of the *polis* that is most significant for the present purposes. Thus, although the Archaic period

---

[50] These estimates are derived from Nielsen (2002: 549–601, app. IX).

witnessed the foundation of a number of settlements and *poleis* in Arkadia, the development of significant urban centres was a phenomenon of the Classical period[51]—and it is here that we must search to observe the dawn of the fortified *polis* in Arkadia.[52] Therefore, while fourth- and third-century BC fortifications are certainly well represented in Arkadia, and as such will form the bulk of this study, it is the late fifth century that represents the *terminus post quem* for the present purposes.[53]

At the opposite end of the spectrum, it seems undeniable that the *polis* did not disappear forever in the summer of 338 BC with the allied Greek defeat at Chaironeia;[54] or, if '[it] did in any way mark the end of the *polis*, this was not noticed in Arkadia'.[55] True, the century before that fateful day witnessed the slow decline of the independent city state; first, during the second half of the fifth century BC as many *poleis* joined the great hegemonic leagues (for example, Peloponnesian and Delian); and, second, during the late fifth and fourth centuries BC as they became members of the regionally based federal states (for example, in Boiotia, Phokis, Lokris, Euboia, Thessaly, Epeiros, Aitolia, Akarnania, Achaia, and Arkadia).[56] What actually disappeared with the rise of Macedon, therefore, was not the *polis*, but the hegemonic *polis* (such as Athens, Sparta, and Thebes).[57] In the true meaning of the word, as a small political community of citizens living in an urban centre and responsible for its own political institutions, the *polis* appears not only to have survived the end of the Classical period, but to have existed and prospered throughout the Hellenistic period.[58]

While acknowledging that Hansen is correct in his assertion that the Greek *polis* continued to flourish into the Hellenistic period (as suggested, for example, by the founding of several new *poleis* at this time), Camp maintains that 'essentially the *polis* ends in the middle years of the second century BC, with the Roman conquests of Greece'.[59] Camp admits that, although hundreds of *poleis* continued to exist after 146 BC, some of them for centuries to come, effectively no new city states were founded in Greece after this period.[60] Underlying this conviction is his belief that fortification walls are the domain of *poleis*, and, since the construction of walls ends in the mid-second century BC, then the *polis* too must end in this same period. Whether city walls were no longer necessary or because the 'polis was now only a fossilized remnant [and] no longer a creative phenomenon',[61] it is clear that there are no fortifications

---

[51] Jost (1999: 203).
[52] In his comprehensive study of Greek fortifications in Archaic period, Frederiksen (2011: 176) records the city of Oresthasion as the only fortified Arkadian site from this period. Still, this identification is uncertain, based solely on the observation of a small fragment of wall by Pikoulas (1988: 102). See the Appendix for more information on Oresthasion.
[53] Jost (1999: 203).   [54] Hansen (1993: 21).   [55] Nielsen (1996a: 142).
[56] Hansen (1993: 21).   [57] Hansen (1993: 21).   [58] Hansen (1993: 21).
[59] Camp (2000: 50).   [60] Camp (2000: 50); cf. Lawrence (1979: 111).
[61] Camp (2000: 50).

in Arkadia that should be dated after the Roman conquest of Greece. The destruction of Corinth in 146 BC, therefore, provides an appropriate *terminus ante quem* for the chronological scope of this book.

LIMITATIONS OF THE STUDY

Before exploring the methodology employed, it is necessary to provide a brief word about the limitations of the study and about the themes that, although related, lie beyond the scope of the present work. There are two associated areas of study that are immediately notable by their absence: Arkadian territorial defences and the fortification of the *poleis* of Triphylia. Although the study of known Arkadian extra urban military installations would certainly contribute to the overall understanding of a *polis*'s territorial boundaries and defence of its *chora*, it would not significantly contribute to the overall focus of this book—that is, the fortifications of Arkadian *poleis* themselves. Moreover, because personal observation comprised a crucial methodological component, the time and resources required to visit every such known site, in addition to the numerous *poleis* under investigation here, were simply beyond the means of the author at the present time.[62]

It was partly this same combination of methodological considerations, scope, and resources that is responsible for the omission of Triphylian fortifications. Again, there were limitations because of the importance of personal observation and the time required to conduct appropriate and thorough investigations; but it could also be argued that the *poleis* of Triphylia, although technically Arkadian, are beyond the range of a study focusing on 'original' Arkadian settlements. As a subregion (or tribe), Triphylia was not incorporated into Arkadia until the early fourth century BC, at which time it had fully formed *poleis* and associated fortification works. Any attempt to discern regional patterns in regards to the fortifications, therefore, would be unproductive. Finally, it should also be noted that Triphylia remained a part of Arkadia for only a short time, reverting to Elian hands during the second half of the third century BC.[63]

The state of preservation of the remains of the fortifications also imposes a number of limitations on the present work. Although enough of the walls often exist to deduce their original course with a high degree of accuracy, very rarely do the foundations of the circuits of Arkadian *poleis* exist in their

---

[62] On extra-urban military installations in Arkadia, see Pikoulas (1984, 1990–1b, 1991; 1995: 27–8, 244–55, 332–46; 1999c); Tausend (1998a, 1999b); Topouzi et al. (2000, 2002); Tausend and Tausend (2014: 23–5); Maher and Mowat (forthcoming).

[63] Nielsen (1997: 152). On the *poleis* of Triphylia, see Nielsen (1997; 2002: 603–12).

entirety. Similarly, as the population of many *poleis* inhabited unfortified areas—relying on a nearby fortified acropolis as a refuge in case of emergencies only—determining the extent of these extramural settlements is difficult without intensive archaeological survey. For these reasons, attempting to reconstruct the population size, and by association the available manpower to build and/or patrol the different circuits, would be a futile exercise and is, therefore, not attempted. Furthermore, owing to the limited preservation (and lack of excavation) characteristic of many Arkadian city walls, precise architectural details and the methods of internal construction are often unavailable. For instance, as the superstructure does not survive from any of the circuits in question, reconstructions of the original heights of the different city walls would be largely conjectural, and are thus also not provided in the majority of cases. That being said, some general observations are possible.

Although Frederiksen is certainly correct in his assertion that 'the height of the wall depends on the width',[64] there is still no exact proportional formula on which we might rely. Furthermore, if Frederiksen is correct in his opinion that Archaic city walls probably averaged around 6 m in height,[65] it follows then that, as a response to the widespread use of artillery, the curtains employed in Classical and Hellenistic period fortifications should be taller. How much taller is difficult to determine and depends on both the archaeological evidence and surviving comparanda. As the best-preserved fortification circuit in the Peloponnese, and one that is contemporary to many of the Arkadian systems comprising this study, the walls of Messene perhaps provide the best comparanda.[66] The height of the early fourth-century BC curtains at Messene is between 7 and 9 m.[67] Regarding archaeological evidence, in his study of the Arkadian city of Gortys, Martin hypothesizes about the original height of the curtain by cleverly reconstructing a stairway that probably once led to the wall-walk (that is, the internal height of the curtain). Basing his calculation on cuttings indicating the width and height of the lowest steps and knowing the length of the base of the stairway, he determined that a wall-walk at a height of *c.*6.75 m would have been required to accommodate the calculated twenty-five steps.[68] Employing a discovered parapet block in his reconstruction, Martin determined that the external face of the wall (to the top of the parapet) would have measured 8.25–8.50 m in height.[69] Here we see Martin's proposed height for the walls of Gortys falls within the range for the height of the early fourth-century BC curtains at Messene. Thus, while

---

[64] Frederiksen (2011: 95).   [65] Frederiksen (2011: 95).
[66] Also significant in this regard is the fact that the walls of Messene, Megalopolis, and Mantineia (and perhaps others in Arkadia) were constructed together as part of a larger Theban defensive initiative. For a concise summary of the chronological arguments regarding the circuit at Messene, see Ober (1987: 573, n. 14).
[67] Fields (2006: 35).   [68] Martin (1947–8: 112–13).
[69] Martin (1947–8: 113). The towers, of course, would be taller still.

acknowledging that circuits and towers might vary slightly in height throughout a given circuit (as strategy and/or the topography demanded), until future excavations change or modify the picture, it is I think safe to assume a height averaging between 7 and 9 m for the curtains of the fortified Arkadian *poleis*.[70]

METHODOLOGY

Simply stated, for a site to be included in this study it must have satisfied only two conditions: that the settlement was an Arkadian *polis* and that it possessed a fortification circuit to some extent.[71] Discounting the *poleis* of Triphylia, between the Archaic and Hellenistic periods there are no fewer than thirty-three known Arkadian sites whose existence is testified to in either the ancient literary, archaeological, or epigraphic record.[72] When those sites without fortifications or whose location and/or *polis* status is suspect are removed, the list is reduced to only nineteen candidates appropriate for this study:

Alea	Kynaitha*	Stymphalos
Alipheira	Mantineia	Tegea*
Asea	Megalopolis	Teuthis
Bouphagion*	Methydrion*	Thaliades*
Brenthe*	Nestane	Theisoa (Lavda)
Dipaia	Orchomenos	Theisoa (Karkalou)
Eutaia*	Oresthasion*	Thelphousa*
Halous	Pallantion*	Torthyneion*
Heraia*	Paos	Trapezous*[73]
Kaphyai*	Pheneos	
Kleitor	Phigaleia	
Gortys	Psophis	

[70] Although they provided a different function, the isolated signal towers in the *chora* of Mantineia have been reconstructed to a height of 8 m (Pikoulas 1990–1a: 251; Topouzi et al. (2002: 560); Maher and Mowat (forthcoming), which fits this suggested range.

[71] The evidence used to determine whether a settlement was a *polis* is outlined in detail in Chapter 1.

[72] This number is derived from Nielsen (2002: 549–601, app. IX), where the author, employing the same lines of evidence as dictated by the general *Copenhagen Polis Centre* methodology, has determined the probability of a settlement's *polis* status.

[73] Although the fourteen Arkadian sites marked with an asterisk were probably fortified, they are excluded from the main study because no remains of the walls exist, and/or their location/*polis*-status is uncertain. These sites are catalogued in the Appendix, including the reason for their exclusion and the most relevant literature pertaining to each site.

As the focus and nature of this study demanded that data be collected at the level of the individual site, for each fortified *polis* data were assembled from two equally important sources: the published historical and archaeological literature, and personal reconnaissance or observation. After a careful reading of the literature pertaining to both the *polis* in question and, if published, its fortifications, the next step was to visit the identified Arkadian sites (as listed).[74] This part of the data collection process included walking the trace in order to gain an overall impression of its relationship with the natural topography; carefully recording and photographing of the details of the extant remains (including building materials, construction technique, and where possible visible surface pottery);[75] recording the different defensive elements (number and types of towers, gates, and posterns), and measuring with as much precision as possible the dimensions of these defensive elements.[76]

The use of detailed topographical maps, published plans, and satellite imagery available online were invaluable supplements to the personal observation of each site and represent an important part of the data collection process. For more detailed topographical elements, including distances between sites, site elevations, and the presence of tributaries and/or seasonal streams, the high resolution 1:50,000 scale Anavasi maps were consulted.[77] The satellite images provided by Google Maps, Google Earth, and the specifically Greek website of *Κτηματολόγιο*[78] were employed to trace parts of circuits not visible on the ground, to provide measurements (for example, between towers, approximate lengths of stretches of walls, and so on), and, often, to trace the path of (dry) watercourses that were not clearly discernible by personal observation alone.

As the product of both personal observation and a detailed review of the published literature, much of the data include relatively irrefutable observations. Still, not every observation or deduction was completely black or white, and some of the data were more open to interpretation. Consequently,

---

[74] These sites were visited (and some revisited) during winter 2009, spring 2010, spring 2011, summer 2015, and summer 2016.

[75] All photographs included in the book are the author's unless otherwise stated.

[76] Measurements of these elements were conducted by the author only on those sites for which a study permit was granted by the Greek Archaeological Service.

[77] Almost all of ancient Arkadia is available at this resolution in the combined Anavasi maps of Mt Chelmos (Anavasi 2003), Upland Corinthia (Anavasi 2007), and Mt Menalo (Anavasi 2008). Moreover, ancient structures (including the trace of some site's fortifications) are accurately noted on these maps by consulting scholars such as Y. Pikoulas and Y. Lolos.

[78] Google Maps is available at: http://maps.google.ca; *Κτηματολόγιο* is available at: http://gis.ktimanet.gr/wms/ktbasemap/default.aspx (both accessed May 2010). These two applications were especially useful because they provide satellite images taken at different parts of the year. Those on the *Κτηματολόγιο* website, for example, appear to have been taken at the height of summer, while the greenery presented in the images from Google Earth suggest that some were taken in the spring or autumn.

methodological clarification is required to explain how the more subjective elements of the dataset, specifically masonry style and chronology, were established for a given fortification circuit. Although masonry style was often the easier of these two elements to determine, it was rarely a straight-forward task. The subjectivity and limitations of establishing unambiguous categories of masonry style are explored in Chapter 2, and examples demonstrating how the traditional classification system breaks down in Arkadia are found throughout this book.[79] When the style of masonry encountered did not wholly fit the established categories—for example, completely 'polygonal', 'coursed polygonal', 'isodomic trapezoidal', and so on—a record was made of which style was predominant and which appeared to be intrusive or secondary. Generally, it appears that the fortifications of the Arkadian *poleis* are for the most part one of two types, either predominantly (coursed) polygonal or predominantly (coursed) trapezoidal.

As establishing a reliable chronology for the city walls in question was one of the main objectives, it is important to outline the methodology employed in the process. The chronology for each of the city walls was deduced by the carefully weighing of all the available evidence, which can be broadly grouped into three main categories: external evidence (ceramics, coins, inscriptions, ancient texts); internal evidence (established defensive architectural affinities, style of masonry, as well as comparanda from other Arkadian sites); and historical probability. Because few of the sites in question have been systematically excavated, the amount of external evidence available was often limited, and, consequently, much of the dating involved relevant comparanda and historical probability. Avoiding circular reasoning was paramount, as it is easy to fall into the trap of relying on a single piece of evidence. It is important to remember that the very nature of the evidence itself guarantees that the established chronologies for the unexcavated circuits are the most uncertain aspect in the present study. Nonetheless, even if we are able to speak only in generalities, by employing multiple categories of evidence we are able to get that much closer to the truth.

ORGANIZATION OF THE BOOK

This book is divided into two parts. Part One (Chapters 1–5) presents the background information for this study as well as the most significant findings, discernible patterns, arguments, and conclusions, while Part Two (Chapters 1–19) represents an extensive catalogue of the individual Arkadian sites

---

[79] i.e., the traditional classification system as developed by Scranton (1941).

comprising the data for the discussions in Part 1. At the root of any larger regional archaeological synthesis is the need for an awareness of how exactly the study area of ancient Arkadia is defined geographically and politically. These themes are explored in Chapter 1. Chapter 2 examines the choice of site, the types of fortifications, and the different building materials employed in the construction of Arkadian fortifications, including a discussion on the limitations of using masonry for stylistic dating of a city's fortifications. Chapter 3 explores the constituent parts of a city wall and the architectural responses of these structures resulting from the rise and spread of *poliorketics* in Greek warfare from the early fourth century BC onwards. Chapter 4 provides the detailed topographical, architectural, and historical analyses, including an examination of the discernible patterns shared and differences exhibited in the geographical distribution of sites, the local topography, and the specific architecture employed in the various Arkadian fortification systems. The chronological patterns established in this synthesis are viewed in the light both of the recognized history of Arkadia as well as of the historical probability that can reasonably and plausibly be inferred. A summary of the principal observable patterns as well as suggestions for further research are presented in Chapter 5. Part Two of this book comprises an extensive Catalogue, which supplies extensive information and detail regarding all nineteen of the fortified Arkadian *poleis* comprising this study. For each site evidence for its *polis* status and relevant bibliography are provided; then, in addition, each *polis* is explored through the local history, the geographical and topographical setting, the architectural components of the fortifications themselves, and, finally, the strategy, tactics, and overall defensive planning inherent in its construction. Based an understanding of all of these factors, including historical probability, a tentative chronology for each circuit in question is provided.

A list of Arkadian sites that were probably fortified but are excluded from the main study because no remains of their walls exist, and/or their location and/or *polis* status is uncertain, is provided in the Appendix, including the reason for their exclusion and the most relevant literature pertaining to each site.

Part One

Methodology

1

Arkadia, City Walls, and the *Polis*

Underlying the present work are a number of general theoretical assumptions held by the author on the subjects of Arkadia, fortifications, and the *polis*. If we consider city walls, it is difficult to find in the published literature anyone willing to use a fortification circuit alone as proof of a settlement's identity as a *polis*. Perhaps this is rightly so. Instead, city walls are often listed among other traits as 'features *commonly connected* with the concept of the *polis*'.[1] That is to say, a community's *polis* status cannot be inferred from walls alone, but from a number of characteristics, among which one may count the presence of a fortification circuit. Moreover, the fact that the second half of the fifth to the fourth century BC witnessed the decline of the truly independent city state is better understood as a decline in political independence and is not to be confused with civic autonomy. Thus, while a *polis* may have sacrificed its larger political identity and individuality with regards to foreign affairs by joining a regional federation or hegemonic league, civic autonomy was nonetheless a crucial aspiration—one that required fortifications.[2] Accordingly, it is assumed that the city walls functioned both to reflect and to protect a community's civic autonomy, and as such are a fundamental characteristic of the *polis* itself. Consequently, a fortification circuit was just as much (if not more) of an imperative for truly independent *poleis* as it was for dependent ones.

In addition to the practical function of defending a settlement's civic autonomy, it is also held that fortification circuits encompass a variety of symbolic or psychological functions. As is explored in the case of Sparta and the creation of the Arkadian League, opposition to different foreign groups is an important factor for the maintenance of the identity of any ethnic group. Similarly, as Nielsen and Roy maintain, any 'analysis of ethnicity should

---

[1] Hansen (1995: 9; emphasis added). Similarly, Ducrey (1995: 254) notes: 'peut-on dire dans ces conditions que la muraille est un element constitutive d'une cité? Sans doute non, en tout cas au moment de la constitution des cites, à la fin des "ages obscures" et de l'époque archaïque.'

[2] Camp (2000: 47–8).

ideally include an exploration of boundary maintenance [between groups]'.[3]
Thus, just as each *polis* had its own physical territory to which it belonged and
was identified, each also had a fortification circuit that embodied a symbolic
boundary for maintaining the ethnicity with which it identified. Another
function inherent in a *polis*'s fortifications was as a means of preserving central
authority. A populace is more likely to comply with the directives of an acting
government so long as there is at least the promise granted of protection from
outsiders. Therefore, besides physically protecting a population, the defences
afforded by city walls may also be seen as a psychological force that acts both
to control dissent and to bind social allegiance.

With regard to the physical construction and general layout of a city's
fortifications, it is held that city walls were constructed in response to the
geographical demands of the city, and natural features such as rivers, lakes,
hills, mountains, plains, and passes not only determined the layout of a trace,
but in most cases were actively exploited by the form and placement of the
circuit. A picture of the different fortifications characteristic of Arkadian *poleis*
will be truly comprehensive only after the choice of site, its available natural
resources, its natural defensive capabilities, and the historical circumstances
behind its construction have been considered.[4] These convictions form the
theoretical foundation for the present book and for realizing the objectives
contained therein.

As for the region of Arkadia itself, it is held that its ancient inhabitants
constituted an ethnic group, that Arkadia was perceived as a clearly defined
geographical region, and that Arkadian ethnic identity was manifested at both
the regional level (*ethnos*) and the local level (tribe/*polis*). At the local level,
moreover, the tribe and/or *polis* also represented the main unit of political
organization for the region as a whole. Thus, as the ultimate objective of the
present study is a comprehensive inventory and investigation of the fortifications of Arkadian *poleis*, it is important to outline how the these study units
are defined. The remainder of this chapter establishes Arkadia and its *poleis* as
a clearly defined area of focus for the present study by outlining the evidence
for an Arkadian identity at the regional level and how a *polis* status may be
determined for individual settlements.

ARKADIA AS A GEOGRAPHICAL CONCEPT

As the only landlocked region in the Peloponnese, Arkadia is distinguished
geographically from other regions largely by its almost exclusively mountainous

---

[3] Nielsen and Roy (1999: 21).
[4] All these elements are addressed for each site in Part Two, the Catalogue.

Fig. 1.1. Map of ancient Arkadia. (© *Matthew Maher*)

character (including the valleys and plains lying among them) and its associated system of drainage (Fig. 1.1).[5] The main beneficiaries of this system, the Alpheios River in the south and both the Erymanthos and Ladon Rivers in the north and west respectively, are able to collect the winter rains and spring thaws. In eastern Arkadia and parts of the north, there are no major rivers or tributaries to direct the flow of surface drainage outwards, and instead the system relies on the drainage of excess water into sinkholes (*katavothroi*) in the limestone.[6] Although most of Arkadia is mountainous, there is very fertile land to be found in the well-watered valleys, basins, terraced hillsides, and especially in the great plain of eastern Arkadia, dominated in antiquity by the *poleis* of Tegea and Mantineia.

---

[5] Jost (1999: 192). Contemporary maps show the prefecture of Arkadia to include the prefecture of Kynouria—a stretch of coast on its eastern side, approximately between the towns of Kiveri in the north and Fokiano in the south. This is a modern geographical division, and the eastern extent of Arkadia in antiquity did not extend to the Argolic Gulf, but to the mountains defining the eastern limits of the plains of Tegea and Mantineia (Nestane).

[6] e.g., as at Stymphalos and Pheneos.

The physical geography of the region, however, can go only so far in defining Arkadia, since it is clear that the ancient borders of the region, rarely static, were defined by historical and social organization, as well as by geography. Nielsen maintains that, between the late Archaic and Classical periods, Arkadia did not so much form its own borders but had its borders negatively formed—that is, the region of Arkadia was defined when the surrounding regions became settled and developed with fixed borders.[7] Nielsen is also surely correct in supposing that this trend arose from the fact that Arkadia itself was not a regional political concept before the foundation of the Arkadian League.[8] If this is accepted, it remains to determine exactly when the territorial boundaries were formed and Arkadia became a clearly defined geographical concept. We know that Herodotus,[9] Thucydides,[10] and Xenophon[11] perceived Arkadia as a distinct region within the Peloponnese by the fifth century BC. Keeping in mind that the geographical borders of Arkadia were known to fluctuate to some extent over time, enough evidence exists reasonably to establish the geographical extent of Arkadia before the Classical period.

Although limited by the paucity and consistency of sources for the period, by employing a combination of literary/historical, epigraphic, and archaeological evidence, a number of settlements can be seen to have existed and already been considered 'Arkadian' in the late Archaic period.[12] From Homer's 'Catalogue of Ships', it would appear that Archaic Arkadia included Pheneos, Orchomenos, Tegea, Mantineia, Stymphalos, and the communities of Parrhasia, Stratie, Enispe, and Rhipe.[13] Basing his observation on the assumption that all eponymous Arkadian-named towns should be Arkadian, Nielsen maintains that Hesiod's mention of Pallas as a son of the Arkadian king Lykaon means that Pallantion too should be considered as part of Arkadia by the late Archaic period.[14] Hekataios supplements this list with the settlements of Mainalos, Kleitor, Trapezous, and Psophis;[15] while from Herodotus we get Nonakris, Phigaleia, and Paos being described as Arkadian.[16] Finally, based on inference (that is, on the geographical location between attested Archaic period sites) as well as epigraphic verification, Heraia and Lousoi were also probably Arkadian in the late Archaic period.[17]

From the early sources, therefore, the late Archaic borders of Arkadia appear to have extended from Psophis in the north-west to Phigaleia in the south-west (including Heraia), eastward to include Parrhasia, Trapezous,

[7] Nielsen (2002: 22); see also Morgan (1999: 429).   [8] Nielsen (2002: 22–3).

[9] Hdt. 7.202.   [10] Thuc. 5.29.1.   [11] Xen. *Hell.* 7.4.36.

[12] What follows is a brief overview. All relevant historical and archaeological evidence is explored on an individual site basis in Part Two, the Catalogue.

[13] Hom. *Il.* 2.605–8. Parrhasia is an area west north-west of Lykosoura and Trapezous. Stratie, Enispe, and Rhipe are otherwise unknown.

[14] Nielsen (2002: 92–3).   [15] Hekataios [*FgrHist* 1] fr. 6.

[16] Hdt. 6.74.1–2, 6.83.2, 6.127.3   [17] Nielsen (2002: 95).

Pallantion and Tegea, north towards Mantineia, Orchomenos, Stymphalos, Pheneos and Nonakris, and north-westward to Kleitor, and Paos. Nielsen reasonably considers Thelpousa, Thaliades, Kaphyai, and Methydrion also to be Arkadian, as they are areas situated within these borders.[18] Constrained by the nature and scarcity of evidence, this 'picture of Arkadia in the late Archaic period probably represents its minimum extent'.[19] Nonetheless, this brief review of the territorial limits of the region demonstrates that most of the settlements that constitute Classical Arkadia could already be considered Arkadian by the late Archaic period.[20]

The geographical extent of Arkadia is better documented in the Classical period. While it would be an argument from silence to assume that the communities attested for the first time in the Classical period (for example, Kynaitha, Alea, and Alipheira) may not have belonged to Arkadia earlier in the Archaic period, evidence suggests that the region of Arkadia was certainly enlarged during this period (Fig. 1.2).[21] Also, as Nielsen contends, there is 'no reason to believe that Arkadia "lost" any of its Archaic communities in the Classical period; in fact, Arkadia seems to have slowly grown throughout the Classical period'.[22] If we employ the same logic that determined Pallantion was Arkadian in the Archaic period, to the fact that Kynaitha and Alipheira are mentioned as sons of Lykaon by Apollodoros (probably citing a fifth-century BC source), it could be argued that these settlements belonged to Arkadia at least in the Classical period, if not earlier.[23] A further example of this growth is the acquisition of the Elian settlement of Lasion, which, according to Xenophon, was laid claim to by the Arkadians in 390 BC;[24] thus, in Lasion we may have an example of a city 'becoming' Arkadian during the first quarter of the fourth century BC.[25]

In the Classical period and into the Hellenistic period, a further number of communities in the region are explicitly attested to as Arkadian; these include Alea, Amilos, Asea, Euaimon, Kaphyai, Gortys, Kynaitha, and Lykaia.[26] The fact that the expansion of the region during this time was limited and occurred soon after the foundation of Megalopolis is a reflection of the larger political history of the Peloponnese. In contrast to the Archaic period, when it appears that the borders of Arkadia were formed only as the more powerful and stable surrounding regions were settled with defined borders (that is,

---

[18] Nielsen (2002: 96).   [19] Nielsen (2002: 109).
[20] Nielsen (2002: 96). See also Hansen (1994: 16–17).
[21] Nielsen (2002: 105). The growth of the region is best attested to by the addition of Triphylia. This region, however, for reasons outlined in the Introduction, is omitted from the present study.
[22] Nielsen (2002: 97).   [23] Apollod. 3.8.1.   [24] Xen. *Hell.* 3.2.30.
[25] Nielsen (2002: 99); see also Nielsen (1996b: 75–7).
[26] Nielsen (2002: 108).

Methodology

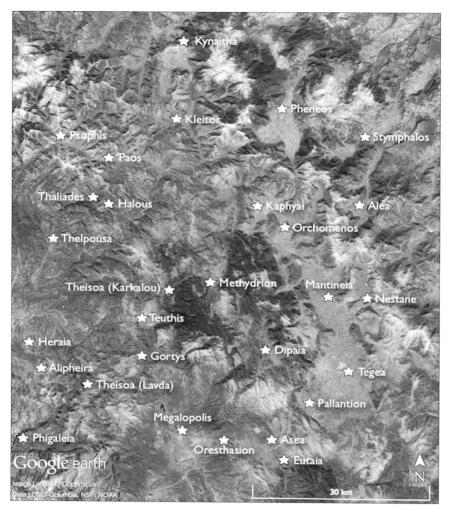

Fig. 1.2. Map of Arkadian *poleis* from Archaic through Hellenistic Period. (© *2011 Google-Map data* © *2011 Tele Atlas*)

Lakonia, Argolid, and Elis),[27] the acquisitions of Arkadia in the middle of the fourth century BC were based on its own strength and facilitated by the weaknesses of the major powers surrounding it.[28] The years following Leuktra not only witnessed Spartan supremacy being largely eliminated in the Peloponnese,

[27] Elis was not really 'settled' until the synoikism of 471 BC. For a detailed account of Elian and Arkadian relations, see Roy (2000).

[28] Nielsen (2002: 111).

but also the creation of Megalopolis and the foundation of the Arkadian Confederacy (*c*.370 BC).[29] Arkadia, arguably for the first time in its history, gained a distinctly formalized regional political identity.[30] Important for the present purposes is to keep in mind that, while it is true that the oscillations of the borders of Arkadia experienced were largely conditioned by the shifting political power of the region in relation to the major Peloponnesian states, it should not obscure the fact that, by the late Archaic period, the region comprised what we traditionally take to be ancient Arkadia.[31]

DEFINING *POLIS* STATUS

Neilson and Roy have demonstrated that the people of Arkadia comprised an ethnic group in which identity was manifested on both a regional (*ethnos*) and a local (tribe/*polis*) level, and it is this local level of identity that corresponded to the internal social and political organization.[32] It is this point that will be explored in greater detail here; specifically, the *polis* and how this characteristically ancient Greek institution developed in Arkadia. As the present work considers the fortifications of Arkadian *poleis*, it is important to establish the criteria as to how a *polis* is defined, and, by association, to identify which Arkadian states were in fact *poleis*.[33]

In their attempt to answer the seemingly simple question of what defines a *polis*, research from the Copenhagen Polis Centre (CPC) has shown the answer to be anything but straightforward. In fact, recent research has shown that many of the characteristics previously used to define a *polis* are in fact unreliable.[34] With the ultimate aim of producing a comprehensive inventory of all Archaic and Classical *poleis*, the CPC has turned away from the many (and often conflicting) definitions of what a *polis* is or should be, and instead has focused on the ancient evidence for individual city states by collecting detailed information about all the communities actually called *poleis* in the sources.[35] The historical and archaeological evidence employed by the CPC thought to be supportive of a community's identity as a *polis*

---

[29] It is generally held that the Arkadian League lasted until dissolved by Alexander the Great in 324 BC, but Roy (1968: 238–79) believes it lasted into the third century BC, breaking down only when Arkadian communities like Megalopolis joined the Achaian League.

[30] For arguments of whether there existed an earlier fifth-century BC Arkadian League, see Roy (1972a) and Nielsen (1996c).

[31] Nielsen (2002: 111).

[32] Roy et al. (1988); Nielsen (1996a; 1999; 2002: 45–88, 271–308); Roy (1996); Nielsen and Roy (1998).

[33] The specific evidence for each settlement's *polis* status is provided in Part Two, the Catalogue.

[34] e.g., see Hansen (1993, 1994, 1995, 2000).   [35] Hansen (1994: 9).

largely include the use of the city ethnic,[36] epigraphic data (public enactment of laws/decrees[37] and attestations of *theorodokoi*[38]), some types of political architecture, the striking of coinage, and also the ancient literary sources.[39] A catalogue of Archaic and Classical *poleis*, identified by these criteria, is not the only objective established by the CPC, but merely provides the foundation for addressing a number of issues (including the revision of a number of accepted beliefs), which, as they have a direct bearing on the present work, are briefly summarized here.

First is the commonly held belief that, as an institution, the *polis* was formed before the colonization movement of the mid-eighth century BC. In fact, the evidence suggests that it is more likely that the features central to the *polis* (urbanization, splitting of population into citizens and foreigners, introductions of political institutions) may have developed in the colonies before they became prominent in Greece itself.[40] Second is the idea that by definition *poleis* had to have autonomy. Evidence gathered through the CPC does not support the idea that *autonomia* was an essential aspect of the concept of the *polis*. As long as a community still had its political institutions, the loss of autonomy (for example, joining a confederation or hegemonic league) did not affect its identity as a *polis*.[41] Third is the misconception that, when the term *polis* designates a town, it must be distinguished from *polis* in the sense of political community. There are examples of *poleis* in the Archaic period whose political centre was not focused around an urban centre. But, by the Classical period, every attested *polis* seems to have been centred around an urban core (walled or unwalled), and 'whenever the term *polis* is used in the sense of conurbation it denotes a town which was also the political centre of the *polis* in the sense of the political community'.[42] Fourth is the notion that the division of territories into clearly defined regions can be traced back to the Archaic period, if not earlier. This hypothesis is certainly true in the case of Arkadia, as already demonstrated. And fifth is a rejection of the belief that the *polis* ended with the Greek defeat at Chaironeia. Although

---

[36] Although the city ethnic could often be used as a geographical adjective, it was most often used in a political sense (Hansen 1995: 7). On the use of city ethnics, see Nielsen (1996a).

[37] The public enactments of laws (*nomoi*) and decrees (*psephismata*) were usually the jurisdiction of *poleis* and larger federations; and such decrees, of course, 'presuppose the existence of *boule* and a *boule* is characteristic of the *polis* or larger political unit such as a federation' (Hansen 1995: 7). For laws and decrees as evidence, see Rhodes (1995).

[38] The epigraphic attestation of *theorodokoi* (those who received the people sent to announce Panhellenic festivals, the *theoroi*) is also suggestive of a *polis*, since most of the communities visited by the *theoroi* were indeed *poleis* (Hansen 1995: 7). See Perlman (1995).

[39] Although not characteristics of *poleis* in their own right, when taken together some main types of political architecture (e.g., a *bouleuterion*, a fortification circuit, a *prytaneion*, etc.) and the striking of coinage, may suggest a community's designation as a *polis* (Hansen 1995: 7). On architecture and the *polis*, see Hansen and Fischer-Hansen (1994) and Miller (1995); and on the minting of coins, see Guettel Cole (1995).

[40] Hansen (1994: 15–16).   [41] Hansen (1994: 16).   [42] Hansen (1994: 16).

the truly independent *polis* began its decline a century before Chaironeia, the *polis* as a functioning political institution did not end in 338 BC, but survived until the end of the Hellenistic period.[43]

This work will follow the methodology and explore the assumptions laid out by the CPC as it pertains to specifically Arkadian *poleis*.[44] Essential in this regard, however, is not only what evidence is to be employed in establishing the characteristics corresponding to Arkadian *poleis*, but how and when the *polis* as a social, political, and cultural institution developed in Arkadia. As demonstrated, evidence suggests that Arkadia existed as a geographic concept with a distinct regional ethnic identity by the late Archaic period. It does not necessarily follow, however, that, at that time, all the communities comprising the Arkadian *ethnos* or existing in its clearly defined territory were *poleis*, or, indeed, even significant urban centres. Still, although Roy convincingly argues that in most cases the tribal states developed before the widespread development of *poleis*, he admits that there were still communities that had a fully developed *polis* identity before the Classical period.[45] Yet how do we identify which settlements were *poleis* before the Classical period, and how do we reconcile this information with the fact that true urban centres do not appear to develop in Arkadia until the fifth century BC?

In his *Arkadia and its Poleis in the Archaic and Classical Periods*, the only definitive study devoted to Arkadian *poleis*, Nielsen aims to identify 'those Arkadian communities that ranked as *poleis* in the eyes of the Greeks at different points in time from the Archaic period to the end of the Classical period'.[46] At the core of this work are the evidence and criteria utilized to establish a settlement's *polis* identity, and, more importantly here, when *poleis* developed in Arkadia.[47] Although Nielsen believes that some Arkadian settlements were viewed by the ancient Greeks as *poleis* in the late Archaic period, he is careful to draw attention to the fact that there is no general agreement as to when *poleis* developed in Arkadia.[48] In defence of his view, however, Nielsen finds support in the historical and archaeological record.

Basing his conclusions largely on the work of Morgan[49] and Jost,[50] Nielsen points to the large number of Archaic temples in Arkadia as verification of the

---

[43] Gauthier (1993); Hansen (1994: 17; 2000a); Camp (2000: 50).

[44] The general methodological rules established by the CPC are set out in detail by Hansen (1994).

[45] Roy (1996: 109–10).   [46] Nielsen (2002: 20).   [47] Nielsen (2002: 159–228).

[48] Nielsen (2002: 159); e.g., Callmer (1943: 67–70) maintains that Tegea was already synoikized into a *polis* in the seventh century BC; Borgeaud (1988: 10) vaguely maintains that the important centres in Arkadia appeared relatively early; Jeffery (1976: 170–2) believes that the significant settlements of Orchomenos, Tegea, Phigaleia, and Mantineia existed as *poleis* as early as the mid to late eighth century BC; Gehrke (1986: 154) argues that *poleis* developed in Arkadia in the sixth century BC; while Snodgrass (1980: 154) denies *polis* status to all the settlements of Archaic Arkadia.

[49] Morgan (1999).   [50] Jost (1985; 1999: 206–16).

existence both of organized local communities concerned with a desire to
express local identity, and of local territories (that is, temples as territorial
boundary markers) by the late Archaic period.[51] Furthermore, by the end of
the Archaic period, at least some communities had begun the minting of
coinage.[52] Coinage, like the act of temple-building, 'indicates that the community responsible had developed a high degree of complexity and capacity
for communal decision making'.[53] As suggestive as the archaeological evidence may be, it must be noted that nowhere in the Archaic sources is any
Arkadian settlement referred to as a *polis*.[54] We are not completely in the
dark, however, and there are other sources at our disposal from which
inferences can be drawn. Pausanias, for example, preserves a late Archaic
inscription erected at Olympia by the Kleitorians recording the dedication of
the spoils of many defeated *poleis*.[55] If we assume that these *poleis* were
neighbouring Arkadian *poleis*, then it follows that the people of Kleitor
found it conventional to use the term *poleis*, and, because it was set up at a
great Panhellenic sanctuary, that the use of the term had the same meaning to
all Greeks.[56] This example demonstrates just one of the ways in which it
may be shown that by the late Archaic period Arkadia did have *poleis*, even if
we cannot identify them in this specific case. Basing his work on deductions
similar to this, as well as on a careful examination of the historic and
archaeological record (including epigraphic and numismatic evidence), Nielsen
has identified no fewer than sixteen Arkadian communities that might have
been *poleis* before the Classical period.[57]

If these communities can be considered *poleis* as defined by the criteria of
the CPC, then, as Nielsen maintains, their appearance at the end of the sixth
century BC is explained by local Arkadian communities joining 'the panhellenic network of *polis*-interaction, something which was bound to have an
influence on self-perception and the way of organizing themselves'.[58] Such a
network, involving the interaction of Greek *polis* culture, may explain why
certain characteristics (for example, increased temple-building, minting of
coins, and so on), appear around the same time in different parts of late
Archaic Greece.[59] While this may go some way to explain the development of
Arkadian *poleis* as political communities, we still know very little about the

[51] Nielsen (2002: 184).   [52] e.g., Heraia in *c*.510 BC (Nielsen 2002: 185).
[53] Nielsen (2002: 185).
[54] For the problematic cases of Lousoi and Ptolis (Old Mantineia), see Morgan (1999: 390–3,
417–20) and Nielsen (2002: 199).
[55] Paus. 5.23.7.   [56] Nielsen (2002: 199).
[57] These include Heraia, Kaphyai, Gortys, Kleitor, Lousoi, Mantineia, Nonakris, Orchomenos,
Paos, Pheneos, Phigaleia, Psophis, Stymphalos, Tegea, Thaliades, and Thelphousa (Nielsen 2002:
212–28).
[58] Nielsen (2002: 220).   [59] Nielsen (2002: 223).

physical organization of Arkadian communities before 600 BC.[60] In other words, although there is little evidence of significant urbanization before the late Archaic period that can be established archaeologically, what evidence does exist suggests that the beginnings of urbanism came relatively late to Arkadia.[61] For the present, therefore, the fact that it is very likely that certain Arkadian *poleis* existed by the late sixth century BC is in no way irreconcilable with the fact that the development of true urban centres in Arkadia was a product of the Classical period.[62]

---

[60] Nielsen (2002: 225).   [61] Nielsen and Roy (1999: 12).
[62] Roy (1996); Jost (1999: 203); Nielsen (2002: 171).

2

Arkadian Fortification Types and Construction

In order to investigate the defences of specific Arkadian *poleis*, it is necessary to appreciate the various architectural components, their relationship to each other and the landscape, as well as the larger historical, political, and social factors that influenced not only their appearance but their very existence. In order better to understand these concerns, several diverse yet related elements are addressed here and in the subsequent chapter. Beginning with an examination of the factors that determined the choice of site, this chapter also examines the relationship between Arkadian settlement patterns and the type of fortification employed. The different methods and building materials employed in a city wall's construction, including the type of masonry and its limitations for stylistic dating, are also addressed.

CHOICE OF SITE

Identifying the criteria behind a site's 'ideal' location is easily done on paper, yet it is important to remember that many of the major mainland *poleis* had some form of settlement that went back centuries and difficulties encountered in the Classical and Hellenistic periods had to be dealt with. In other words, even if there was an increased need for water to meet the requirements of an expanding settlement, or developments in offensive siege warfare revealed inadequacies in the natural terrain, it was rarely practical to abandon and re-establish a city elsewhere.[1] Defensive military engineering was, therefore, forced to keep pace with its offensive counterpart in order to compensate both for a site's topographical inadequacies as well as for the evolving theatre of

---

[1] Winter (1971a: 4). Not surprisingly, it is in these older more established centres that we see the most rapid advances in the sciences of fortifications to compensate for any topographical shortcomings.

Greek warfare.[2] The experience accumulated in the Iron Age and Archaic periods was beneficial when town planners began to lay out new cities in the late Classical and Hellenistic periods to meet the new circumstances of their times. Military engineers of the Classical and Hellenistic periods had at their disposal 'a wealth of experience of the features which did not constitute an ideal site, [and] were far better qualified to pronounce in favour of one location over another than they would have been without the hard-won knowledge of earlier centuries to guide them'.[3] To this extent, the development of military strategy in the Hellenistic period can be said to have grown directly out of the earlier achievements of the fifth and first half of the fourth century BC. Similarly, the nature of those achievements was in large measure determined by the historical background of the early Iron Age and Archaic periods.[4]

From the beginnings of Greek urbanization in the Archaic period, defensibility appears to have been the main motivation for choice of site as well as plans for the defences of its acropolis.[5] But the security of a city, prompted by the beginnings of systematic siege craft, came to depend increasingly on its fortifications in the Classical period.[6] Such security required that the walls both were strong and took every possible advantage of the surrounding natural topography, including access to water. If, however, inhabitants were forced to choose between a site's natural strength and a reliable water supply, founders of a new city would often select the former.[7] Although sites suitable for an acropolis are extremely common almost everywhere in the Greek mainland (especially in rugged Arkadia), 'there are not nearly so many locations that combine the defensive qualities of the early acropolis with a good local water supply and enough space for the building of a complete city'.[8] Consequently, many cities were forced to restrict the length of their circuits. In Arkadia, where many circuits date to this period, we see that compact and easily defensible sites are common.[9] Accordingly, the expansion of settlements from the acropolis into the surrounding lowlands also saw the defensive

---

[2] This idea is discussed in greater detail in Part One, Chapter 3.

[3] Winter (1971a: 4).

[4] Winter (1971a: 4). On early Iron Age and Archaic fortifications throughout the Greek world, see Frederiksen (2011).

[5] Jost (1999: 193); Frederiksen (2011: 71).   [6] Lawrence (1979: 111).

[7] Although some opted for the latter; e.g., Winter (1971a: 52 n. 14) notes that a great deal of the Arkadian settlements mentioned by Pausanias did possess a good water supply. This is an especially significant observation. As demonstrated in Part One, Chapter 1, urbanization in Arkadia was a relatively late phenomenon. As most Arkadian *poleis* were founded at a time after the main military aspects of town planning had already been developed on the mainland, the presence of abundant mountain springs and streams, characteristic of many Arkadian sites, 'may well have determined, or at the least influenced, the final choice of site' (Winter 1971a: 52).

[8] Winter (1971a: 57).   [9] Winter (1971a: 59).

importance of its original citadel decrease in proportion to the strengthening of the man-made defences of the outer city.[10]

ARKADIAN FORTIFICATION TYPES

Whether in the Bronze Age, the early Iron Age, or the Archaic period, the most important *poleis* of the Greek mainland of the Classical period had some form of earlier settlement. Still, new cities appear in more remote areas in the fifth and fourth centuries BC, in regions that were primarily agricultural and pastoral, Arkadia being one of them.[11] Similarly to other regions of Greece, Arkadia possessed several different types of these fortified settlements, three of which seemed to have been particularly popular; here I categorize them as the 'acropolis type', the 'horizontal type', and a combination of the first two, the 'uneven type'.

The 'acropolis type' is found in the smaller settlements and is characterized by a more or less isolated peak or rock face rising sharply from the surrounding landscape (often above a deep river gorge), with some gently sloping land within reach of the summit.[12] Arkadian sites of this type that most readily come to mind include Teuthis, Nestane, and Halous.[13] While many of these smaller fortified mountain sites appear to conform closely to the typical acropolis of earlier *poleis*, Winter cautions that it was not uncommon for even small villages to have a small fortified citadel.[14] At any rate, whether *polis* or village, such sites rarely provided sufficient space for an intramural settlement of any size.[15]

The second or 'horizontal type' of fortified settlement is a category reserved exclusively to *poleis* in the larger agricultural regions of Arkadia.[16] Unlike in the 'acropolis type' of settlement, here the situation is reversed and we see inhabitants entrusting their safety completely to the security provided by a

---

[10] Winter (1971a: 58). This sometimes resulted in the absence of an acropolis altogether. In Arkadia, while many cities still possessed an acropolis, it generally bore little resemblance to the steep and hard-to-attack citadels of earlier times. Instead, it functioned more as a strategic post from which one could observe the whole trace and direct defensive operations.

[11] Winter (1971a: 40).

[12] Roughly equivalent to Winter's 'acropolis' type (1971a: 32), Jost's 'villes acropoles' type (1999: 193–8), and Frederiksen's 'hilltop fortification wall' type (2011: 50–3).

[13] Jost (1999: 193–8) lists Alipheira, Torthynion, Paos, Dipaia, Methydrion, Teuthis, Nestane, Theisoa (Lavda), Gortys, and Theisoa (Karkalou) as Arkadian examples of the 'villes acropoles' type.

[14] Winter (1971a: 31).   [15] Lawrence (1979: 112); Frederiksen (2011: 8).

[16] The 'horizontal' type of settlement is roughly equivalent to Jost's 'villes de plaine' type (1999: 201–3), and some examples fall into Frederiksen's category (2011: 50–1) of the 'city wall' type.

man-made circuit.[17] The *poleis* of Mantineia and Tegea in the great eastern
plains of Arkadia are the most obvious examples of this type.[18] As suggested
by the label, the main characteristics of this type of circuit include a trace laid
out over generally even terrain without a recognized acropolis. This type of
fortified settlement supports the conclusion drawn from other Arkadian sites
that, from the mid-Archaic period to the fourth century BC, the importance of
an acropolis to the overall defensive structure of the defences of a Greek city
steadily decreased, and was frequently dispensed with altogether.[19]

The third and final category of Arkadian fortified sites is the 'uneven type'.[20]
This type is characterized by those larger settlements for which some high
ground, either level or unevenly terraced, was incorporated into the overall
trace. Although some of the circuit may be located on relatively flat terrain, these
fortifications take advantage, wherever possible, of natural defences and consequently are usually rather rugged and forbidding in their appearance.[21] This
type is found, for example, at Phigaleia, Psophis, Kleitor, Stymphalos, and
Alea,[22] where, instead of focusing on a small strong acropolis or trusting
completely to the walls themselves, the circuits sought to incorporate a much
larger defensible area—one that found balance in the active interaction between
the defensible topography and the strengths of the walls themselves. That is not
to say, however, that in this category of sites the inclusion of an acropolis was
abandoned altogether, as many of these later Arkadian cities did possess a
separate acropolis, which was maintained until relatively later times. Nonetheless, while in earlier times the acropolis alone had been chosen for its defensive
qualities, in the Classical and Hellenistic period, such defensive considerations
were often sought around the whole perimeter of the settlement.[23]

It must be noted that, although such categories may exhibit some chronological patterns, they are not primarily chronological classifications.[24] That is,
there is no sense of sequential evolution from one type to another. Thus, even
into the fourth century BC and through the Hellenistic period, we see *poleis*
relying heavily on natural defences. Similarly, the acropolis almost always
remained a prominent feature in the city plan, even if it came to lose much

---

[17] Winter (1971a: 32–3).

[18] While I agree with Jost (1999: 201–3) that Mantineia and Tegea are certainly examples of
this type, I disagree with her inclusion of Megalopolis and Kleitor in this category. Because some
high ground was incorporated into the plan of these two settlements, they are more accurately
understood as being representative of the 'uneven' type of site.

[19] Winter (1971a: 33).

[20] The 'uneven' type of settlement is roughly equivalent to Jost's 'villes mixtes' type (1999:
198–201) , but some examples also fit Frederiksen's 'city wall' type (2011: 50–1), which can
include horizontal and uneven types.

[21] Winter (1971a: 32).

[22] Jost (1999: 198) correctly lists Alea, Orchomenos, Stymphalos, Psophis, Phigaleia, and Asea
as examples of this type.

[23] Winter (1971a: 31).   [24] McNicoll (1997: 4).

of its original social and political significance.[25] Even so, these settlement types form convenient categories, with little overlap, into which the extant fortifications of Arkadian *poleis* explored in subsequent chapters may be placed.

The sheer number of surviving fortifications in Arkadia not only demonstrates a relative lack of continuous occupation through post-Classical, medieval, and modern times,[26] but also testifies to the extensive spread of urbanization in the region during the Classical period. By the time many city walls appeared in Arkadia, therefore, regular siege techniques had already been developed and the inclusion of a large population within the walls often had to be considered from the very beginning.[27] Accordingly, in order to keep pace with developments in offensive siege warfare, the larger defensive strategies involved in site selection, water procurement, and type of fortification trace had also to incorporate important tactical strategies. Ultimately, such strategies were manifested in the form and placement of the individual features of a fortification circuit.[28]

FORTIFICATION BUILDING MATERIALS AND CONSTRUCTION TECHNIQUES

The only regular materials for building a fortification circuit were stone and mudbrick.[29] Apart from the availability of water, therefore, the ideal location for a site would also have possessed a suitable stone supply and clay deposits in its vicinity. Greek military architects rarely missed an opportunity to exploit the landscape in the constructions of their fortifications, whether it be in the placement of the walls to take maximum advantage of the natural defences afforded by the topography, or in the exploitation of the natural resources necessary for its assembly. In the case of the latter, it was discovered early that sun-dried mudbrick was an effective and expedient building material. Unskilled workers could make a mudbrick circuit rapidly and with little equipment, unquestionably saving a great deal of money and labour.[30] Perhaps more importantly for military engineers, mudbrick is virtually fireproof and practically

[25] Winter (1971a: 34).
[26] For example, Teuthis, Tegea, and perhaps Kynaitha are the only Arkadian *poleis* now buried beneath modern settlements: Teuthis by Dhimitsana, ancient Tegea by modern Tegea, and Kynaitha by Kalavryta. On the various processes affecting the preservation of a city wall over time, see Frederiksen (2011: 41–9).
[27] Winter (1971a: 34).
[28] McNicoll (1997: 6). These features are explored in detail in Part One, Chapter 3.
[29] Frederiksen (2011: 54–5). The main materials could also be supplemented by timber, but its use was normally restricted to providing accessories to the brick and stone (Lawrence 1979: 208).
[30] For a concise summary of the process whereby mudbricks are made, see Lawrence (1979: 210–11).

indestructible by the weather when its surface is properly protected.[31] Moreover, many Greeks believed that a mudbrick wall could withstand the assault of rams and artillery better than their stone counterparts.[32] Yet the advantages of mudbrick have to be carefully weighed against their limitations. The manufacture of mudbrick required copious amounts of both water and suitable clay—a type with a consistency that would not crumble or turn to mud.[33] Moreover, although it may withstand the shock of artillery better than a stone wall, a mudbrick superstructure is more easily breached if an enemy succeeded in reaching the base of a wall.[34] Finally, as a building material, mudbrick is very susceptible to water, and there are at least three historically attested examples of a besieging force attempting to use water to cause a breach in a mudbrick fortification circuit.[35]

The limitations of mudbrick and, of course, the availability of material certainly played a part in the preference for a stone (or a partly stone) superstructure over time. Still, since few sites possessed both raw materials in sufficient quantities, it is unlikely that an architect could freely choose between mudbrick or stone; instead the choice would be made for him based on the available resources.[36] Unlike in the building of temples or prominent civic structures, when stone was employed in the construction of fortifications, it was more likely to be taken from the source that was the closest and most accessible. This is especially true on a rocky acropolis, where stone could be quarried at the spot it was required and put together in less time than would be spent in making and setting an equivalent number of mudbricks.[37] Even if few sites could produce the quantities of mudbrick required, suitable rock is available at an immensely larger proportion of sites.[38] The availability of stone and its perceived strength may account for the general tendency of replacing mudbrick with stone witnessed in the Greek world from the fifth century BC onwards.[39] Yet, as the types and quality of stone found in the various parts of Greece could vary considerably (they could vary too within

---

[31] Lawrence (1979: 213); Fields (2006: 10).

[32] Pausanias (8.8.8) tells us that 'against the blows of engines brick brings greater security than fortifications built of stone. For stones break and are dislodged from their fittings; brick, however, does not suffer so much from engines, but it crumbles under the action of water just as wax is melted by the sun.'

[33] Lawrence (1979: 212); Fields (2006: 10).   [34] Lawrence (1979: 213).

[35] Coincidently, two are Arkadian examples. In 385 BC the walls of Mantineia were breached when Agesipolis of Sparta dammed the river that ran through the town, causing the water to rise and melt a section of the mudbrick fortifications (Xen. *Hell.* 5.2.4–5; Diod. 15.12.1–2; Paus. 8.8.7). Similarly, in the early fourth century, Iphikrates attempted and ultimately failed to take Stymphalos by blocking the *katavothros* of the adjacent lake with sponges in the hopes of causing the lake level to rise and undermine the mudbrick walls (Xen. *Hell.* 4.4.16; 6.5.49–51; Stab. 8.8.4).

[36] Lawrence (1979: 213).

[37] Winter (1971a: 77); Fields (2006: 10); Maher and Mowat (forthcoming).

[38] Lawrence (1979: 213).   [39] Winter (1971a: 77).

the same region), the preference for stone walls is perhaps also a reflection of the later emphasis 'on aesthetic, as opposed to purely structural, consider-ations'.[40] It should be noted that, although fortifications with a stone or partly stone superstructure became more common in the later Classical and Hellen-istic period, they never fully replaced the mudbrick ones. This is especially true in Arkadia, where the city walls of every single *polis* were comprised of mudbrick set atop a stone foundation.

Based on how and in what arrangement these raw materials were employed in construction, fortifications can be divided into three main groups: mudbrick walls on a stone socle, walls in which the curtains and ground storeys of towers were of stone and the battlements and upper portions were of mudbrick or wood, and walls built entirely of stone. As there are no examples of Arkadian fortifications built entirely with a superstructure completely in stone, the following discussion is concerned exclusively with the first category.[41]

MUDBRICK WALLS ON A STONE SOCLE

Mudbricks were formed by taking a suitable clay and reinforcing it with straw, animal hair, or even potsherds. The material was then poured into wooden frames, open at the top and bottom, dumped out, and allowed to dry. Although this ensured some variation in height, their lengths and widths remained fairly regular. From the fifth century BC onwards, mudbricks were usually square in section, ranging between 40 and 50 cm^2 with a height between 8 and 10 cm.[42] Like modern baked bricks, dry mudbricks were laid in courses but set with wet clay (identical to that from which they were made) instead of mortar.[43] The dangers of water to the integrity of the superstructure was a constant concern and one that required precautions to be taken from the ground up, at every level of its assembly. The first courses were set atop the stone socle to prevent contact with standing water, the exterior faces of the wall were covered in a waterproof lime plaster,[44] and the top was protected by tiles, or, if it had a *parodos*, by a layer of packed earth, wood, or thin stone slabs.[45]

As attested to by both the literary and the archaeological evidence, fortifi-cations characterized by a superstructure consisting predominately of coursed mudbrick erected atop a stone foundation were fairly common on the main-land and are partially preserved (or assumed to have existed) at sites dating

---

[40] Winter (1971a: 73, 78–9).
[41] On the construction of all or largely stone walls, see Winter (1971a: 73–80).
[42] Lawrence (1979: 211); Fields (2006: 11).   [43] Lawrence (1979: 211).
[44] This whitewash not only prevented damage from precipitation, but would act to absorb moisture from within the wall (Lawrence 1979: 211).
[45] Lawrence (1979: 211).

from the Geometric through the Hellenistic periods. Because mudbrick very rarely survives in Greece, a general rule for identifying circuits of this type is the presence of a stone socle that is noticeably level along the top.[46] Unfortunately, for a variety of reasons, this may be difficult to recognize among the surviving portions of some circuits. In those cases where the socle itself may have been removed or has partially disappeared, it may be impossible to determine whether the upper sections of the wall were originally brick or completely stone. This is not an insurmountable problem, since, if a wall was completely of stone, numerous blocks should be found strewn around the base.[47] It is generally safe to assume a mudbrick superstructure in those cases where the preserved stone foundation is less than 1.50–2 m in height, and both the faces and the fill have a reasonably flat surface.[48] It is also important to consider that a stone socle on which the mudbrick superstructure rested may vary in height, not only between different circuits, but also in different parts of the same trace. The reason for such variation often lies in the nature of the terrain traversed by the wall—for example, at the bottom of hills, where water (rain/snow) was likely to gather, higher foundations would be required than on flatter areas.[49]

INTERNAL STRUCTURE OF CURTAIN WALLS

Whether a curtain was built predominately of mudbrick or worked stone blocks, such components rarely comprised an entire solid wall. As a general rule, masonry would be employed only on the outer and inner surfaces of a wall, leaving a hollow centre behind the facings, which was then filled by inferior material.[50] The cheapest and most expedient filling material for such a double-face wall was gravel, earth, discarded tiles, mudbricks, and pieces of rock—that is, whatever materials lay at hand.[51] Packing with readily available material such as these, preferably in combination, was especially necessary in

---

[46] Winter (1971a: 73, 78–9); Frederiksen (2011: 55). This rule applies to the irregular mass of the central fill as well as to the interior and exterior facing blocks.

[47] Frederiksen (2011: 55).

[48] Winter (1971a: 71); Frederiksen (2011: 55). Lawrence (1979: 212) implies that a mudbrick superstructure can also be identified in cases where the stone foundation rises to a height 'beyond a man's reach'. Indeed, some Arkadian examples (e.g., Gortys) have stone foundations with a flat surface reaching to a height of at least 3.75 m.

[49] Winter (1971a: 69).

[50] Although rare on the mainland, examples of walls with a solid stone core do exist. Of the Themistoklean walls at Piraeus, Thucydides (1.93.5) writes that 'between the walls thus formed there was neither rubble nor mortar, but great stones hewn square and fitted together'.

[51] Lawrence (1979: 214); Frederiksen (2011: 51).

curtain walls where the width to be filled averaged about 2 m.[52] When these materials were used together, the earth worked to keep the larger components from shifting and exerting excessive outward pressure.

The most common approach for combating such pressure and increasing the overall strength and stability of the curtain was the construction of perpendicular bonding courses placed at regular intervals throughout the thickness of the wall. Although Lawrence argues that, 'more often than not, the mere weight of the facings was thought sufficient to ensure their stability',[53] the placement of these partitions dividing the interior into a number of chambers added considerably more stability and, more importantly, permitted the construction of circuit walls on steep gradients. Normally, these cross walls were only one block thick in each course, and the resultant chambers were filled solid. They could be relatively crudely constructed and were rarely bonded to the facings of the curtain, owing to the fear of lateral thrusting.[54] That is, if the pressure exerted by the fill was too great (especially on steep gradients), it might cause the cross wall of its compartment to shift too. In this unfortunate situation, if the cross wall was bonded to the main facings, then any lateral movement could undermine the structure of the facings, and, ultimately, the entire section of the curtain.

CLASSIFICATION AND TREATMENT OF MASONRY

It was first suggested in the 1830s by Dodwell during his travels in Greece that a wall may be dated based on the style of masonry or the details of construction.[55] Subsequent refinements by Noack,[56] Wrede,[57] and Scranton[58] have added significantly to the study, and much of their work still forms the foundation on which rests the dating of many Greek fortifications.[59] Unfortunately, although the idea of an evolutionary sequence of masonry is very appealing (for example, cyclopean to polygonal to ashlar), such a universal succession of styles does not always stand up to close examination.[60] The works of these scholars, therefore, while useful, must always be 'referred to only with extreme caution, since they are oversimplifications of a field which may eventually prove to be almost without order'.[61] That being said, and acknowledging that it is beyond the scope of the present study to attempt to refine or identify a valid

---

[52] Winter (1971a: 132); Lawrence (1979: 214).   [53] Lawrence (1979: 214).
[54] Lawrence (1979: 215).
[55] For Dodwell's contribution, see *Views and Descriptions of Cyclopean or Pelasgic Remains in Greece in Italy* (1834).
[56] Noack (1927).   [57] Wrede (1933).   [58] Scranton (1941).
[59] Winter (1971a: 80); Lawrence (1979: 235); McNicoll (1997: 3); Camp (2000: 41–2).
[60] Snodgrass (1982: 128); McNicoll (1997: 3).   [61] McNicoll (1997: 3).

Panhellenic sequence of masonry, it is held here that, in a particular region at a certain time, a sequence may be arranged or a predominant style identified.[62] Thus, although the scholarship cited is valuable for its contribution towards a general system of classification and a regularity of terminology, again, caution is always warranted because some Greek walls refuse to be categorized so neatly.[63]

In the early 1940s, Scranton observed that, 'until those interested in the subject come to a common ground on the matter of terminology, further progress is impossible'.[64] Accordingly, the following outline of the different categories of fortification masonry is based largely on the work of Scranton and modifications thereof made by Winter[65] and McNicoll.[66] The masonry of any wall belongs to one of three main groups: unhewn, roughly hewn, or carefully hewn and jointed.[67] Whereas the first two categories are almost indistinguishable from one another (both are often classified as rubble masonry), the third category, which inevitably consists of faces of finely joined masonry usually enclosing a fill of packing material, may be further subdivided into uncoursed and coursed masonry. Uncoursed masonry can include curvilinear blocks (Scranton's 'Lesbian'[68]), polygonal blocks, and trapezoidal or rectangular blocks (Scranton's 'Irregular Trapezoidal' and 'Irregular Ashlar' respectively[69]). Walls constructed of coursed masonry can incorporate polygonal, trapezoidal, rectangular, or ashlar blocks (Fig. 2.1).[70] Examples of coursed masonry where the blocks are laid in continuous courses, all of which appear to be of the same height, are referred to as isodomic; pseudo-isodomic refers to walls in which the blocks are laid in continuous courses that vary perceptibly in height among themselves.[71] It should also be noted that, in the construction of a wall, blocks may be laid as stretchers, headers may be introduced at intervals, or courses of headers and stretchers may alternate with each other.[72] In all the styles of the carefully hewn and jointed blocks, further distinctions can also be made based on treatment of the faces and joints.[73]

Curvilinear (or Lesbian) masonry, characterized by blocks with all sides curved to greater or less degree, is easily identified, but, as there are almost no known examples outside the Aeolic and Ionian sphere of influence,[74] this category need not concern us here. Polygonal masonry refers exclusively to

[62] Although this is the important assumption employed by McNicoll (1997) in his study of Hellenistic fortifications outside the Greek mainland, I believe it is an equally valid tenet for a study with a specifically regional Arkadian focus.
[63] Lawrence (1979: 235); Camp (2000: 42).   [64] Scranton (1941: 20).
[65] Winter (1971a: 80–91).   [66] McNicoll (1997: 3).   [67] Winter (1971a: 80).
[68] Scranton (1941: 17–18).   [69] Scranton (1941: 17–19).   [70] Winter (1971a: 80).
[71] Scranton (1941: 73–4).
[72] Winter (1971a: 80). It must have been recognized that headers interspersed in the face increased the cohesion of the wall and enabled it better to resist shocks (Lawrence 1979: 237).
[73] Winter (1971a: 81).   [74] Scranton (1941: 25); Winter (1971a: 81).

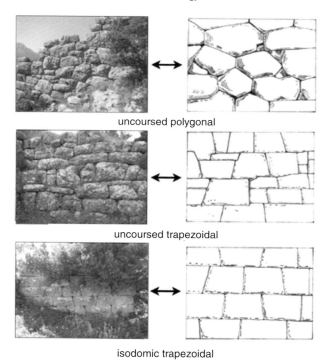

uncoursed polygonal

uncoursed trapezoidal

isodomic trapezoidal

Fig. 2.1. Image showing different masonry types. (© *Matthew Maher*)

blocks that have varying numbers of straight, non-parallel sides, usually more than four, which meet at clear-cut angles.[75] Uncoursed polygonal became widespread on the Greek mainland in the fifth century BC, and coursed polygonal (a variant of the style) appeared in the Peloponnese during the second half of the fourth century BC.[76] Trapezoidal walls, as defined by Scranton, are comprised of blocks in which two opposite sides are parallel (usually the horizontal sides) and the other two opposite sides are cut on the slant and are not usually parallel.[77] Although coursed and uncoursed trapezoidal masonry appears to occur in all parts of the Greek world, there are no clear indications of where exactly the style may have originated.[78] On the other hand, it seems certain that this 'compromise between polygonal and ashlar'[79] developed in the years following the Persian Wars and thrived in fortification

[75] Scranton (1941: 45).
[76] Winter (1971a: 81). Scranton (1941: 54) adds that, in some good examples of normal polygonal style, there are occasional places where the semblance of coursing appears, and in coursed polygonal work there are occasional places that seem highly complex; in some examples, a transitional form seems to have resulted.
[77] Scranton (1941: 71).   [78] Scranton (1941: 77–8).   [79] Fields (2006: 12).

building for at least a century.[80] The last general category of walls is ashlar and is recognized by blocks that are rectangular and usually uniform in size. Although there are but a few examples of uncoursed ashlar, coursed ashlar, beginning in the late fifth century BC, flourished throughout the fourth century BC and became the dominant style of the Hellenistic period.[81]

STYLISTIC CHRONOLOGY OF MASONRY AND ITS LIMITATIONS

The general underlying assumptions concerning the stylistic dating of Greek walls are the belief that fortifications and styles of masonry are not likely to be local in their developments, but, instead, that some sort of international style in fortifications and masonry must have spread through the Greek world;[82] and that the developments of this international style, including the regular and discernible transition from one style to another, are visible in the archaeological record and can be dated relatively. Unfortunately, the classification of masonry styles based on the shape of the blocks and the treatment of the surface is not easily attained. In fact, although there seem to be some stylistic associations, the fact remains that 'a precise and reliable [universal] chronology of styles eludes us'.[83] While the reasons for this are addressed later in this chapter, here it is worth briefly noting the chronological trends that have been *generally established* concerning the stylistic development of polygonal and trapezoidal masonry—the only two styles employed in the fortifications of Arkadian city states.

While examples are known in the Peloponnese from the Archaic period,[84] Scranton maintains that polygonal walls became quite widespread on the mainland during the fifth century BC (specifically 480–400 BC).[85] By the end of the fifth century BC the style had generally declined in popularity, although in the Peloponnese coursed polygonal masonry remained in vogue from the second half of the fourth and beginning of the third century BC.[86] Similarly, Winter argues that, during the fifth and early fourth century BC, polygonal was chiefly employed in the Peloponnese (or areas under Peloponnesian spheres of influence).[87] As aesthetics remained important in city wall construction and

---

[80] Winter (1971a: 81).   [81] Scranton (1941: 99); Winter (1971a: 81).
[82] Scranton (1941: 10–11).   [83] Camp (2000: 42).
[84] e.g., in the late eighth century, a polygonal wall is attested at Asine (Frederiksen 2011: 132) and at Argos a seventh-century polygonal wall has also been identified (Frederiksen 2011: 65, 130).
[85] Scranton (1941: 55).
[86] Scranton (1941: 55). Lawrence (1979: 235) maintains that polygonal masonry was also the most characteristic style of the sixth century.
[87] Winter (1971a: 90).

appearance, architects did not immediately abandon the 'pleasing ruggedness and irregularity of the polygonal style'.[88] Although it appears that *poleis* on the mainland lost much of their enthusiasm for polygonal masonry as soon as they began to build large circuits, a number of Hellenistic examples of polygonal fortifications do exist.[89] Nonetheless, it can be generally stated that, from the last third of the fifth century BC, polygonal steadily lost ground in favour to trapezoidal and ashlar masonry.[90]

Scranton also proposes a few chronological generalizations on the periods in which some of the trapezoidal styles were preferred. He maintains that the use of uncoursed trapezoidal work covers a period from the early fifth century to the early third century BC—that is, the same chronological limits as polygonal masonry.[91] The reason was that uncoursed trapezoidal retained something of the effect and the strength of polygonal work, but was easier to assemble.[92] As the science of siege warfare developed on the mainland, the irregular nature of uncoursed trapezoidal became a liability and it was discovered that the old effect could still be retained in part by using coursed trapezoidal.[93] Uncoursed trapezoidal work, therefore, inevitably gave way in preference to coursed (or isodomic) trapezoidal during the late fifth century and early fourth century BC.[94] With the beginning of the Hellenistic period, we see the rise of pseudo-isodomic trapezoidal masonry.[95]

The limitations of attempting to employ such a stylistic chronology in the dating of fortifications are frequently described.[96] Most obvious is the issue of stylistic overlap. From the general developments already outlined, it is immediately clear that polygonal or trapezoidal were both viable options for a circuit constructed in fourth-century BC Arkadia. Such imprecision is ultimately the result of the scope of the earlier studies in which these observations were based. In other words, if one is looking for universal or even Panhellenic patterns, much of the masonry employed will cover periods that are too long to be of any practical chronological significance. Furthermore, in justifying his stylistic study of city walls, Scranton insists that an international chronology of styles of masonry evolved that will hold for the entire Greek world, except in 'cities too poor or too removed from the outer world to be interested in vying with others'.[97] It is here that Scranton misses the point: namely, that the majority of Greek settlements (and their fortifications) fall into this category and should not be excluded from an attempt to establish a universal stylistic chronology.[98]

---

[88] Winter (1971a: 87).   [89] Winter (1971b: 413); Lawrence (1979: 235).
[90] Scranton (1941: 98); Winter (1971a: 86, 90).   [91] Scranton (1941: 98).
[92] Winter (1971a: 87).   [93] Winter (1971a: 87).   [94] Winter (1971a: 87).
[95] Scranton (1941: 98).   [96] Most recently by Frederiksen (2011: 63–5).
[97] Scranton (1941: 10–11).
[98] The CPC has to date identified no fewer than 800 mainland *poleis* existing in the Archaic and Classical period (Hansen 1994: 9); yet only a few (e.g., Athens, Sparta, Thebes, Sikyon,

Rigid categories of different masonry styles do not really acknowledge the possibility that, in any given circuit, different styles of masonry may simply indicate different workshops or groups of masons rather than different building periods. This would not be uncommon, as a considerable number of contractors must have been employed on the construction of a city wall.[99] Moreover, the classifications of masonry styles are rarely flexible enough to take into account what Winter refers to as 'special solutions to special problems'.[100] Thus, sometimes the masonry style is altered in areas dictated by the terrain (for example, keying courses together to reinforce the facing blocks in the wall against outward pressure exerted by the fill, or where a wall 'stepped' down a hillside). Such alterations, defying the standard categorical definition, may represent 'technical adjustments in the fitting of blocks rather than different styles of masonry'.[101] While such imprecision is a constant drawback, the fallibility of this method is demonstrable on many other points.[102]

At the root of the problem, however, is the basic assumption that the choice of a given masonry style is first and foremost dictated by external influences. In fact, it is clear that styles of masonry were governed not only by external emulation, but by local custom, and could vary from place to place within a region in any given period.[103] Such variation is ultimately the result of conscious choices made by architects at the individual site level. Indeed, the selection of a particular style of masonry could be based on any number of factors: aesthetic ideals, the nature of the terrain, economy, stability, type of stone available, and/or to keep pace with developments in siege warfare at a particular time or place.[104] For these reasons, any rough date established for a circuit based on the stylistic sequence of its masonry is but one chronological consideration. In the end, the problem of dating fortifications can be satisfactorily resolved only when the stylistic evidence is combined with a thorough 'consideration of the military concepts underlying the whole of the system in question [as these] factors do vary from period to period'.[105] In his study of Archaic Greek fortifications, Frederiksen maintains that 'the observations and interpretations based on . . . stylistic grounds in combination with historic arguments, are generally accepted as useful and valid'.[106] This sound methodological approach holds true for the present study.

Mantineia, Tegea, etc.) should be considered major players in the history and politics of their time and place.

[99] Winter (1971a: 83).   [100] Winter (1971a: 83).
[101] Winter (1971a: 84).   [102] Lawrence (1979: 245).
[103] As noted by Camp (2000: 44), 'there are instances where I think we should actually think in terms of regional or local styles of wall-building, which were then exported elsewhere'.
[104] McNicoll (1997: 3); Lawrence (1979: 234–5).
[105] Winter (1971a: 72); cf. Camp (2000: 43).   [106] Frederiksen (2011: 69).

3

Tactical Development of the Constituent Parts of City Walls

In the initial stages of fortification construction, military engineers and architects had to bear in mind a number of different strategic considerations regarding choice of site, procurement of water, access to natural resources, building materials to be used, and how best to take advantage of the natural defences afforded by the surrounding topography. But they also had to consider a number of different tactical concepts. Tactical concepts denote the individual features or constituent parts employed in a fortification system by which a defender is able to gain some particular advantage over an attacker.[1] Thus the form, function, and placement of the curtains, towers, gates, posterns, and outworks were all the result of consciously made decisions based on their role as working parts of the larger defensive system. But because such decisions were largely dictated by the topography of a site, current technology, and historical conditions, there is no standard formula for the collective arrangement of a circuit's constituent parts. This chapter provides a brief examination of the main characteristics and historical development of these individual tactical features of fortifications.[2] Not only does this provide an explanation of the architectural terms and categories that are employed extensively in the rest of the book, it also establishes the variety of evidence, which is often helpful in the relative dating of the Arkadian circuits under discussion.

CURTAINS AND BATTLEMENTS

While fitted masonry was not unknown earlier,[3] arguably the most important and widespread technical development of the fifth century BC was the transition from

[1] McNicoll (1997: 6). Although the trace of a wall is essentially a strategic problem, the shape and constitution of its curtain were a tactical concern.
[2] Detailed structural, chronological, and overall tactical considerations and defensive planning involving these elements are addressed on a site-per-site basis in Part Two, the Catalogue.
[3] For examples and observations of curtains in Iron Age and Archaic period Greek circuits, see Frederiksen (2011: 53–5, 71–2, 76, 78–83, 86–7, 91–5).

rubble to fitted masonry (including mudbrick), whether for the whole curtain or only for its stone foundations.[4] Although this technological advance had aesthetic repercussions, it was essentially a logical and practical improvement developed in response to the ever-increasing desire for higher and thicker walls. Walls that averaged around 2 m or more in thickness required some packing fill between the faces, which rubble facing cannot easily support. In this way, the use of fitted masonry drastically increased the overall strength and stability of the curtains.[5]

The curtains of fortifications generally became taller and thicker with time as city walls increased in size and often expanded to include the lower city, but this is a fact that is not very useful for determining an accurate chronology.[6] Nonetheless, as with the style of masonry employed, there are some general approximations that can be made regarding height and thickness. Relying on his research of defensive architecture throughout the Greek world, Winter maintains that, in the absence of other evidence, walls that are around 3.50–4.50 in height are unlikely to date from earlier than the late fifth century BC, whereas examples that stand over 10 m in height should be regarded as Hellenistic.[7] Although they are admittedly less satisfactory than the use of height,[8] chronological approximations can also be made regarding thickness. It appears that the thickest walls are those of the mid-fourth century BC onwards, especially as thickness was often increased by the addition of a second outer face of masonry.[9]

General developments can also be traced in the internal structure of curtains. As for the nature of the packing material, in walls of the fifth century BC the fill was most often comprised of a mixture of earth, clay, and/or unworked masses of stone.[10] Fill composed predominately of rubble became increasingly frequent throughout the fourth century BC, even when, during the Hellenistic period, headers and stretchers were used regularly to bind the mass of the curtain together.[11] Indeed, during this period, employing headers at regular intervals that ran far back into the fill (to form a compartment or *emplekton*) became much more common.[12] In most cases prior to the fourth century BC, however, binding of the curtain was achieved by leaving the inner faces of the blocks unworked in the rough state in which they were quarried.[13] Although the technical generalities outlined here are of rather limited chronological value individually, taken together they 'carry a considerable cumulative weight'.[14]

---

[4] Winter (1971a: 132).   [5] Winter (1971a: 132); Lawrence (1979: 344).
[6] Winter (1971a: 134). Of course, the overall increase in mass of a curtain over time was also a direct result of the attempt to keep pace with contemporary advances in siege warfare.
[7] Winter (1971a: 134). Frederiksen (2011: 95) maintains that Winter's estimate is too low and instead maintains that walls probably averaged around 6 m in height before the Classical period.
[8] If for no other reason than the fact that curtains in a given circuit were rarely uniform in thickness but varied according to the topography on which they rested and the ground that they were meant to command (Lawrence 1979: 344).
[9] Winter (1971a: 134–5).   [10] Winter (1971a: 135).   [11] Winter (1971a: 136).
[12] Especially in those cases where the outer faces of a curtain were fitted with trapezoidal or ashlar masonry (Winter 1971a: 135; Tomlinson 1961: 139; Lawrence 1979: 215–16).
[13] Winter (1971a: 135).   [14] Winter (1971a: 137).

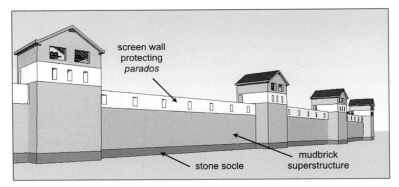

Fig. 3.1. 3D reconstruction of fortification wall with major parts labelled. (© *Matthew Maher*)

The utility of curtains in a given circuit was, of course, not limited to their primary purpose of surrounding and shielding a settlement. More than merely passive elements of the larger defensive whole, curtains were, from the beginning, employed actively as effective platforms for launching offensive manoeuvres. Accordingly, a wall-walk or *parodos* located on top could be used not only for observation but as an advantageous height from which to counter-attack a besieging force (Fig. 3.1). While the earliest walls probably had only a tight packing of earth and stones at the top of the fill, the *parodos* of a mudbrick or stone wall must have consisted of wooden planks, stone slabs, or a thin layer of chips set in mortar (all of which would have protected the bricks from exposure).[15] The introduction of stone-throwing artillery required changes to be made along the top of curtains, as crenellations alone could not provide enough protection against increasing large missiles. Thus, in exposed sectors, crenellated battlements were replaced by battlements comprised of a continuous screen wall, usually 2 m or more in height, with windows protected by wooden shutters at regular intervals (see Fig. 3.1).[16] Although this type of screen wall was not common before the middle of the fourth century BC,[17] when this new feature was adopted, it became almost a universal feature—not only because it provided greater security for defending troops, but because its roof offered protection from the elements for both the artillery and the mudbrick superstructure of the curtain below.[18]

---

[15] Winter (1971a: 138).

[16] Winter (1971a: 140). The term *epalxis* is applied by Hellenistic writers to this new type of screen wall.

[17] Crenellations were still used in the first half of the fourth century BC—e.g., in the walls of Messene and Gortys.

[18] Winter (1971a: 141).

TOWERS

Arguably the greatest and most versatile tactical constituents of a fortification's circuit were its towers. Although the earliest occurrence of such towers seem to be in the late Archaic circuits of Asia Minor, as a rule, towers continued to be employed sparingly and generally unsystematically in Greece until around the time of the Peloponnesian War, when the manifold possibilities of the tower begin to be appreciated and consequently became regular features of most circuits.[19] It cannot be a coincidence that they are employed regularly at a time that also coincided with the appearance of the first effective siege techniques. Undeniably, their development is best understood as a direct response to counter any offensive advantages attackers might have gained with the introduction of the ram and the tentative use of mines.[20]

In many respects, the towers of mainland Greek fortifications show a fairly steady and logical development from the Classical to the Hellenistic periods, except, however, in the one place where we would expect it: their ground plans. In this regard, there appears to be no 'reasonable and logical pattern of development'[21] regarding tower shape. The first true towers were rectangular in shape.[22] Whether they were the cheapest or easiest to build,[23] or whether they developed to conform to the plan of earlier solid bastions,[24] towers of this shape remained the most common.[25] Rectangular towers with long projecting flanks were the most effective shape for protecting the adjacent curtains. For keeping an enemy at a distance from the walls, however, a circular or semicircular tower was most effective, as the defenders could all open fire at once without the 'blind spots' presented by the corners in a rectangular tower.[26] Accordingly, such curvilinear towers were more commonly situated at gateways and sharp angles rather than elsewhere in the circuit. Still, as often as not, round and rectangular towers were used together without any special system.[27]

---

[19] Winter (1971a: 155). For examples and observations of bastions and towers in Iron Age and Archaic period Greek circuits, see Frederiksen (2011: 56, 73, 83–4, 88, 97–8).

[20] Winter (1971a: 155, 157).   [21] Winter (1971a: 191).

[22] The advantages of the different shapes of towers and their relationship to advances in artillery are addressed in detail in the subsequent section. What follows is a brief outline of the various shapes that are encountered in Arkadian circuits.

[23] Lawrence (1979: 378); McNicoll (1997: 8).   [24] Winter (1971a: 191–2).

[25] While failing to mention how he arrived at such a number, Lawrence (1979: 378) observes that 'rectangular towers constitute at least 90 per cent of the total known at all periods'.

[26] Winter (1971a: 192). Curvilinear towers were also advantageous because they did not offer a broad flat surface to enemy artillery.

[27] Winter (1971a: 194) suggests that round and rectangular towers may have been placed side by side for purely aesthetic reasons—that is, as a way of 'enlivening the whole work by varying the appearance of the towers'.

Another type of tower shape can be broadly classified as polygonal (includ-ing pentagonal and hexagonal). Like curvilinear towers, a major advantage of polygonal towers (with blunt angles) was that, with five or more sides, they offered less surface area to enemy fire. Perhaps the main advantage was that a polygonal plan combined the oblique surfaces of a round tower with the economy and material of the square and rectangular types.[28] Although some of the 180° coverage of a semicircular tower was sacrificed (and a polygonal could also probably house fewer weapons), some advantages of the round tower could be recovered by increasing the number of sides on the polygon.[29] Since the best way of protecting the curtains was provided by rectangular towers with long flanks and the most effective way of keeping an enemy from the walls was provided by curvilinear or polygonal towers, it is not surprising to see the development of a 'composite' tower. Essentially comprised of a boldly projecting rectangle terminating in a semicircle or half a polygon, such a tower may have offered the greatest advantage for the least expenditure of money and material.[30]

The first appearance of towers with ground storey chambers in the later fifth century BC[31] brought with it associated structural problems. While towers with a hollow ground storey were no more difficult to construct than the solid variety, the omission of the central fill would have weakened the base and thus necessitated thicker foundations.[32] In order to increase their strength and overall stability, it became necessary to found the towers more securely and to increase both their thickness and the overall size of the blocks used.[33] Consequently, by the Hellenistic period it was not uncommon for the walls of towers to be at least two courses thick, to be unbonded to the adjacent curtain, or to have an increased use of header-and-stretcher systems to bind the whole structure more securely together.[34] Such modifications were made to provide not only better protection to a tower's structural integrity from an enemy assault, but also sufficient support for the discharging of heavy artillery encamped in the upper storeys.

GATEWAYS

The location of gateways must have been primarily dictated by defensive considerations (as with towers) but also convenience. By their very nature,

---

[28] Winter (1971a: 195).   [29] Winter (1971a: 195).   [30] Winter (1971a: 196).
[31] Winter (1971a: 161–2).
[32] Despite the advantages of this type of tower, examples before the time of Epaminondas and the Macedonians are rare (Winter 1971a: 162, 176).
[33] Winter (1971a: 176).   [34] Winter (1971a: 176).

towers were more flexible and could be placed more or less where needed to protect the weaker spots in the circuit. The location of gates, on the other hand, which were openings in the line of a wall and therefore potential weak spots, depended almost entirely on the nature of the terrain and often on the presence of existing roads. Most major roads were generally placed in low-lying parts of the circuit for convenience. Accessibility may not have been a problem for early acropolis circuits, where most of the institutions of trade and commerce would have been located in the lower city, or for those cases where there may not have been a choice of location, with the main roads having been established before the lower city was fortified.[35] Still, in sites where the lower city was fortified, it was a general rule that the main entrances into the city should be fairly easy to reach. In this respect military architects were obviously faced with the problematic condition that, 'the more convenient the approach, the greater was the danger from enemy attack; the more inaccessible the entrance, the greater the inconvenience to those passing in and out about their lawful occasions'.[36]

We know very little of the character of major gates on the mainland before the late Archaic period, but it appears that, from the beginning, the plan of Greek gateways generally conformed to one of two basic types.[37] The first type, the 'frontal gateway', is characterized by an opening in a continuous stretch of wall guarded by a projecting tower or bastion on one or both sides.[38] The second category is the example of 'overlap gates', wherein there is a lateral opening in the walls lying between two overlapping and more or less parallel arms of a wall, which form an entrance corridor.[39] Perhaps here a third type of gate should be introduced, the 'gatecourt' type.[40] These types of entrances

---

[35] Winter (1971a: 209); Lawrence (1979: 304).   [36] Winter (1971a: 206).

[37] Winter (1971a: 208). Although the majority of Archaic, Classical, and Hellenistic gateways conform to one of the following types, as with masonry there are some entrances that defy classification. These rare variants are addressed when encountered in the specifically Arkadian examples presented in Part Two, the Catalogue.

[38] Winter (1971a: 208). There is much inconsistency in the terminology for gates—e.g., Winter (1971a: 208) refers to this first category as 'simple-opening gates' or 'Type I'; Frederiksen (2011: 55) and McNicoll (1997: 6), after Vitruvius (1.5.21), refer to them as 'axial gateways'; and Lawrence (1979: 306) calls them 'frontal gateways'. Although all refer basically to the same form, because the term 'axial' is obscure and 'simple-opening' is misleading (as it can include the complex and monumental examples of the Hellenistic period), I employ Lawrence's classification of 'frontal gateways'.

[39] Winter (1971a: 208); Lawrence (1979: 332). Although Winter (1971a: 208 ff.) refers to examples in this category as 'Type 2', Frederiksen (2011: 55) and McNicoll (1997: 6 ff.) as 'tangential', and Lawrence (1979: 332 ff.) as 'lateral openings', they also continuously use the adjective 'overlap' to describe them. Since this usage is so unambiguous and common in the literature, I have employed it here.

[40] This kind of entrance is usually (and unsatisfactorily) grouped together into one of the first two categories—e.g., based on the standard categories, the Arkadian Gate at Messene is characterized by Lawrence (1979: 318) as a frontal gateway, whereas the Phlious Gate at Stymphalos is

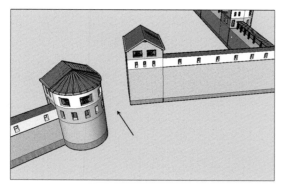

Fig. 3.2. 3D reconstruction of a frontal gate type from Stymphalos. (© *Matthew Maher*)
Note: Opening would have been secured by single or double wooden door—not shown.

have an external opening (lateral or frontal), often protected by towers or bastions on one or both sides, leading to a forecourt and ultimately an inner entrance.[41]

Frontal gateways seem to have been preferred where the entrance to a settlement lay either on a slope or in the depression between two hills, although this type could also be employed on flat ground if the terrain offered some advantage (Fig. 3.2).[42] When these gates were provided with a tower, which was most often the case, they were inevitably placed on the left commanding the attacker's unshielded right side.[43] If, however, the gateway was on a steep slope or its approach was protected by a jog in the curtain, then towers could be omitted altogether.[44] In any event, as the line of the trace was usually governed by natural features, these gates were more often than not placed where their flanks were protected by projecting salients or angles.[45] Variants of the frontal gate can be found in all periods and all places in the Greek world.[46] Early in the fifth century BC, however, when regularity of planning came to be preferred, 'the ideal scheme demanded the symmetrical placing of two identical towers that projected outward'.[47] Before the fourth

---

described by the same author (1979: 334) as an overlap type, although both possess a circular forecourt as their main architectural component.

[41] This type of gate is extremely rare in Arkadia, so much so, in fact, that Stymphalos, Mantineia, and Kleitor possess the only known examples. The courtyard gate, therefore, will be explored when encountered.

[42] Winter (1971a: 209).   [43] Winter (1971a: 210). This is advised by Vitruvius (1.5.2).

[44] Winter (1971a: 210).   [45] Lawrence (1979: 315); Winter (1971a: 212, 223).

[46] For examples and observations on Iron Age and Archaic period gateways, see Frederiksen (2011: 55, 72–3, 79, 83–4, 87–8, 95–7).

[47] Lawrence (1979: 316). On the other hand, although McNicoll (1997: 7) argues that there are no examples of frontal gates with two flanking towers in the 'Greek world earlier than the

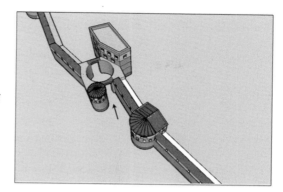

Fig. 3.3. 3D reconstruction of a gatecourt type gate from Stymphalos. (© *Matthew Maher*)

Note: opening would have been secured by single or double wooden door—not shown.

century BC the actual openings of these gates were very narrow, usually no deeper than the thickness of the main curtain, thus leaving room for only a single gate.[48] The great civic gates that would become characteristic of many Hellenistic circuits were most often of this gatecourt type and could reach monumental proportions (Fig. 3.3).[49]

In the periods preceding the Classical period, the overlap gate appears to have been favoured and regarded as the strongest type of entrance (Fig. 3.4).[50] The overlap plan had many advantages. Before the introduction of artillery, any direct attempt to storm the gate would have been impossible, as it did not present its opening to the field, while attempts to scale the walls in the vicinity of a gate would have been met by defensive fire from the overlapping walls.[51] To complement the intrinsic strengths of this type of gate architects would use the natural advantages afforded by the surrounding topography. Thus, overlap gates were generally favoured on level ground and in places where the wall ran along the crest of a hill or traversed a slope—that is, in places that compelled an enemy to advance for some distance at the foot of the adjoining curtain before reaching the gateway, exposing where possible both of their flanks to defensive fire.[52] Herein lies the principle advantage of the overlapping gate, one that was further enhanced by the placement of a tower on the attacker's right.

later fourth century', early fourth century BC examples of this type are found in Arkadia at Paos and Stymphalos.

[48] Winter (1971a: 213).   [49] Lawrence (1979: 334).

[50] Lawrence (1979: 332). Indeed, until the serious use of artillery, when the main dangers to a circuit 'lay in direct attempts at forcing the gate and assaults on the flaking stretches of wall by means of scaling-ladders, the overlap gate had certain obvious advantages over the simple-opening type' (Winter 1971a: 208–9, n. 6).

[51] Winter (1971a: 208–9, n. 6).   [52] Winter (1971a: 215, 209).

Fig. 3.4. 3D reconstruction of overlap gate type from Stymphalos. (© *Matthew Maher*)

Note: opening would have been secured by single or double wooden door—not shown.

Although overlap gates show considerable diversity in their plans and the Greeks used this type 'habitually from a very early period',[53] some chronological developments can be traced.[54] Generally, in the course of time, the length of the overlaps increased, the opening between them became wider, and the passage was often lengthened as the inner wall continued to be prolonged far within (see Fig. 3.4).[55] While the opening was often commanded from all directions by a round tower constructed on the end of the outer curtain, it was also common to have another tower projecting from the inner wall just outside the entrance to the passage.[56] With the rapid development in siege craft in the fifth and fourth centuries BC, the overlap gate often became more complex, usually by making the corridor L-shaped or (less frequently) Z-shaped in plan.[57] Despite the advantages presented by the overlap gate, as demonstrated by its popularity from the Bronze Age through the Classical period, of the two it was the frontal gate that became almost standard in the Hellenistic period.[58] One of the main reasons often cited is that the frontal or gatecourt is better suited (structurally and aesthetically) to main civic entranceways.[59] Whatever the reason, from around the time of Alexander onwards, overlap gates are more frequently confined to secondary entrances.

[53] Lawrence (1979: 332).

[54] It should be noted that because the choice of gate was based on a number of factors through time, not least of all terrain, both frontal and overlap gates 'are chronologically valueless' (McNicoll 1997: 6). Nonetheless, some general patterns of development, and the impetus behind such, can be observed.

[55] Winter (1971a: 209); Lawrence (1979: 333).

[56] Winter (1971a: 209); Lawrence (1979: 333).

[57] Winter (1971a: 223). Neither of these advanced forms of the overlap gate is found in Arkadia.

[58] Winter (1971a: 209); Lawrence (1979: 334).

[59] Winter (1971a: 223); Lawrence (1979: 334); McNicoll (1997: 6).

POSTERNS AND OUTWORKS

Posterns are found in all periods of Greek military architecture, serving two primary functions. In times of peace, posterns provided citizens from the settlement quick access to the *chora*.[60] In times of war, the postern functioned as a means for defenders to sally out from the walls and attack the besiegers.[61] The latter was its most important function, and, consequently, posterns were commonly placed next to towers (which could provide flanking cover), or, later, in the flanks of the towers themselves.[62] Although there may exist some examples as early as the fifth century BC, as a general rule the use of posterns is less common in the earlier circuits, where defenders still relied on the strength of their walls.[63] By the fourth century BC posterns became increasingly common, as 'city-walls lost much of their efficacy owing to the vast improvements in siege-equipment'.[64] In theory, the construction of posterns, especially in areas more accessible to the enemy, would allow a team to sally out speedily and disable an enemy machine before retiring to the safety of the circuit. It is not surprising, therefore, that, from the fourth century BC onwards, the advances in offensive siege craft are paralleled so closely by the increasing frequency of posterns in a city's fortifications.[65] As the Hellenistic period advanced, posterns continued to become more numerous and to become more complex in plan, but their location was generally dictated by the same considerations as before.[66]

The Hellenistic period also witnessed outworks becoming more common (although rarely in Arkadia).[67] Today it is often difficult to assess this important complement to Greek fortifications, for in many cases outworks have left no trace on the surface.[68] But, based on the ancient literary sources and the scanty archaeological remains, some conclusions may be drawn. The virtual absence of these outworks in the Archaic period is easy to understand, as most circuits were confined to an acropolis or clung to easily defensible terrain, making ditches unnecessary.[69] What is less easy to understand, however, is why, from the later Archaic and Classical periods, when more large

---

[60] Winter (1971a: 234); Garlan (1974: 191); Lawrence (1979: 336); McNicoll (1997: 7).

[61] Hence the synonym for posterns, 'sally-ports'.

[62] Winter (1971a: 235); McNicoll (1997: 7). Posterns in the flanks of towers had another advantage: defending troops could muster in the tower chamber until the exact moment arrived for them to strike (Winter 1971a: 240).

[63] Winter (1971a: 235). [64] Lawrence (1979: 338).

[65] Winter (1971a: 240). [66] Winter (1971a: 244).

[67] Winter (1971a: 244). In Arkadia, only the fortifications of Phigaleia and possibly Stymphalos contain examples.

[68] Frederiksen (2011: 41).

[69] The earliest outworks do not appear until the seventh century BC (Frederiksen 2011: 97). For examples and observations on Iron Age and Archaic period gateways, see Frederiksen (2011: 56, 84, 88, 97–8).

Greek cities were fortified, or refortified, outworks were not more common.[70] Frederiksen argues that outworks were unnecessary in the Archaic period, as most fortified sites were securely located on hilltops.[71] Winter adds that because the primary aim of outworks such as ditches and *proteichismata* (out walls) was to meet the combined threat of siege towers, rams, mines, and artillery, and not to hinder the approach of enemy infantry, 'there was never any compelling reason for employing outer defences before the Macedonian period'.[72]

FORTIFICATIONS AND THE EVOLUTION OF GREEK WARFARE

A city's defences are more than the sum of its parts, and the placement of a circuit, its relationship to the natural topography, and the interaction of its various architectural components can take us only so far down the road to understanding a fortification's form and function. This picture is bound to remain incomplete without due consideration of the nature of ancient Greek warfare and its evolution in the Classical and Hellenistic periods. As is so often the case, spurred on by the shifting political and historical happenings of the time, this evolution witnessed several new technological innovations, which developed in its wake. And here the shift in emphasis from the time-honoured pitched hoplite battles to the introduction of artillery and its use in siege warfare had a direct impact on the fortifications. While artillery was initially developed as an offensive weapon in the fourth century BC, it was not long before its defensive capabilities were realized and fortifications were built or rebuilt accordingly. Since the science of fortifications is inseparable from the study of siege craft, 'and an understanding of one is essential to the understanding of the other',[73] the development of this relationship and its repercussions for Arkadian fortifications specifically are also addressed.

THE DECLINE OF HOPLITE WARFARE

When Greek warfare emerged from the shadowy depths of prehistory into the light of history, it was dominated by the heavily armoured, citizen soldier, the hoplite. For the next three centuries (*c.*675–350 BC), military disputes between Greeks would be decided by 'a head-to-head collision of summertime soldiers

---

[70] Winter (1971a: 272).   [71] Frederiksen (2011: 98).
[72] Winter (1971a: 273).   [73] Winter (1971a: p. x).

on an open plain in a brutal display of courage and physical prowess'.[74] For most of the period dominated by hoplite armies, fortifications did not have a place in the main ethic of Greek warfare—the clash of opposing phalanxes. Although relatively heavily armed, the average Greek hoplite was still too vulnerable to risk a direct assault on an enemy wall. Consequently, in the sixth and first half of the fifth century BC, military architects employed a 'passive' rather than 'aggressive' defensive strategy, seeking protection, when necessary, behind their walls and the steep slopes on which they were built.[75] Things changed in the second half of the fifth century BC, and with the beginning of the Peloponnesian War the Greeks witnessed more or less continuous military activity, including important developments in siege warfare. While there were no real innovations in the field of *poliorketics* at this time, as the Greeks basically just copied the techniques employed by the Persians (rams, mounds, and mines), their increasing use of such methods certainly made military architects sit up and take notice.[76]

The increasing deployment of siege craft during the latter half of the fifth century BC probably 'stemmed in large measure from the increasing incidence of city-circuits built on open and easily accessible terrain'.[77] Since the earliest settlements had an outer city that was often partly or entirely unwalled, and siege engines could not easily be brought up against the steep terrain characteristic of their fortified acropoleis, before the Peloponnesian War siege warfare had been of limited importance.[78] Yet, as soon as the walls had been extended to include the level quarters of the outer city, it became possible to employ siege engines effectively, and the relative merits of *poliorketics* began to receive more careful study.[79] It is clear that the increasing risk of enemy machines being brought up against city walls had a direct and lasting effect on the fortifications of the time and those that followed. In order fully to understand and appreciate the evolution of the science of *poliorketics*, we must be constantly aware of the political and economic limitations imposed upon the construction of defence systems in different periods.[80]

FORTIFICATIONS AFTER THE ASCENDANCY OF ARTILLERY IN THE FOURTH CENTURY BC

In his pioneering work *Greek and Roman Artillery* (1969), Marsden makes a very convincing case for the accuracy of Didodorus' statement that arrow-shooting

---

[74] Fields (2006: 48).   [75] Winter (1971a: 299).

[76] Although by *c.*400 BC, the average Greek city must have been much better protected than it had been a century earlier, no radical improvements were made in siege techniques until the first half of the fourth century (Winter 1971a: 308).

[77] Winter (1971a: 57).   [78] Winter (1971a: 57).   [79] Winter (1971a: 57).

[80] Winter (1971a: pp. xvi–xvii).

catapults were first invented in Syracuse in 399 BC.[81] The earliest artillery to which Diodorus refers was a catapult known as a *gastraphetes* ('belly-bow' or 'belly-shooter').[82] As non-torsion machines, these weapons relied instead on the principles of strength and resilience. As such, the early prototypes are best understood as functioning like a large composite bow, where the bow was fixed to a wooden case in which moved a wooden slider that was grooved to receive a missile (resembling a smaller arrow).[83] While estimates vary, Marsden maintains that the maximum effective range of these machines is between 180 and 230 m.[84] Although it had only a slightly greater range than a regular composite bow, its design facilitated better accuracy, and thus its 'introduction must have produced a significant impact'.[85] Indeed, these earliest catapults, when set up at a distance from the walls of a city, would have clearly given the tactical advantage to the attackers.

Because of the limitations imposed by the inherent properties of the composite bow, it did not take long for military engineers fully to exploit and exhaust the potential of these early machines. In order fully to achieve their objective of projecting larger missiles over greater distances, these engineers had to employ a new and more resilient material. By isolating the sinew (which they believed contributed the major force in the composite bow), and combining it with the principle of torsion, by the second half of the fourth century BC they had discovered what they were looking for.[86] This important innovation probably took place in Macedonia under Philip II sometime between 353 and 341 BC.[87] The basic form of the torsion catapults resembled their earlier non-torsion counterparts in most respects, except that in place of the bow were two pivoting arms each anchored to a box spring containing the sinew cord. Furthermore, with some experimentation and modification of the frame, it was also discovered early on that these torsion catapults could also be used to throw large stones.[88]

---

[81] Diod. 14.50.4. For Marsden's argument, see Marsden (1969: 48–55).

[82] Essentially an overly large composite crossbow, it acquired this unthreatening name because the shooter had to place his stomach on the rear of the wooden stock and use the weight of his body to force back the bowstring to its maximum extension (Marsden 1969: 5).

[83] Ober (1987: 570) provides a range of 200–300 m for small stones or bolts. For detailed analysis of the *gastraphetes,* its constituent parts, and its description by Heron of Alexandria, see Marsden (1969: 5–13).

[84] Marsden (1969: 12).   [85] Marsden (1969: 12).

[86] Marsden (1969: 17, 56–7). Two inscriptions recording military inventories discovered on the Athenian Acropolis mention parts of torsion catapults. One (*IG*² ii.1467, B) dates to the Lykourgian period (338–326 BC) based on its letter forms, while the other (*IG*² ii.1627, B) is attributed to the year 330/29 BC. Thus, it is certain that torsion catapults existed by 326 BC at the latest.

[87] While admitting the evidence is tenuous, Marsden (1969: 60–1) combines the fact that there exists no mention of torsion catapults before Philip's reign, with the ancient sources that mention the Macedonians employing these machines at the sieges of Perinthus and Byzantium in 340 BC. Ober (1987: 570) also argues for a date in the 340s BC.

[88] Marsden (1969: 61–2); Ober (1987: 570).

From the last quarter of the fourth century BC until the early years of the second century AD, variations of both the torsion arrow-firers and stone-throwers[89] remained the standard artillery throughout the Mediterranean.[90] Not only could these machines clear the curtains of the defenders; they could also take a heavy toll on any defenders who dared to venture out and attempt to disable them. It is not surprising that the revolutionary development of this mechanical propulsive device would come to exemplify the acme of military technology in the Greek world and would eventually come to threaten fortifications by the sheer amount of force it could produce.

Despite the promising capabilities of these machines, the earliest examples did not possess the strength to hurl stones large enough to threaten well-built walls, and they were also heavy, relatively fragile, and difficult to transport.[91] These machines, therefore, were inefficient for use as field artillery and instead were largely limited to anti-personnel fire.[92] But, as Ober explains, 'none of these factors limited their usefulness as defensive weapons and the fact that a catapult's range was increased by placing it in an elevated position naturally led to the employment of catapults in towers'.[93] In the end, although the first non-torsion catapults were originally developed as offensive weapons to be employed in the siege of a city, the true defensive potential of catapults was soon realized, and we see Greek fortifications responding accordingly. It took some time for this technological innovation to disseminate from Sicily, but the housing of catapults on towers appeared on the Greek mainland by the second quarter of the fourth century BC.[94] While towers of some sort remained prominent defensive features of almost all Greek fortification circuits from the late Archaic period onwards, with the development of improved siege techniques, as well as the introduction of offensive and defensive artillery, they soon changed their function and appearance.

It was not until the time of the Peloponnesian War that the diverse potential of the tower began to be appreciated. That this change coincided with the appearance of the first effective siege techniques—the introduction of the ram and the tentative use of mines—cannot be coincidental.[95] The more wide-spread use of artillery from the mid-fourth century BC onwards, however, necessitated a more aggressive (or active) defensive strategy than in earlier times; no longer was it feasible simply to withdraw and trust in the impenetrability of the walls.[96] The earliest artillery was housed in what Ober refers to as first-generation catapult towers, which, based on historical probability, were

---

[89] Marsden's Mark IVA and Mark IVB respectively.   [90] Marsden (1969: 64).
[91] Ober (1987: 571).   [92] McNicoll (1997: 4).   [93] Ober (1987: 571).
[94] Marsden (1969: 126) maintains that the first changes can be seen in the towers of Messene, constructed beginning in 369 BC. Ober (1987: 571), on the other hand, points to an inscription from the Athenian Acropolis (*IG* II², 1422) dated to 371/70 BC, which mentions the possession of stores of catapult bolts.
[95] Winter (1971a: 155).   [96] Winter (1971a: 243).

developed over a span of about fifty years (c.375–325 BC).[97] It is in the second-generation towers of the Hellenistic period that we see artillery beginning 'to find its true place as a defensive rather than offensive weapon'.[98] As the most obvious place to mount artillery was in the towers, in Hellenistic systems this became their most important function, and a number of architectural developments can be traced.

Generally, from the late fourth century BC onwards, we see military architects employing larger, higher towers, with thicker walls and in greater numbers,[99] both in an attempt to counteract the offensive threat that accompanied the introduction of the much-improved torsion catapult, and to provide the strength and stability required in the towers themselves to support the defensive use of the same machines (that is, the recoil). The most obvious change in the towers, however, occurred when architects began to 'consider which tower shapes provide the most advantageous fields of fire for catapults in any given set of circumstances'.[100] Although rectangular and semicircular towers were employed on the mainland during the Archaic and Classical periods, it is likely that the appearance of hexagonal towers was a direct result of innovations in siege craft of the fourth century BC.[101] In other words, it was no secret that the trajectory of a missile would remain constant if the same calibre machine was fired from the same height. It was the shape of the tower, however, that determined the field of fire.

One of the first changes brought about by the introduction of artillery was the conversion of the platform on the roof of older towers into an enclosed chamber with arrow slits covered by a pitched roof from which artillery could be housed and deployed.[102] Once this crucial first step had been taken, architects were able to explore the advantages afforded by different tower shapes. Marsden examines the various technical details involved in determining a tower's field of fire, but for the purposes of this study a concise outline will suffice.[103] Briefly, the fields of fire of artillery fired from a rectangular tower with three embrasures (one on the front and one on each flank) are fairly substantial, covering an area of no less than 150°.[104] What is immediately apparent is the presence of two blind spots (15° each), resulting from the corners that are inherent in the tower's rectangular shape. This is not an insurmountable difficulty, as the range from the adjacent towers would have covered these gaps, and vice versa. The problem of blind spots in a field of fire

---

[97] Ober (1987: 572).   [98] Winter (1971a: 156).
[99] Marsden (1969: 126); Ober (1987: 572).   [100] Marsden (1969: 140).
[101] Marsden (1969: 147).
[102] It is unlikely that these first-generation artillery towers were ever designed to house stone-throwers, unless they were extremely small (Marsden 1969: 139).
[103] For a technical and detailed account of the relationship between artillery and tower shape, see Marsden (1969: 126–54).
[104] Marsden (1969: 140).

is resolved in semicircular and circular towers. In these curvilinear examples, a complete 180° is achieved, and what is more, there are actually three narrow strips of area that are covered by more than one machine.[105] In hexagonal towers, we see an even greater coverage in the field of fire. Like the curvilinear examples, hexagonal towers possess a complete 180° range with no blind spots, but have the added advantage of an increased area covered by multiple machines. In this design, we see architects fully exploiting the advantages afforded by the defensive installation of artillery. In effect, by replacing the blind spot corners with straight sides, they have combined the cost and labour efficiency of constructing a rectangular tower with the superior fields of fire of a curvilinear tower.

'The greatest "discovery" of the second half of the fourth century was the realization that artillery could serve the defenders as well as the attackers, and do a great deal of damage with a minimum of danger.'[106] It is certain that the improvements made to towers were designed to make the greatest possible use of artillery and ultimately to restore the balance between offence and defence that had been upset with its invention.[107] Further to restore this balance (or, hopefully, to tip it in favour of the defenders), fortifications began to employ a more active, rather than passive defensive approach characteristic of the fifth and first half of the fourth century BC. Accordingly, besides the towers, improvements were also made in the construction of curtains, gates, and posterns of many fortifications of the Hellenistic period.

To be able better to withstand the payload of stone-throwers, curtains of circuits of the late fourth century BC were generally higher and thicker than before, the fill was often more solid, and the header-and-stretcher and compartmented styles of building were increasingly common.[108] The crenellated battlements atop earlier curtains were replaced by the solid screen wall of Hellenistic times (see Fig. 3.1). Stone slowly continued to supersede brick as the preferred material, but otherwise very few changes were made in the actual building materials and constructions.[109] The growing threat of new siege engines also led to a more systematic use of flanking devices. In addition to building taller and more massive towers, architects also began to exploit more fully the possibilities of the indented trace, which, when combined with the heavy concentration of artillery in neighbouring towers, added greatly to the security of gateways (which often were already so strong as to be in little danger of attack).[110] Another example of the tendency towards an active type of defence can be seen in the gates, which were now designed with a view to

---

[105] Because they do not present a flat surface, curvilinear towers have the extra advantage of superior resistance to enemy artillery.
[106] Winter (1971a: 323).   [107] Winter (1971a: 310).   [108] Winter (1971a: 323).
[109] Winter (1971a: 325); Garlan (1974: 199).
[110] Winter (1971a: 329); Garlan (1974: 245).

entrapping a large body of enemy troops.[111] With the exception of the changes made to towers, arguably the greatest advances in the move towards an active defence from the late fourth century BC onwards can be seen in increasing the frequency of posterns.

It is fair to say that no fortified Greek city, however large or small, would have had enough citizen soldiers to defend an entire circuit.[112] Consequently, it was important where possible to be able to harass an enemy position before the attackers got too close to the walls. The most effective way to achieve this was to have a number of posterns, especially in the areas of the circuit most vulnerable to a frontal assault. The increasing use of posterns is one of the earliest signs of the emergence of an active rather than a passive concept of defensive strategy.[113] Although this strategy, which compelled defenders to obstruct the approach of enemy machines by sallying forth and destroying them, has its beginnings in the later fifth century BC, it was increasingly adopted throughout the fourth century BC and would come to form the cornerstone of defensive planning during the Hellenistic period.[114] While the walls themselves remained the main barrier confronting the attacker, the increasing incidence of posterns from the middle of the fourth century BC onwards demonstrates an active defensive strategy aimed at keeping enemy machines at a distance. It is not that defenders no longer trusted the impregnability of their walls, but that in time the walls became the last line of defence— the first being outworks, the second being the use of artillery mounted on the curtain and in towers; the third being the use of sallies in force; and the fourth and last barrier being the wall itself. The effective and specific use of towers as artillery emplacements (especially curvilinear and hexagonal) suggests that, by the third century BC, artillery had found its true place as a defensive rather than an offensive weapon. Still, the incredible advances in siege craft and siege warfare developed and employed on the mainland up to the time of the Roman Conquest ensured that the balance between offense and defence remained more or less even, with neither side possessing a decisive advantage— it would remain this way until the invention of gunpowder.[115]

---

[111] This idea differed from the fifth-century concept of relying simply on impregnability (Winter 1971a: 310).

[112] McNicoll (1997: 6).   [113] McNicoll (1997: 7); Winter (1971a: 325).

[114] Winter (1971a: 305).   [115] Winter (1971a: 331).

4

Topographical, Architectural, and Historical Analysis

In an effort to gain a better understanding of the fortifications from every known Arkadian *polis*, Part Two of this book, the Catalogue, explores in detail the history, the natural features and topography, the architecture, the use of strategy and tactics, and, finally, the chronology of each defensive system in the region on an individual site level. While the cataloguing of extant defensive works is an important aspect of this study, it is only one part, and a truly comprehensive and detailed study of the historical development of Greek military architecture and defensive planning in Arkadia during the Classical and Hellenistic periods requires an equally inclusive interregional synthesis. What follows is an examination of the discernible patterns shared and differences exhibited in the geographical distribution of sites, the local topography, and the architecture employed in the various fortification systems. The chronological patterns established in this synthesis are then viewed in the light both of the recognized history of Arkadia as well as of the historical probability that can be reasonably and plausibly inferred.

GEOGRAPHIC DISTRIBUTION OF SITES

Although the attribution of cardinal points for the location of each site (northern Arkadia, southern Arkadia, and so on) is employed in Part Two, the Catalogue, largely for organizational convenience, the general geographic distribution of the fortified *poleis* does display interesting spatial and chronological patterns. It is not surprising to find all the fortified sites distributed throughout the inhabitable areas of Arkadia (Fig. 4.1). Thus we find sites located on the plains without an acropolis (for example, Mantineia, Kleitor), on the summit of independent hills (for example, Theisoa (Lavda), Dipaia), on mountain spurs (Theisoa (Karkalou), Halous, Teuthis), or in areas combining flat and elevated terrain (for example, Stymphalos, Alea, Psophis). Similarly,

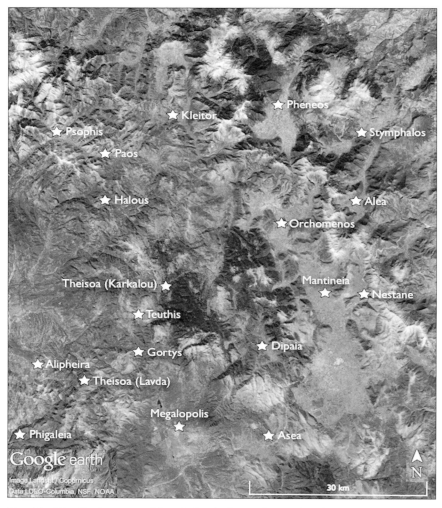

Fig. 4.1. Distribution map of fortified Arkadian *poleis* explored in this study. (© *2011 Google-Map data © 2011 Tele Atlas*)

we see that the distribution of *poleis* is usually limited to a single settlement in areas with territories clearly defined in basins. Stymphalos, Pheneos, Kleitor, and Alea, for example, were the only *poleis* located in their respective basins. The larger and more open plains, however, attracted more settlements, and we see a number of *poleis* occupying different parts of the same plain. Thus, the same plain was occupied by Mantineia, Tegea, and Pallantion, another was occupied by Orchomenos and Kaphyai, another by Asea and Eutaia, and one by Megalopolis, Oresthasion, and Trapezous.[1] Conversely, those sites that did not possess a considerable amount of flat terrain were confined exclusively to the banks above the major rivers: the Helisson (Dipaia), the Alpheios (Alipheira, Theisoa (Lavda), Heraia), the Ladon (Halous, Thaliades, Thelphousa), the Neda (Phigaleia), the Lousios/Gortynios (Gortys, Teuthis, Theisoa (Karkalou)), and the Lopesi/Sireos (Paos, Psophis).[2] In addition to the obvious spatial patterns, there is also a marked relationship between the geographic distribution of the sites and the date of their city walls (Fig. 4.2).[3]

The earliest fortifications, appearing at *poleis* in the late fifth/early fourth century BC, are found in three geographical areas, the south-west (Alipheira, Phigaleia), the north-west (Psophis, Paos), and the east (Tegea and Mantineia). That Phigaleia was fortified at such an early date should not come as a surprise, considering its historical animosity and constant skirmishes with Sparta.[4] Although exactly why the other three should have been fortified at that time is more difficult to account for, their specific locations and close grouping do betray an apparent pattern—one perhaps associated with their membership of the Peloponnesian League and Sparta's larger hegemonic interests. That Alipheira was fortified sometime during the Peloponnesian War is not a coincidence. Indeed, with Phigaleian control of the Neda, the long east–west valley commanded by the hill of Alipheira would have represented Sparta's most convenient point of access to the Ionian Sea, without the need to traverse Messenia or either Taygetos or Mt Lykaion. Furthermore, as the cities of Achaia were not members of the Peloponnesian League, a fortified Paos and Psophis would also have been in the interests of Sparta, since these *poleis* controlled one of the main north–south routes from Achaia into Arkadia. Sparta's hegemony in the Peloponnese and its interest in strategic communication routes might also have played a part in the original fortification of both Mantineia and Tegea in eastern Arkadia. Although the extant walls of Mantineia belong to the earlier fourth century BC,[5] the archaeological record and the historical sources agree that the city was certainly fortified sometime prior to the Spartan siege in 385 BC, probably in the fifth century BC.[6] Similarly,

[1] On Pallantion, Kaphyai, Eutaia, Oresthasion, and Trapezous, see the Appendix.
[2] On Thaliades, Thelphousa, and Heraia, see the Appendix.
[3] The dates provided for all the sites in question refer only to when the settlement was fortified, not founded. With the exception of Megalopolis, presumably all the sites (or the general area around them) were occupied for a time prior to when they were actually fortified.
[4] See Part Two, Chapter 14, for a more detailed history of the site of Phigaleia.
[5] Xen. *Hell.* 6.5.3–5.
[6] Basing his argument on stylistic grounds and the historical evidence, Scranton (1941: 59) believes that the earlier polygonal sections of the trace belong to the fifth century BC and the time of first synoikism. Certainly they should date to before the time Mantineia ceded from the Peloponnesian League in 421 BC (Thuc. 5.29.1). On the Spartan siege in 385 BC, see Xen. *Hell.* 5.2.4–5; Diod. 15.12.1–2; Paus. 8.8.7.

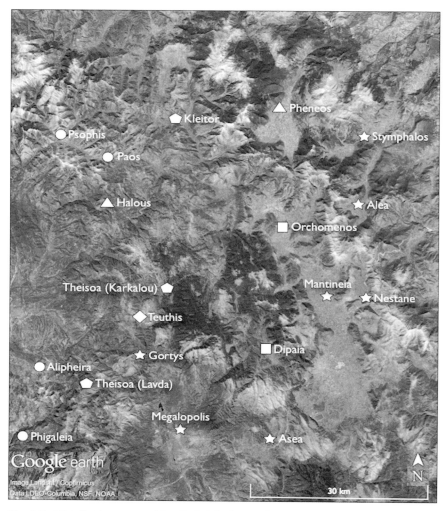

Fig. 4.2. Distribution map of fortified Arkadian *poleis* explored in this study by date of construction: circle = late fifth/early fourth century; star = early fourth century; triangle = first half fourth century; square = mid-fourth century; pentagon = late fourth/third century; diamond = fourth or third century. (© *2011 Google-Map data © 2011 Tele Atlas*)

it appears that Tegea (a long-time Spartan ally) must also have been fortified by the fifth century BC, and probably much earlier.[7] The presence of these two (fortified) Peloponnesian League allies, together occupying almost the entirety

---

[7] On historical grounds alone, Winter (1971a: 30, n. 60) believes that Tegea may have been fortified by the early sixth century BC. Scholars from the Norwegian Institute at Athens continue to search for the exact line of fortifications. Although a small section of the fortifications has

of eastern Arkadia, provided Sparta with a safe corridor—one that linked Lakonia to allied Corinthian territory.[8] In this way, Spartan troops could move north towards the Isthmus while avoiding hostile Argive territory.

The most perceptible distribution pattern is represented by the explosion of fortification building (and rebuilding) that occurred in early fourth-century BC Arkadia. As opposed to the later fifth-century BC fortifications, whose distribution reflected Spartan or Peloponnesian League interests, the early fourth century BC—especially the years around *c*.370 BC—witnessed a marked shift in the distribution of the fortified sites: instead of looking north to Achaia, all eyes were now firmly fixed on Sparta in the south and Orchomenos and Phlious in the north-east. Indeed, in an attempt to limit any future Spartan aggression, a confederation of Arkadian cities was established and Megalopolis and Mantineia were founded and refounded as defensive consolidations under the guidance of the Theban general Epaminondas. Also at this time we see the fortification of Nestane, Gortys, Asea, and possibly Dipaia—*poleis* that may have been part of the same defensive strategy. Finally, as discussed in greater detail later in this chapter, it is no coincidence that this period also saw the fortification of Alea and refoundation and fortification of Stymphalos. That Elis was an ally of the Arkadian League during the early fourth century BC[9] probably explains why no new fortifications were built at this time in western Arkadia.

LOCAL TOPOGRAPHY AND CHOICE OF SITE

On the topography of ancient Stymphalos, Gourley and Williams note that the site was so well equipped with natural defences that 'we must assume that its very form and its position in the valley were largely dictated by defensive considerations'.[10] Not limited to Stymphalos, this phenomenon observable at every fortified Arkadian *polis*. Indeed, while informative in some regards, the geographic distribution of fortified *poleis* is ultimately a product of the local topography at the individual site level. The geographic location for a settlement is based on the consideration of a number of local topographic factors, such as the quantity and quality of arable land, an adequate water supply, and, particularly important here, its natural defensibility. As repeatedly stressed throughout this book, in both form and function, a city's fortifications are a reflection of the local topography. Thus, it is the topographic patterns that are

---

appeared recently in the geophysical survey Ødegård (forthcoming), the walls of Tegea remain strangely elusive (K. Ødegård, pers. com.). See the Appendix for more information on Tegea.

[8] Pretzler (forthcoming).   [9] Xen. *Hell.* 6.5.5.
[10] Gourley and Williams (2005: 220).

the most revealing concerning the strategy behind the choice of site, its perceived defensibility, and its relationship with the fortifications.

As in most areas of Greece, the larger topography of Arkadia restricted the choice of sites to basins, relatively open plains, or the mountainous heights above the major rivers. Within these areas, to use the terminology employed in this book, the fortifications are categorized as horizontal, uneven, or acropolis types (Fig. 4.3). Of the nineteen *poleis* with extant fortifications, Mantineia

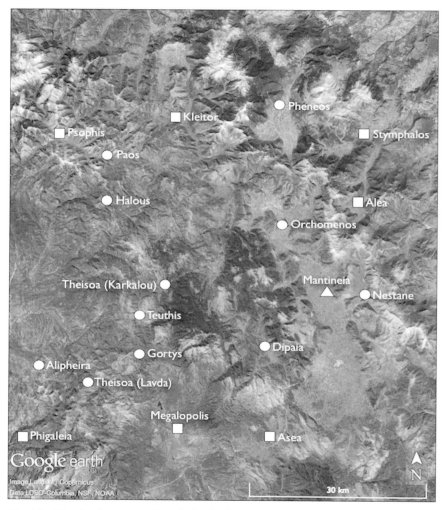

Fig. 4.3. Distribution map of fortified Arkadian *poleis* explored in this study by type of construction: circle = acropolis type; square = uneven type; triangle = horizontal type. (*© 2011 Google-Map data © 2011 Tele Atlas*)

represents the only example of a horizontal type, and, with seven and eleven examples respectively, we see that the uneven and acropolis type of fortification circuits predominate in Arkadia. Yet, even within these broader categories, there are subtle similarities and differences. Uneven type fortifications, for example, are found both at sites primarily comprised of flat terrain, but in which some elevated height is incorporated for defence (Stymphalos, Alea, Kleitor, Asea), as well as at places that occupy predominately 'high ground, either level or unevenly terraced, and preferably at an angle between two rivers'[11] (Psophis, Phigaleia, Megalopolis). Interestingly, the uneven type sites are found almost exclusively along the northern and southern peripheral edges of the region. The acropolis type of fortification circuits differ slightly in the topographical details and are found encircling both isolated hilltops—with intramural habitation (Theisoa (Lavda)), without intramural habitation (Dipaia, Pheneos), or with a fortified lower city on its slopes (Alipheira)—and, more commonly, mountain spurs where habitation was most often limited to the unfortified slopes or adjacent saddle (Gortys, Paos, Nestane, Halous, Theisoa (Karkalou), Teuthis, Orchomenos). Taken together, the examples of the acropolis type of circuit are found throughout Arkadia, most commonly on the banks above the major rivers.

The types of fortifications encountered in Arkadia are first and foremost a reflection of the specific local topography and are thus specific to individual choice of site. The choice of the location for a settlement was based primarily on two inclusive factors: that the surrounding territory was more or less self-sustainable (including land suitable for agriculture and pastoralism, a ready water supply, and a situation on an important communication route), and that the site was naturally defensible, at least in part. If we take for granted the fact that the respective territories could support and sustain the local populations of all the *poleis* in question, we are left to consider the second, more variable, motivation behind the choice of sites—its natural defences. Winter maintains that, 'in all periods of Greek urbanization, the choice of site was a fundamental defensive consideration'.[12] Arkadia is no exception, and a study of the natural defences inherent in the local topography of these sites demonstrates interesting and revealing patterns. These established patterns are based on the exploitation of three natural defensive variables common to all the sites (individually or in combination), including the incorporation of elevated terrain, the surrounding mountains, and/or local watercourses.

[11] Winter (1971a: 32). [12] Winter (1971a: 3–4).

NATURAL DEFENCES

Neolithic remains found scattered on hilltops across Greece and late Bronze Age
circuits at Mycenae, Athens, and Tiryns, for example, demonstrate that the
defensive advantages afforded by elevated terrain have long been recognized.[13]
Predictably, therefore, we see that all the Arkadian *poleis* employing acropolis
and uneven types of fortifications (that is, all sites except Mantineia) have at
least some high ground incorporated into their respective circuits (Table 4.1).
The advantages of occupying elevated ground are obvious and do not need to
be recounted in detail. Briefly, according to the main principle of physics
inherent in artillery towers, defensive missiles fired from a height could reach
greater distances than those fired from the ground. Moreover, occupation of
elevated terrain gave advantage to defending infantry, as it was easier to fight

Table 4.1. Geographic and topographic data

Arkadian poleis	Region	Fortification type	Natural defences	First building phase
Alea	East	Uneven	Acropolis	Early 4th (*c.*370 BC)
Alipheira	West	Acropolis	Acropolis, 2 rivers	Late 5th (*c.*425–400 BC)
Asea	South	Uneven	Acropolis, 1 river	Early 4th (*c.*370 BC)
Dipaia	West	Acropolis	Acropolis, 1 river	Early–mid 4th (*c.*375–350 BC)
Gortys	South	Acropolis	Acropolis, 1 river, streams	Early 4th (*c.*370 BC)
Halous	West	Acropolis	Acropolis, 2 rivers	Early–Mid 4th (400–350 BC)
Kleitor	North	Uneven	Elevated terrain, 2 rivers	Late 4th–early 3rd (325–275 BC)
Mantineia	East	Horizontal	1 river	Early 4th (*c.*370 BC)
Megalopolis	South	Uneven	Elevated terrain, streams	Early 4th (*c.*370 BC)
Nestane	East	Acropolis	Acropolis, streams	Early 4th (*c.*370 BC)
Orchomenos	East	Acropolis	Acropolis, 1 river	Mid 4th (*c.*375–325 BC)
Paos	North	Acropolis	Acropolis, 2 rivers	Late 5th–early 4th (*c.*425–375 BC)
Pheneos	North	Acropolis	Acropolis, 2 rivers	Mid–late 4th (350–300 BC)
Phigaleia	West	Uneven	Acropolis, 2 rivers	Late 5th–early 4th (*c.*425–375 BC)
Psophis	North	Uneven	Acropolis, 2 rivers	Late 5th–Early 4th (*c.*425–375 BC)
Stymphalos	North	Uneven	Acropolis, lake, streams	Early 4th (*c.*370 BC)
Teuthis	West	Acropolis	Acropolis, 1 river, streams	Early 4th–late 3rd (*c.*370–200 BC)
Theisoa (Karkalou)	West	Acropolis	Acropolis, 1 river, streams	Late 3rd (*c.*250–200 BC)
Theisoa (Lavda)	West	Acropolis	Acropolis, 1 river, streams	Late 4th–early 3rd (325–275 BC)

[13] For a survey of the distribution of prehistoric remains in eastern Arkadia, see Howell (1970).

moving downhill than up. Finally, as extolled by Aristotle, the high ground facilitated the observation of one's territory, allowing it 'to be taken in at one view'.[14] To these clear advantages could be added the local geology, which often consists of rough and irregular veins of exposed bedrock. Sites fortunate enough to possess elevated terrain exhibiting this geology had a double defensive advantage: not only could the bedrock be fashioned and substituted for stone blocks in the foundations of the wall, as seen at Gortys and Theisoa (Lavda), for example, but steep and rocky terrain could often make additional, man-made fortifications superfluous—as at Nestane, and possibly Teuthis and Dipaia.

The same mountains that often defined a *polis*'s territory also represented a form of natural defence, as they dictated the approaches to the city and often protected at least one flank. This is expected at those sites that occupy a mountain spur connected to a larger mountain by a saddle. Thus, we see a larger mountain protecting at least one side of a settlement at Halous, Nestane, Orchomenos, Paos, Teuthis, Theisoa (Karkalou), and Alea. The same defensive principle applies to the acropoleis of Asea and Dipaia, which, although not connected to larger mountains, are comprised of hills that are one among several in series of low foothills. Even in sites that are laid out over predominately flat terrain, such as at Mantineia, Stymphalos, Kleitor, and Pheneos, we see in their location a concern for this notion. All these sites were situated extremely close to surrounding mountains or high hills, separated usually by only a couple of hundred metres. The proximity to or occupation of elevated terrain ensured that the main approaches to the sites were predictable and, thus, defensible. A final natural defence sought in and exploited by the choice of site was, simply put, water.

Of all the demonstrable topographic observations in this study, the role water played in the defence of Arkadian *poleis* was both the most widespread and the most surprising: the most widespread, since every site without exception has some form of natural hydraulic defence, and the most surprising, since it is a fact that is easily overlooked on the ground. Of course the role played by water as a natural defence is obvious at sites such as Stymphalos, Gortys, and Halous. But the existence of waterways at other sites is often less perceptible, especially if reconnaissance is limited to the dry summer months. Still, a careful examination of the ancient sources, the early modern travel reports, and satellite imagery establishes that all of the sites in question exploited water in some form for defensive purposes.[15]

---

[14] Arist. *Pol.* 7.1327ᵃ.
[15] Even a dry river bed (essentially a ditch) would be defensively advantageous and can also be considered a form of natural outwork.

How the water was exploited is evident in two primary patterns. There are those sites at which tributaries, rivers, or *katavothroi*-lakes flanked at least one whole side of the settlement. This arrangement can be seen at Dipaia, Orchomenos, Pheneos, Theisoa (Karkalou), Asea, Nestane, and Alea. The other and more common pattern, those sites where watercourses and lakes protected two sides of the settlement, is exemplified at Alipheira, Gortys, Halous, Paos, Teuthis, Theisoa (Lavda), Kleitor, Megalopolis, Phigaleia, Psophis, and Stymphalos. Although Mantineia too exploited water as an additional measure of defence, because its course was altered (after the 385 BC Spartan attack) to circumvent the city, it is the only site that does not fit neatly into either of these patterns. In any case, the choice of site flanked by one, or more often two, watercourses had a number of defensive advantages. Ultimately the presence of such water-courses functioned to impede, and thus dictate, approaches to the city, and, in this way, they worked like natural outworks.[16]

When we consider that all the sites (except Mantineia) took care to incorp-orate some elevated terrain into the course of their circuit, that all the sites (except Megalopolis) were located very close (or were attached) to the sur-rounding mountains, and that all the sites (without exception) also had a watercourse protecting one or two flanks, we can appreciate the perceived importance of natural defences and the important role they played in the choice of site. That being said, it is important to remember that natural defences provided only part of the equation. As settlement at these sites almost always preceded the construction of the fortifications, it follows that, even if the location of these settlements was chosen based on its natural defensibility, the strength of such defences was viewed against the backdrop of contemporary warfare practices—that is, traditional hoplite warfare. With the development and increasingly frequent use of siege machinery—from around the time of the Peloponnesian War onwards—the inhabitants of these sites must have immediately realized the necessity of fortifications for secur-ity. Indeed, no site was naturally impregnable or completely safe—a fact that became all too apparent to people everywhere with the invention of artillery. Thus, as will be discussed, when these *poleis* were finally fortified, they were done so with careful strategic and tactical consideration, and deliberate care was taken to ensure that the city wall complemented and amplified the already present natural defenses, while at the same time compensating for inadequacies in the terrain.

---

[16] While a prevalent tactic in the landlocked region of Arkadia, the use of natural outworks like rivers or riverbeds is not solely a phenomenon of the Classical and Hellenistic periods. As noted by Frederiksen (2011: 77), beginning in the seventh century BC, as settlements began to be founded 'entirely or partly on level ground, a river would often be used as an extra obstacle for access to the settlement on one side'.

FORTIFICATION ARCHITECTURE

The increasing development and deployment of siege craft during the latter half of the fifth century BC, and the invention of the catapult by *c.*399 BC especially, had lasting and far-reaching effects on the security of Arkadian *poleis*. Like the ripples on a pond radiating from its centre, this technology spread throughout the Mediterranean from Syracuse, the place of its invention.[17] The transmission of this new technology and its offensive potential must have been accompanied by real defensive concerns. It is certainly unlikely to be a coincidence that the majority of Arkadian *poleis* were fortified in the generation after its invention.[18] Since siege engines could not easily have been brought up against the steep terrain characteristic of most Arkadian settlements, in the past these settlements would have been able to trust the natural defences or, in a few cases, the impregnability of their circuits.[19] Artillery machines, however, were not party to the same restrictions and could inflict substantial damage from considerable distances—a fact that defenders soon realized worked both ways. It is clear that the increasing risk of catapults being brought up against one's walls and, later, the appreciation of the catapult's defensive applications, had direct and lasting effects on the fortifications of the time and those that followed. The effects of this relationship are visible in the architecture and implicit tactics of the fortifications of the Arkadian *poleis*.

Curtains

The limitations in the use of masonry style for relative dating have been expressed by others and already voiced in this study.[20] In most cases, other forms of external and internal evidence have been employed whenever possible to supplement the stylistic evidence provided by the type of masonry. Still, it would be specious to claim that the polygonal walls of Dipaia, for example, fit the pattern of the other fourth-century BC walls if the walls themselves have been dated based solely on this style. To avoid circular reasoning, therefore, those circuits in which the masonry provided the only date for the circuits' construction (Dipaia, Theisoa (Karkalou), Teuthis) are absent from consideration in the chronological discussion. That being said, an

---

[17] Diod. 14.50.4.

[18] The creation of the Arkadian League and the end of Spartan hegemony in the Peloponnese after the Battle of Leuktra were also important factors for the appearance of fortifications at this time in Arkadia. This point is discussed in detail later in this chapter.

[19] e.g., Alipheira, the pre-385 BC wall at Mantineia, or the early site of Stymphalos thought to be near modern Lafka (B. Gourley, pers. com.).

[20] See Part One, Chapter 2.

examination of the style of masonry and construction of the walls does reveal interesting spatial and chronological patterns (Table 4.2).

The curtains of the fortifications established in the survey of sites are nowhere consistent, and we see examples of coursed polygonal, regular (uncoursed) polygonal, irregularly coursed trapezoidal, isodomic trapezoidal, trapezoidal with some polygonal, coursed polygonal with some trapezoidal, dry rubble, or combinations of the above. Minor discrepancies aside, however, these masonry styles can be categorized into two primary groups: those circuits constructed in a predominately polygonal style (Alipheira, Phigaleia, Paos, Nestane, Asea, Megalopolis, Stymphalos, Alea, Halous, Pheneos, Mantineia (pre-385 BC circuit), Theisoa (Lavda), Dipaia), and those that are predominately coursed trapezoidal (Psophis, Mantineia (c.370 BC circuit], Gortys, Orchomenos, Kleitor, Theisoa (Karkalou), Teuthis). Since one person may see coursed trapezoidal with the occasional polygonal block, another might see polygonal with the occasional trapezoidal block. A binary division

Table 4.2. Architectural data: masonry and superstructure

Arkadian *poleis*	Fortification type	Masonry	Superstructure	First building phase
Alea	Uneven	Polygonal	Mudbrick	Early 4th (c.370 BC)
Alipheira	Acropolis	Coursed polygonal	Mudbrick	Late 5th (c.425–400 BC)
Asea	Uneven	Coursed polygonal	Mudbrick	Early 4th (c.370 BC)
Dipaia	Acropolis	Coursed polygonal	Mudbrick	Early–mid 4th (c.375–350 BC)
Gortys	Acropolis	Trapezoidal	Mudbrick	Early 4th (c.370 BC)
Halous	Acropolis	Coursed polygonal	Mudbrick	Early–mid 4th (400–350 BC)
Kleitor	Uneven	Trapezoidal	Mudbrick	Late 4th–early 3rd (325–275 BC)
Mantineia	Horizontal	Trapezoidal	Mudbrick	Early 4th (c.370 BC)
Megalopolis	Uneven	Polygonal	Mudbrick	Early 4th (c.370 BC)
Nestane	Acropolis	Coursed polygonal	Mudbrick	Early 4th (c.370 BC)
Orchomenos	Acropolis	Trapezoidal	Mudbrick	Mid 4th (c.375–325 BC)
Paos	Acropolis	Coursed polygonal	Mudbrick	Late 5th–early 4th (c.425–375 BC)
Pheneos	Acropolis	Coursed polygonal	Mudbrick	Mid–late 4th (350–300 BC)
Phigaleia	Uneven	Coursed polygonal	Mudbrick	Late 5th–early 4th (c.425–375 BC)
Psophis	Uneven	Trapezoidal	Mudbrick	Late 5th–early 4th (c.425–375 BC)
Stymphalos	Uneven	Polygonal	Mudbrick	Early 4th (c.370 BC)
Teuthis	Acropolis	Trapezoidal	Mudbrick	Early 4th–late 3rd (c.370–200 BC)
Theisoa (Karkalou)	Acropolis	Trapezoidal	Mudbrick	Late 3rd (c.250–200 BC)
Theisoa (Lavda)	Acropolis	Coursed polygonal	Mudbrick	Late 4th–early 3rd (325–275 BC)

Fig. 4.4. Distribution map of fortified Arkadian *poleis* explored in this study by type of masonry: circle = predominately polygonal; square = predominately trapezoidal. (© *2011 Google-Map data* © *2011 Tele Atlas*)

between polygonal and trapezoidal is, therefore, the most representative way to separate the types of masonry in a way that is not subjective or arbitrary.

The number of sites with predominately polygonal versus predominately trapezoidal masonry are thirteen and seven respectively, or roughly 65 and 35 per cent (Fig. 4.4).[21] These numbers clearly demonstrate that, in terms of

---

[21] Including the pre-385 BC polygonal walls of Mantineia, but not later repairs or modifications, both of which are discussed later in this chapter.

masonry style alone, polygonal masonry is the predominate type employed in the fortifications of Arkadian *poleis*. Moreover, when those walls with an uncertain date or a chronology derived from only the masonry style are removed,[22] sixteen sites remain. With eleven examples of polygonal walls (70 per cent) and five with trapezoidal (30 per cent), these numbers establish the same general predilection for polygonal over trapezoidal masonry. When the type of masonry employed in these sixteen sites is compared to the date of the circuits' construction, interesting and significant patterns emerge. First of all, we see that eleven of the sixteen sites have walls dated between the late fifth and early fourth centuries BC, of which eight were built in a polygonal style and three in a trapezoidal style. In the more inclusive chronological frame of the first three-quarters of the fourth century BC, we see two polygonal and one trapezoidal example. Finally, of the two walls that date between the late fourth and early third century BC, one was built in a polygonal style, the other in a trapezoidal style. This analysis tells us two important things. First, this breakdown confirms the problems of relying solely on masonry style to establish a date for a circuit, as it demonstrates that both polygonal and trapezoidal styles were used throughout the fourth century BC (if not longer). Second, it demonstrates that the polygonal style decreased in popularity from its peak in the early fourth century BC, slowly giving way to the trapezoidal. This shifting trend in masonry styles is perhaps best explained by the fact that trapezoidal curtains could be constructed more quickly, more cheaply, and more easily, while still retaining something of the effect and the strength of polygonal work.[23]

When the masonry style of the curtains is compared to the type of fortification, we see the same preference (at the same general ratio) for polygonal over trapezoidal in the construction of both acropolis and uneven type circuits. For example, of the eleven acropolis circuits, seven were built with polygonal blocks (65 per cent) and four with trapezoidal (35 per cent), and, in the uneven type of fortifications, we see five examples of polygonal (70 per cent) and two of trapezoidal (30 per cent). The circuit at Mantineia—the only example of a horizontal type—had both styles: the pre-385 BC wall was polygonal, while the *c.*370 BC wall was trapezoidal. An interesting pattern that emerges is the recognition that all the uneven type circuits erected in the early fourth century BC were built with polygonal style masonry (Alea, Asea, Megalopolis, Stymphalos). Furthermore, it is interesting to consider that the only two acropolis type circuits to employ trapezoidal masonry were Theisoa (Karkalou) and Teuthis. As they are separated by only 8 km, that these two acropolis sites alone used trapezoidal blocks may not be a coincidence. Indeed, an examination of the spatial distribution of the different masonry styles brings to light a number of interesting patterns.

[22] i.e., Mantineia (pre-385 BC circuit), Dipaia, Theisoa (Karkalou), and Teuthis.
[23] Winter (1971a: 86–7).

Proximity appears to have played a role in the type of masonry employed, since the territory of every *polis* with polygonal masonry lies immediately adjacent to the territory of another *polis* with the same (see Fig. 4.4). In other words, there are no isolated examples of polygonal masonry in Arkadia and all examples lie within close proximity to other examples in the style. This relationship between geographic location and polygonal style is represented by the extremely short distances between Mantineia (pre-385 BC circuit) and Nestane, between Nestane and Alea, between Alea and Stymphalos, between Phigaleia and Alipheira, between Alipheira and Theisoa (Lavda), between Megalopolis and Asea, and between Paos and Halous. The same pattern is demonstrable for the sites using predominately trapezoidal masonry. Thus we see sites in close proximity using the same trapezoidal style, such as Orchomenos and Mantineia (*c.*370 BC circuit), Kleitor and Psophis, as well as Gortys, Teuthis, and Theisoa (Karkalou).[24] Finally, it should come as no surprise to discover that the only other style of masonry used anywhere in Arkadia, dry rubble masonry, also fits this pattern of distribution. Only two examples of curtains in this style exist—at Gortys and Megalopolis—both of which appear to represent later repairs to the original circuits.[25] As the original walls at Gortys were trapezoidal and those at Megalopolis were polygonal, it is clear that dry rubble style was used indiscriminately with regard to the original type of masonry—probably because it was the fastest and cheapest way to make repairs.

Our understanding of construction techniques and appreciation of any characteristics shared by the different circuits are severely limited by the poor state of the extant remains themselves. Still, some general observations and probable deductions can be made based on what does survive. The majority of circuits appear to have been constructed with the typical double facing of blocks with a core in between comprised largely of rubble and packed earth. It was also common to leave the interior facings of the blocks in a rough state so as to adhere better to the core inside. Moreover, if Alea and Nestane are representative, then we might expect the other Arkadian fortifications to have employed relatively smaller blocks for the interior facing wall. The walls at Gortys provide the exception that proves these general rules. The eastern wall of Gate B at Gortys, for example, did not have the usual rubble filling between the faces, but was instead comprised of a solid core of tightly packed blocks. Furthermore, while the rest of the curtains in the circuit did possess a

---

[24] This preference for trapezoidal masonry may have been politically motivated, since Pausanias (8.27.4) implies that both Theisoa (Karkalou) and Teuthis (and Methydrion) were dependent *poleis* of Orchomenos, a city that also employed trapezoidal masonry in the construction of its fortifications.

[25] It is also likely that the rubble wall repairs at Gortys and Megalopolis were contemporary and might even have been constructed by the same architects. See Part Two, Chapters 5 and 9, for more on the chronology of these repairs.

rubble core, they also possessed a backing revetment of small stones stacked vertically between the facings and the fill.[26] While this treatment of the core is seemingly unique, because of the advantages it affords concerning internal cohesion and strength, 'although the ruins give no visible indication…the system found at Gortys should, hypothetically, have been much used [at other sites]'.[27]

The range provided by the thicknesses of the curtains among the different circuits is so broad as to be of little value in any larger synthesis. Still, while some walls are less than 1.50 m thick and others exceed 4.50 m, in general, curtains between 3 and 4 m thick were common. The problem is exacerbated by the presence of thin walls (less than 1.50 m) among unexcavated and/or poorly preserved circuits, because it is not always clear whether they represent the total thickness of the wall or only half (that is, one of originally two facings). If the former is the case, it could be argued that the thin walls of Megalopolis, the so-called South Fort at Gortys, and of Theisoa (Karkalou) may be representative of a third-century BC trend towards thinner walls. On the other hand, it could equally be argued that, as the thin walls of Megalopolis and Gortys were repairs to the original circuit, economy and speed were the reasons behind their slimness. The nature of the surviving remains similarly hinders an accurate assessment of the original heights of the foundations. From what does remain, however, it appears that the stone foundations across the different sites vary considerably in height, ranging from a couple of courses (less than 1 m) high to numerous courses reaching almost 4 m.

Only curtains from two sites representing clearly defined examples of the indented trace have been discovered—Gortys and Theisoa (Lavda). Although the example at Theisoa (Lavda) is short and consists of only a few jogs, like the north-north-east (NNE) and west-south-west (WSW) walls at Gortys, it is representative of the fully developed form. The defensive advantages in terms of enfilading as well as the architectural benefits of the indented trace with regards to the navigation of steep slopes in these two sites is discussed in Part Two, Chapters 5 and 10. While the existence of only two attested examples precludes any larger appreciation of the role of the indented trace in Arkadian fortifications in general, if nothing else, the proximity between these two sites does warrant brief mention. Separated by the Alpheios and only 8 km apart (as the crow flies), Gortys and Theisoa (Lavda) were the respective *poleis* closest to each other. Because the original indented trace at Gortys (both on the NNE and WSW sides) appears to have been constructed in the early fourth century BC, while that at Theisoa (Lavda) was a product of the late fourth/early third century BC, it is likely that the latter was influenced by the former. As both

---

[26] Martin (1947–8: 120).   [27] Lawrence (1979: 217).

poleis were members of the Arkadian League,[28] it seems inconceivable that Theisoan architects would have been unfamiliar with the form and layout of the circuit at nearby Gortys.

Although they varied in height, masonry style, and thickness, the fortifications had one thing in common. Indeed, it is clear that the superstructure of all of the fortifications in Arkadia were comprised of mudbrick—even at those sites such as Alea, Gortys, Nestane, Stymphalos, and Theisoa (Lavda), where the stone foundations in places approached 4 m in height.[29] Mudbrick does not survive, of course, so reconstructing the upper elevations of the walls is more difficult.[30] It is reasonable to suppose that the thinnest walls, those less than 2 m in width, may have been widened at the level of the *parodos* by wooden scaffolding (*ikria*), as Winter proposes for the walls of Gortys's South Fort.[31] As for battlements, again we must look to Gortys, where Martin discovered a fragment of a stone crenellation.[32] If this fragment—the only surviving example of a parapet from anywhere in Arkadia—is representative of other fortifications, then we may assume that they presented a crenellated battlement, not unlike Messene (even if in mudbrick rather than stone)—with which so many of the Arkadian sites appear to be contemporary. Similarly, in the light of the established chronology, the use of fully developed Hellenistic *epalxis* seems less likely.

Towers

It has been established that, on the Greek mainland, towers were employed sparingly and generally unsystematically until around the time of the Peloponnesian War, at which time their manifold possibilities began to be appreciated and consequently they became regular features of most circuits.[33] This development accelerated with the introduction of the catapult. Although catapults were originally developed as offensive weapons to be employed in the siege of a city, their true defensive enfilading potential was soon realized, and Greek fortifications responded accordingly. Thus, by the early fourth century BC, the tower represented the greatest and most versatile tactical constituent of a fortification circuit. This statement certainly holds true in

---

[28] Both were also voted to participate in the synoikism of Megalopolis, although, as mentioned, this seems to have been a decision that was implemented only in the case of Theisoa (Lavda).

[29] The one possible exception is Phigaleia, which may have had a stone wall to the height of the *parodos*, presumably surmounted with battlements and upper tower chambers of mudbrick.

[30] On the problems and assumptions in reconstructing the height of a wall, see the Introduction to this book.

[31] Winter (1971a: 147).   [32] Martin (1947–8: 113–15).   [33] Winter (1971a: 155).

Arkadia, as can be confirmed by the patterns established by an examination of the different shapes, distribution, style of masonry employed, spacing, and construction of the towers from the various fortified *poleis* (Table 4.3).

As previously voiced, from the Archaic through the Hellenistic periods, the towers of the fortifications in mainland Greece display a fairly steady and logical development in deployment and function, but not in the one place where we might most expect it: their ground plan.[34] Although there appears to

Table 4.3. Architectural data: tower shapes and spacing

Arkadian *poleis*	Fortification type	Tower shapes	Tower spacing	First building phase
Alea	Uneven	Rectangular	Regular	Early 4th (*c*.370 BC)
Alipheira	Acropolis	Rectangular	Strategic	Late 5th (*c*.425–400 BC)
Asea	Uneven	Rectangular, semicircular	Strategic	Early 4th (*c*.370 BC)
Dipaia	Acropolis	Unknown	Unknown	Early–mid 4th (*c*.375–350 BC)
Gortys	Acropolis	Rectangular, semicircular	Strategic	Early 4th (*c*.370 BC)
Halous	Acropolis	Rectangular, semicircular	Regular	Early–mid 4th (400–350 BC)
Kleitor	Uneven	Semicircular	Strategic	Late 4th–early 3rd (325–275 BC)
Mantineia	Horizontal	Rectangular, semicircular, hexagonal	Regular	Early 4th (*c*.370 BC)
Megalopolis	Uneven	Rectangular, semicircular	Unknown	Early 4th (*c*.370 BC)
Nestane	Acropolis	Rectangular, semicircular	Strategic	Early 4th (*c*.370 BC)
Orchomenos	Acropolis	Rectangular	Regular	Mid 4th (*c*.375–325 BC)
Paos	Acropolis	Rectangular	Strategic	Late 5th–early 4th (*c*.425–375 BC)
Pheneos	Acropolis	Rectangular, semicircular	Regular	Mid–late 4th (350–300 BC)
Phigaleia	Uneven	Rectangular, semicircular	Strategic	Late 5th–early 4th (*c*.425–375 BC)
Psophis	Uneven	Rectangular, semicircular	Strategic	Late 5th–early 4th (*c*.425–375 BC)
Stymphalos	Uneven	Rectangular, Semicircular, Hexagonal	Regular	Early 4th (*c*.370 BC)
Teuthis	Acropolis	Rectangular	Unknown	Early 4th–late 3rd (*c*.370–200 BC)
Theisoa (Karkalou)	Acropolis	Rectangular	Strategic	Late 3rd (*c*.250–200 BC)
Theisoa (Lavda)	Acropolis	Rectangular, semicircular	Regular	Late 4th–early 3rd (325–275 BC)

[34] See Part One, Chapter 3.

be no 'reasonable and logical pattern of development'[35] concerning tower shape, there are still patterns that are observable when the frequencies of the circuits employing the different shapes of towers are compared with relevant variables. Three tower shapes are attested in the fortifications of Arkadia: rectangular, semicircular, and hexagonal.[36] Rectangular and semicircular towers comprise the majority of the examples, and only two hexagonal towers are known, one at Mantineia, another at Stymphalos. Of the eighteen circuits with attested examples of towers, only Pheneos and nearby Kleitor possessed all semicircular examples. The rest of the sites can be divided into two groups: those with only rectangular towers and those with both rectangular and semicircular towers. We see six sites belonging to the former category (Paos, Theisoa (Karkalou), Orchomenos, Teuthis, Alipheira, Alea), and ten to the latter (Phigaleia, Stymphalos, Asea, Psophis, Megalopolis, Mantineia, Gortys, Nestane, Theisoa (Lavda), Halous).

A closer look at these frequencies establish important functional and chronological patterns. For example, of the six sites employing rectangular towers only, five of them are acropolis type fortifications (Paos, Theisoa (Karkalou), Orchomenos, Teuthis, Alipheira) and only one has uneven type circuits (Alea).[37] On the other hand, the sites using both rectangular and semicircular towers are more evenly distributed by fortification type, and include five uneven type circuits (Phigaleia, Stymphalos, Asea, Psophis, Megalopolis), four of the acropolis type (Gortys, Nestane, Theisoa (Lavda), Halous), and one horizontal type (Mantineia). This pattern clearly suggests that, in general, circuits with only rectangular shaped towers were preferred for the smaller acropolis circuits, while the larger uneven and horizontal sites preferred to employ either towers of both shapes or exclusively semicircular ones. The different form and function of acropolis and uneven circuits perhaps explain this pattern. That is, the 180° view afforded by semicircular towers may have been in greater demand on uneven sites, which could be approached from a number of directions. Conversely, it is possible that, because acropolis sites are typically characterized by a more limited approach, they could afford the strategic placement of solely rectangular towers. Still, it is not impossible that such a functional distribution is largely a coincidental consequence of the larger chronological pattern or local taste.

When the types of tower shapes employed are considered with an eye to the date of their construction, a striking association is immediately discernible. If we compare the frequency of sites using only rectangular towers with

---

[35] Winter (1971a: 191).

[36] With no confidently attested examples of towers, Dipaia is excluded from the present discussion.

[37] Although it must exist, the lower city wall of Alea has not been discovered. But, from the observable patterns, it would not be surprising to find that it did contain semicircular and rectangular towers.

the date of the circuit, we find one site dating to the late fifth century BC (Alipheira), two to the late fifth or early fourth century BC (Paos, Alea), one site to 375–325 BC (Orchomenos), one to the third century BC (Theisoa (Karkalou)), and one conceivably to either the fourth or the third century BC (Teuthis). Of those sites incorporating both tower shapes in their circuit, two belong to the late fifth/early fourth century BC (Phigaleia, Psophis), six are firmly early fourth century BC (Stymphalos, Gortys, Asea, Megalopolis, Nestane, Mantineia), one is possibly of the early fourth century BC but certainly of the first half of the fourth century BC (Halous), and one is of the late fourth/early third century BC (Theisoa (Lavda)). The only two sites employing exclusively semicircular towers (Kleitor and Pheneos) possess circuits that probably date to the late fourth or early third century BC. This chronological dissection establishes three significant patterns. First, while the use of only rectangular towers can be traced from the fifth through the third centuries BC, it generally appears to be an early phenomenon, most apparent in the late fifth and early years of the fourth century BC. Second, while the use of semicircular towers was not unknown earlier, the sudden increase of fortification building that occurred in early fourth-century BC Arkadia was characterized by their widespread use and deployment alongside the traditional rectangular-shaped towers. Finally, the exclusive use of semicircular towers appears to be an early Hellenistic period phenomenon and is perhaps reflective of the development and widespread use of torsion artillery.

When the tower shapes are evaluated by their style of masonry, we see further associations. In the circuits possessing only rectangular towers, the type of masonry employed is evenly divided, with three polygonal (Paos, Alipheira, Alea) and three trapezoidal (Theisoa (Karkalou), Orchomenos, Teuthis). The circuits employing both tower shapes tell a markedly different story. Indeed, of the ten circuits employing rectangular and semicircular towers, seven were constructed in the polygonal style (Phigaleia, Stymphalos, Asea, Megalopolis, Nestane, Theisoa (Lavda), Halous), and only three in the trapezoidal (Psophis, Gortys, Mantineia (c.370 BC circuit)). Other considerations based on the construction of the towers are limited by the same factors of preservation affecting the curtains. Thus, in only a few cases is it possible to determine which circuits possessed towers bonded to the curtains, which had ground storey chambers, and which were accessible through posterns in their flanks. The known examples of these features comprise a sample too small to be certain whether they are architectural traits truly representative of Arkadian fortifications in general. The preservation of the towers, however, does permit an appreciation of the tactics envisioned in their relative spacing, from which larger conclusions may be drawn.

The method of tower spacing employed in the different circuits can be broadly categorized as representing either strategic or regular spacing. Strategic spacing is here defined as those cases where the deployment of towers is limited largely to the most vulnerable points of the circuit, while regular spacing denotes the more or less systematic distribution of towers at regular intervals throughout the circuit. Of course, as a proper distinction between these two categories requires the survival of three or more towers in succession, the fortifications whose remains do not meet this condition are excluded from the following discussion.[38] There are sixteen sites, however, that do meet this requirement,[39] seven of which have regularly spaced towers (Orchomenos, Mantineia, Alea, Stymphalos, Theisoa (Lavda), Asea (lower city circuit), Halous), while nine contain towers displaying strategic spacing (Phigaleia, Gortys, Nestane, Kleitor, Psophis, Alipheira, Asea (acropolis circuit), Paos, Pheneos).

The overall frequency is not the only similarity shared between these two categories. When the type of fortification is considered, we see that the seven circuits with regular spaced towers include three acropolis type circuits (Orchomenos, Halous, Theisoa (Lavda)), three uneven (Stymphalos, Alea, Asea (lower city circuit)), and one horizontal type site (Mantineia). This pattern is mirrored almost exactly in the sites with strategically spaced towers, which include five acropolis type (Pheneos, Gortys, Paos, Nestane, Alipheira) and four uneven type of fortifications (Phigaleia, Kleitor, Psophis, Asea (acropolis circuit)). Furthermore, when the shape of the tower is considered, again there is little difference in regard to the type of spacing exhibited by the towers. Thus, of the seven circuits with regularly spaced towers, three contain only rectangular towers (Orchomenos, Alea, Theisoa (Lavda)) and four possess both rectangular and semicircular (Mantineia, Stymphalos, Asea (lower city circuit)], Halous). Similarly, of the nine circuits with strategically placed towers, we see that three contain only rectangular towers (Paos, Asea (acropolis circuit), Alipheira), two only semicircular towers (Pheneos, Kleitor), and four towers of both shapes (Psophis, Phigaleia, Gortys, Nestane). While the circuits with regularly spaced and strategically spaced towers show almost no difference regarding frequency, fortification type, or the shape of the towers employed, there is one variable that distinctly sets these two categories apart.

When the chronology of the circuits is taken into consideration, a definite pattern emerges. The nine circuits with strategically spaced towers include one circuit dating to the late fifth century BC (Alipheira), three belonging to the late fifth/early fourth century BC (Psophis, Phigaleia, Paos), three to the early fourth century BC (Gortys, Asea (acropolis circuit), Nestane), and two to the late fourth/early third century BC (Kleitor, Pheneos). On the other hand, the seven circuits with towers deployed at regular intervals include three erected in the early fourth century BC (Mantineia, Alea, Stymphalos), one from the first

---

[38] i.e., Megalopolis, Teuthis, Dipaia, and Theisoa (Karkalou).
[39] As the towers of Asea are strategically spaced on the acropolis and regularly spaced in the lower city circuit, it is counted twice—once for each category.

half of fourth century BC (Halous), one example from the middle two quarters of the fourth century BC (Orchomenos), as well as two built in the late fourth/early third century BC (Theisoa (Lavda), Asea (lower city circuit)). These data suggest that the strategic placement of towers appears to be largely a phenomenon beginning in the late fifth/early fourth century BC, after which time the regular spacing of towers becomes the general rule. The change in this trend must correspond to the type of site and the invention and development of artillery.[40]

In the late fifth/early fourth century BC, before the invention of the catapult, siege craft was limited to mines and rams, which, dictated by the terrain, could be brought up only against certain parts of a circuit. In the rugged terrain of Arkadia, a minimal number of towers strategically placed to protect the main approach, the gate(s), and/or the especially vulnerable areas would have provided sufficient protection—and the natural defences would have done the rest. Apart from the continued use and development of both mines and rams, circuits of the early fourth century BC had to respond accordingly to the threat posed by the invention, development (tension to torsion), and dissemination of the catapult. Because of the distances the catapult was capable of reaching, most parts of the circuit were now vulnerable, and no part of the circuit could be trusted to natural defences alone. Furthermore, as the larger uneven and horizontal type circuits appear at this time, most of which incorporate a substantial amount of flat terrain, an array of regularly spaced towers was an absolutely essential defensive necessity, since a hostile approach could come from any direction.

Defence in the circuits with regularly spaced towers was never sacrificed for uniformity or symmetry. Like earlier examples with strategically situated towers, although towers were regularly deployed, care was still taken to provide cover at gates, to incorporate high ground whenever possible, and generally to provide cover for the more vulnerable parts, especially places where an enemy force might mass and launch an assault on the walls.[41] Generally during the early fourth century BC, the distance between the towers when regularly spaced was around 25–30 m (Alea, Orchomenos, Mantineia, Stymphalos, Halous). Interestingly, at Theisoa (Lavda), the one example displaying regular spacing from the late fourth/early third century BC, we find the towers deployed approximately every 60–70 m. The reason for such a relatively wide spacing, presumably, lies in the fact that fewer towers were needed because the artillery machines could cover the space between.[42]

What can be said about the relationship between tower size and artillery appears to conform to Ober's chronological distinctions between first- and

---

[40] Marsden (1969: 12); Winter (1971a: 49, 54, 57, 58, 155, 243); Lawrence (1979: 111).
[41] Winter (1971a: 154).   [42] Winter (1971a: 169); Lawrence (1979: 386, 390).

second-generation artillery towers.[43] As the vast majority of the Arkadian fortifications date to the first half of the fourth century BC, it is not surprising that most of the towers are of the first-generation type—designed to house the smaller rudimentary (tension) artillery machines. The years after *c*.325 BC, however, witnessed the introduction of second-generation towers. Generally larger, higher, and with thicker walls, these towers aimed not only to counteract the offensive threat that accompanied the introduction of the much improved torsion catapult, but to provide the strength and stability required in the towers themselves to support the defensive use of the same machines (that is, the recoil). Although limited by the general degree of preservation, a number of second-generation towers are demonstrated in Arkadia. All the semicircular towers in the circuit of Kleitor, all the rectangular towers from Theisoa (Lavda), and possibly the large rectangular tower west of the ramp gate at Theisoa (Karkalou) are examples of this type of tower, designed to house large artillery machines. To keep pace with the new technological advances, circuits that were built in the early fourth century BC—before the widespread use of artillery—were forced to compensate for any inadequacies or obsolete elements in their defensive systems. Thus we see first-generation towers modified to meet the new offensive threat posed by the torsion catapult. This is best documented at Stymphalos, where excavations have revealed three first-generation towers of the original circuit that were rebuilt (after destruction) in the late fourth or early third century BC. Atop the highest point on the Stymphalian acropolis, a large rectangular bastion was one of these new structures. Measuring 21 m long by 11 m wide, this bastion has a remarkably similar parallel at nearby Alea, which possessed a similarly shaped bastion, also on the highest point of the hill, and measured a comparable 23 by 8 m. These physical similarities, not to mention the extremely close proximity of the two sites, suggest that the bastion at Alea is also a second-generation tower, probably dating to the late fourth or early third century BC.

Gateways

Owing to the same problems of preservation affecting the other components of the fortifications, of the nineteen fortified sites in this study, only eleven of them have attested or extant remains of gateways (Alea, Dipaia, Gortys, Kleitor, Paos, Stymphalos, Theisoa (Lavda), Nestane, Asea (acropolis circuit), Theisoa (Karkalou), Mantineia). Nevertheless, by studying the relationship between the topography and what does remain of the circuit, we can plausibly deduce the location and frequency of now vanished gateways at other sites,

---

[43] That is, the smaller and earliest artillery towers date to between 375–325 BC, and the larger second-generation towers appear in the last quarter of the fourth century BCE (Ober 1987: 571).

including Halous, Teuthis, and Alipheira. Similarly, the itinerary of Pausanias suggests that Megalopolis once had eight gates, even if we can only speculate about their architectural forms and approximate locations. What is certain, however, is that the extant remains establish that the Arkadian *poleis* employed four main types of gates in their fortifications: the frontal opening type, the overlap type, the ramp gate, and/or the monumental gatecourt type (Table 4.4).[44] In terms of overall frequencies, we see seven circuits with frontal opening gates (Alea, Dipaia, Gortys, Kleitor, Stymphalos, Theisoa (Lavda), Paos), three with overlap gates (Mantineia, Nestane, Stymphalos), three possessing a monumental gatecourt (Kleitor, Mantineia, Stymphalos), and three that include an example of a 'ramp' gate (Asea, Stymphalos, Theisoa (Karkalou)).

Table 4.4. Architectural data: gates

Arkadian *poleis*	Fortification type	Gate types	Number of gates	First building phase
Alea	Uneven	Frontal	1	Early 4th (*c.*370 BC)
Alipheira	Acropolis	Frontal (?)	2 (?)	Late 5th (*c.*425–400 BC)
Asea	Uneven	Ramp	1	Early 4th (*c.*370 BC)
Dipaia	Acropolis	Frontal	1	Early–mid 4th (*c.*375–350 BC)
Gortys	Acropolis	Frontal	3	Early 4th (*c.*370 BC)
Halous	Acropolis	Frontal (?)	1 (?)	Early–mid 4th (400–350 BC)
Kleitor	Uneven	Frontal, gatecourt	2	Late 4th–early 3rd (325–275 BC)
Mantineia	Horizontal	Overlap, gatecourt	10	Early 4th (*c.*370 BC)
Megalopolis	Uneven	Unknown	8 (?)	Early 4th (*c.*370 BC)
Nestane	Acropolis	Overlap	1	Early 4th (*c.*370 BC)
Orchomenos	Acropolis	Frontal, overlap (?)	2 (?)	Mid 4th (*c.*375–325 BC)
Paos	Acropolis	Frontal	1	Late 5th–early 4th (*c.*425–375 BC)
Pheneos	Acropolis	Unknown	Unknown	Mid–late 4th (350–300 BC)
Phigaleia	Uneven	Unknown	2 (?)	Late 5th–early 4th (*c.*425–375 BC)
Psophis	Uneven	Unknown	2 (?)	Late 5th–early 4th (*c.*425–375 BC)
Stymphalos	Uneven	Frontal, overlap, ramp, gatecourt	7	Early 4th (*c.*370 BC)
Teuthis	Acropolis	Unknown	2 (?)	Early 4th–late 3rd (*c.*370–200 BC)
Theisoa (Karkalou)	Acropolis	Ramp	1	Late 3rd (*c.*250–200 BC)
Theisoa (Lavda)	Acropolis	Frontal (?), overlap	3 (?)	Late 4th–early 3rd (325–275 BC)

---

[44] Because Mantineia, Stymphalos, and Kleitor all possessed several of these gate types, they appear more than once in the following discussion.

A close examination of the form, function, and chronology of these different types brings to light a number of interesting relationships.

As noted, the circuits of seven sites possess examples of frontal opening type gates.[45] This type of gate is characterized by 'an opening in a continuous (though not necessarily straight) stretch of wall, with the approaches [often] guarded by a projecting tower or bastion on one or both sides'.[46] As they provide functional and practical portals, it is not surprising to see frontal gates represented from the late fifth to the late third century BC. They are attested in circuits of the late fifth/early fourth century BC (Paos), the early fourth century BC (Alea, Gortys, Stymphalos), the second quarter of the fourth century BC (Dipaia), and the late fourth/early third century BC (Theisoa (Lavda), Kleitor). Similarly, as they are the most basic form of opening in the wall, examples are relatively equally represented in both acropolis type (Paos, Gortys, Theisoa (Lavda), Dipaia) and uneven type circuits (Alea, Stymphalos, Kleitor).[47] The most interesting pattern that emerges is the style of masonry employed. Although the number is perhaps biased by the remains that are preserved, it is still interesting to note that five of the seven circuits with frontal opening type gates were constructed in polygonal style masonry (all except Kleitor and Gortys). Any opening in the curtain is a potential weak spot in the circuit, and thus, by their very form, frontal opening gates represent the most vulnerable part in the system. In addition to providing the usual towers on the flanks to protect the openings, perhaps polygonal masonry was preferred for its rugged appearance, which gave the impression of strength. Such concern is clearly evident even in the predominately trapezoidal masonry employed in the construction of Gate B at Gortys, where the blocks are significantly larger than in any other part of the circuit.

Overlap, or Type 2 gates, are comprised of 'an entrance corridor lying between two overlapping and more or less parallel arms of a wall',[48] often with a tower at the end. Despite the apparently strong and sound defensive outlook inherent in their general plan, examples of overlap type gates are limited to the circuits of only three *poleis* (Mantineia, Nestane, Stymphalos). There appears to be no difference in the type of site in which overlap gates are found, since they are equally represented across acropolis, horizontal, and uneven types of circuits. There is, on the other hand, an unmistakable correlation between both the geographical distribution and the chronological frame for this type of gate. With examples at Mantineia, Nestane, and Stymphalos, the use of the overlap gate appears to have been exclusively a north-eastern

---

[45] Frontal opening gates are also known as tangential (Frederiksen 2011: 55) and Type 1 (Winter 1971a: 208).

[46] Winter (1971a: 208).

[47] The South Gate at Theisoa (Lavda), while technically of the overlap type, does not have long parallel stretches of wall and thus resembles more the frontal type of gate.

[48] Winter (1971a: 208).

Arkadian phenomenon.[49] Similarly, it also cannot be a coincidence that all these gates belong to circuits erected in the early fourth century—most likely in the years around *c*.370 BC. Although it is not conclusive, it is possible that Orchomenos too may have had an example of an overlap gate. If so, because of its location and date, the Orchomenos circuit would generally fit the same chronological and geographical pattern exhibited by the distribution of the other attested examples.

Like the overlap gates, the gatecourt type of gate is also limited to only three sites, all concentrated in north-eastern Arkadia. These include Gate A from Mantineia, the West Gate at Kleitor, and the Phlious Gate at Stymphalos. The parallels in both form and function between these gates and the Arkadian Gate at Messene are clear and have been commented upon by others.[50] Briefly, they are characterized by their monumental size, their plans comprised a round or rectangular court accessed by a small opening at either end and protected by towers, and that they were all laid out on completely flat terrain. Constructed around *c*.370 BC, Gate A from Mantineia represents the earliest of the Arkadian gatecourts, while the examples from both Stymphalos and Kleitor appear to date to the late fourth/early third century BC—contemporary with Messene's Arkadian Gate.[51] Chronologically, therefore, the Arkadian examples conform to what has been generally established for this type—namely, that they increased in popularity after their appearance in the fourth century BC (especially the 360s BC onward).[52]

As Mantineia, Stymphalos, and Kleitor are among the largest Arkadian settlements (and circuits), and since only a single example of this gate is found at each site, we might suppose that such costly and monumental gates would have been limited to one per circuit in the fortifications of only the most affluent *poleis*—perhaps in the future examples will be found at the comparable sites of Tegea, Megalopolis, or Heraia. In any case, although it is easy to get lost in the relative splendour and monumentality of these gates, it is important to remember that, like all the constituent parts of a circuit, aesthetic concerns were secondary to defensive interests. Thus we see that the form and development of the gatecourt is directly related to the history of siege craft, specifically from the fourth century BC onwards. Indeed, as their popularity coincides with the regular use of offensive artillery and the increasing use of both mines and rams, Winter notes, 'it is certainly tempting to connect the two developments, and to suppose that it was the increasing threat of mines and artillery that led to the new popularity of the courtyard type of gate'.[53]

---

[49] On the gate at Nestane, see Lattermann (1913: 411–12). On the overlap gates at Stymphalos, see Gourley and Williams (2005: 227) and at Mantineia, see Fougères (1898: 150–7).

[50] e.g., Fougères (1898: 153); Frazer (1898: iv. 204); Winter (1971a: 217); Gourley and Williams (2005: 232–3).

[51] Scranton (1941: 128–9).   [52] Winter (1971a: 219).   [53] Winter (1971a: 219).

Finally, of the last type, the 'ramp' gate, there are three circuits with known examples (Asea (acropolis circuit), Theisoa (Karkalou), Stymphalos). This type was a largely practical device directly related to the local topography, so there are few discernible chronological or geographical patterns associated with its occurrence. Examples are attested in southern, northern, and central Arkadia at sites with both early fourth-century and third-century BC circuits. The only real difference among these types perhaps relates to their primary function. The ramp gate at Stymphalos, for example, was a secondary entranceway, providing access for primarily wheeled traffic to the acropolis directly from the extramural area.[54] The ramp gate on the acropolis at Asea may have provided a similar function, although it provided access directly from the intramural area of the lower city. The ramp gate at Theisoa (Karkalou), however, appears to have been the only gate in the entire circuit, providing access to the acropolis from the (unfortified) settlement located on the saddle to the south.

When the various gates are considered collectively, it appears that, in general, the acropolis type circuits are characterized by their almost exclusive use of the frontal type gate. Uneven and horizontal sites, however, display much greater variability. When it comes to the type of gates used in their circuits, it is not uncommon to find two, three, or even all four of the different types of gates represented. This pattern is obvious at the majority of sites where more than one gate survives in the circuit. The fortifications at Mantineia, for instance, include both the gatecourt and overlap types; Kleitor possesses frontal and gatecourt types; while Stymphalos can boast examples of frontal, overlap, gatecourt, and ramp types. It appears, therefore, that very few of the larger circuits possessing more than one gate relied solely on a single type. Even at Gortys, where all three gates are technically of the frontal type, we see that the funnel-shaped Gate B is markedly different in form from Gates A and C. Theisoa (Lavda), too, possessed at least one overlap-like gate and possibly two frontal gates.

Posterns

Nowhere is the present analysis more limited by the preservation of the remains than in considering the question of whether or not a circuit possessed posterns.[55] Determining their presence requires not only a thorough investigation of the entire circuit, but also that the trace of the fortifications in question survives more or less in totality. And, even when a postern can be

---

[54] Ancient wheel ruts are still visible on the ramp today.
[55] The following discussion pertains to posterns in the curtains only, not those in the flanks of towers.

confidently identified, without excavation or obvious signs of architectural alterations there is usually no way of determining whether the said postern was original to the circuit or a later addition. Until evidence to the contrary is uncovered, therefore, perhaps in the course of future excavation, it is here assumed that all the posterns in question are contemporary with the circuits' original phase of construction. Finally, a study of posterns must consider function, and a number of factors can help determine whether they had a primarily military function, intended for defensive sorties, or whether they were envisioned largely for use by civilians as a quick point of access to the *chora*.

Of the nineteen fortified sites in this study, only ten meet the criterion of possessing a circuit whose outline can be traced more or less in its entirety (Table 4.5). Of these ten sites, however, only six Arkadian *poleis* had posterns in their curtains (Alea, Asea (acropolis circuit), Gortys, Phigaleia, Theisoa (Lavda), Stymphalos), while the fortifications of four settlements appear to have possessed none (Mantineia, Nestane, Orchomenos, Paos). There does seem to be a slight correlation between both the presence and absence of posterns and the type of fortification employed. Of those sites with posterns, four are examples of the uneven type (Phigaleia, Alea, Asea, Stymphalos), while only two are of the acropolis type (Gortys, Theisoa [Lavda]). Conversely, we see that those sites without posterns are predominately of the acropolis

Table 4.5. Architectural data: posterns

Arkadian *poleis*	Fortification type	Number of posterns	First building phase
Alea	Uneven	1	Early 4th (*c.*370 BC)
Alipheira	Acropolis	Unknown	Late 5th (*c.*425–400 BC)
Asea	Uneven	2	Early 4th (*c.*370 BC)
Dipaia	Acropolis	Unknown	Early–mid 4th (*c.*375–350 BC)
Gortys	Acropolis	4	Early 4th (*c.*370 BC)
Halous	Acropolis	Unknown	Early-Mid 4th (400–350 BC)
Kleitor	Uneven	Unknown	Late 4th–early 3rd (325–275 BC)
Mantineia	Horizontal	0	Early 4th (*c.*370 BC)
Megalopolis	Uneven	Unknown	Early 4th (*c.*370 BC)
Nestane	Acropolis	0	Early 4th (*c.*370 BC)
Orchomenos	Acropolis	0	Mid 4th (*c.*375–325 BC)
Paos	Acropolis	0	Late 5th–early 4th (*c.*425–375 BC)
Pheneos	Acropolis	Unknown	Mid–late 4th (350–300 BC)
Phigaleia	Uneven	2	Late 5th–early 4th (*c.*425–375 BC)
Psophis	Uneven	Unknown	Late 5th–early 4th (*c.*425–375 BC)
Stymphalos	Uneven	1	Early 4th (*c.*370 BC)
Teuthis	Acropolis	Unknown	Early 4th–late 3rd (*c.*370–200 BC)
Theisoa (Karkalou)	Acropolis	Unknown	Late 3rd (*c.*250–200 BC)
Theisoa (Lavda)	Acropolis	3	Late 4th–early 3rd (325–275 BC)

type (Paos, Orchomenos, Nestane), with three examples, while the only horizontal type site was without posterns (Mantineia).

There also appears to be a chronological relationship between the sites with attested examples of posterns, and we see that the vast majority of these circuits date to the early fourth century BC (Stymphalos, Asea (acropolis circuit), Gortys, Alea), with only one late-fifth/early fourth-century BC example (Phigaleia) and one late-fourth/early third-century BC example (Theisoa [Lavda]), representing the limits of the chronological spectrum. On the other hand, there seems to be no correlation between chronology or type of fortification and those sites without posterns. Thus, we have examples from the late fifth/early fourth century BC (Paos), the early fourth century BC (Mantineia, Nestane), and the second and third quarter of the fourth century BC (Orchomenos). When the total frequencies are considered chronologically, we see that in the late fifth/early fourth century BC there is one site with posterns and one without; in the early fourth century BC there are four sites with and two without; while in the middle fourth to late fourth/early third century BC, there is one site with posterns and one without.

Although the sample size is admittedly small, when the type of site and chronology are considered, not surprisingly, the frequencies generally suggest that the use of posterns was most popular in Arkadia in the early fourth century BC, primarily in the larger circuits characteristic of uneven type fortifications (Stymphalos, Alea, Phigaleia, Asea), but also in the larger acropolis type circuits (for example, Gortys, Theisoa (Lavda)). While posterns in the flanks of towers made additional posterns in the curtains unnecessary at Mantineia, the absence of posterns at the other sites may be explained by their small size, their function as an acropolis, or a local topography that limited the approaches to the summit (for example, Nestane, Orchomenos, Paos). It is also interesting to consider the geographical distribution of the *poleis* with and without posterns. It might not be a coincidence, for instance, that, with the exception of Stymphalos and Alea, all the sites with posterns are concentrated in south-west Arkadia (Theisoa (Lavda), Phigaleia, Gortys, Asea). Similarly, with the exception of Paos, all the sites without posterns are to be found in north-east Arkadia (Nestane, Orchomenos, Mantineia).

The location of the posterns within the larger circuit, their frequency and proximity to each other, and the surrounding topography all help to establish which posterns had a primarily military function and which were built for civilian means of access. Phigaleia possessed two posterns, both located on the east side of the circuit between flanking towers. The fact that they were the only two posterns in an otherwise extensive circuit and were positioned where the concentration of towers was greatest clearly demonstrates that these openings were envisioned primarily for defensive sorties at a part of the circuit that was considered vulnerable. This situation is mirrored at Gortys and on the acropolis of Asea, where the circuits' posterns are placed close together, purposely where the concentration of towers was greatest and where the topography facilitated the approach—in other words, the most exposed parts of the circuit. The one attested postern at Stymphalos varies slightly from this pattern, but its position just outside the north overlap gate is curious, and suggests a military function. A postern placed just outside the gate would have permitted defenders to sally forth and attack the unshielded right and rear sides of any enemy occupying the area between the overlapping stretches of curtain in front of the gate.

On the other hand, the posterns at Alea, Theisoa (Lavda), and the one example on the north-east side of the circuit at Gortys appear to have been largely designed for simple access, rather than primarily defensive use. Not only are they all situated at the top of relatively steep slopes, where an attack would be less likely, but the postern at Alea was placed directly opposite the entrance to the citadel, and one from Theisoa (Lavda) was built directly into the wall of the citadel, which further suggests they must have been used primarily for access. Similarly, it is not a coincidence that the one example from Gortys is found on the north-east side of the circuit, where it could be reached by civilians from the main area of habitation directly below.

Outworks

The detailed survey of fortified Arkadian *poleis* demonstrates that only Phigaleia and Mantineia (and possibly Stymphalos) possessed defensive outworks, and, although all were man-made, they differ considerably in form and function.[56] The defensive system at Phigaleia employed both *hypoteichismata* (cross-walls) and *proteichismata* (outwalls).[57] Two examples of the former are found—one running due north from the highest point of the site for a length of *c*.30–40 m, and the other stretching for *c*.165 m from the westernmost part of the circuit. One example of the latter was discovered—oriented north–south, and spanning a small ravine approximately 150 m west of the main circuit. Collectively, both of these types of outworks operated with

---

[56] Although it appears that there are no examples of man-made outworks employed as part of a city's defence system before the seventh century BC, Frederiksen (2011: 84, 97, 98) provides examples that demonstrate that they were certainly used with increasing frequency from the middle Archaic period onwards; e.g., ditches are attested at Megara Hyblaea (pp. 79, 98), Vroulia (p. 84), Alalie (p. 88); Paphos (p. 88); Siris (p. 98). Numerous ancient authors (e.g., Thuc. 3.22.1; Xen. *Hell.* 4.7.6; Dem. *Phil.* 2.23–4) refer to ditches in the Classical period and it is safe to assume that they were regularly employed in concert with fortifications (Frederiksen 2011: 98, n. 182). Still, compared to 'natural' outworks, man-made outworks are rare in Arkadia, with Mantineia and Phigaleia (and perhaps Stymphalos) providing the only known examples for the whole of the Classical and Hellenistic periods. See Part Two, Chapter 16, for more information about this possible outwork at Stymphalos: the enigmatic 'West Wall Structure'.

[57] See Part Two, Chapter 14, for more detail on these interesting structures at Phigaleia.

the local topography to command the main routes to the city by actively dictating the possible approaches. At Mantineia we see something different. At the same time as it was decided that the *c.*370 BC city walls of Mantineia would follow the same course as the original, it was also determined to modify the course of the Ophis River, turning it into a defensive advantage rather than a liability. Thus, in order to avoid a repeat of the disaster of 385 BC, which saw the Spartans cleverly dam and redirect the course of the river against the walls—a feat made possible by its original course, which ran through the city—the Ophis was now redirected to circumvent the city. Essentially functioning as a moat, the course of the river now provided several defensive advantages. It not only created a narrow strip of land between itself and the walls, taking away any numerical advantage held by an enemy by limiting the amount of space it could actually occupy; it also worked to keep an enemy effectively at a distance from the walls. Carefully placed (and surely carefully protected) bridges represented a further measure to control access to the city.

Although this is speculative, that the majority of Arkadian *poleis* did not have any outworks may be explained by the topography and perhaps the type of the fortified site. The majority of the acropolis sites in Arkadia, for example, were small settlements in which the main area of habitation was unfortified and the acropolis functioned primarily as a refuge when required. These sites were chosen first and foremost because of defensive considerations, and man-made outworks would more often than not have been superfluous additions to an already strong local topography. Similarly, as demonstrated, the locations of even the larger, more exposed uneven circuits were chosen because of the natural defences afforded by the local topography. Protected by one, or more often two, watercourses, almost every single uneven type of fortified site (and acropolis types for that matter) was already provided with a natural outwork, making further man-made outworks unnecessary. Finally, since every Arkadian site was protected by at least some form of watercourse (for example, river, seasonal stream, lake), even in the hot summer months when they were dry or largely so, such courses could be considered a form of natural outwork, essentially functioning as ditches.

Chronological Summary

Late-fifth/early fourth-century BC patterns

- Fortified sites are limited to the western edge of Arkadia.
- Sites incorporate substantial amount of high ground; protected by rivers on at least two sides.
- There is an equal number of acropolis and uneven type sites.
- Style of masonry is predominately coursed polygonal.

- All sites employ strategic spacing of towers, predominately only rectangular; semicircular towers are rare.
- Frontal or simple opening is only attested type of gate.
- Posterns and man-made outworks are rare.

Early fourth-century BC patterns

- New fortified sites are found throughout Arkadia, especially in the south, east, and north.
- Sites incorporate substantial amount of high ground as well as relatively flat terrain; protected by watercourse on at least one, but usually two sides.
- There is an equal number of acropolis and uneven type sites; Mantineia is the only site laid out on completely flat terrain.
- Style of masonry is predominately polygonal; more trapezoidal masonry than in previous period.
- Sites begin to employ regular spacing of towers, especially when deployed over flat terrain; acropolis sites continue to use strategic spacing of towers; the combined use of rectangular and semicircular towers predominates; the use of only rectangular towers in a single circuit is rare.
- Frontal or simple opening is the dominate type gate; overlap and gate-court type gates appear at sites in north-east Arkadia, but are still comparatively rare; ramp gates also appear.
- Posterns become more common; man-made outworks are rare.

Late-fourth/early third-century BC patterns

- New fortified sites are found in northern and western Arkadia; modifications made to circuits in north-eastern Arkadia.
- New sites incorporate substantial amount of high ground or relatively flat terrain; protected by rivers on two sides.
- There is an equal number of acropolis and uneven type sites.
- Both coursed polygonal and trapezoidal masonry are used evenly; see only example of pure isodomic trapezoidal masonry.
- Sites use both strategic and regular spacing of towers; see preference for only one tower type in the circuit, either all semicircular or all rectangular towers; towers become generally larger (second generation); greater distances between towers than in previous periods; see repairs/modifications of early fourth-century BC towers into large bastions.
- Frontal or simple opening is the dominate type gate; both gatecourt and an overlap gate modified into a gatecourt appear in northern Arkadia.
- Posterns are rare; man-made outworks are not attested.

Third-century BC patterns

- New fortified site appears in central Arkadia; see fortification of existing lower city in southern Arkadia; repairs made to existing circuits in northern and southern Arkadia.
- New site is acropolis type, incorporating exclusively high ground; protected by river on one side; fortified lower city is laid out on relatively flat terrain.
- See use of both polygonal and trapezoidal masonry; repairs made to existing circuits employ predominately dry rubble masonry.
- Sites use both strategic and regular spacing of towers; see preference for only one tower type in the circuit, either all semicircular or all rectangular towers; towers become generally larger (second generation).
- Only ramp gate attested in this period.
- Posterns and man-made outworks are not attested.

HISTORICAL PROBABILITY

We are indeed fortunate in those rare cases where the precise year of a circuit's construction is mentioned in the ancient sources (for example, Mantineia, Megalopolis); or when the date of repairs may be inferred from a recorded attack on the walls (for example, Gortys, Megalopolis); or when excavation in particular can shed light on the chronology of a city wall (for example, Gortys, Stymphalos, Pheneos, Theisoa (Lavda)). As mentioned, however, these are rare occurrences, especially where the fortified *poleis* of Arkadia are concerned. Thus, in the majority of cases, it is necessary to establish relative chronologies using regional architectural affinities and historical probability. Accordingly, the use of ancient texts, excavation, regional comparanda, and historical probability, employed on an individual site level, have yielded chronologies for the circuits that are not just plausible, but indeed probable.[58] With reliable chronologies established for the individual circuits, we are able to understand the *polis* and its walls within the larger regional and historical context. A late fourth/early third-century BC date for the upgrades made at Stymphalos and Alea, for example, as well as the large towers in the circuit at Kleitor, can be appreciated as defensive responses to the contemporary advances in siege warfare.

The relationship between technology and the architecture of the walls has been touched on already, both here and regarding fortifications elsewhere in

---

[58] See Part Two, the Catalogue, for the evidence and arguments for determining the chronology of each individual site.

the Greek world. But what of the larger and more predominant patterns that are observable in Arkadia specifically? Can historical probability, for instance, explain why the majority of Arkadian *poleis* threw walls around their settlements in the early fourth century BC? And can it provide an explanation for why these sites are located largely in the north-east and south? Finally, can it clarify why many of the *poleis* that were voted to participate in synoikism appear not to have participated, and were instead actually fortified?[59] To all of these questions, the answer is, I believe, yes. And, what is more, the answers to all of these questions lie with the formation of the Arkadian League. In an effort to answer these questions under the umbrella of what is not only historically possible, but ultimately historically probable, the discussion that follows employs not mere speculation, but informed speculation, derived from the collective weight of the data presented in this study.

It cannot be a mere coincidence that, of the total nineteen sites in question, seven of them (Mantineia, Megalopolis, Nestane, Alea, Stymphalos, Gortys, Asea) belong securely to the early fourth century BC, while the fortifications at a further six sites (Phigaleia, Paos, Psophis, Halous, Dipaia, Orchomenos) may also conceivably have been built (or rebuilt) around this time. The most probable historical catalyst for this sudden and widespread regional development is the foundation of the Arkadian League.[60] Not only did the Spartan defeat at the Battle of Leuktra in 371 BC see an end to its centuries-old hegemony in the Peloponnese; this event also had far-reaching consequences for the cities of Arkadia. In an effort to limit any future Spartan aggression, a confederation of Arkadian cities was established, and Mantineia and Megalopolis came together in defensive consolidations. These cities provided local centralized habitation, but their geographical position shows that they also functioned as a system of fortresses.[61] Including Messene and extending across the Peloponnese to the Argolid, these communities were fortified specifically to control the major routes from Lakonia into neighbouring Arkadia. Indeed, both the influence of Epaminondas and the *raison d'être* behind the foundation of Megalopolis, Mantineia, and Messene are well documented in the ancient historical record.[62] But what of the other Arkadian *poleis* that were fortified at this time—were they part of some Arkadian and/or Theban defensive master plan, or did these cities simply seize the opportunity offered by the defeat of the Spartans at Leuktra to fortify their settlements? That all of

---

[59] Jost (1999: 228–9) also observed in the location of these cities a coherent defensive network and notes the defensive value of maintaining inhabitation (and fortifying) many of the cities thought to have participated in the synoikism.

[60] Maher (2014: 272–8; 2015a: 18, 32–42; forthcoming); Maher and Mowat (forthcoming).

[61] Jost (1999: 234) seems to believe this was the case, writing that the synoikism was 'accompagne d'une véritable politique de maintien des villages fortifiés.'

[62] For the argument against Theban involvement in the second synoikism of Mantineia, see Demand (1990: 109–10).

the *poleis* fortified at this time (with the exception of Orchomenos) were original members of the Arkadian League suggests the former and provides a crucial clue behind the observable pattern in the geographical distribution of these sites.

Stymphalos, Alea, Nestane, Asea, Gortys, and perhaps also Dipaia were almost certainly part of the same overall defensive strategy envisioned with the foundation of Megalopolis and Mantineia.[63] The geographic location of these cities, their recognized membership in the Arkadia Confederacy, the architectural affinities shared by their fortifications, and, above all, the early fourth-century BC date of their walls add considerable support to this supposition. Furthermore, Xenophon tells us that 'some of the Arkadian cities sent men to help the Mantineians in their building [of their fortification]'[64]—such amity clearly suggests communal unity and purpose. Xenophon also adds that the Elians contributed three talents to the rebuilding of the Mantineian circuit, suggesting that they were allied with the Arkadians and united against their common enemy Sparta.[65] While such an alliance may go a long way to explaining why the early fourth century BC saw no new fortifications erected along the shared border in the west,[66] it does not clarify why the proliferation of early fourth-century BC Arkadian fortifications was limited to the south and northeast; nor how this is to be reconciled with the fact that most of the *poleis* fortified at this time were voted to participate in the synoikism of Megalopolis.[67]

It is conceivable that, in the rush to consolidate their strength at Megalopolis, the more influential League members indiscriminately voted for all of the smaller *poleis* and settlements in the area to participate in the synoikism. After careful reflection—no doubt prompted in part by the inevitable dissension issued by the supposed participants—a new defensive strategy was established—one that was complementary to the existing strategy embodied in the foundations of Megalopolis and Mantineia. It would not have taken long to realize that in putting all their proverbial eggs in one basket at Megalopolis and abandoning the strategically significant positions held by some of these settlements, the League would have weakened rather than strengthened their underlying defensive strategy. Asea provides a particularly appropriate example.

[63] Gourley and Williams (2005: 219, n. 10) briefly suggest this possibility for Stymphalos. See Maher (2015a: 18, 32–42) for the case for Stymphalos and Alea.

[64] Xen. *Hell.* 6.5.5.

[65] Xen. *Hell.* 6.5.5. See Maher and Mowat (forthcoming) for the contributions of Arkadians and Elians towards the defences of Mantineia specifically.

[66] An alliance with Elis may also explain why Theisoa (Lavda) appears to be the only *polis* in this study that actually participated in the synoikism. In other words, without fear of incursion from the west, perhaps it was decided that Theisoa (Lavda) could be abandoned without compromising the larger defensive interests of the Arkadian League.

[67] It should be noted that Pausanias (8.27.3–6) is our only source for those settlements thought to have participated in the synoikism of Megalopolis, and his accuracy in this regard has recently been called into question by Pikoulas (forthcoming).

A small and relatively minor *polis* close to the Megalopolitan frontier, Asea, according to Pausanias, voted to participate in the synoikism.[68] It is known, however, that Asea continued to exist as a *polis* after the synoikism.[69] Perhaps the reason was that the geographic position occupied by Asea was too strategically important to the security of both Megalopolis and Arkadia for it simply to be abandoned. Indeed, its situation due north of and sharing a border with Lakonia meant that, if the plain of Asea were unoccupied, this would have allowed the Spartans to circumvent both the plains of Tegea and Megalopolis and drive straight to the heart of central Arkadia, thus negating the whole *raison d'être* of Megalopolis.[70] While the same argument explains why we find the fortification and continued occupation at other *poleis* although they initially voted to participate in the synoikism, the geographic distribution of these settlements demonstrates that keeping Sparta out of Arkadia was not the only concern for the new Arkadian League, and that there was a perceived internal threat to their security.

It is well known that Mantineia was a leading and influential member of the League, one whose opinion held considerable sway. Not only did the foundation of the League probably begin there; it was also the home of the important federal leader Lykomedes, who was one of the two *oecists* provided by Mantineia for the foundation of Megalopolis.[71] Located only 16 km to the north of Mantineia, and separated from it by only a series of low hills, stood Orchomenos—a city whose residents initially 'refused to be members of the Arkadian League on account of their hatred toward the Mantineians'.[72] This hatred manifested itself as early as 370 BC, when Orchomenos began to raise a mercenary force, the perceived threat of which was so great that, when the rest of the Arkadian League assembled at Asea, the Mantineians decided to remain at home to 'keep watch upon them'.[73] Such concern was justified, for, shortly after raising this army, Orchomenos joined forces with Sparta, whose soldiers they 'recognized as friends'.[74] Xenophon recounts the events of 370 BC, which saw Orchomenos, as well as the Arkadian city of Heraia, allied with Sparta in several skirmishes against the army of the Arkadian League and their Elian allies.[75] As soon as Sparta had departed on its invasion of Arkadia in 370 BC, the League army 'made an expedition against the Heraians, not only because they refused to be members of the Arkadian League, but also because they had joined with the Lakedaimonians in invading Arkadia'.[76] Although the fate of Orchomenos is not recorded by Xenophon, as it too refused to join the League

---

[68] Paus. 8.27.3.   [69] Evidence for this is presented in Part Two, Chapter 3.
[70] In 370 BC, the Spartans under King Agesilaos took this exact route via Eutaia on their way to attack Mantineia (Xen. *Hell.* 6.5.12).
[71] Xen. *Hell.* 7.1.23–4, 7.1.39, 7.4.2; Paus. 8.27.2.   [72] Xen. *Hell.* 6.5.11.
[73] Xen. *Hell.* 6.5.11.   [74] Xen. *Hell.* 6.5.17.   [75] Xen. *Hell.* 6.5.13 ff.
[76] Xen. *Hell.* 6.5.22.

and took up arms with Sparta, the city may have received similar treatment at the hands of the Arkadian army.

In the earliest days of the Arkadian League, therefore, it is clear that Orchomenos was an ally of Sparta, but also, as Xenophon maintains, of Corinth and Phlious.[77] It is equally clear that Orchomenos and its allies were initially attending interests contrary to those of Mantineia and the Arkadian League, and they constituted a serious threat to the League's security. It is possible that, at the urging of Mantineia specifically or the League as a whole, a defensive strategy was established to protect the settlements surrounding Orchomenos and its allies. Indeed, it cannot be a coincidence that at this time we see the fortification of Alea and Stymphalos—*poleis* that border both Orchomenos, on one side, and its Phliasian allies, on the other.[78] Although it is likely that the city of Alea already existed in its present location in the early fourth century BC, that Stymphalos represented a refoundation suggests it was part of this new Arkadian defensive policy. Its new location within the valley is also telling: instead of being tucked away in the far western end of the valley, it was now confidently situated directly across from the main road leading to Phlious.[79] Furthermore, at the same time that the fortifications were being built around Mantineia, Nestane, Stymphalos and Alea, Gortys and possibly Dipaia also received city walls. As these cities are located on important communication routes linking southern and central Arkadia, their fortification in the early fourth century BC perhaps reflects a desire to curb the mobility of the Orchomenians into central Arkadia, where they traditionally held a lot of influence.[80]

In the end, we may never know whether the explosion of fortification building witnessed in early fourth-century BC Arkadia was conceived as one inclusive grand defensive strategy or whether such a strategy arose from that envisioned by the foundation of Megalopolis and Mantineia. What is certain, however, if we consider historical probability, is that the establishment of the Arkadian League, and the threat to its security from the very beginning represented by Orchomenos, Sparta, and their allies, were certainly catalysts in this process.

---

[77] Xen. *Hell.* 6.5.30.   [78] Maher (2015a).

[79] Gell (1823: 384) reports that the main pass in the Stymphalian Valley leading to the territory of Phlious was 'fortified by two walls'. Because of modern quarrying activities, no trace of these walls exist. But, if they were contemporary with the early fourth-century circuit of Stymphalos, then Gell's valuable description not only adds considerably to our knowledge of rural defensive planning in the area around the ancient city of Stymphalos, but might be further evidence of the Stymphalians' concern with the perceived threat posed by Phlious.

[80] Before the foundation of Megalopolis, Orchomenos was at the head of a political organization that included the central Arkadian *poleis* of Teuthis, Methydrion, and Theisoa (Karkalou).

5

The Fortifications of Arkadian City States

In his landmark study of the walls at Gortys published in the 1940s, Martin wrote that a comprehensive study of a given fortification circuit should consider not only the architecture, history, and historical probability, but also the 'histoire des enceintes de la même région, classées en séries typologiques et chronologiques'.[1] More recently, Camp has echoed this view, writing that, where the study of fortifications is concerned, 'there are instances where . . . we should actually think in terms of regional or local styles of wall-building'.[2] Although the advantages of studying fortifications on a regional level have long been recognized, very little has been done to advance the discipline in this regard. That is not to say that scholars of Greek fortifications have been idle, as the last seventy years have witnessed influential and instructive scholarship, without which the present study would not have been possible.[3] With the notable exception of Typaldou-Fakiris's study of the fortifications in Phokis[4] and Coutsinas's monograph on the fortifications of Crete,[5] however, these fundamental works were carried out with primarily an architectural, technological, and/or chronological scope—not with a regional focus. The value of an exclusively Arkadian focus for shedding light on a number of architectural, topographical, and historic issues is demonstrated by the present work.

The architectural and topographical synthesis made possible by the data gathered from the published literature and collected during the field reconnaissance of every site in question and assembled in Part Two of this book, the Catalogue, has confirmed a number of interesting and noteworthy regionally specific patterns. Related to the chronology of the walls, it is significant that there is no evidence for fortified *poleis* in Arkadia during the Archaic period. That is not to say that *poleis* did not exist in the Archaic period, only that they were not yet fortified. This point accords with Fredericksen's recently published survey of Greek fortifications of the Archaic period, which establishes

---

[1] Martin (1947–8: 120).   [2] Camp (2000: 44).
[3] e.g., Scranton (1941); Winter (1971a); Lawrence (1979); Adam (1982); Frederiksen (2011).
[4] Typaldou-Fakiris (2004).   [5] Coutsinas (2013).

that, although there are numerous examples of Archaic city walls on the Greek mainland, none is to be found in Arkadia.[6] Both the lack of archaeologically attested settlements of significant size and the lack of fortifications in the Archaic period seem to affirm 'the general opinion that the development of "true urban centres" in Arkadia was a development of the Classical period'.[7] When the *poleis* of Arkadia were eventually fortified in the Classical period, the fact that most appeared in the early fourth century BC, strategically distributed in limited geographic areas, suggests that the larger defensive concerns of the Arkadian League were a factor. Effectively, the majority of these new fortifications appear to have been erected as defensive bulwarks, specifically in areas in the south and north-east, where they could both observe and limit the movement of troops from Sparta, Orchomenos, and Phlious— the League's enemies. At the same time, the lack of fortifications being erected in western Arkadia is explained by the peaceful relationship with Elis—an ally of the Arkadian League.

Regarding the construction and architecture of the city walls, the fortifications of every *polis* in Arkadia were comprised of a mudbrick superstructure set atop a stone foundation. Similarly, it is evident that, although foundations were more often constructed in polygonal masonry, in all time periods trapezoidal masonry was an equally viable option. In this regard, it is established that, when used alone, the type of masonry is not necessarily a reliable stylistic indicator for establishing the relative date of a circuit. Although there are no definite patterns in the architecture of the city walls at the subregional level, there are hints that proximity had an influencing affect in the decisions made by military architects. Thus, we see, for example, that Stymphalos and nearby Alea possess the only Arkadian examples of regular (that is, uncoursed) polygonal masonry; that the overlap type of gate is most common in the circuits of the north-eastern *poleis*; that the indented trace is found at only Gortys and the adjacent city of Theisoa (Lavda); and that there was a general preference for trapezoidal masonry in the circuits of the northern Arkadian *poleis*. Finally, one of the most interesting patterns to emerge in this study is the defensive role played by the local topography at each site. While it is not surprising to find that all the sites but one took care to incorporate some elevated terrain into their circuits, the location of every single site chosen was provided with protection in the form of some sort of watercourse (river, tributary, lake, and/or seasonal stream).

---

[6] Although Frederiksen (2011: 176) does include the Arkadian *polis* of Oresthasion in his catalogue, I do not count it here because it is presumably based, not on personal observation, but solely on Pikoulas's opinion (1988: 102 ff.) that a small fragment he observed there was Archaic. No rationale beyond this opinion is presented, nor has any plan or photograph of this wall fragment been published. On Oresthasion, see the Appendix.

[7] Nielsen (2002: 171).

Concerning innovations in siege warfare and improvements to offensive artillery, the defensive responses of the Arkadian fortifications follow the same general developments observable in the circuits found throughout the Greek world. For example, the use of semicircular towers became more widespread as circuits lengthened to cover larger areas of flat terrain (especially at gates). Once this type of tower was established, the circuits deployed them—often indiscriminately—in combination with rectangular towers. Although the strategic spacing of towers was never completely abandoned in the smaller acropolis circuits, as towers became regular features of the circuits in the fourth century BC, there was an accompanying shift towards regular spacing. Finally, in order to house and support higher calibre artillery, the towers built (or rebuilt) in the late fourth and early third centuries BC were most often larger than the early fourth-century BC examples.

Before one of their numerous invasions of Arkadia, the Spartans consulted the oracle at Delphi, who warned them that they would find there 'many acorn-fed Arkadians to stop you'.[8] This famous, if unfortunate, proclamation undoubtedly echoed the view held by the ancient Greeks themselves and was inherited by the earliest scholarship, which focused on the idea of Arkadia as a cultural and political backwater, inhabited by the proverbial 'acorn-eaters'. But Arkadia was not the land of acorn-eaters. Arkadia was the land of Pelasgos, Lykaon, Agapenor, Lykomedes, Aeneas Tacticus, Polybius, and Philopoimen— admired by Pausanias as the greatest of all Greek men who performed deeds for Greece in the face of tyranny and invasion.[9] Nor was Arkadia either 'marginal in terms of its cultural development'[10] or 'the most backward district in the development of the πόλις'.[11] Instead, as demonstrated by the most recent modern scholarship—characterized by a move away from traditional stereotypical interpretations of a poor and isolated Arkadia—it appears that this region was a moderately prosperous one whose inhabitants followed generally the same patterns of social, political, and cultural development seen elsewhere in ancient Greece.[12] Just as this most recent scholarship has been responsible for leading the theoretical assumptions and disciplinary predispositions away from the idea of the backward and culturally poor Arkadia that had dominated earlier scholarship, so too it is hoped that the present book will dispel the idea that the fortified *poleis* of Arkadia possessed a 'less advanced social and military outlook'.[13]

Indeed, the comprehensive and detailed study of the fortifications demonstrates that Arkadian military architects possessed a keen awareness and appreciation of strategy, tactics, and defensive planning—elements reflected in the city walls of even the most modest *poleis*. It is often all too easy to get lost in the architectural and topographical details and to forget that the function of

---

[8] Hdt. 1.66.   [9] Paus. 8.49.1–8.52.6.   [10] Hunt (1998: 197, n. 1).
[11] Parke (1933: 14).   [12] Nielsen and Roy (1999: 12–13).   [13] Winter (1971a: 34).

a *polis*'s fortifications in the larger context was both to reflect and to protect a city's autonomy. In this way a city's walls represent a fundamental characteristic of the *polis* itself. But, even at the level of their function for the individual citizen, the often poorly preserved state of the remains can lead us to forget that these walls were built to protect people, their loved ones, their homes, and their possessions. For these reasons, nothing in the fortifications was random and nothing was left to chance. The trace of every Arkadian *polis* was carefully plotted to maximize the efficiency of the natural defences afforded by the topography. Every stone foundation block was quarried, carved, and positioned with care. Every mudbrick was thoughtfully laid, and every tower, gate, and postern was aligned and built with purpose.

Part Two

Catalogue

1

Alea, Eastern Arkadia

LOCATION

Alea is located in a small valley in eastern Arkadia, approximately 3 km east of the modern village that bears its name (Fig. C1.1).[1] The acropolis comprises the summit and south slope of a small spur attached by a narrow saddle to a larger mountain to the north. Inhabitation was largely limited to the fortified lower city, where scattered remains of houses have been reported.[2]

POLIS STATUS

Two *proxenia* grants, the internal and external use of the city ethnic, a civic mint, as well as a *theorodokos*, are all demonstrable for Alea in the Classical period.[3] Alea is called a *polis* by Pausanias in his list of Arkadian cities that are said to have participated in the synoikism of Megalopolis.[4]

HISTORY

The earliest reliable evidence suggests activity on the site during the late fifth century BC.[5] Alea was probably a member of the Peloponnesian League, and

---

[1] Formerly the village of Bougiati. Although Alea was originally part of Arkadia, Pausanias (8.23.1) mentions that Alea, like Stymphalos, belonged to the Argives in his day. Today the site and nearby village continue to belong to the Argolid prefecture.

[2] Nielsen (2002: 550).

[3] One grant of *proxenia* (*IvO* 30) was to an Athenian and is the oldest known public enactment of Alea (c.450–350 BC). The other is a fifth-century BC grant (*IG* I³ 80) by Athens of *proxenia* to a man from Alea. The city ethnic Ἀλειός (*IvO* 30) and Ἀλεός (*IG* I³ 80) are attested on both of the *proxenia* inscriptions. *SEG* xxiii. 189.25 (c.330 BC) records an Argive *theorodokos* in Alea.

[4] Paus. 8.27.3.

[5] Alea appears to have produced its own coinage by the last quarter of the fifth century BC (Head 1963: 446).

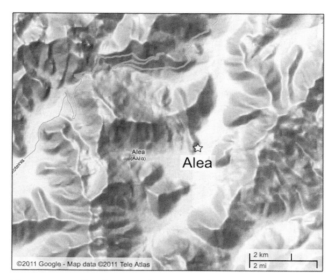

Fig. C1.1. Alea, topographical map of territory. (© *2011 Google-Map data © 2011 Tele Atlas*)

was certainly later a member of both the Arkadian and Achaian Leagues.[6] As the site has never been excavated and is virtually absent in the ancient sources, unfortunately, besides the evidence already given, next to nothing is known about the history of the ancient city.[7]

LOCAL TOPOGRAPHY

The site of ancient Alea is ideally situated on the south-east side of a narrow spur that extends from Mt Skiathis southward into the plain below (Fig. C1.2).[8] The hill of Alea rises *c.*140 m from the surrounding plain and is linked to Mt Skiathis by a narrow saddle on the north. While the hill tapers southwards relatively gradually from its highest point, the east and west sides of the hill fall away more steeply. Here it commands the greater part of an S-shaped plain to the south as well as access to a narrow valley that continues north-east

---

[6] Nielsen (1996b: 87, 94–5; 2002: 550).

[7] For a summary of the history of scholarship of Alea, see Maher (2015a: 21–2).

[8] I would like to thank the 4th Ephorate of Prehistoric and Classical Antiquities for granting me a study permit to examine the remains of ancient Alea. Unless otherwise cited, all photographs and measurements are based on personal observation from my visits to the site in autumn 2009, winter 2011, and the summers of 2014 and 2015.

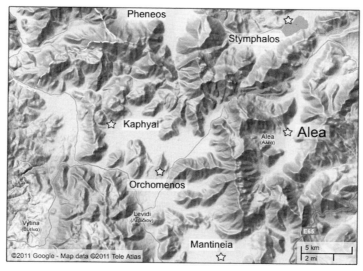

Fig. C1.2. Alea, topographical map of Alea and neighbouring territories. (© *2011 Google-Map data © 2011 Tele Atlas*)

Fig. C1.3. Alea, the site (facing north-east). (© *Matthew Maher*)

from the plain towards the Stymphalos Valley.[9] With the exception of this north-east passage, the main southern plain is essentially enclosed on all sides by mountains. The mountains that surround the main valley not only defined the territory of Alea (determined to be *c*.110 km²),[10] but also separated it from those of neighbouring *poleis* (Fig. C1.3). To the north,

[9] Jost (1999: 198).
[10] All territorial sizes are from Nielsen (2002: app. 9), based on the map in Jost (1985).

Mt Skiathis and Oligyrtos divided Alea from the territory of Stymphalos; eastwards, Mt Pharmakas marked the boundary with Phlious and the Argolid; in the south, Mt Lyrkeio and Artemisio separated Alea from the *chora* of Mantineia; while, in the west, the Trachy Mountains formed a continuous barrier between Alea and Orchomenos.

NATURAL DEFENCES

The height offered by the acropolis, and the steep slopes on its north-east and western sides (Fig. C1.3), provide natural defences to the site. The surrounding mountains limit the approaches to the site from routes from the north-east and south.

FORTIFICATION TYPE

Uneven type.[11] The extant remains of the acropolis are comprised of three main elements, which together form a rough triangle: a west wall, a north-east wall, and, at the highest point, a separately fortified citadel (Fig. C1.4).[12] Although nothing remains, the lower city in the plain must have been surrounded with walls connected to those of the acropolis circuit.[13]

PRESERVATION

The stone foundations of the acropolis circuit (including the citadel) are very well preserved, surviving in places to over 4 m in height.[14] Nothing remains of the lower city circuit.

[11] Listed as a 'ville mixtes' type by Jost (1999: 198).
[12] Because the fortifications included a lower city, the word 'acropolis' here denotes all the intramural area on the hill and 'citadel' refers only to the separately fortified enclosure on its peak. The combined total of these elements is 1,110 m, enclosing an area of 14.3 ha. For a more detailed discussion of the course of the wall and its constituent parts, see Maher (2015a: 27–32).
[13] Lawrence (1979: 133) does not acknowledge the existence of a lower city, instead maintaining the acropolis of Alea 'must have been solely intended for a garrison'. Evidence for the existence of a lower city wall is discussed in more detail under Comments.
[14] I first visited the site on 22 November 2009. Cf. with Frazer's description (1898: iv. 276) on his visit on 14 October 1895.

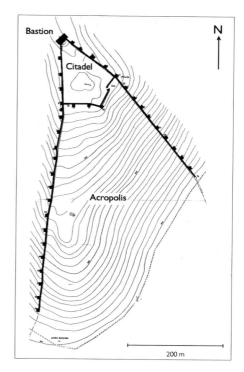

Fig. C1.4. Alea, plan after Meyer (1939a: pl. II).

CONSTRUCTION

The foundations of the acropolis walls and towers were constructed pre-dominantly in an uncoursed polygonal style (Fig. C1.5). The acropolis bas-tion and the adjacent west wall of the citadel are the only exceptions, built instead of trapezoidal blocks laid in isodomic courses (Fig. C1.6). The stone foundations of all the curtains and towers in the circuit once supported a mudbrick superstructure (not preserved). The curtains measure 2.80–3.25 m in thickness.

SUMMARY OF TACTICAL COMPONENTS

The acropolis circuit contains twenty-six rectangular towers (*c.*5 m × 2.50 m), spaced fairly regularly at *c.*28–30 m. The citadel contains a further eleven rectangular towers of similar size and one bastion on the summit, measuring

Fig. C1.5. Alea, exterior north-west curtain below citadel (facing east). (© *Matthew Maher*)

Fig. C1.6. Alea, exterior acropolis bastion (facing north-east). (© *Matthew Maher*)

23 by 8 m. There is one postern in the acropolis circuit and one small frontal opening type gate providing access to the citadel from the intramural area.

Towers

The west wall of the circuit (*c.*485 m long) contains fifteen rectangular towers spaced fairly evenly at intervals between 28 and 30 m.[15] These towers are typically *c.*5.10 m wide and project an average of 2.50 m from the walls.[16] The north-east wall (*c.*296 m) is furnished with ten rectangular towers regularly

[15] The exceptions are Towers 28 and 30, which are 39 m apart, and Towers 30 and 32, which are separated by only 18 m (Meyer 1939a: 24).

[16] Meyer (1939a: 24). Excluding the inexplicably small Tower 40 (4.70 m wide and projecting 2.0 m).

Fig. C1.7. Alea, postern (exterior) in north-east curtain (facing south-west). (© *Matthew Maher*)

spaced at intervals comparable to those of the west wall. Although the majority here are 5 m wide and project 2 m from the curtain,[17] there are several exceptions, most notably Tower 60, which is some 9 m wide.[18]

Gates

There is one postern (1.25 m wide) in the acropolis circuit (Fig. C1.7) and one small frontal opening type gate (3 m wide) providing access to the citadel from the intramural area.[19]

Citadel

The citadel occupies the relatively flat area on the top of the hill, and its irregular quadrangle shape is defined both by the convergence of the west and north-east walls on the north, as well as by a set of three cross-walls on the south. The citadel contains a Π-shaped bastion on the summit, measuring 23 by 8 m,[20] and a further eleven rectangular towers, most of which are similar

---

[17] Meyer (1939a: 24).

[18] All tower numbers are taken from the plan in Meyer (1939a: pl. 2).

[19] When Rangabé (1857: 121) visited the site in the mid-nineteenth century, the lintel above the postern door was still intact, comprised of 'de deux pierres penchées, et se servant mutuelle-ment d'appui'. Although in a ruinous state today, a small 1.25 m wide opening can still be observed. See Rangabé (1857: pl. XI) for sketch of the postern. Meyer (1939a: 24) found the opening to be 1.20 m wide. Lawrence (1979: 257), presumably based on Rangabé's sketch, dates this opening to the end of the fourth century BC.

[20] On the types and number of artillery machines this bastion may have housed, see Winter (1997: 260).

Fig. C1.8. Alea, citadel gate (facing north-east). (© *Matthew Maher*)

in size to those on the slopes. The polygonal style of masonry preferred for the rest of the circuit was abandoned in the construction of the bastion in favour of trapezoidal blocks laid in regular isodomic courses (see Fig. C1.6).[21] The circuit's only gate can be found in the south-east corner of the citadel wall (Fig. C1.8). This gateway, 3 m wide with a 7 m long passage, does not wholly conform to the established types. Although it more closely resembles a frontal gateway than an overlap type, the opening itself is neither flanked by towers nor set perpendicular to the curtain. Instead, we see an oblique opening formed by small returns in the adjoining curtains.

COMMENTS

Although the full and exact course of the lower city circuit is impossible to trace today, perhaps the partitioning of different tracts of land can provide some clues.[22] Satellite images and photos of the lower city reveal a curious feature (Fig. C1.9). An oblique field boundary is clearly discernible, extending in a curved line from the point where the north-east wall meets the modern road on the plain below. Not only is such a boundary apparently at odds with the surrounding rectilinear land partitions, but its alignment with

---

[21] Scranton (1941: 167) lists the masonry of the walls of Alea as irregular trapezoidal work and dates them tentatively to 390 BC. Because his designation was based on a photograph and he provides no more specifics, it is uncertain whether he is referring to the masonry of the bastion or of the acropolis walls (although I suspect the latter). In any event, this is especially problematic, since neither can really be described as irregular trapezoidal.

[22] The lack of any remains did not prevent Meyer (1939a: 28) from estimating the length of the lower city circuit to be 1,220 m. Much of this argument for the existence of a lower city wall appears in Maher (2015a: 31–2).

Fig. C1.9. Alea, view of lower city from north-east wall (facing south-east). (© *Matthew Maher*)

the north-east fortification wall is certainly suggestive and may represent the lower city wall's eastern course.[23]

OVERALL DEFENSIVE PLANNING

Incorporating ample natural resources, an advantageous geographical position, and a suitable topography that could easily be enhanced by man-made fortification works, the *polis* of Alea is ideally located. Like the valleys of Stymphalos and Pheneos, the valley of Alea is extremely well watered, and contains no fewer than fourteen seasonal streams as well as a number of mountain springs.[24] Arable land is also plentiful in the flat valley floor, while the maquis and holly-oak-covered slopes of the surrounding hills provide

---

[23] Jost (1999: 198) also believes that the lower city was fortified, even if its course is not clear.

[24] Meyer (1939a: 26–7) notes: 'Geschiebe führenden Bäche zusammenlaufen und die Talsohle jeden Winter in einen See verwandeln.'

suitable fodder for grazing livestock. The surrounding hills—and the hill of
Alea itself—probably provided the limestone employed in the fortifications.
Besides access to natural resources such as these, larger defensive strategies
also had to take topography and geography into account.

Topographically, the hill of Alea is very practically fashioned. Located at the
edge of a plain on the tip of a spur that extended from the flank of a mountain
and was linked to its main mass by a narrow saddle, it was defendable without
being too high or inaccessible, and was close enough to protect the arable land
in its territory. The saddle separating it from the main mass of the mountain to
the north was especially crucial, as it took away any advantage an attacker
might have held from holding the high ground above the city. The hill's
geographical position in relation to the valley was also advantageous from a
defensive point of view. Located at the north of the valley, the hill not only
commanded the plain to the south, but also controlled access into the valley
itself. Specifically, the acropolis and the hill immediately across the plain to the
south-east combined to create a small bottleneck at the terminus of the narrow
valley to the north-east, which was the main point of access to the territory of
Alea.[25] Finally, as noted by Frazer, 'the view from the hill of Alea embraces the
valleys on both sides, with high barren mountains rising from them and
bounding the horizon in all directions. The outlines of the mountains on the
east, south, and north are bold and fine.'[26] But, more than being a picturesque
site, the position of the acropolis and its natural topography facilitated the
optimal lines of site for defence of the surrounding area. Thus, from the
citadel, almost the whole of the territory is visible, including the two minor
entrances into the valley.[27]

To make Alea defensible, corresponding tactical considerations were combined with the general defensive strategy founded on the natural topographical and geographical advantages of the site.[28] In this regard, the most
observable feature is the effort made to strengthen the north-eastern defences.
For example, with the exception of Tower 9, it is on this side of the trace that
the largest artillery towers were constructed. It could be argued that such
precaution on this side of the hill was necessary to defend the approach to the
acropolis's (and the citadel's) only gateway. But certainly the slope of the
hill and the formidable and appropriately placed Tower 17 could have effectively protected the small postern. Furthermore, the fact that the north-eastern
wall is, on average, 0.50 m thicker than its western counterpart implies that

---

[25] This gap between the two hills is less than 800 m, and would be considerably smaller when
the lower city fortifications, which extended from the hill into this area, are taken into account.

[26] Frazer (1898: iv. 278).

[27] The only part of the territory not visible from Alea is a small area in the extreme south-west
part of the valley, immediately north of the modern village of Frousiouna.

[28] With the absence of extant remains in the lower city, we are here confined to tactical
analyses of the acropolis fortifications.

protecting the gate is only part of the answer. The other, and main part, of the answer is that this wall was the first line of defence for both Alea and its territory.

Any aggressors intent upon laying siege to the city or invading its country-side would be required to approach the territory by way of the narrow valley that opens north-east of the city.[29] Upon exiting this narrow passage and entering the plain, they would immediately find the north-eastern fortifications set at a 90° angle in front of them. The construction of this wall perpendicular to the main approach into the valley ensured that an enemy would be presented with the maximum artillery fire possible. Moreover, if an enemy attempted to stay out of range of the acropolis artillery by sticking close to the hill opposite the city to the south-east, it would have brought itself into both the range of the artillery fired from the towers in the lower city fortifications, and the bottleneck effect already mentioned.

Finally, as the western approach was too steep for siege engines to be brought against it effectively—and in any case would have required getting past the north-eastern defences—the only other area vulnerable to attack was the north. If an enemy wanted to avoid the imposing fortifications of the north-east wall, it might have attempted to launch an attack from the relatively flat saddle north of the acropolis citadel. Not surprisingly, the fortifications also reflect the attempt to gain the tactical defensive advantage in this direction. The larger Tower 60 was advantageously positioned to control easterly access to the saddle from the small hollow at its base, and it is likely that the relatively large Towers 17 and 21 of the citadel performed a similar function. Because of their position, however, these towers would be of little use if an enemy succeeded in reaching the saddle itself. The protection of this vulnerable area was instead entrusted to the citadel's bastion. Like the north-eastern wall, the bastion was oriented perpendicularly—presenting its long side to the north—in order to cover the greatest area and offer the maximum amount of artillery fire. As the bastion occupied the highest point of the citadel, the potential range of its artillery would have given the advantage to the defenders and would guarantee that any attack from the north would be a costly one for the enemy.

CHRONOLOGICAL SUMMARY

The proposed date for the entirety of the original circuit, based on historical probability and architectural affinities, is *c*.375–350 BC. It appears modifications

---

[29] For traces of the road network in the territory of Alea, see Pikoulas (1999a: 266).

were made to the bastion and the west wall of the citadel sometime in the late third/early fourth century BC.

CHRONOLOGICAL ARGUMENTS

The first to offer any kind of chronology for the walls of Alea is Lattermann, who, in the minutes of a meeting published after a visit to the site, vaguely proposes that they date to the time of the Achaian League.[30] The only other observation he makes, besides the favourable preservation, is that 'die Türme nicht im Verband mit den Kurtinen stehen'.[31] Lattermann does not, however, provide any reason for a proposed third-century BC date. Meyer, on the other hand, while subscribing to Lattermann's chronology, at least offers grounds, however unpersuasive, for a Hellenistic date.[32] For instance, he maintains that the bulkiness of the construction, the size of the citadel bastion, the size of the blocks, historical considerations, and the presence of ground-storey tower chambers all suggest the walls were built when the city was affiliated with the Achaian League.[33] The size of blocks employed in the construction of a settlement's fortification, however, is of little chronological value, and assuming the walls of Alea must be Hellenistic because they are made of large blocks is flawed reasoning.[34] Although the rest of Meyer's arguments for a Hellenistic date are not as easily dismissed, there are elements of Alea's fortifications that do suggest an earlier—perhaps late Classical period—date.

One of the most obvious architectural features (or lack thereof) that speaks to an earlier date is the paucity of posterns in the Alean circuit. Since generally, from the later fourth century BC onwards, posterns (in the curtains and flanks of towers) became increasingly common[35]—especially in large circuits incorporating a lower city—the deficiency of such features at Alea may suggest an earlier date. On the other hand, perhaps it was thought that siege engines could not be brought against the naturally defensible terrain of the acropolis, thus precluding the need for posterns. Although the presence of only a single

---

[30] Lattermann (1914: 106). This is only true of the north-east and western sections of the circuit. The towers on the acropolis, as noted by Meyer (1939a: 26), are integrated with the adjacent curtains—a fact that also suggests a Classical period date.

[31] Lattermann (1914: 106).

[32] Jost (1999: 198) also subscribes to a Hellenistic date (third century BC).

[33] Meyer (1939a: 25–6).

[34] e.g., one has to look no further than to the walls of Nestane, located in a neighbouring valley just south of Alea. Although the walls of Nestane were constructed with blocks comparable in size to those of Alea, they have long been thought to date to the first half of the fourth century BC. On dating the walls of Nestane, see Lattermann (1913: 413–15) and Hodkinson and Hodkinson (1981: 247).

[35] Winter (1971a: 239, 305).

extant postern, and one that functioned more to provide access to the citadel rather than for offensive sorties, may suggest an overall passive approach, the number of towers employed in the circuit points to the opposite conclusion. Indeed, the existence of thirty-seven acropolis towers demonstrates an active defensive policy, one in which the use of mounted (small calibre) artillery played a significant role in the plan to keep the enemy at a distance from the walls. Ultimately, such a policy is paralleled at Stymphalos, Orchomenos, and Mantineia, and speaks to a date in the second quarter of the fourth century BC. Conversely, Winter mentions in passing that the 'close-set towers of Alea obviously belong to the Hellenistic age'.[36] In the same article, however, he also states that the 'numerous close-set towers' are 'characteristic of the period in which the new Mantineia was founded and fortified [i.e., 370 BC]'.[37] The style of masonry is, unfortunately, no more conclusive, as Scranton and Winter have both commented on the difficulties in establishing the chronological limits of polygonal masonry.[38] Nonetheless, Winter believes that polygonal was chiefly employed in the Peloponnese in the early fourth century BC, and Scranton maintains that by the late fourth century BC the style had all but run its course. [39]

Neither does a closer examination of Meyer's 'historischen Gründen'[40] support the notion that Alea's fortifications date to the time of the city's affiliation with the Achaian League; instead it indicates that their origin may pre-date this membership by nearly a century. For example, if Pausanias is to be believed, then Alea was one of the settlements persuaded to participate in the synoikism of Megalopolis c.370 BC.[41] The city, however, does not seem to have been abandoned, or at least not completely, as an inscription dated to c.330 BC records and an Argive *theorodokos* in Alea.[42] Still, as it is commonly held that Pausanias' description of the participating cities is derived from an inscription he had personally read, the idea cannot be dismissed completely.[43] Whether all or only some of the population left to join Megalopolis, it follows that a construction project on the scale of Alea's fortifications would demand the full economic resources and labour force of a unified settlement, and thus should not post-date the 360s BC.[44]

---

[36] Winter (1989: 195).
[37] Winter (1989: 191). Averaging c.28–30 m, the towers at Alea are very similarly spaced to the first-generation towers at Stymphalos, which have been dated to c.375–350 BC (Gourley and Williams 2005: 219, 241).
[38] Scranton (1941: 50); Winter (1971a: 83 ff.).
[39] Scranton (1941: 50, 69); Winter (1971a: 90). By way of comparison, on the polygonal circuit of Oiniadai, Winter (1971a: 236) maintains that 'it seems to me unlikely that so vast a circuit would have been built in the polygonal style during the Hellenistic period'.
[40] Meyer (1939a: 26).
[41] Alea is mentioned first in Pausanias' list of Arkadian cities that joined Megalopolis (8.27.3).
[42] SEG xxiii. 189.25.   [43] See Nielsen (2002: 573).
[44] Lawrence (1979: 396) takes the opposite stance, maintaining that the walls were built after the Arkadian League had collapsed and people returned to their cities. He goes on to say,

Another historical consideration to be taken into account regards the origin of the settlement itself. Although without excavation there is no way of determining when the settlement was founded, the earliest reliable coin evidence suggests activity on the site during the late fifth century BC.[45] This evidence, combined with the fact that Alea was probably a member of the Peloponnesian League, and certainly was later a member of the Arkadian League, demonstrates an active political history going back over a century before its affiliation with the Achaian League. It would be extremely unlikely, not to mention unusual, for the city to have remained unfortified during this extended period.[46] But perhaps the best historical evidence for an early fourth-century BC date for the fortifications comes by way of comparanda from the surrounding sites.

The construction of the walls of Alea at a time that also witnessed comparable fortifications erected at nearby Stymphalos, Nestane, and Mantineia adds considerable weight to the argument for an early fourth-century BC date.[47] Comparisons with the fortifications at Stymphalos, located a mere *c.*15 km to the north, are especially revealing.[48] Although the construction of the walls differ, the layout, size, use of towers, and utilization of the natural terrain by both circuits are extremely similar.[49] Moreover, as mentioned, the size of the towers and their spacing (*c.*28–30 m) are especially comparable. Fortunately, sections of the Stymphalian fortifications have been excavated, and evidence suggests that, besides the modification of a few components, the bulk of the circuit was constructed with the refounding of the city in the first third of the fourth century BC.[50] Furthermore, because of Stymphalos' strategic location and the date of its foundation, Gourley and Williams 'suspect that the refounding of Stymphalos is to be associated with new cities at Mantineia, Megalopolis and Messene built to control Sparta'.[51] It is not inconceivable that Alea performed a similar function, more specifically, as an Arkadian League bulwark against Orchomenos and Phlious—both of which were initially allied with Sparta against the League and both of which bordered the territory of Alea.

---

somewhat inexplicably, that the walls were built and paid for in the late fourth century by Alea's 'overlord' and that the citadel 'was, no doubt, reserved for his mercenaries'.

[45] Head (1963: 446).

[46] Kleitor appears to have been the only sizeable Arkadian *polis* not to receive a city wall by the end of the fourth century.

[47] For a more detailed argument on why Alea was probably part of the same defensive system envisioned with the foundations of Megalopolis and Mantineia around 370 BC, see Maher (2015a: 35–8, 39–40).

[48] For a detailed comparison of the walls of these two cities, see Maher (2015a, forthcoming).

[49] So much so, in fact, that, if you rotate the plan of Alea counter-clockwise 90°, it becomes almost indistinguishable from the plan of Stymphalos' circuit.

[50] Gourley and Williams (2005: 219).

[51] Gourley and Williams (2005: 219, n. 10). Especially since passing through Stymphalian territory could be avoided completely by a route through Alea's valley. In other words, in passing through Alea, Spartans on the move could eventually reach Achaia, the Corinthia, or the Argolid.

Finally, another feature held in common by both Stymphalos and Alea is the existence of a large bastion as the focal point of the fortifications. Again, although these are constructed differently, it is unlikely that their position in relation to the rest of the circuit and their almost identical dimensions are coincidental.[52] Excavation has demonstrated that the bastion at Stymphalos was adapted into its present state early in the third century BC, perhaps under Macedonian influence.[53] Excavation at Stymphalos has also determined that, like the bastion, during the late fourth and early third centuries BC several other components of the fortifications were modified in response to advances in siege warfare.[54] A similar scenario at Alea involving the adaptation of existing features in response to advances in siege warfare may explain those tactical features not easily reconcilable with date of the early fourth century BC.[55]

In the end, future excavation may demonstrate that, as at Stymphalos, the bastion of Alea and the larger citadel towers were enlarged from existing structures in the later fourth or early third century BC.[56] On the basis of historical probability, therefore, although it is far from conclusive, I would suggest that the fortifications of Alea were largely constructed in more or less their present form during the second quarter of the fourth century BC, while the enlargement of the bastion and several of the citadel towers were responses to advances in *poliorketics* of the late fourth and early third centuries BC.[57]

BIBLIOGRAPHY

Pausanias (8.23.1, 8.27.3); Gell (1817: 168); Dodwell (1819: ii. 432); Boblaye (1836: 47); Leake (1846: 383); Curtius (1851: i. 208–9); Rangabé (1857: 119–22);

[52] Alea's bastion measures 23.30 m by 8 m and Stymphalos' bastion measures 21 m by 11 m (Gourley and Williams 2005: 246).
[53] Gourley and Williams (2005: 249).   [54] Gourley and Williams (2005: 249).
[55] e.g., the ground-storey tower chambers, which Winter (1971a: 162) notes were relatively uncommon before the time of Epaminondas and the Macedonians. It is not inconceivable that the entire separately fortified citadel and the bastion are contemporary and post-date the rest of the circuit.
[56] Chronologically, the isodomic trapezoidal masonry of Alea's bastion also fits with the aesthetic appeal of the Hellenistic period, which arose from the 'natural structural qualities of the coursed styles' (Winter 1971a: 88). The larger towers too are consistent with Ober's second generation of artillery towers intended to house larger-calibre torsion machines, which appear in the late fourth and early third centuries (Ober 1987: 570).
[57] Lawrence (1979: 396) believes the bastion is contemporary with the rest of the circuit (late fourth century BC). Winter (1989: 195) expresses his doubt of Lawrence's assertion that the bastion is contemporary with the rest of the circuit.

Bursian (1862: ii. 198); Rochas d'Aiglun (1881: 58–9); Frazer (1898: iv. 275–78); Lattermann (1914: 106); Meyer (1939a: 19–29); Scranton (1941: 167); Martin (1944: 113); Levi (1971: 424, n. 155); Winter (1971a: 193, n. 108; 1989: 191, 195; 1997: 260); Lawrence (1979: 133, 257, 396–7, 398, 440, 458); Jost (1985: 107–9, 526; 1999: 198); Papachatzis (1994: 265–6); Nielsen (1996b: 87, 94–5; 2002: 549–50); Pikoulas (1999a: 266); Maher (2012a: 108–32; 2015a; forthcoming).

2

Alipheira, Western Arkadia

LOCATION

Alipheira is located in western Arkadia on an isolated hill near the borders of Triphylia and Elis, on the south side of the Alpheios River Valley (Fig. C2.1). The acropolis encompassed the apex of a narrow but high and precipitous hill sharply delineated by adjacent river valleys. The lower city was located on the eastern slope of the acropolis[1] and was surrounded by a wall connected to the acropolis circuit.

POLIS STATUS

A third-century BC inscription has been found that refers to Alipheira as a *polis*,[2] as well as a number bearing the use of the city ethnic.[3] Polybius refers to Alipheira as a *polis*, as does Pausanias.[4] In the Hellenistic period, we can be confident that a Delphic *theorodokos* resided in the city.[5] Because there is little evidence that makes the political identity of the settlement clear in the Archaic and Classical periods, the most we can say on the subject is that, since Alipheira certainly existed before the Hellenistic period, '[it] may possibly have been a *polis*'.[6]

HISTORY

Alipheira was one of the settlements voted to be incorporated into the new city of Megalopolis in *c.*370 BC.[7] At that time, Pausanias tells us that the city was

---

[1] Jost (1999: 193).   [2] *SEG* xxv. 447.9.
[3] *SEG* xxv. 449; *IvO* 48; *CIG* 1936 (Hell.). For a review of the toponym and city ethnic, see Orlandos (1967–8: 9–10).
[4] Polyb. 4.78; Paus. 8.27.4, 8.27.7.   [5] Plassart (1921: ii. 80).
[6] Nielsen (2002: 550).   [7] Paus. 8.26.5, 8.27.4, 8.27.7.

Fig. C2.1. Alipheira: Topographical map of area. (© *2011 Google-Map data © 2011 Tele Atlas*)

'abandoned by *many* of its inhabitants'[8]—the implication being that not all the population participated in this Arkadian union and the city was not completely deserted. Alipheira was almost certainly a member of the Arkadian League and, before that, presumably also a member of the Peloponnesian League.[9] Alipheira appears to have remained a member of the Arkadian Confederacy until 244 BC, when Lydiadas—then tyrant of Megalopolis—ceded the city to Elis.[10] The alliance of Achaians and Macedonians led by Philip V would not suffer an Elian garrison to hold such a valuable and strategic position for long and in 219 BC, just weeks after they had wrestled Psophis from Elian control, the Achaian and Macedonian troops laid siege to Alipheira.[11] Although the defenders briefly resisted the advance of Philip, they soon capitulated, and their lives were spared.[12] The city was annexed again by Megalopolis a few years later in 207 BC, and in 191 BC Alipheira joined the Achaian League and began to mint its own coinage.[13] Finally, although by the time Pausanias visited the site Alipheira was a town 'of no great size',[14] scant remains from the early Christian period demonstrate that inhabitation in the area continued to some degree.[15]

---

[8] Paus. 8.26.5; emphasis added.   [9] Nielsen (2002: 551).
[10] Polyb. 4.77.   [11] Polyb. 4.77–8.
[12] Polyb. 4.78. This siege will be discussed in more detail later in this chapter. For a commentary on Polybius' account of Philip's attack with reference to the local topography, see Pikoulas (1983).
[13] Orlandos (1967–8: 21).   [14] Paus. 8.26.5.
[15] Hellenic Ministry of Culture (2007a).

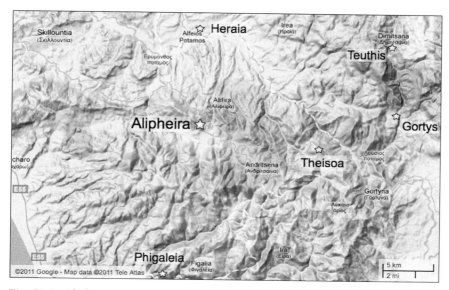

Fig. C2.2. Alipheira, topographical map of south-west Arkadia. (*© 2011 Google-Map data © 2011 Tele Atlas*)

LOCAL TOPOGRAPHY

The acropolis of Alipheira encompassed the summit of a narrow, high, and very steep hill (see Fig. C2.1).[16] This hill rises *c.*160 m above, and is sharply delineated by, the Phanari and Zelechovitiko River Valleys to the east and west respectively. While the slopes of the hill fall away on all sides—though considerably more steeply to the west and south-west—the top consists of a narrow crest, about 800 m by 65 m.[17] The southern end of the acropolis is fashioned into terraces—artificial and natural—which descend to the south in a series of steps: the separately fortified citadel occupying the highest point, followed by the sanctuary of Athena below, and finally, a long narrow tongue of land representing the southernmost part of the hilltop. The numerous mountains, small hills, and tributaries represented the natural boundaries of the territory (Fig. C2.2). South of the southern plain is Mt Minthi, demarcating the border with Phigaleia; to the north and north-west Mt Arithas formed the boundary with the territory of Heraia; while the Phanari and Mylaon Rivers, tributaries of the Alpheios, constituted the eastern limit of the territory and boundary with

---

[16] The modern village of Alifira lies on the northern slope of the hill, below the ancient acropolis.

[17] Orlandos (1967–8: 32). The hill is not oriented east–west, as on the early plans of Leake (1830: ii. 72) and Curtius (1851: pl. 7).

Theisoa (Lavda).[18] The city's fortified acropolis, known to the early travellers as Kastro Nérovitsa, commanded a territory of *c*.100 km² comprised of a small plain that extends northwards towards the Alpheios River, and a larger narrow plain in the valley running north-west–south-east, which is located south of the site.

NATURAL DEFENCES

The height offered by the acropolis, and the steep slopes on its long south-west side, provide the site with natural defences. The Zelechovitik and Phanari Rivers flank the acropolis and lower city on the west and east respectively.

FORTIFICATION TYPE

Acropolis type.[19] A wall encircles the entire summit of the acropolis, while another extends from the acropolis to envelop the lower city on its eastern slope (Fig. C2.3).[20] There is a separately fortified citadel on the acropolis.[21]

PRESERVATION

The walls are fairly well preserved, especially the western section on the north side of the hill, the southern section (including the citadel), and parts of the northern trace, where courses of the wall stand in places to heights of over 3 m. The total length of the acropolis circuit is *c*.1,440 m.

CONSTRUCTION

The superstructure was mudbrick (not preserved), while the stone foundations of both the lower city and acropolis circuit (including citadel and towers) were

---

[18] Orlandos (1967–8: 32).   [19] Jost (1999: 193).

[20] The lower city wall does not appear on Orlandos's plan.

[21] Basing his decision on his interpretation of Polybius, Orlandos labels this separately fortified enclosure the acropolis. But from an interpretation of Pikoulas (1983), I agree with him that the entire hill is better understood as the acropolis, and employ the word citadel to differentiate between the two.

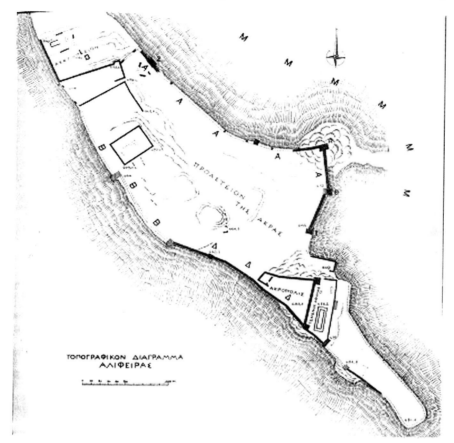

Fig. C2.3. Alipheira, plan of the site from Orlandos (1967–8: pl. 2).

constructed in a style best described as a predominately coursed polygonal with irregular trapezoidal (Fig. C2.4).[22] For the most part, the walls on the acropolis appear to be around 2.75–3 m thick.[23] The walls forming the southern terminus of the Athena Sanctuary are limited to a thickness of *c.*2 m.[24]

---

[22] Basing his comment on a photograph alone, Scranton (1941: 81–2, 167) lists the walls among his examples of irregular trapezoidal. The limestone employed is friable, with clearly visible veins of differing consistency. That it is so similar to the type of stone used in the nearby circuit of Theisoa (Lavda) suggests it is a type found locally. Frazer (1898: iv. 298) maintains 'it is the native rock of the hill, as may be seen by the numerous rocks of this sort which crop up on the surface at the northern end of the ridge'.

[23] See Orlandos (1967–8: 29, fig. 10, 38, fig. 21).

[24] Orlandos (1967–8: 29, fig. 10, 38, fig. 21).

Fig. C2.4. Alipheira, photo of exterior west wall of citadel showing predominately coursed polygonal masonry (facing north-east). (© *Matthew Maher*)

SUMMARY OF TACTICAL COMPONENTS

The acropolis circuit contains ten rectangular towers (ranging *c*.7.50–12 m × 2–8 m), strategically, rather than regularly, spaced (see Fig. C2.3). The citadel contains a further two rectangular towers (*c*.7 m × 7 m) and one larger tower or keep (12.40 m × 15.30 m). There are no attested posterns in the acropolis. One (possibly two) simple frontal opening type gates provided access to the acropolis from the lower city. Nothing is known of lower city towers or gates.

Towers

The acropolis circuit at Alipheira contains ten rectilinear towers of differing dimensions.[25] The ten acropolis towers range in size (averaging *c*.7–8 m in width and projecting 2 m from the curtain), though one example is *c*.12 by 8 m. These towers are spaced strategically rather than regularly and do not appear to be bonded to the curtains.[26]

Gates

It appears that access to the acropolis of Alipheira was facilitated by at least one, and possibly two, gates. Although today no traces of these gates are

[25] Following Orlandos, I will refer to these towers according to their elevation provided on the site plan (see Fig. C2.2).
[26] Jost (1999: 194) maintains the circuit must date to the late fourth century BC because 'l'indépendance des tours vis-à-vis des courtines semble interdire de remonter plus haut'.

visible, their existence is attested by several early travellers[27] as well as by the detailed surveys of the hill conducted by both Orlandos and Pikoulas.[28] All these writers perceived a gate on the eastern side of the hill, north of the citadel, in the area south of Tower 644. The only substantive description is provided by Leake, who writes: 'the entrance appears to have been in the middle of the eastern wall, between two square towers, of which only the left now remains.'[29] We may surmise from its location and this description that it was a simple frontal gate on an east–west axis, protected by rectangular towers on its north and south side. The other acropolis gate, as suggested by Pikoulas, may lie somewhere on the north-west part of the hill in the area of the Asklepieion.[30]

Citadel

The southern wall of the citadel, basically a continuation of the acropolis wall continuing south-east from Tower 667.7, runs for 73 m between the entrance and the southern tower (Fig. C2.5).[31] From this southern tower— square in shape and measuring 7.50 by 7.50 m—the eastern wall of the citadel runs north–south for 61 m, where it joins the south-west corner of the northern tower.[32] This tower is also roughly square, and, with dimensions measuring 6.20 by 6.60, is only slightly smaller than its southern counterpart.[33] Finally, the northern side of the citadel is enclosed by a 43 m long stretch of wall, the western end of which forms the north wall of the citadel's large western tower or keep.[34] This tower, according to Orlandos, measures some 12.40 by 15.30 m, has walls 1.20 m thick, and is preserved in places to seven or eight courses totalling some 2.80 m (see Fig. C2.4).[35]

[27] e.g., Leake (1830: ii. 73); Curtius (1851: i. 361).
[28] Orlandos (1967–8: 36); Pikoulas (1983: 55).
[29] Leake (1830: ii. 73). The tower on the left (south) observed by Leake may be the tower located in the north-east corner of the citadel. This would place the gate just north of the Athena Sanctuary, near the elevation marked 669 on Orlandos's plan. This is approximately where Pikoulas (1983: 54) places this gate.
[30] Pikoulas (1983: 54–5).
[31] Orlandos (1967–8: 28). All the curtains of the citadel are *c.*3 m in thickness.
[32] Orlandos (1967–8: 28).   [33] Orlandos (1967–8: 28).
[34] Orlandos (1967–8: 28). Orlandos believes this tower/keep functioned as a guardhouse, the entrance to which can be found in its south-east corner.
[35] Orlandos (1967–8: 28).

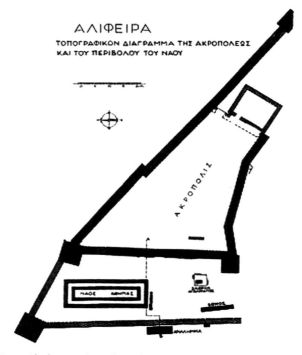

Fig. C2.5. Alipheira, plan of citadel from Orlandos (1967–8: 29, fig. 10).

COMMENTS

As noted by others,[36] nowhere in Orlandos's monograph are there allusions to a lower city wall, nor does any trace of such appear on any of his plans. It is difficult to understand such an omission, since the idea that a fortification wall did indeed once surround the lower city was first suggested a century before Orlandos began his work at the site. Writing of his observations at Alipheira, Leake tells us that, 'after winding around the eastern side of the hill . . . I find the foundations of one of the gates of the lower city. This part of the fortification was flanked with towers, of which there are the remains of two or three, together with considerable pieces of the intermediate walls' (Fig. C2.6).[37]

In his survey of the site based on Polybius' account of Philip's siege, Pikoulas too encountered parts of the lower city wall on the lower slopes

---

[36] Pikoulas (1983: 54); Pritchett (1989: 43).   [37] Leake (1830: ii. 73–4).

Fig. C2.6. Alipheira, possible gate/tower in the lower city wall (facing west). (© *Matthew Maher*)

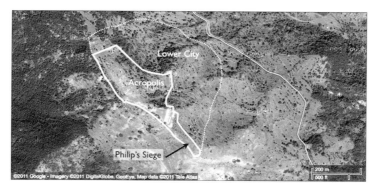

Fig. C2.7. Alipheira, satellite image and proposed location of lower city walls. (© *2011 Google-Map data © 2011 Tele Atlas*)

east of the acropolis, thus confirming Leake's testimony.[38] Pikoulas's discovery was instrumental to his establishing 'what seems to be the correct solution of Polybius' account',[39] and, consequently, has not only confirmed the very existence of a lower city wall, but has provided a clue to its course. If his interpretation is correct, and the forces of Philip laid siege to the lower city walls while the king himself and a select group of men scaled the south-west side of the southernmost part of the acropolis, then it stands to reason that the lower city walls did not completely encircle the acropolis (Fig. C2.7). Instead,

[38] Pikoulas (1983: 54). Most recently, Pritchett (1989: 44–5, pls 84–6) traced (and photographed) *c.*50 m of this wall located about 100 m north of the ruined church of St Nikolaos near the modern road east of the acropolis.

[39] Pritchett (1989: 45).

we may suppose that the lower city wall encircled part or all of the north-eastern side of the hill, while the south-western half of the hill, perceived as being too steep either for habitation or to necessitate additional defences, did not receive parts of the lower city circuit.

OVERALL DEFENSIVE PLANNING

Despite the successes of Philip, we see at Alipheira a careful strategic and tactical awareness reflected in the choice of site and utilization of the terrain. The site of Alipheira appears to have been blessed with the natural environmental elements of a successful city state: it was well watered, it enjoyed a small but fertile plain, and was founded in an easily naturally defendable position. Apparently not satisfied with the already considerable defensive position of the site, military architects took supplementary measures to increase the safety of the city's inhabitants: the construction of a lower city wall and the reinforcement provided by a fortified acropolis. It is in the latter where we can catch a glimpse of both the defensive concerns of these architects and the solutions put forward to meet them.

Foremost we see the line of the fortification circuit embracing the entirety of the hilltop. This immediately presented two advantages: first, placing the circuit on the very edges of the crest meant that any attacker would first have to negotiate the steep slopes before even attempting an attack on the walls above. Furthermore, even if an enemy succeeded in reaching the base of the wall, because it was built right on the edge, it would quickly find itself without a foothold from which to proceed. Second, the course of the circuit around the entire hill ensured the inclusion of its most advantageous and highest topographical features. For example, the inclusion of the small knoll on the northeast side of the hill within the circuit not only prevented its use against the acropolis if taken by an enemy, but created a dogleg in the course of the walls from which further protection was afforded to the curtains to the north and east. Finally, while the defensive advantages inherent in the incorporation of the highest part of the hill and the construction of an independently fortified citadel are obvious, less obvious is the fact that elements of this citadel clearly betray an apprehension for the security of the south-eastern part of the circuit.

Even with the advantage of hindsight, the southern tongue of land—where Philip's forces successfully breached the acropolis—was, it seems, a defensive concern from the very beginning (see Fig. C2.7).[40] This concern is manifested in the fortifications of the citadel and the southern part of the acropolis, where

[40] Especially if this area did indeed lie outside the area enclosed by the lower city fortifications.

we see a concentration of military architecture unparalleled in any other part of the site. While the northern and southern towers in the eastern wall of the citadel certainly can be seen as logical parts of the structure as a whole, additionally they would have functioned to block access to the acropolis from a south-easterly direction. It is Towers 675 and 672.7, however, that provide the best support for this argument. Too far away for them to protect the eastern gate or to prevent a circumvention of the citadel to the north, the location of these towers reflects a concern for protecting an approach from the south. Such a concern was certainly warranted, as the southern side of this tongue of land is the most navigable slope on the acropolis. Although no traces survive on the surface today, it is reasonable to expect that another tower or two may one day be discovered south of Tower 672.7 on the southern side of the hill.

In the location of the eastern gate, and conceivably the northern one also, we see further examples of the relationship between the natural terrain and the man-made defences. Of the former, if its location is to be reconciled with the area marked 669 on Orlandos's plan, then the small return of wall to the north may represent the remnants of the northern tower alluded to by Leake.[41] Whether or not the northern citadel tower represented the tower to the south of the gate mentioned by Leake, the location of this gate was strongly defendable. It is, I believe, safe to assume that this part of the acropolis was enclosed within the lower city circuit and the gate was intended to provide access between the two. Even to reach this gate, therefore, the lower city fortifications would first have to be taken. In this worst-case scenario, the location of the gate ensured that accessing the acropolis itself would be no easy task. Flanked on the south by the north *temenos* of the Athena Sanctuary, the northern citadel tower, and the steep slope of the citadel itself, this gate would have funnelled movement in a western direction through a very narrow corridor running below and parallel to the north wall of the citadel. Finally, if an enemy managed to navigate the missiles raining down from the citadel and continued to advance, it would be forced by the terrain in a north-west direction, where it would meet resistance from the southern flank of Tower 644.

The other acropolis gate, while equally well positioned and presumably also accessible from the lower city, had less in the way of natural defences. Accordingly, to increase the strength of this entrance and to compensate for the generally flat approach in front, the north gate was provided with a number of tactical elements. The south *temenos* of the Asklepieion, for example, appears to extend further east than its function required, limiting a direct approach on the gate to a space of only around 20 m. Moreover, Orlandos's strangely named Tower 'βουβάλας', would have provided protection from any unwanted approach from

---

[41] Leake (1830: ii. 73).

the slopes on the north-east side of the acropolis hill. Finally, any hostile force funnelled directly towards the gate from the north would find its unshielded right side vulnerable to missiles fired from Tower 652.6, immediately to the right of the gate.

In terms of general defensive planning, the acropolis of Alipheira is very practically suited to its purpose. Located just north of an arable plain, on the crest of a considerable hill, it was for the most part defendable without being too high or inaccessible. The western and southern halves of the hill are precipitous to the point that some scholars have questioned the existence of a circuit on these sides at all.[42] The acropolis and lower city fortifications compensated for any shortcomings in the topography on the east and north sides. Furthermore, not only was the hill flanked by the Phanari and Zelecho-vitiko River Valleys to the east and west respectively, adding to the already considerable natural defences of the site, but, at a height of some 160 m, the defensive advantages afforded by the elevation of the acropolis were considerable. Frazer writes, 'from the citadel, and indeed from the whole summit of the ridge, there is a magnificent view [to the north] over the valley of the Alpheus for miles and miles. All the mountains of northern Arcadia are spread out like a panorama.'[43] From the city of Heraia and the Alpheios Valley to the north, to the plain stretching below on the south, from the mountains defining the territory to the west, to the city and *chora* of Theisoa (Lavda) to the west, nearly the whole territory of Alipheira was visible from its acropolis.

CHRONOLOGICAL SUMMARY

It is likely that the entire circuit was constructed in the late fifth century BC—a date based on historical probability, external evidence, and architectural affinities.

CHRONOLOGICAL ARGUMENTS

Based on the history of the site, the known archaeological record, and the style of the walls themselves, a provisional chronology for the fortifications at Alipheira may be ascertained. Regarding the recorded history of the site, two events are especially relevant to the story of the city walls. We know from

---

[42] e.g. Gavrili (1976: 41); Lawrence (1979: 461); Hellenic Ministry of Culture: http://odysseus.culture.gr/h/3/eh351.jsp?obj_id=2412; (accessed 18 January 2010).

[43] Frazer (1898: iv. 299).

Polybius' detailed account that Philip and his forces laid siege to the city in 219 BC.[44] As at ancient Psophis, this attack seemingly provides a fitting *terminus ante quem* for the fortifications of both the acropolis and the lower city.[45] While Polybius brings us no closer to a possible date for the circuits' inception, fortunately, Pausanias does provide a clue. He maintains that in *c*.370 BC, Alipheira was one of the settlements that participated in the synoikism of Megalopolis.[46] Moreover, as he implies that only a part of the population actually relocated to the Great City, 'it is certain that the city was not abandoned'.[47] Orlandos is undoubtedly correct in supposing that the fortifications must have been built before some (or even most) of its population was displaced to Megalopolis.[48] Although it is logical to assume that a construction project on the scale of Alipheira's fortifications would demand the full economic resources and labour force of a unified settlement, part of Orlandos's argument for a pre-370 BC date for the circuit derives from evidence gathered from the archaeological record.

Although Orlandos did not excavate any part of the fortifications, his work to uncover the Sanctuary of Athena has a bearing on the present discussion. For example, excavations determined that the Temple of Athena probably dates to *c*.500–490 BC, and the nearby statue base—presumed to have held the famous Athena statue commented upon by Pausanias—has also been dated to the fifth century BC based on the letter forms of the partial surviving inscription.[49] Orlandos maintains, therefore, that it is unreasonable to suppose that, by the middle of the fifth century BC, the acropolis would have possessed a great temple of Athena and a colossal statue of the goddess, but not a fortification circuit.[50] While the argument derived from this evidence is suggestive, even credible, it is far from conclusive. A closer look at the walls themselves, however, does lend support to an early, probably fifth-century BC, date for their construction.[51]

From the style of masonry of the fortifications, Scranton corroborates Orlandos's opinion, maintaining that that the walls of the acropolis were probably in place during the fifth century BC.[52] Lawrence too feels that the circuit was constructed 'probably in the fifth century, certainly before 370'.[53]

---

[44] Polyb. 4.77–8.   [45] For Psophis, see Part Two, Chapter 15.
[46] Paus. 8.27.4.   [47] Nielsen (2002: 551).
[48] Orlandos (1967–8: 32). Although Orlandos is referring only to the acropolis fortifications, the same should hold true for the lower city circuit.
[49] Paus. 8.26.6–7; Orlandos (1967–8: 95, 114, 125–32); Jost (1985: 79–81).
[50] Orlandos (1967–8: 32).
[51] Jost (1999: 194) believes that, while the settlement may date to *c*.500 BC, the walls themselves date to the late fourth century.
[52] Scranton (1941: 81). Logically enough, Scranton (1941: 82) adds that, since Alipheira apparently participated in the synoikism of Megalopolis, that it must have had an earlier history.
[53] Lawrence (1979: 461).

The actual trace of the acropolis, moreover, accords surprisingly well with Winter's general criteria for fifth-century BC circuits in the Greek world. For example, of these early systems Winter writes that, 'wherever possible, the wall followed a natural line of defence...the top of steep hill or the edge of a ravine, the rim of a plateau, and so forth. Occasionally some unused territory may have been included within the walls for the sake of the natural defences it afforded.'[54] To be sure, attempting a more accurate description than this one, relating the relationship between the walls and topography at Alipheira, is hardly possible.

The form and function of both the curtain and the towers are also indicative of a fifth-century BC date and a time before the widespread use of artillery. As mentioned, the curtains on the acropolis are only c.2.75–3.00 m thick, while those south of the Athena Sanctuary are limited to a thickness of c.2 m. The relative slenderness of these curtains—compared to most of the other Arkadian examples in this study—suggests they were conceived before the invention of artillery, when their main function was not to withstand heavy missiles, but to keep enemy soldiers out. Furthermore, the limited use of towers, widely distributed strategically at irregular intervals, and with long stretches of unflanked curtains between them, is also characteristic of fifth-century BC defensive systems.[55] In describing these systems, Winter again offers a general explanation that describes the situation at Alipheira perfectly; he writes, 'fifth-century systems generally employed towers only at specially vulnerable points: at angles, or where the wall traversed a stretch of level ground, or stood on a gentle slope'.[56] Finally, the complete lack of posterns in the acropolis circuit is also in harmony with an early date. As Winter notes, in the fifth century BC, the impregnability of the circuit remained the most important consideration and 'we should not expect posterns to be widely employed in early-acropolis circuits'.[57]

While the lower city fortifications were probably in place by 370 BC, those on the acropolis were certainly in position by that time. Ultimately, the trace of the circuit, the style of masonry, the specific tactical elements such as the utilization of the towers and curtains, and the lack of tactical elements such as posterns, are all characteristic of a 'passive' defensive outlook. They are also all general characteristics of a fifth-century BC defensive system conceived before the widespread use of offensive or defensive artillery. In short, without the aid of excavated material to narrow the scope, the evidence suggests that the acropolis circuit at Alipheira was constructed sometime in the late fifth or early fourth century BC.

---

[54] Winter (1971a: 108).   [55] Winter (1971a: 154).
[56] Winter (1971a: 154).   [57] Winter (1971a: 235).

BIBLIOGRAPHY

Polyb. 4.77–8; Paus. 8.26.5–7, 8.27.4, 8.27.7; Gell (1817: 86, 114); Cramer (1828: iii. 327); Leake (1830: ii. 71–80); Boblaye (1836: 160); Ross (1841: i. 102–4); Curtius (1851: i. 360–3); Bursian (1862: ii. 234); Frazer (1898: iv. 297–300); Scranton (1941: 81–2, 167); Orlandos (1967–8); Winter (1971a: 35, n. 75, 52, n. 14); Gavrili (1976: 41); Lawrence (1979: 461); Pikoulas (1983); Jost (1985: 77–81; 1999:193–4); Pritchett (1989: 41–6); Papachatzis (1994: 282–8); Nielsen (2002: 550–1); Alevridis and Melfi (2005); Maher (2012a: 308–38).

3

Asea, Southern Arkadia

LOCATION

Asea is located in central Arkadia in the northern part of a basin (with *katavothroi*) defined by mountains on all sides (Fig. C3.1). The small table-top hill comprising the acropolis is the easternmost rise in a series of low hills emanating from a mountain to the north-west. Inhabitation was largely limited to a fortified lower city in the plain directly east and south-east of the acropolis.

POLIS STATUS

Three main types of evidence suggest that Asea reached *polis* status some time in the second half of the sixth century BC.[1] This evidence includes the existence of peri-urban religious sanctuaries, the size of the settlement, and parallels with neighbouring and contemporary Arkadian sites.[2] Survey data have also revealed that during this time the settlement at Asea was by far the largest in the area (of some twenty to thirty sites), exceeding 10 ha in size. Thus, in overall size and distribution of border sanctuaries, Asea appears to have followed the main developments of Tegea, Mantineia, and Orchomenos, all of which also probably became *poleis* during the second half of the sixth century BC.[3] Although listed among other *poleis* voted to participate in the synoikism of Megalopolis,[4] it appears that Asea survived as an independent *polis* at least until the end of the third century BC (and possibly as late as 146 BC), as suggested by the city's listing in the Delphic catalogue of *theorodokoi*.[5]

---

[1] Forsén (2003: 251).
[2] Forsén and Forsén (1997); Forsén et al. (1999); Forsén (2003: 247–52).
[3] Forsén (2003: 252).   [4] Paus. 8.27.3.
[5] Plassart (1921: iii. 9, 52); Perlman (1995: 130 and n. 62); Forsén (2003: 247, 260).

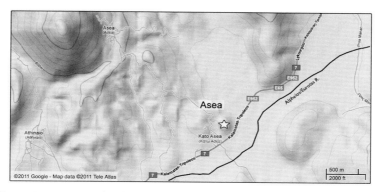

Fig. C3.1. Asea, topographical map of area. (© *2011 Google-Map data © 2011 Tele Atlas*)

HISTORY

Perhaps soon after developing into a *polis*, Asea joined the Peloponnesian League.[6] Likewise, membership in the Arkadian Confederacy can be assumed, not only from the fact that the Mainalians were members, but from Xenophon, who records that the Arkadian League army congregated at Asea in 370 BC.[7] Asea was one of the *poleis* that supposedly participated in the synoikism of Megalopolis.[8] It remains uncertain whether all, or even parts of, the population relocated to the Great City because Asea continued to exist after the synoikism. Xenophon, for example, lists Asea along with Tegea, Pallantion, and Megalopolis as those Arkadian *poleis* that sided with Thebes against Sparta in 362 BC.[9] Very little is known of the city's history during the Hellenistic period.[10] Although Asean coinage issued by the Achaian League would suggest active membership in the first half of the second century BC,[11] after the defeat of the league in 146 BC the city gradually declined. Strabo refers to Asea as 'κώμη' of Megalopolis,[12] while a century and a half later the settlement observed by Pausanias lay in ruins.[13]

LOCAL TOPOGRAPHY

Occupying a substantial plain in a valley bounded on all sides by mountains, Asea lies almost exactly halfway between ancient Megalopolis and Tegea,

---

[6] Nielsen (1996b: 87, 100; 2002: 553); Forsén (2003: 254). [7] Xen. *Hell.* 6.5.11.
[8] Paus. 8.27.3. [9] Xen. *Hell.* 7.5.5.
[10] For a concise summary of the major political and military events in Arkadia from the late Classical through the Hellenistic period and the *possible* role played by Asea in these events, see Forsén (2003: 254–8).
[11] On the coins, see Head (1963: 417–18). [12] Strab. 8.3.12. [13] Paus. 8.44.3.

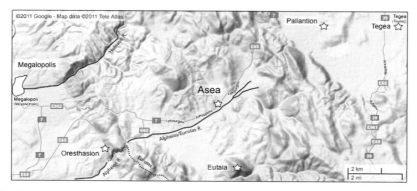

Fig. C3.2. Asea, topographical map of southern Arkadia. (© *2011 Google-Map data* © *2011 Tele Atlas*)

separated from each by only *c.*18 km (Fig. C3.2). The site itself is centred on and around a small but conspicuous flat-topped plateau. This, the Asean acropolis, rises 54 m from the plain below and measures 240 m north–south by 120 m east–west.[14] The lower slopes of the acropolis are relatively gentle all around, and the upper slopes are especially precipitous on all sides except the east. Although seemingly freestanding and independent, the acropolis is actually the easternmost rise in a series of low hills emanating from Mt Kandreva to the north-west.[15]

The Asean territory is more or less surrounded by mountains on all sides; the Forséns estimate it measures *c.*60 km^2.[16] While the bulk of Mt Tsimbarou marked the southern limit of Asean territory and the boundary with Lakonia beyond, a long north-west running spur from the same mountain separated the territory of Asea from the territories of Megalopolis and Oresthasion to the west. To the south-east, the foothills of the smaller Mts Tsoukna and Boziki represented a further boundary with Lakonia and also with the southern edge of the Tegean plain. The eastern edge of Asean territory and the western limit of the *chora* of Pallantion were defined by Mt Boreion. Finally, separating Asea from the *poleis* in the Helisson River Valley to the north were the foothills of Mt Renissa, while the Helisson River itself as it curved towards Megalopolis must have formed the north-west limits of Asean territory.

[14] Nielsen (2002: 552). The acropolis is alternatively often referred to as Paleokastro in the published literature.
[15] Incidentally, Kandreva is the old name for the modern village of Asea located on its eastern slope (Pikoulas 2001: 87). The village of Asea should not be confused with the village of Kato Asea, which lies immediately south-west of the ancient site on the modern Tripoli–Megalopoli highway.
[16] Forsén and Forsén (1997: 175). This presumably also includes the territory of Eutaia, located *c.*4 km due south of ancient Asea. For more on Eutaia, see the Appendix.

Fig. C3.3. Asea, the site (facing east). (© *Matthew Maher*)

The Helisson was not the only major river in Asean territory, and the sources of both the Alpheios and the Eurotas can be found close together in the valley, just to the east of the site (see Fig. C3.2). After the confluence of these two rivers, the united stream skirts the southern side of the site before continuing in a south-westerly direction to the modern village of Marmaria. At this point, the ancient authors agree that the river disappears, taking an underground route through the northern arm of Mt Tsimbarou, where it divides again—with the Eurotas coming to the surface in Lakedaimonian territory to the south, and the Alpheios in the territory of Megalopolis to the west.[17]

NATURAL DEFENCES

Asea's most prominent natural defences are the height provided by the acropolis and the precipitous slopes on its western side (Fig. C3.3). The surrounding mountains and hills limit the approaches to the site to routes from the north-east and south-west. The Alpheios/Eurotas River flanks the lower city along most of its east and south sides.

FORTIFICATION TYPE

Uneven type.[18] A wall encircles the entire summit of the acropolis, while another extended from it via two surviving spur walls to envelop the lower city on its eastern slope and in the plain below (Fig. C3.4).

---

[17] Polyb. 16.17; Strab. 8.3.12; Paus. 8.44.3–4.
[18] Listed as a 'ville mixtes' type by Jost (1999: 199).

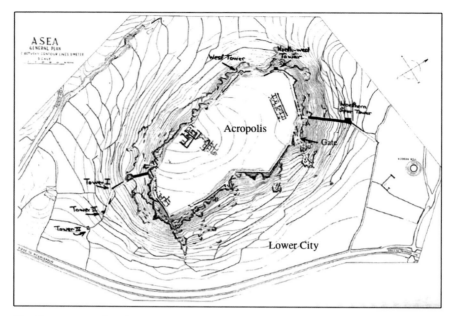

Fig. C3.4. Asea, plan from Forsén et al. (2005: 316, fig. 1). (© *Jeannette Forsén, Björn Forsén, and Lars Karlsson*)

PRESERVATION

The stone foundations of the acropolis circuit and northern spur wall are poorly preserved; the southern spur wall is well preserved. The intramural area of the acropolis is 2.50 ha. Almost nothing remains of the lower city wall, but it is estimated to have been *c.*1,000 m in length and to have enclosed an area of *c.*11 ha.[19]

CONSTRUCTION

The foundations of the acropolis walls and towers were constructed in the polygonal style (whether coursed or uncoursed is unclear) (Fig. C3.5); the southern spur wall was constructed with polygonal blocks laid in clearly defined courses (including header courses running through its width to form compartments) (Fig. C3.6).[20] The stone foundations of all the curtains and

---

[19] Forsén et al. (2005: 310).
[20] Forsén et al. (2005: 309). Basing his comments on a photograph, Scranton (1941: 165) lists the walls of Asea as coursed polygonal but does not indicate whether he is referring to the

Fig. C3.5. Asea, southern spur wall (facing south-east). (© *Matthew Maher*)

Fig. C3.6. Asea, polygonal masonry of acropolis wall (facing east). (© *Matthew Maher*)

towers in the acropolis circuit (including spur walls) once supported a mud-brick superstructure (not preserved). The width of the acropolis wall is 3.10 m and is comprised of the typical parallel faces filled with earth and rubble.[21] The lower city walls had a width of 3–3.30 m (similar to the southern spur wall).[22]

SUMMARY OF TACTICAL COMPONENTS

The acropolis circuit contains at least two rectangular towers, and possibly as many as six. No less than three regularly spaced semicircular towers (*c.*5 m

acropolis or spur walls; from the degree of preservation, however, I suspect he is describing the latter.

[21] Holmberg (1944: 134); Forsén et al. (2005: 309).   [22] Forsén et al. (2005: 310).

Fig. C3.7. Asea, photo of North-West Tower (facing west). (© *Matthew Maher*)

diameter) and one large rectangular tower (6.60 m × 6.45 m) are attested for the lower city circuit. There is one postern in the acropolis circuit (with the possibility of another one) and one simple ramp gate provided access to the acropolis from the lower city.

Towers

The acropolis circuit contains at least two rectangular towers (the West and North-West Towers), and possibly as many as six. Although the two towers were cleaned and studied in the early 2000s, no details or measurements are provided in the Forséns' report, other than that the North-West Tower was solid (that is, there was no ground-storey chamber) (Fig. C3.7).[23]

No less than three regularly spaced semicircular towers (*c.*5 m diameter) and one large rectangular tower (6.60 m × 6.40 m) are attested for the lower city circuit. The three semicircular towers are found in the stretch of wall emanating from the southern spur (Fig. C3.8), and all these towers are regularly spaced 33 m apart or exactly 100 Greek feet.[24] The one rectangular example, the Northern Spur Tower, as its name suggests, is located on the northern spur, situated 40 m from the acropolis wall.[25] This tower, apparently marking the point where the northern spur changes direction to the east, 'is of special interest because there exists an inner wall face which shows that it was not filled with rubble and earth, but must have had an inner room just above ground level.'[26]

---

[23] Forsén et al. (2005: 309).   [24] Dogan and Papamarinopoulos (2003: 247).
[25] Forsén and Forsén (2003: 51). Holmberg (1944: 141) claims the distance to the acropolis wall is 54 m.
[26] Forsén et al. (2005: 309).

Fig. C3.8. Asea, lower city towers and proposed trace (facing south-west). (© *Matthew Maher*)

Fig. C3.9. Asea, acropolis gate (facing east). (© *Matthew Maher*)

Gates

The circuit at Asea contains only at a single gate located along the east side of the acropolis just south of where the northern spur meets the acropolis wall (Fig. C3.9). The original gateway consisted of a simple opening (*c.*3.75 m wide x 12 m long) with a stepped ramp.[27] Each step (0.6–0.85 m in depth) is comprised of a row of flat stones.[28] At least one and perhaps two posterns (widths unknown) have been identified: one to the east of the Northern Spur Tower,[29] the other, possibly on the acropolis, just north of the West Tower.[30]

---

[27] Lawrence (1979: 333) mistakenly refers to this gate as an overlap type.
[28] Holmberg (1944: 138).   [29] Forsén et al. (2005: 309).
[30] Forsén et al. (2005: 309).

COMMENTS

Although the exact course of the lower city wall remains tentative, it is certain that there was indeed a lower city wall, as Loring suggested in the late nineteenth century.[31] Parts of the buried lower city wall were discovered by geophysical survey employed to penetrate the layers of alluvium and debris in the area of the terminal spur walls east and south of the acropolis.[32] The preliminary results of this work suggest that the lower city walls had a width of 3–3.30 m (similar to southern spur wall), and may have totalled *c.*1 km in length.[33]

OVERALL DEFENSIVE PLANNING

Consisting of a small, easily defendable but accessible hill located on the edge of a well-watered plain, Asea possesses many of the strategic characteristics sought after when a suitable location for a site is being chosen. In terms of satisfying the requirements of an acropolis specifically, the high, frequently precipitous, and flat-topped plateau is especially superlative. Accordingly, we clearly see the natural topography of the hill itself dictating the course of the wall. In order to take full advantage of an already considerably defensible site, however, the walls were thrown up on the edges enclosing the whole perimeter of the acropolis—even on the east and south sides facing the lower city.[34] While the main defensive advantages inherent in fortifying such a naturally suited acropolis are obvious and need not be belaboured, the incorporation of more subtle, easily overlooked tactical elements are points that do deserve to be expanded upon.

The topography of the acropolis is not uniformly steep on all sides. Even as the long west side is especially precipitous and the north-east slope is also considerably steep, there is a narrow corridor in the north-west part of the hill that is easily navigable. While the analysis of the Asean fortifications is limited by the poor condition of the remains, it is still clear that the architects observed precaution by taking active measures to strengthen this north-west corner of the acropolis circuit (see Fig. C3.4).[35] To compensate for the defensive weakness of the topography and to protect this route, two artillery towers (the West and North-West Towers) were constructed on either side of the approach, only 40 m apart.

---

[31] Loring (1895: 32). The plausibility of the course of the lower city wall as reconstructed by Forsén et al. (2005) is discussed in greater detail under Overall Defensive Planning.
[32] Forsén et al. (2005: 310).   [33] Forsén et al. (2005: 310).
[34] This was a strategy also employed by the architects of the circuit at Alipheira.
[35] Holmberg (1944: 136).

Concern for this vulnerable area can be further recognized by the insertion of a postern here, just north of the West Tower. While creating an opening in the most vulnerable section of trace may at first glance seem ill-considered, as demonstrated in the composition of Arkadian fortifications, every element had a reasoned purpose and nothing was left to chance. Thus, while conceivably risky, a postern here would have actually been well within the protective range of fire provided by both the West and North-West Towers on its flanks. Furthermore, since the gently sloping terrain on the north-east makes it the most vulnerable section of the entire circuit to attack, a postern here would be well placed for a defensive sortie. Placing it next to the West and not the North-West Tower ensured that any attempt by enemy forces to breach it would require them to advance with their unshielded right side exposed to enfilading from the flank of the West Tower.

Although next to nothing remains of the walls of the lower city and much is speculative, some deductions can be made regarding the inherent defensive strategy and tactical components envisioned in its conception. Obviously important in this regard is the proposed reconstruction of the trace. The Forséns maintain that the preliminary work of the geophysical survey suggests that 'the lower circuit wall may have had a total length of *c*.1 km, enclosing an area of about 11 ha'.[36] This statement—and the (approximate) reconstruction of the lower city wall published in 2003—was made despite the fact that the geophysical prospection was limited to only thirteen 'lines', all in the vicinity of the northern and southern spurs.[37] Thus, it is important to remember that, while the course of the northern and southern parts of the lower city wall are attested by the resistivity survey, the reconstructed trace south and to the west of the Tripoli–Megalopoli highway (that is, the eastern wall) is conjectural. Finally, although it seems unlikely that the eastern lower city wall neatly and conveniently followed the course of a ravine and the railway track—as the reconstruction would have us believe[38]—what is important is that a lower city wall existed and extended into the plain.

Construction of this lower circuit into the plain was a logical decision ultimately governed by the topography of the acropolis. That is, since the eastern slope of the acropolis is the most moderate, it was crucial to include it within the lower city walls, which, in turn, compelled the lower city (and the city wall) to extend into the plain east and south of the acropolis.

---

[36] Forsén et al. (2005: 307).

[37] Dogan and Papamarinopoulos (2003: fig. 2); Forsén et al. (2005: 318, fig. 4).

[38] Although the geophysical results demonstrate the wall might follow the ravine (at least for an interval), the subsurface remains that were identified could also be the remains of a retaining wall or a wall from the intramural settlement (Dogan and Papamarinopoulos 2003: 247). At any rate, it should be remembered that the authors repeatedly stress that their reconstruction is based only on 'preliminary results, and further geophysical work is needed in order to establish the exact course of the lower city wall' (Forsén et al. 2005: 311).

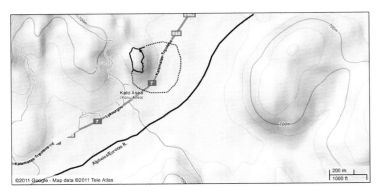

Fig. C3.10. Asea, topographic plan showing acropolis circuit and reconstructed course of lower city walls. (© *2011 Google-Map data* © *2011 Tele Atlas*)

This arrangement had important defensive implications. Instead of retreating to the slopes below a separately fortified acropolis off the main roadway—like the settlements at Halous or Nestane, for example—the creation of a lower city circuit assertively extending into the plain produced a bottleneck and a means of controlling access into the valley from the east (Fig. C3.10). While the large hill less than 1 km to the east, the Alpheios/Eurotas River, and the lower city walls of Asea together defined this bottleneck approach, the topography of the Asea Valley itself ensured that any traffic from the east would be funnelled right through it. Thus, like the lower city walls of Alea and Stymphalos, this bottleneck would have decreased the options for an offensive approach or deployment of troops, and at the same time ensured that traffic passing through the territory was constrained by being brought close to the city and in the shadows of its artillery towers.[39]

That we can expect the lower city walls to have had more or less regularly spaced towers distributed throughout can be inferred from what we know of Arkadian fortifications and of the Asean circuit. Of all those Arkadian *poleis* examined with a fortification circuit completely or partly set out over flat terrain, the majority have been found to have relatively evenly spaced towers.[40] Certainly, without the advantage afforded by naturally defendable terrain, such towers were indispensable. Furthermore, based on the analogy of the presence and even spacing of Towers I, II, and III, it is reasonable to expect that a similar pattern was employed in the rest of the circuit.[41]

---

[39] Protection of this route is important, considering the armies that probably passed through the Asean Valley in the fourth and third centuries BC (Forsén 2003: 256–7). This is discussed in greater detail under Chronology Arguments.

[40] e.g., Mantineia, Stymphalos, and Psophis.

[41] Traces of at least one more tower were discovered during the resistivity survey north-east of the Northern Spur Tower near a well (Dogan and Papamarinopoulos 2003: 247).

Still, the Forséns interpret the occurrence of these semicircular towers quite differently. Regarding Towers I, II, and III, they inexplicably maintain that semicircular 'towers are unusual, and usually occur only in connection with gates'.[42] Basing their comments on this belief, they add that it is 'quite possible that the three round towers in Asea have framed one of the main gates, the important gate towards Megalopolis'.[43] First, while semicircular towers were commonly built to protect gateways—as seen in the gates at Stymphalos, Mantineia, and Kleitor—that was certainly not their only or even their primary purpose. Indeed, their use as independent artillery encampments in curtains is extremely well attested, and examples are frequent in Arkadia. Not to dwell on this point, but as demonstrated, examples of such are found at Pheneos, Phigaleia, Kleitor, Nestane, Theisoa (Lavda), Stymphalos, and Halous.[44] Second, exactly how three towers (semicircular or otherwise), spaced 33 m apart—and therefore with 66 m separating the Towers I and III—can be interpreted together as somehow 'framing' a gate is incomprehensible. Still the existence of a western gate facing Megalopolis is likely, and perhaps one of these towers was part of such a gate. We might equally envision a gate leading to Pallantion/Tegea having been located somewhere in the north-east part of the lower circuit.[45]

CHRONOLOGICAL SUMMARY

From a combination of historical probability, the external evidence, and known architectural affinities, it seems likely that the acropolis circuit of Asea was constructed *c.*400–370 BC. Unfortunately, based on the same evidence, the chronology for the erection of the lower city wall cannot be dated much more precisely than *c.*300–220 BC.

CHRONOLOGICAL ARGUMENTS

Two basic chronologies have been proposed for the construction of the walls of Asea.[46] First proposed by Holmberg is the idea that both the acropolis and

---

[42] Forsén et al. (2005: 309).   [43] Forsén et al. (2005: 309).

[44] Interestingly, Holmberg (1944: 141) actually mentions the semicircular tower at Halous in his analysis of the Asean fortifications.

[45] Like the gates at Kleitor and Phigaleia, which still flank the roads today, perhaps the Asean gates should be sought in the vicinity of the modern highway.

[46] These chronologies do not include any later modifications of the gate in the Byzantine period, for which see Holmberg (1944: 138) and Forsén et al. (2005: 312–13).

the lower city walls were erected in the Hellenistic period, specifically in the third century BC.[47] Until the publication of the most recent work on the walls, Holmberg's date was the only one suggested, and appears to have been accepted by most.[48] As a result of their detailed study, however, which revealed that the upper and lower circuits are not of the same construction, the Forséns now argue that, while the lower circuit may indeed be a third-century BC creation, the walls of the acropolis are, in fact, probably fourth century BC in origin.[49] This revised chronology is probably closer to the truth, as it accords best with the available historical and archeological evidence.

Holmberg's chronological assessment is flawed in many regards, not least of all in its attempt to date both the acropolis and the spur walls based on the evidence provided by the latter and the adjacent round towers alone. For example, he believes that the walls of Alea represent the best parallel for 'this type of fortification with a citadel wall and from it two spur walls encircling a lower city'.[50] Following Meyer's proposed chronology of Alea as an equivalent, therefore, Holmberg would see the Asean circuit as Hellenistic also. Even though Meyer's date for Alea is probably too late,[51] the layout of a circuit is not a very reliable chronological indicator, since it was always dictated by the local topography.[52] Furthermore, Holmberg's belief that round towers were a late feature in the science of Greek fortifications and not common until Hellenistic period is unmistakably false.[53] Finally, he argues that the pseudo-isodomic masonry characteristic of the southern spur wall also 'points to the beginning of Hellenistic time'.[54] The point is largely academic, however, since one look at this masonry reveals a polygonal style roughly laid in isodomic courses, with no evidence of pseudo-isodomic coursing (see Fig. C3.5).

As so little remains of the acropolis circuit, so too is there very little evidence on which to construct a reliable chronology. Still, certainly the uncoursed polygonal masonry employing (on average) considerably smaller blocks sets the acropolis walls apart from the lower city circuit. Based on analogy with other Arkadian sites, it could also be argued that such features suggest a fourth-century BC date. The polygonal masonry, for example, could easily be of the fourth century BC.[55] It could also be argued that a comparison could be made based on the presence of a ramp gate at Asea. Otherwise rare in Arkadia, such a gate does find a parallel in the system at Stymphalos, which has been dated to the early fourth century BC. Finally, if the acropolis walls did post-date

---

[47] Holmberg (1944: 141–2).

[48] Lawrence (1979: 463), for example, maintains that the city (and presumably its walls) were 'founded after 300 [BC]'.

[49] Forsén et al. (2005: 311–12).   [50] Holmberg (1944: 141).

[51] See Part Two, Chapter 1, under Chronological Arguments.

[52] If it was reliable, then Alipheira, not Alea, would represent the best parallel and we might be inclined to date the Asean circuit to the early fifth century.

[53] Holmberg (1944: 141).   [54] Holmberg (1944: 142).   [55] Scranton (1941: 69).

the widespread use of artillery, as supposed by Holmberg, we might expect to see the distribution of more and larger towers, especially in the vulnerable northern part of the trace.

Admittedly, if we consider the limited nature of the remains, none of these reasons is enough on which to base a solid chronology. Even together, they do not necessarily form the basis of an infallible argument. Still, when the archaeological record is accompanied by evidence supplied by the historical record, the assignment of an early fourth-century BC date for the acropolis circuit becomes plausible. Xenophon records that in 370 BC, as the Spartan army prepared to march on Eutaia, located just on the south-east edge of the Asean plain, the Arkadian army gathered at Asea.[56] As the Arkadians would have naturally chosen a gathering point they felt was safe and secure, it stands to reason that (at least) the acropolis walls were in place at that time. The Forséns also maintain that the acropolis circuit dates to the Classical period, but note that the poor condition restricts a more precise date. Finally, while cautiously noting the possibility of different phases, they do admit that 'Pikoulas has in his doctoral dissertation suggested an early fourth century date for the acropolis walls, and we see no reason to disagree with him'.[57] On the other hand, the evidence suggests that the lower city circuit was a later addition, but perhaps not as late as that which has been proposed.

While Holmberg suggested a third-century BC date for the lower city walls, the Forséns are more precise, suggesting they belong to 'the second or third quarter of the third century, with a terminus ante quem *c.*220 BC'.[58] Indeed, although they claim to base this date on stylistic grounds, it appears to be based first and foremost on historical considerations. In other words, instead of looking for historical events that may explain the appearance of the archaeological evidence, it seems that here the archaeological evidence is made to fit a known historical event—the so-called Kleomenic War of 229/228–222 BC. In this regard, their brief summary of the archaeological evidence is worth citing in full; they write that:

> The rustic polygonal technique points towards the 3rd century B.C. However, the walls of Asea clearly ante-date the polygonal technique without any kind of such horizontal arrangements that developed *around* 220 B.C. Another important chronological feature of the lower city wall is the existence of an inner room in the ground floor of the square tower. Inner rooms like this were used for placing catapults at the foot of the wall and are not common until the advanced Hellenistic period. Although *no clear date* can be given for the first time when such inner rooms appeared, we *probably* have to get down to the 3rd century before they become common.[59]

---

[56] Xen. *Hell.* 6.5.11–12.
[57] Forsén et al. (2005: 311). For his dissertation, see Pikoulas (1988).
[58] Forsén et al. (2005: 311–12).   [59] Forsén et al. (2005: 312); emphasis added.

Under this broad chronological umbrella based on 'stylistic grounds' (that is, 275–220 BC), the Forséns specifically argue that the walls were constructed in the 220s BC on historical grounds, and this brief discussion of the chronological evidence is followed by a lengthy discussion on how the wall was built in haste, its necessity triggered by the start of the Kleomenic War.[60] Yet, the stylistic evidence provided by the masonry and tower chambers they mention does not neatly fit this chronological scenario. Basing his conclusions on his extensive survey of masonry types, Scranton, for example, found that coursed polygonal masonry was a largely Peloponnesian phenomenon that appeared during the second half of the fourth century BC and the beginning of the third century BC.[61] Furthermore, as noted by Winter, while the use of ground-storey tower chambers was restricted in the fourth century BC, they do appear after the time of Epaminondas.[62] The coursed polygonal walls and ground-storey tower chambers, therefore, while stylistically falling into the broad half century suggested by the Forséns (that is, 275–220 BC), could arguably also be products of the later fourth century BC—and certainly from before the start of the Kleomenic War.

Nonetheless, the Forséns' grasp of 'historical probability'[63] to postulate a chronology based on the factors that may have prompted the construction of the lower city walls is admirable. Unfortunately, there are a number of historical events besides (and prior to) the Kleomenic War that might have instigated the fortification of the lower city. The geographic location of Asea and its political association with Megalopolis made certain that the fourth and early third century BC witnessed the considerable armies of Sparta and, later, of the Successors passing through their territory. Indeed, the catalyst could conceivably have been Antipater's march to Megalopolis against the army of Agis III in 331 BC; or when Polperchon traveled from Pallantion to attack Megalopolis in 318 BC; perhaps Kassander's march through en route to Messene in 315 BC; or Pyrrhos' invasion of Lakonia via Megalopolis in 272 BC. Possibly it was Asea joining the Achaian League in 235 BC that prompted the construction of a lower city wall.[64] Regrettably, historical probability suggests that any one of these events could have threatened Asean security and prompted the construction of a lower circuit.

The Forséns, however, argue that the evidence suggesting that the wall was built in haste points to the fact that it was built quickly as protection against the Spartans at some stage during the Kleomenic War. The physical evidence is comprised solely of a statue found incorporated into one of the round towers and an unconfirmed report that an inscription was also built into

---

[60] Forsén et al. (2005: 312).   [61] Scranton (1941: 69, 140).
[62] Winter (1971a: 162, 176).   [63] See Ober (1985: 208).
[64] The year Megalopolis became a member and perhaps also when Asea joined the league (Forsén et al. 2005: 312).

part of the wall.[65] In their belief that 'apparently any stones found were used in building the wall, which gives the impression that it was constructed in haste during a period of war',[66] the Forséns miss the most obvious point. Although the use of available material to build a wall in haste is not unknown,[67] if the Aseans wanted to build a wall as quickly as possible, they would not have constructed it using polygonal blocks. This technique was not only expensive but, more importantly, time consuming.[68] If haste was a prime motivator, surely they would have employed ashlar and/or trapezoidal blocks—both cheaper and faster options available at the time.

To summarize, therefore, the acropolis circuit is probably the product of the early fourth century BC and may have been in place by the time the Arkadian army assembled there (c.400–370 BC). The lower city wall, on the other hand, exhibits stylistic features (for example, coursed polygonal masonry, ground-storey tower chambers, use of stretchers forming compartments in the curtain) that range from the later fourth century through the third century BC. That it was built to deter Spartan aggression during the Kleomenic War is one of several third-century BC options based on historical probability, but it is impossible to confirm. Certainly this event must represent the latest possible date for its construction, as the Forséns suggest.[69] Determining the *terminus post quem*, however, is more difficult with the evidence at hand. In short, then, however broad and unsatisfactory, the safest and most inclusive date for the construction of the lower city wall is c.300–220 BC.

BIBLIOGRAPHY

Xen. *Hell.* 6.5.11–21, 7.5.5; Strab. 8.3.12; Paus. 8.27.3, 8.44.3; Gell (1817: i. 137); Cramer (1828: 348); Leake (1830: i. 83–4, ii. 46); Boblaye (1836: 173–4); Curtius (1851: i. 264–7); Clark (1858: 152–4); Bursian (1862: ii. 226–7); Loring (1895: 32); Frazer (1898: iv. 4.414–15); Scranton (1941:165); Holmberg (1944: 132–42); Howell (1970: 101); Lawrence (1979: 333, 463); Cooper and Myers (1981:. 131); Jost (1985: 195; 1999: 199); Pikoulas (1988a); Sarantakes (1993: 36–7); Papachatzis (1994: 282–8); Forsén and Forsén (1997); Neilson (2002: 551–3); Dogan and Papamarinopoulos (2003); Forsén and Forsén (2003); Forsén et al. (2005); Maher (2012a: 424–55).

---

[65] Forsén et al. (2005: 311–12). Parallel to the situation at Theisoa (Lavda), perhaps after the general breakdown of the Arkadian League, the displaced Aseans returned home from Megalopolis and incorporated otherwise neglected material into their new wall.

[66] Forsén et al. (2005: 312).

[67] The Themistoklean Wall near the Kerameikos in Athens is perhaps the most obvious example.

[68] Winter (1971a: 90).   [69] Forsén et al. (2005: 312).

4

Dipaia, Central Arkadia

LOCATION

The remains of Dipaia are found in central Arkadia south-west of the modern village of Davia (Fig. C4.1).[1] Located on the west bank of the Helisson River, the small triangular-shaped acropolis rises at the narrowest point of an hourglass-shaped plain defined by mountains on all sides. Inhabitation was probably limited to the south slope of the acropolis. It is uncertain whether the lower city was fortified.

POLIS STATUS

Herodotus provides the first of two surviving examples of the external use of Dipaia's city ethnic.[2] The other example comes from a fourth-century BC inscription discovered at Nemea, the exact nature of which is unclear.[3] Pausanias provides further support that Dipaia was probably a *polis* by retroactively referring to it as such in his list of settlements voted to participate in the synoikism of Megalopolis.[4] Pausanias also records that Dipaia produced an Olympic victor, sometime around the middle of the fifth century BC.[5] While inferring a *polis* status from any one of these pieces of evidence alone would be dubious, taken together they form a more solid foundation for establishing Dipaia's probable *polis* identity.

[1] On the debate concerning the two possible locations for the site of ancient Dipaia, see under Comments.
[2] Hdt. 9.35.2.   [3] *SEG* xxiii. 179. On this inscription, see Bradeen (1966: 321).
[4] Paus. 8.27.3.   [5] Paus. 6.7.9; *Olympionikai*, no. 314 (*c*.440 BC).

Fig. C4.1. Dipaia, topographical map of Lower Helisson Valley. (© *2011 Google-Map data © 2011 Tele Atlas*)

HISTORY

The only documented episode in the history of this small city is as the place where a battle between the Spartans and Arkadians was fought sometime in the 470s or 460s BC.[6] Unfortunately, we know next to nothing about the specific details of the battle.[7] The only documented evidence of this battle comes from one sentence in each of Herodotus, Isocrates, and Pausanias, all of whom state that the Spartans were victorious over a group of Arkadians (not including the Mantineians), while Isocrates alone alludes to the fact that the Spartans may have also been outnumbered.[8] There is no clue as to the nature of this alliance, but presumably the soldiers of Dipaia, if they in fact participated, fought on the side of their fellow Arkadians. Pieces of the subsequent history of this small Mainalian community is derived almost exclusively from plausible inference. Although the city was probably a member of the Peloponnesian League,[9] and later a member of the Arkadian League, as can be inferred by its inclusion in the list of settlements participating in the synoikism of Megalopolis,[10] it is not certain if the decision to relocate was actually implemented.[11] It may be assumed that Dipaia was a member of the Achaian League in the late third/early second century BC, since League coins bearing the name '*ΔΙΠΑΙΕΩΝ*' were issued *c.*194 BC.[12]

---

[6] Hdt. 9.35.2; Isoc. 6.99; Paus. 3.11.7. The exact date is not clear. Nielsen (2005: 553) mentions the 460s BC, Pikoulas (1999b: 126) says 469/468 BC, and, in his translation/commentary of Isocrates' *Archidamus*, Norlin (1980: vi. 99) gives the precise date of 471 BC.

[7] Ray (2011: 121–2) provides an interpretation of this battle that stretches the fragmentary information to its logical limits.

[8] Hdt. 9.35; Isoc. 6.99.   [9] Nielsen (1996b: 95–6, 100–1).   [10] Paus. 8.27.3.

[11] Nielsen (2002: 553).   [12] Head (1963: 418).

LOCAL TOPOGRAPHY

The ancient site of Dipaia is located in the middle of the southern half of the upper Helisson Valley, approximately 1 km south-west of the modern village of Davia (Fig. C4.2). Sandwiched between Mt Menalo to the north and east, and Western Menalo to the west and south-west, the valley itself, oriented northwest–southeast, is about 8 km long by 2 km wide at its maximum dimensions. Besides defining the valley itself, these two mountains also served to separate it from the plains and *poleis* of Megalopolis, Asea, Methydrion, Mantineia, and Tegea to the south-west, south, north, east, and south-east respectively.

Located on the edge of an hourglass-shaped plain, Dipaia was one of the few central Arkadian communities fortunate enough to have commanded an area of flat terrain (see Fig. C4.1). The site itself occupies a small hill, which projects from the west side of the plain at its narrowest point. The plain opens up immediately north and south of the site, bordered on the east by the steep lower slopes of Mt Aidinis (southern part of Mt Menalo), and on the west by a series of low hills radiating from Mt Kakotsouroumi.[13] Continuing its journey from Alonistena, the Helisson River enters the plain north-west of Dipaia (just south of modern Piana), from which it travels in a south-east direction before swinging due south immediately east of the site. From Dipaia, the river continues south-east down the middle of the plain before making a 90° turn to the south-west on its way to Megalopolis and its eventual confluence with the Alpheios. In the plain itself, the Helisson River is served by a number of

Fig. C4.2. Dipaia, topographical map of Helisson Valley and surrounding areas. (*© 2011 Google-Map data © 2011 Tele Atlas*)

---

[13] With its location on a small hill, with a number of other small hills behind, the topographical situation at Dipaia is very similar to the composition of the acropolis of Asea.

Fig. C4.3. Dipaia, hill of Dipaia (facing south-east). (© *Matthew Maher*)

tributaries and seasonal streams, especially from the foothills immediately west of the site.

The hill of Dipaia represents the known limit of the site. It measures about 200 m long from east to west, and *c.*150 m north to south, and rises only around 40–50 m from the plain below (Fig. C4.3).[14] Roughly triangular in shape, it slopes away gradually to the north-east (and more considerably towards the east) from its highest point in the south-west corner. Exposed bedrock abounds on the hill, especially along its edges, where it rises to form a natural crest or plateau, which is visible around most of the hill's circumference. As in antiquity, today the only practical access to the hill is from the east. Not only is this side the lowest part of the hill, but it also possesses its only moderate slope; the south, west, and north sides of the hill are characterized by their precipitous slopes and inaccessibility. This is most apparent on the west and south sides, where the edges of this plateau are especially sheer and in places nearly vertical.

NATURAL DEFENCES

The height offered by the acropolis, and the precipitous slopes on its north, west and south sides, provide the site with natural defences. The surrounding mountains and hills limit the approaches to the site to routes from the north and south. The Helisson River flanks the lower city along its north and east sides, and series of rolling hills offer protection to the west.

---

[14] Howell (1970: 100).

Fig. C4.4. Dipaia, satellite image with reconstruction of original line of walls. (© *2011 Google-Map data © 2011 Tele Atlas*)

FORTIFICATION TYPE

Acropolis type. A wall encircles the entire summit of the acropolis (Fig. C4.4).

PRESERVATION

The site is generally poorly preserved as isolated sections around the hill; parts of the western and eastern curtains are moderately preserved. None of the surviving sections of curtain is more than a couple of courses high or exceeds more than a few metres in length. The internal composition of the walls is nowhere visible on the site—having been largely obscured by the later medieval additions (Fig. C4.5).

CONSTRUCTION

The superstructure was mudbrick (not preserved), while the stone foundations of the acropolis circuit were constructed in a coursed polygonal style (see Fig. C4.5).

Fig. C4.5. Dipaia, photo of eastern curtain showing medieval additions atop original polygonal section (facing west). (© *Matthew Maher*)

SUMMARY OF TACTICAL COMPONENTS

The acropolis was accessed on the east by one frontal opening type gate. No towers or posterns are preserved.

Towers

There are no surviving examples of towers on the site nor are any mentioned in the accounts of the early travellers.

Gates

The acropolis of Dipaia was accessed by a single gate, located at the east end of the summit, and approached by a moderately inclined and zigzagging path, the last stretch of which ran below, and almost parallel to, the hill's eastern curtain. Although later medieval additions have obscured much of the gate, traces of the original are still visible beneath (Fig. C4.6). Apparently a simple frontal opening type, this gate possessed a narrow opening only *c.*2 m wide and oriented east–west. While no towers are evident, the fragmentary remains hint that the northern half may have been a small bastion. No confident examples of posterns have been discovered in the circuit.

Catalogue

Fig. C4.6. Dipaia, gate on east side of acropolis (facing north-west). (© *Matthew Maher*)

COMMENTS

Two main possible locations for the site of ancient Dipaia have been put forward: one beneath the medieval remains at modern Piana,[15] the other, on an isolated rock beside the village of Davia. Using the order of Pausanias' narrative, which (from north to south along the upper Helisson Valley) mentions the settlements of Helisson, Dipaia, and Lykaia,[16] Leake was the first to suggest that Dipaia occupied the site near Davia,[17] a point on which most scholars agree today.[18] In this generally accepted scenario, ancient Helisson is placed either at the source of the river at modern Alonistena or further south at Piana; ancient Dipaia is situated at modern Davia; and ancient Lykaia lies somewhere near the southern end of the valley.[19]

OVERALL DEFENSIVE PLANNING

The fragmentary condition and paucity of the remains restrict our understanding of the individual tactical decisions employed by the fortifications' architects, but not the inherent defensive strategy behind their choice of site. Taken together, its geographic location within the Upper Helisson Valley and the local topography around the site demonstrate just how well suited the hill

---

[15] As held by Ross (1841: 117–18), Frazer (1898: iv. 317), and Levi (1971: 447, n. 220).

[16] Paus. 8.30.1.   [17] Leake (1830: ii. 52).

[18] e.g., Howell (1970: 100); Jost (1973: 253); Pikoulas (1999b: 126); Nielsen (2002: 553). Curtius (1851: i. 316), Bursian (1862: ii. 228), and Philippson (1903: 1151) do not exclude either Davia or Piana as possibilities.

[19] For a detailed appraisal on the settlements and their locations, see Pikoulas (1999b: 125–8).

is for the acropolis of a small *polis*. For the same reason that it would be reoccupied during the medieval period, the acropolis of Dipaia comprised arguably the most defensively advantageous position in the valley. Its location at the narrowest part of a narrow plain not only ensured that any approach to the city (hostile or otherwise) would be predictable from the north or south, but that any approach through the territory would not go unnoticed from the acropolis. Indeed, Dipaia was strategically located astride one of the major arteries of central Arkadia. Like the major east–west road across central Arkadia (occupied by Methydrion, Theisoa (Karkalou), and Teuthis), the Upper Helisson Valley also represented an important link to the great plains of both eastern and southern Arkadia.[20] As this valley extended all the way to Methydrion in the north, it would also have facilitated travel within central Arkadia itself as the north–south equivalent of the main east–west road.

Besides ensuring a ready water supply for the city's inhabitants, the Helisson River and its tributaries represented a further element of protection for the acropolis. Located only *c.*100 m to the east, the Helisson River runs parallel to both the north-east and east sides, mirroring the base contour of the hill. Seasonal streams and tributaries originating in the low hills west of the site provided additional natural defences to the north and west sides and further restricted the approaches to the acropolis. Nor were the west and south-west sides of the hill devoid of natural protection. Here, the rolling and heavily forested hills emanating from Mt Kakotsouroumi—the easternmost of which is actually the acropolis—ensured an incredibly difficult approach from those directions. In the event that an enemy was able to navigate this forest or even command the east side of the river, it would have to contend with the second line of defence—the topography of the hill itself. The natural defensive strength of the hill is unparalleled in any other part of the valley and must have been a key factor behind its choice as the Dipaian acropolis. The near vertical slopes of the plateau-like bedrock shelf representing the uppermost elevation of the hill made it virtually impregnable on its west and south sides, and, to a lesser extent, on the north-east side. This, of course, raises the question of whether the defence of parts of the hill was trusted to the topography or whether the circuit—the third line of defence—enveloped all sides of the hill.

Substantial remains of the eastern curtain in the vicinity of the gate suggest that the entire eastern side was fortified. Even without this evidence, that it faced the main approach and the only navigable (and thus most vulnerable) part of the hill would be sufficient reason to suppose that the whole eastern side was provided with a wall. Isolated, but seemingly associated remains of the curtain on both the west and south sides also indicate that these sides were

[20] Jost (1999: 229).

fortified along most (if not their entire) length. If the architects thought it necessary to fortify the already strong and precipitous sides on the south and west, it stands to reason that the same precaution was taken for the weaker north-west side of the acropolis. Finally, the fact that traces of the wall appear once again at the north-west and north-east corners of the hill, and that this, the north-east side, is the section closest to the modern village—and thus the area most likely to have been stripped for building material—suggests the north-east side of the acropolis must surely also have been fortified.

The paucity of remains, the poor condition of what does survive, and a general lack of identifiable features limit what can be said about the tactical elements and larger defensive planning originally envisioned by the system's architects. Besides the existence of a single gate and the reasonable hypothesis that the circuit once enveloped the entire hill, little can be said with certainty. Still, there are some suppositions that may be plausibly put forward based on what is known and what is reasonable. It is likely, for example, that the extant gate, as is the case with other fortified acropolis sites,[21] was the only one in the circuit. This is a simple deduction based on the fact that a small functioning acropolis needs only one gate—not to mention it is safer with only one—as well as the fact that the topography of the hill precludes access to the summit from any other side but the east. As the gates from the analogous examples directly faced the main area of habitation, it raises the question of where exactly the lower city of Dipaia was located. As the settlement should presumably be sought on the west side of the river—the purpose of an acropolis is defeated if the people cannot get to it quickly and relatively easily—then the south side of the acropolis presents the likeliest candidate. The course of the river and its proximity to both the east and the north slopes of the acropolis rule out habitation on those sides, as does the unsuitably uneven terrain on the west. On the other hand, the even and moderate slope characteristic of the terrain south of the acropolis provides the only setting appropriate for the population of this small *polis*.

When we consider other tactical elements envisioned in the defensive planning of the acropolis, we shift from the realm of what is probable to what is merely plausible. For example, although there are no remains that are recognized as conclusively belonging to towers, it is plausible that the circuit once employed several. The low and relatively exposed east side (including the gate) would have benefited greatly from the additional protection that towers could have provided to the main approach. Similarly, it is not hard to imagine towers advantageously placed at the other two corners of the triangularly shaped plateau, at the north-west and south-west corners of the circuit—the

---

[21] e.g., Nestane, Paos, Theisoa (Karkalou), Halous.

Fig. C4.7. Dipaia, 'opening' cut into bedrock on edge of acropolis (facing south). (© *Matthew Maher*)

latter occupying the highest elevation on the hill. The natural strength of the acropolis notwithstanding, it is also reasonable to suppose that other towers would have once lined at least the south and north-east sides—the latter to protect encroachment on the lower city, and the former to reinforce the only moderate natural defences provided by the acropolis on that side. Finally, although the extremely precipitous slopes on the south and west sides of the acropolis would have negated the use of posterns, the remains do preserve at least one opening on the south side (Fig. C4.7).

It is unclear just what was the function of this *c.*1 m wide rectangular opening, which is carved out of the bedrock and located at the top of and opening onto a *c.*10 m vertical drop. While a number of practical civilian and or/military functions may be conjectured, none is mutually exclusive. For example, as it is located on the south side, perhaps this cutting was made for the operation of cranes or some sort of winch that could be used to lift supplies to the acropolis from the lower city below. Similarly, perhaps it housed a rope or ladder used in times of peace to provide a quick way of accessing the acropolis from the lower city. Or perhaps, instead of being used for the construction of a tower, the bedrock here was simply carved away to form a regular opening to be used as an artillery port—like the shuttered windows of a tower.

CHRONOLOGICAL SUMMARY

From the only available evidence (historical probability and the style of the masonry), the it would seem that the fortifications of ancient Dipaia were probably constructed c.375–350 BC (?).

CHRONOLOGICAL ARGUMENTS

With the paucity and character of the poorly preserved remains and the infrequent mention in the historical record, determining a precise chronology for the walls of Dipaia is beset with many of the same difficulties as those encountered at Teuthis and Theisoa (Karkalou). Herodotus' mention of the Battle of Dipaia, on the one hand, and Achaian League coins issued, on the other, provide a wide chronological spectrum for inhabitation at the site. Still, a *terminus post quem* of *c*.470 BC and a *terminus ante quem* of *c*.194 BC frame a period of some 275 years in which the acropolis fortifications could have been erected. In order to narrow down a more precise date under this wide chronological umbrella, however problematic, we are left with no choice but to rely on the only two pieces of evidence at our disposal: the style of the masonry and historical probability.

The walls of Dipaia were constructed in roughly laid courses of polygonal blocks, a style that Scranton maintains appeared in the Peloponnese during the second half of the fourth century, generally lasting until the early third century BC.[22] Even if the date of this style should be revised downwards, as Winter suggests, as polygonal slowly gave way to trapezoidal and ashlar in the Hellenistic period, a stylistic date for the walls at Dipaia covering sometime in the fourth century BC would still be acceptable.[23] Comparable to the archaeological evidence of the walls, the corpus of information pertaining to the known history of the site is also incredibly limited. What little is known finds direct parallels in the histories of the other central Arkadian *poleis*. For example, like Teuthis and Theisoa (Karkalou), Dipaia was voted to participate in the synoikism of Megalopolis, and was a member of the Arkadian League, and later, the Achaian League. Unlike these two other *poleis*, however, Dipaia was not a member of the συντελέια headed by Orchomenos.[24] And it is this fact that may have an important bearing on the date of the walls, based on historical possibility.

Although Dipaia was initially voted to participate in the synoikism of the Great City, what if, in a situation perhaps mirrored at Alea and Gortys, for example, the decision was not implemented? What if, again perhaps as at Alea and Gortys, it was considered more defensively advantageous to the Arkadian League as whole to keep Dipaia inhabited and, more importantly, fortified?[25] In this scenario we again see Orchomenos as the lone important *polis* initially refusing to join the Arkadian League, and the fortification of Dipaia around the time of the synoikism could reflect a need to keep the major north–south central Arkadian artery (that is, the Upper Helisson Valley) free from overt Orchomenian influence. Indeed, with the συντελέια *poleis* Teuthis, Theisoa,

---

[22] Scranton (1941: 55).   [23] Winter (1971a:. 81–2, 90).
[24] Paus. 8.27.4.   [25] Jost (1999: 228).

and Methydrion, Orchomenos already effectively controlled the major east–west route through the region. The fortification of Dipaia would have ensured that Orchomenians would not have had free rein to move through the valley and into the plains of Megalopolis, Asea, Tegea, or Mantineia beyond—the last being especially important because of their historical animosity with the Mantineians. Although this is admittedly far from conclusive, until further archaeological evidence comes to light, a date for the fortification of Dipaia sometime in the second quarter of the fourth century BC is in agreement with both the stylistic and the historical evidence at hand.

BIBLIOGRAPHY

Hdt. 9.35; Isoc. 6.99; Paus. 3.11.7, 8.27.3; Leake (1830: ii. 52); Boblaye (1836: 171); Ross (1841: 117–18); Curtius (1851: i. 315–16); Bursian (1862: ii. 228); Frazer (1898: iv. 317); Philippson (1903: 1151); Howell (1970: 100); Levi (1971: 447, n. 220, 483, n. 327); Jost (1973: pls 9.1–3; 1985: 193); Norlin (1980: vi. 99); Pikoulas (1992: 204; 1999b: 126); Sarantakes (1993: 49–52); Nielsen (2002: 553–4); Maher (2012a: 562–81).

5

Gortys, Southern Arkadia

LOCATION

Gortys is located in southern Arkadia in the middle of a small basin within the Lousios/Gortynios River Valley (Fig. C5.1). The acropolis comprises the summit and south-east slope of a low hill extending towards the river, where it ends abruptly at the edge of a deep river valley. Inhabitation was largely limited to the area north of the acropolis.

POLIS STATUS

The external and individual use of the city ethnic comes from an inscription dating to the late sixth century BC.[1] An inscription from Delphi dated to the first half of the fifth century BC provides a further example, this time of the external and collective use of the city ethnic.[2] The only source that explicitly classifies Gortys as a *polis* is Pausanias. Because he reports that it was one of the *poleis* voted to participate in the synoikism of Megalopolis, we may assume it retained its *polis* status at least into the first quarter of the fourth century BC.[3]

HISTORY

The first attested historical event is an inscription recording the dedication of spoils by the city of Gortys after a military victory[4] some time during the first

---

[1] *IG* I² 488. See Nielsen (1996a: 122) for commentary.   [2] *Syll.*³ 49.
[3] Paus. 8.27.4. As for many of these cities chosen to participate in the synoikism, it is uncertain whether the decision was implemented.
[4] ‘Κορτύνιοι δεκάταν πολεμίου’ (*Syll.*³ 49).

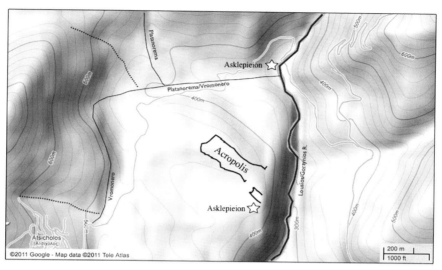

Fig. C5.1. Gortys, topographical map of area and course of fortifications. (© *2011 Google-Map data © 2011 Tele Atlas*)

half of the fifth century BC.[5] The inscription does not mention whom they fought, and so the larger repercussions of this engagement are uncertain.[6] Still, as Gortys was probably a member of the Peloponnesian League,[7] it remains possible that the campaign was conducted under its auspices. Since Gortys is listed among those Arkadian cities selected to join in the synoikism of Megalopolis,[8] membership in the Arkadian League may also be assumed. Because Polybius tells us that in 219 BC the city was captured by an Elian general during the First Social War between the Aitolian and Achaian Leagues, Gortys was likely to have been a member of the latter at that time.[9] By 194 BC, Gortys issued Achaian League coinage in its name.[10] By the mid-second century AD, Gortys was no longer a *polis*, but a '*κώμη*' of Megalopolis.[11]

LOCAL TOPOGRAPHY

Gortys lies high on the western bank of the Lousios (or Gortynios) River, approximately 1 km north-east of the modern village of Atsicholos (Fig. C5.2).

[5] *Syll.*³ 49.   [6] Maher (2014: 266).
[7] Nielsen (1996b: 87; 2002: 562) assumes membership in the Peloponnesian League for Gortys.
[8] Paus. 8.27.4.
[9] Polyb. 4.60. Interestingly, Polybius also adds that at the time Gortys was a city of Thelphousa.
[10] Head (1963: 418).   [11] Paus. 8.27.7.

Catalogue

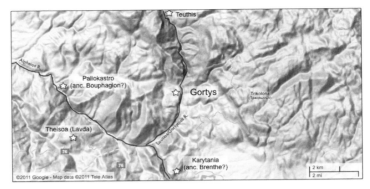

Fig. C5.2. Gortys, topographical map of area. (© *2011 Google-Map data © 2011 Tele Atlas*)

Geographically, the site is centrally positioned, lying almost exactly in the midpoint between ancient Teuthis (*c.*10 km due north), Bouphagion (*c.*11 km to the east), and Brenthe (*c.*8 km to the south).[12]

Ancient Gortys also stands at the juncture of a number of prominent natural features. Not only did its position at the southern terminus of the Lousios Gorge ensure command over the southern stretch of the river and access to central Arkadia from that direction,[13] but the site also commanded the only navigable valley linking the Lousios/Gortynios and Alpheios Rivers (and Elis beyond), which guaranteed that Gortys controlled the eastern end of this important artery.[14] As noted by others,[15] its location also secured a key entrance to the northern part of the plain of Megalopolis.

While these strategic features were undoubtedly important factors in dictating the choice of site, in fact the location chosen represents the only spot along the Lousios/Gortynios River that is really amenable to habitation. As observed by Frazer over a century ago, 'in spite of its height above the river, Gortys lies essentially in a basin shut in on all sides by mountains'.[16] To the west and south-west of the site stand the slopes of Mt Pera Rachi; to the north, the basin is defined by the steep southern slope of Mt Varvoudha; while the east side of the basin site is defined by the west bank of the Lousios/Gortynios River, the slopes of Mt Klinitsa, and the western foothills of Mt Menalo. These mountains not only defined the small basin in which Gortys was located, but must also have represented the natural borders of its territory.

---

[12] Teuthis stands at modern Dhimitsana, Bouphagion at Paleokastro (?), and Brenthe is believed by some to lie beneath modern Karatina (?). The incredibly winding modern road to Dhimitsana from Gortys makes the actual travelling distance closer to 20 km.

[13] Jost (1999: 197).   [14] Jost (1999: 197).

[15] Martin (1947–8: 82–3); Jost (1999: 197).   [16] Frazer (1898: iv. 309).

The fortified acropolis of Gortys comprises a narrow hill oriented north-west–south–east, measuring approximately 425 m in length from the summit to the river and 160 m at its widest point near the top (see Fig. C5.1).[17] From the summit, the intramural area does not slope consistently towards the river. Instead, the slope of the north-west and uppermost third of the site is broken by a number of descending plateaus, which meet the slopes of a low and narrow hill occupying the centre third of the acropolis. The south-eastern third of the intramural area slopes down from the central hill gradually towards the edge of the river valley, where it ends abruptly, falling over 100 m to the river below. Beyond the circuit, the slopes of the acropolis are not uniform on all sides. Disregarding the sheer eastern precipice, the acropolis is steepest on its north and north-east sides. While the west and south slopes are neither as steep nor as high as in the north, it has the advantage of exposed sections of rugged bedrock as additional protection. Finally, immediately south of the acropolis is a small plateau on which stand the remains of the so-called South Fort. While this area is separated from the acropolis by a narrow depression to the north-west, the north-east and east sides of the plateau are delineated by the precipice of the Lousios/Gortynios River Valley. Its exposed south side is comprised of a low, but relatively steep slope broken on its north-western end by a very narrow perpendicular gap.

NATURAL DEFENCES

The height offered by the acropolis, the steep slope on its north-east side, and the precipitous south-east side, provide natural defences for the site (Fig. C5.3). The river valley and surrounding mountains limit the approaches to the site to routes from the south-west and north. The Lousios/Gortys River flanks the site to the east, while its tributaries, the Vromonero and Platanor-ema, surround the base of the acropolis on the west and north.

FORTIFICATION TYPE

Acropolis type.[18] The fortifications of the acropolis can be divided into three sections, which, using the terminology applied by Martin, include the north-north-east (NNE), north-west (NW), and west-south-west (WSW) stretches

---

[17] Martin (1947–8: 85).   [18] Jost (1999: 197).

Fig. C5.3. Gortys, the site (facing south-west). (© *Matthew Maher*)

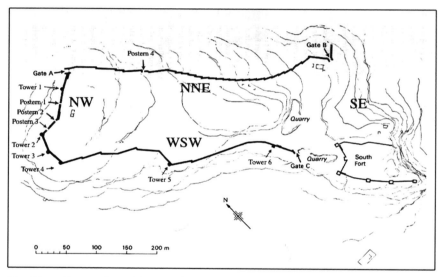

Fig. C5.4. Gortys, plan of the site after Lawrence (1979: 354, fig. 82). (© *A.W. Lawrence*)

(Fig. C5.4).[19] From the highest point of the hill to the north-west, the acropolis circuit embraces the south-eastern slope of the hill with two roughly parallel sections, all the way to the edge of the river valley (including a small plateau comprising the southernmost part of the hill).[20]

[19] I would like to thank the 39th Ephorate of Prehistoric and Classical Antiquities for granting me a study permit to examine the remains of ancient Gortys. Because much of the circuit was concealed by overgrowth, however, I was unable to make many useful measurements and had to rely instead on those made and published by Martin (1947–8). Unless otherwise cited, all photographs are based on personal observation from my visit to the site in autumn 2009.

[20] For a detailed examination of the course of the circuit, see Maher (2014: 267–8).

PRESERVATION

The stone foundations of the acropolis circuit are moderately preserved on the north-west and parts of the southern side. Gate B is especially well preserved, surviving in places to its original height of *c*.3.75 m. The total length of the acropolis circuit is *c*.1,000 m.

CONSTRUCTION

The foundations of the walls and towers in the NW and WSW sections of the circuit are best described as predominately coursed trapezoidal with occasional polygonal blocks (Fig. C5.5).[21] The NNE section (indented trace) and parts of the southern acropolis wall (the area of the so-called South Fort) were constructed of dry rubble masonry.[22] The stone foundations of all the curtains and towers in the circuit once supported a mudbrick superstructure (not preserved).[23] The interior of the curtains was filled with the standard combination of earth and rubble packing, but also with a stack of small flat

Fig. C5.5. Gortys, western curtain adjoining Gate B (facing south-west). (© *Matthew Maher*)

[21] Maher (2014: 268). Describing the walls as semi-polygonal or semi-trapezoidal, Martin (1947–8: 120) sees them as an intermediate style between pure quadrangular and pure polygonal. Scranton (1941: 162, 165, 159, 184) notes four different styles of masonry in the walls of Gortys. He describes them only as 'first of four', 'second of four', etc., with the exception of the NNE indented trace, so it is difficult to determine to which parts of the circuit he is referring.

[22] Maher (2014: 269).

[23] Martin (1947–8: 112) maintains that the superstructure of the walls was formed entirely out of stone. For arguments why they were almost certainly mudbrick, see Maher (2014: 269–70).

stones, which was raised against the rough interiors of each facing block to separate them from the rubble fill. In the NW section the curtain measures 3.60–3.80 m in thickness, in the WSW section it measures 2.50–2.60 m in thickness, while in the NNE section the wall is 2–2.50 m thick. The walls of the South Fort are only 1.20–1.30 m in width.[24]

SUMMARY OF TACTICAL COMPONENTS

The acropolis circuit contains five semicircular towers (*c*.7.5 m in diameter), strategically, rather than regularly, spaced, and (including the south fort) at least five rectangular towers (see Fig. C5.4). There are four posterns located in the upper (north-west) part of the circuit and three gates. All are simple frontal opening type gates set at oblique angles to the surrounding curtain; Gate B is set back, essentially located at the end of a funnel produced by the narrowing curtains. The wall in parts of the WSW curtain and in the majority of the NNE side are arranged in a highly developed form of the indented trace.

Towers

Although measuring almost 1 km in length, the circuit of Gortys was fitted out with only six towers, the foundations of which were constructed in the same manner as the curtains. The acropolis circuit contains five semicircular towers (most of which measure *c*.7.5 m in diameter), strategically, rather than regularly, spaced, and one rectangular tower (6.35 × 3.30 m).[25] None of the faces of any of these six towers was bonded to the wall behind, nor is their evidence that any of these towers had ground-floor chambers (Fig. C5.6).[26] The South Fort contained at least four regularly spaced rectangular towers (*c*.6–7 × 3–4 m), and possibly as many as six (Fig. C5.7). Tower 4 had a ground-storey chamber that was accessible from the fort by a narrow door in its north corner.

Gates

With three large gates (Fig. C5.8) and four posterns, the circuit contained more openings than towers.

Providing access to the summit from the north and marking the boundary between the north-west and NNE sections of the circuit is Gate A. This gate is

[24] Martin (1947–8: 117).   [25] Martin (1947–8: 96).
[26] Martin and Metzger (1940–1: 276); Martin (1947–8: 87).

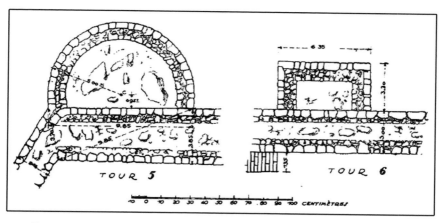

Fig. C5.6. Gortys, plans of Towers 5 and 6 from Martin (1947–8, pl. XIV).

comprised of a straight and narrow corridor (extending for 9.77 m and widening slightly from 4.64 m to 4.90 m), interrupted only by two small piers for the door.[27] Gate B, located at the bottom of the hill in the easternmost part of the circuit, is comprised of a frontal opening, 5.30 m long and 3.20–3.60 m wide, with similar piers as provisions for a door (Fig. C5.9).[28] As this was the city's main gate, measures were taken to ensure that it was sufficiently protected. Not only was it assembled using massive blocks on the exterior, but the core of the eastern half of the gate and adjoining curtain was of solid stone masonry, instead of the usual earth and rubble fill.[29]

Occupying the southernmost part of the acropolis circuit is Gate C. Although it is poorly preserved, its relatively intact western half confirms that it is a frontal opening type, similar in both size and layout to Gate B.[30] Four posterns survive in the circuit—three are located in the north-west part of the system and one in the NNE—each *c*.1.15 m wide and, as suggested by cuttings in the surviving thresholds, would have once been secured by wooden doors.[31]

COMMENTS

The NNE part of the circuit is the poorest preserved in the system, which prompted Martin to comment that 'cette face de l'enceinte mérite de retenir

---

[27] Martin (1947–8: 100).   [28] Martin (1947–8: 103).   [29] Martin (1947–8: 121).
[30] Martin and Metzger (1940–1: 278). The most interesting feature of this gate is the discovery of a small shrine and associated votive remains, which Martin (1947–8: 109–12) believes were dedicated to Pan.
[31] Martin (1947–8: 90–1).

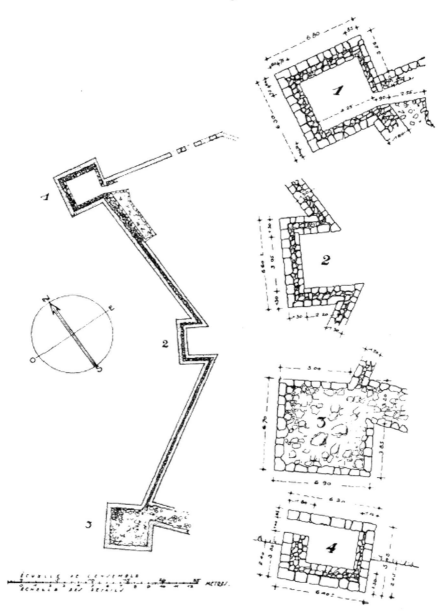

Fig. C5.7. Gortys, plans of the towers of the South Fort from Martin (1947–8: pl. XVIII).

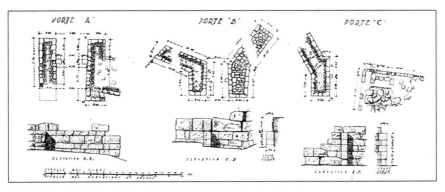

Fig. C5.8. Gortys, plans of Gates A, B, and C from Martin (1947–8, pl. XV).

Fig. C5.9. Gortys, photo of Gate B (facing south). (© *Matthew Maher*)

l'attention moins par son état de conservation que par l'unité de son tracé et de sa conception'.[32] Indeed, it is the only section of the system not provided with towers, and we see here that architects chose to employ an indented trace instead. Between Gate B and Postern 4, this *c.*300 m stretch of indented trace is 'articulées suivant une courbe harmonieusement adaptée aux lignes du terrain'.[33] The small, overlapping sections of curtain that define this trace are relatively uniform in size, averaging between *c.*10.50 m and 12 m in length and 2 m and 2.50 m in thickness.[34] Following the long concave section is a more linear, yet still indented, section of trace that continues to climb the slope between Postern 4 and Gate A. As the slope above Postern 4 is milder than

---

[32] Martin (1947–8: 97).   [33] Martin (1947–8: 97).

[34] Martin (1947–8: 98). The three overlapping sections at the bottom of the hill closest to Gate B are narrower, measuring 1.90 m, 1.50 m, and 1.40 m in thickness (Martin 1947–8: 98).

the one below, the four overlapping sections of curtain, measuring 31.25 m, 10.50 m, 32 m, and 36 m respectively, are considerably longer here.[35]

OVERALL DEFENSIVE PLANNING

The choice of site for the *polis*, acropolis, and the South Fort of Gortys was carefully and strategically selected. The location was well watered, it possessed arable land, building material (that is, quarries), and considerable natural defences, and it ensured command of the hub where some of the major arteries linking southern, central, and western Arkadia came together.[36] Surrounded by mountains on all sides, the basin in which Gortys stood was effectively provided with natural defences on all sides. It had the additional protection on the east afforded by the 100 m high and precipitous west bank of the Lousios/ Gortynios River Valley.

While the choice to fortify the acropolis ridge was a strategic decision conceived to complement the natural advantages of the area, the course of the fortifications themselves was ultimately dictated by the topography of the ridge on which they were built. Thus, its elongated shape and north-west–south-east axis conform to the shape and contours of the hill. This is most obviously reflected in the north-west section, where the wall skirts the summit to enclose the highest part of the ridge, and in the WSW section, where the wall descends the edge of the hill, sticking close to its natural contours. In the final NNE section, where the slope is steeper and the edge of the ridge is not strictly defined, a potential course for the defensive wall is less obvious. Accordingly, we see that military architects turned again to the topography and constructed a concave and indented trace that both reflected and complemented the natural terrain. Besides a practical approach to navigate the NNE slope, the indented trace also represents a conscious tactical decision with the aim of enhancing the defensive strength of the system as a whole. A closer examination of the composite parts of the fortifications, their form and function, as well as their distribution, demonstrates the same objective of ensuring that the acropolis defences were as strong as possible.

The construction of four of the acropolis's six towers along the north-west section strongly suggests apprehension for the safety of this part of the site. There were two main reasons at the root of such concern. First, while this section occupied the summit of the ridge and was the highest point of the acropolis, the extramural terrain to the west was still elevated and flat enough

[35] With a thickness of 2.75 m, the wall here is also thicker than below Postern 4 (Martin 1947–8: 97, 98).
[36] Jost (1999: 197).

to be a liability if held by an enemy.[37] Second, the easiest approach and access to the acropolis from the south would have required passing past this part of the circuit. In order to command access to the acropolis from the south and to minimize the threat imposed by the uncooperative terrain to the west, architects both increased the width of the curtain and erected a cluster of semicircular towers. The curtain between Postern 1 and Tower 2, for example, was strengthened to 3.60 m, while the wall between Towers 2 and 4 was increased to 3.90 m in width.[38]

As for the towers, we see that Tower 1 was well placed both to exploit the unshielded right side of anyone approaching Gate A and to protect any defenders who sallied forth from Postern 1. Its semicircular shape, moreover, eliminated blind spots and ensured a 180° view of the gate and the postern. Like Tower 1, it is both the semicircular shape and position of the adjacent Towers 2, 3, and 4 that arguably provide their greatest tactical advantage. The fact that they were placed on the 'hinges' (that is, where the curtain changes direction), combined with their shape, provided a greater than 180° view; the projection of Tower 2, specifically, would have ensured a viewing angle closer to 270°—more than enough to safeguard both Posterns 2 and 3. The close spacing of these three towers also guaranteed that they could protect each other.[39] The semicircular Tower 5 further down the hill possessed similar tactical abilities, although its size meant it could probably have housed a greater number of artillery machines. Furthermore, as in the north-west section, the stretch of curtain issuing north of this tower was strengthened to 3.80 m in width, rather than the 2.50 m thickness characteristic of the rest of the section.[40] Finally, Tower 6—an otherwise fairly typical rectangular example of a first-generation artillery tower—was well sited to provide enfilading cover for Gate C, located just under 50 m away. Arguably, a semicircular tower would have been equally (if not more) effective here, and as this was the only rectangular tower in the system, the choice behind its shape raises questions without obvious answers. Perhaps Frazer was correct in his observation that several other rectangular towers had existed along this WSW stretch,[41] even if Martin and Metzger maintain that these 'pseudo-tours ne sont que les ruines d'habitations tardives, sans doute médiévales, qui se sont appuyées au rempart en utilisant les blocs tombés'.[42]

Further tactical considerations can be discerned in the frequency and distribution of the circuit's posterns. As with the concentration of towers in the north-west section, that three of the four posterns (Posterns 1, 2, and 3) are also located here further demonstrates a concern for the defence of this part of the circuit. These posterns, placed only around 30 m apart, are *c.*1.15 m

[37] Martin (1947–8: 88).   [38] Martin (1947–8: 89).   [39] Martin (1947–8: 89).
[40] Martin (1947–8: 94).   [41] Frazer (1898: iv. 309).
[42] Martin and Metzger (1940–1: 276).

wide.[43] These posterns were positioned where they could receive enfilading protection from flanking towers—Postern 1 is easily within range of Tower 1, while Tower 2 was close enough to protect defenders sallying forth from Posterns 2 or 3. That a further measure of protection was envisioned is suggested by what appears to be the remains of a staircase behind the curtain separating Posterns 1 and 2. From this staircase, defenders could quickly access the wall-walk directly above the posterns and provide further defence if required. Finally, the frequency of posterns in the north-west section immediately suggests they had a military rather than a civilian function. If these were conceived primarily for citizens passing to or from the countryside, then certainly one postern here would have sufficed. Postern 4, on the other hand, located above in the upper part of the NNE section, may have served such a civilian function. Standing alone on this side of the circuit, this postern directly faces what is thought to have been the residential area of Gortys and would have been a convenient access point to the acropolis from the lower city.[44] Still, as any opening in the wall is a potential weak spot, and this section of the circuit was not provided with towers, architects constructed a small bastion-like projection flanking the north side of the 1.10–1.20 m wide opening.[45]

As the NNE section did not contain any artillery towers, it appears that the form and course of the curtain itself were regarded as the primary defensive tactic. Certainly, the indented trace on this side is the architectural feature most often remarked about in connection with the fortifications of Gortys. Similar to Theisoa (Lavda), the topography of this part of the acropolis must have been a factor in its conception. Still, that an indented trace was also constructed between Towers 4 and 5 in the WSW section—in an area with more negotiable terrain—does not suggest, as maintained by Lawrence, that 'the sole motive [of this feature] was probably to enhance stability'.[46] Instead, as towers could easily have been accommodated in the WSW indented section and at least in the stretch north-west of Postern 4 in the NNE section, we must concede that the use of the indented trace, while perhaps somewhat dictated by the terrain, was a conscious decision introduced purely for purposes of enfilading. In the WSW section, like the north-west defences as a whole, the faces of these jogs or indents look towards the north-west. In the NNE stretch, however, the faces of the jogs stand facing downhill towards the south-east and east. Because the depth of the jogs measures about 2.40 m, each face could have held a couple of archers or a light artillery machine,[47] which may not sound too formidable, but, when this is multiplied by the number of closely spaced jogs, the enfilading capabilities possible in the NNE arrangement would have been considerable. Indeed, the concentration of defensive

[43] Martin (1947–8: 90–1).   [44] Reekmans (1955: 335).   [45] Martin (1947–8: 98).
[46] Lawrence (1979: 353).   [47] Lawrence (1979: 353).

firepower would probably have surpassed that provided by towers spaced even 30 m apart. Even in the WSW section, where the jogs are much further spaced, the overlapping sections would have created a small platform on which machines and defenders could be placed. Finally, how are we to explain the obvious differences between the forms of the indented traces in the NNE and WSW sections? Martin maintains that 'c'est plutôt dans une différence d'époque et dans des raisons d'ordre historique que nous trouverons l'explication de ces divergences'.[48]

Although technically examples of the simple opening type, all three gates of the Gortys's circuit display sophisticated tactical considerations. Set at the end of a narrowing funnel, Gate B is arguably the most obvious in this regard. At *c.*45 m at its widest, this funnel had two tactical purposes: first, provided with two solid flanks for defensive fire, its form would have forced an attacking foe through the imposed bottleneck—reducing any strength in offensive numbers; second, and related to the first, simply put, Gate B was meant to be imposing to anyone approaching. Combined with the daunting funnel-shaped approach, the fact that the gate employed massive (almost cyclopean) masonry, including the use of polygonal blocks to add to its ruggedness and perceived strength, demonstrates that Gate B was designed to send a strong message. Furthermore, the curtain forming the eastern half of the funnel was constructed with a solid stone core, and this indicates that this was not all bluster, and that the gate was as daunting and as strong as it was meant to appear.

Gates A and C are more closely related in form than either is to Gate B. Both are set at oblique angles, had projecting flanks on either side, and were protected by a nearby tower. As Lawrence maintains, 'sometimes obliquity appears to have conferred a purely military advantage'.[49] The oblique gates suggest that the road towards both of them must have approached obliquely from the defenders' left.[50] Thus, not only would an enemy be forced to advance for some distance along the foot of the wall, but when this oblique position was combined with the gates' projecting flanks, defenders would have been able to attack from both sides of the gate simultaneously.[51] To add further protection, we see Tower 1 well positioned to cover the left side of Gate A and the unshielded right side of an approaching enemy. Gate C was also provided with a flanking tower, yet one is left to wonder at the effectiveness of Tower 6 to cover this entrance. The rectangular shape of this tower would have limited enfilading in a direction parallel to the curtain, which was blocked at Gate C by its protruding western flank. Furthermore, Tower 6 was not well positioned to protect the south or south-east, which the oblique angle of the gate suggests were the directions of the main approach. The relative

---

[48] Martin (1947–8: 99). See under Chronological Arguments.
[49] Lawrence (1979: 307).   [50] Winter (1970a: 212, n. 13).
[51] Winter (1970a: 212, n. 13).

ineffectiveness of Tower 6, therefore, hints that we might expect Gate C to have had another tower on its right side (similar to Gate A), in the area where no remains of the circuit survive today.

Because the acropolis fortification system would have been useless if the area in the south-east between Gate B and Gate C was left open, we may confidently assume that a wall once existed here.[52] Martin discovered a block or two here and there and believed that a wall certainly linked these two gates,[53] and, although its direct course could not be traced, like the rest of the circuit its position must have been dictated by the terrain and probably proceeded all the way to the edge of the Lousios/Gortynios River Valley. Fortunately, there are clues in the area that may permit a more precise reconstruction of the original south-east part of the circuit. Because of its proximity to the acropolis, the small plateau on which the South Fort stands would have been a defensive liability and too valuable to have been left outside the original circuit. Furthermore, the South Fort is deemed by all authorities to be a later structure that was built quickly, cheaply, and probably by cannibalizing parts of the now missing south-east wall in question.[54] If we can accept that this plateau would have been included in the original circuit, and that the quickest and cheapest way to build a wall is to use or modify an existing wall, we might envision that the south-west and north-west walls of the South Fort more or less followed the course of the original circuit, and a now missing wall (reused in the construction of the fort) would have existed between Gate C and the South Fort's Tower 1 (Fig. C5.10). Here it is significant to point out that two of the earliest plans of Gortys (by Blouet and Aldenhoven) show just this: that the circuit embraces the small plateau in the south-east and the South Fort as a separate entity does not exist.[55] Whether the south-east side along the edge of the Lousios/Gortynios River Valley was fortified or not remains uncertain. In this reconstructed scenario, looking to build the South Fort as quickly and cheaply as possible, architects followed the course of the original circuit for its south-west and north-west sides, while the north-east wall of the fort (if it existed at all) was added to close the final side of the fort.

As for the defensive planning of the South Fort, the preservation of the remains limit the discussion to its north-west and south-west sides. The south-west section, as mentioned, contains at least one, and perhaps two, further rectangular towers. Otherwise typical and unexceptional, Tower 4 is interesting because its flanks continue through the thickness of the wall. The north-west side contains two true rectangular towers at the corners and a tower-like projection inset in between them. Interestingly, as the two corner towers

---

[52] Much of the following argument regarding the original trace as it relates to the South Fort complex appears in Maher (2014: 271–2).
[53] Martin (1947–8: 104).   [54] Martin (1947–8: 129); Winter (1971a: 147).
[55] Blouet (1833: pl. 31, fig. 1); Aldenhoven (1841: 232).

Fig. C5.10. Gortys, satellite image with reconstruction of original circuit. (© *2011 Google-Map data* © *2011 Tele Atlas*)

(Towers 1 and 3) are attached to the curtain at the corner, they presented all four of their sides. Thus, unlike the usual placement of rectangular towers, Towers 1 and 3 could have placed machines on all four sides, ensuring a near 360° viewshed. Moreover, the 'saw-tooth' inset between them presented a concave angle into which fire from both towers could reach simultaneously.

Additional defensive fire could be provided by the so-called Tower 2, easily the most interesting architectural feature of the South Fort. With no back walls to support chambers or firing platforms, enfilading from this pseudo-tower would have been limited to the top of its curtain. Even if wooding scaffolding once supported such chambers, the rectangular shape would have produced the usual blind spots at its corners, making it useless for protecting not only Towers 1 and 3, but the curtains linking them. Thus, Tower 2 could effectively protect the flanking curtains and towers only from the top of its curtains. Constructing what was essentially a fake tower is in keeping with the fact that the South Fort appears to have been constructed quickly and cheaply. What could be cheaper or quicker, in fact, than building only the external edifice of a tower? While compromising some of its defensive firing capabilities, building such a fake tower would still present to an enemy something resembling a real tower while reaping the benefits of speed and economy.

From the reconstruction outlined here, it is likely that the north-west and south-west walls of the South Fort incorporated the foundations of the original acropolis circuit. In this scenario, again in the interests of speed and economy, with the exception of two small surviving sections, the vast majority of the fort's curtains were erected at a considerably thinner width (*c.*1.25 m).[56] Consequently, these walls represent 'a good candidate for a system in which long stretches of wall were provided with wooden *ikria* and *parodos*, now completely vanished'.[57] Indeed, as calculated by Winter, once the width of the screenwall/crenellations was removed from the thickness of the curtain, the wall-walk would have been reduced to only *c.*0.60 m.[58] While noting that patrolling and even fighting could in theory be performed from such a narrow *parodos*, Winter continues: 'it is not unreasonable to suppose that the width was increased by laying wooden planks on a wooden scaffolding, which has since disappeared.'[59]

CHRONOLOGICAL SUMMARY

The most likely chronological scenario—one based on historical probability, external evidence, and architectural affinities—would include a date of *c.*400–370 BC for the entire circuit, with repairs (of dry rubble) made to the indented trace on the NNE side and to the southern part of the circuit (that is, in the area of the so-called South Fort) during the last quarter of the third century.

CHRONOLOGICAL ARGUMENTS

Minor discrepancies aside, on the whole, there is a consensus among modern scholars that Martin's proposed chronology for the fortifications of Gortys is essentially correct.[60] In general, he maintains that the acropolis fortifications were constructed in the early fourth century BC (*c.*370 BC), that the indented trace on the NNE side was a Hellenistic repair, and that the South Fort was built after the acropolis circuit, sometime during the second half of the third century BC.[61] Winter, however, makes an important addition to the chronological discussion. Since an indented trace was employed in the original

---

[56] Immediately south-west of Tower 1 and south-east from Tower 3, the curtain is considerably thicker at 3.20 m and *c.*3 m respectively (Martin 1947–8: 117). These thicker curtains may represent unaltered remnants of the original circuit incorporated into the South Fort.

[57] Winter (1971a: 147).   [58] Winter (1971a: 147).   [59] Winter (1971a: 147).

[60] e.g. Bölte (1912b: 1672); Winter (1971a: 103, n. 8, 213, n. 15, 222; 1971b: 414); Lawrence (1979: 440); Adam (1982: 179); Jost (1999: 197); Nielsen (2002: 562). Scranton (1941: 184, 186) appears to be alone in his belief that the indented trace on the NNE side is of the Archaic period. The following argument for the dates of construction for the different sections of the circuit appears in Maher (2014: 272–9).

[61] Martin (1947–8: 120 ff.); Jost (1999: 197).

early fourth-century BC circuit on the WSW side, he is probably correct in his belief that, before the Hellenistic repair, the original course on the NNE side 'followed substantially the same course as the later, which simply re-used the surviving parts of the earlier foundations'.[62] Winter's argument here, as well as the rest of the archaeological and historical evidence, appears to be consistent with these three chronological phases.

Although conceivably inconclusive on their own, when all aspects of the archaeological evidence are taken together, they establish convincingly that the original circuit must have been laid out during the first third of the fourth century BC. Briefly, as far as the curtains are concerned, the coursed trapezoidal masonry of Gortys, as Scranton maintains, is a style that belongs to the last quarter of the fifth century to the first quarter of the fourth century BC.[63] Internally, we know that the use of headers running back through the walls forming compartments becomes 'much more common'[64] from the fourth century BC onwards. The construction and form of the towers provide further evidence. For example, none of the towers on the acropolis of Gortys is bonded to the curtain. Although admitting the presence or lack of bonding between a tower and curtain is inconclusive on its own, Winter maintains that 'by the second quarter of the fourth century, when mines, artillery, and rams were all in common use, the indivisibility of bonding towers and curtains together must have been quite evident'.[65] The apparent lack of ground-floor chambers and their relatively small size further suggest the acropolis towers are first-generation types, conceived in the early fourth century BC before the wide-spread defensive use of artillery.

The gates and posterns too present evidence that is consistent with this chronological range. Although Martin is confident that the grouping of the acropolis posterns is 'd'une tactique défensive mise au point dans les premières années du IVᵉ siècle',[66] Lawrence argues that 'early posterns are never grouped close to a main gateway with the same outlook, as are the two of a late period…near Gate A at Gortys'.[67] While the frequency and concentration of posterns at Gortys suggest an 'active' defensive strategy characteristic of the later fourth century BC and Hellenistic period, because the use of posterns becomes increasingly common throughout the fourth century BC,[68] a precise date for these features is difficult to pin down. Perhaps one or two posterns were included in the original early fourth-century BC circuit, and, later, another one or two were deemed necessary and installed. In either case, an early fourth-century BC date cannot be dismissed for the acropolis posterns. The gates are also instructive, since the frontal opening and single door type,

---

[62] Winter (1971a: 103, n. 8).   [63] Scranton (1941: 90, 98).
[64] Winter (1971a: 135).   [65] Winter (1971a: 167, n. 51).
[66] Martin (1947–8: 92).   [67] Lawrence (1979: 454).
[68] Winter (1971a: 239).

such as Gates A, B, and C at Gortys, appear to have been the standard form until at least the middle of the fourth century BC, when advances in siege warfare necessitated the use of the double gate.[69]

The second chronological period and second phase of construction are represented by the indented trace on the NNE side of the circuit, which, as mentioned, appears to be a Hellenistic repair. Martin and Winter both agree that this indented trace at Gortys is probably a third-century BC repair to the original early fourth-century BC circuit.[70] They differ, however, as to the form of the wall that preceded the repair. Martin maintains that the indented trace in general is largely a Hellenistic invention that should not pre-date *c.*350 BC, which implies that the earlier trace on the NNE side was not indented.[71] Winter, on the other hand, suggests the possibility that an earlier NNE wall followed substantially the same course as the later, which simply reused the surviving parts of the earlier foundations.[72] This is certainly a plausible interpretation, since the original wall apparently employed another indented trace, along the northern end of the WSW section. Without excavation, perhaps at this point the question is purely academic. What is important is that the advanced form of the trace, the intrusive rubble masonry, and the improbability that the original fourth-century BC wall would have needed repairs so soon after its creation, all suggest that the current remains are a product of the Hellenistic period.[73]

The final period of construction at Gortys is demonstrated in the walls of the South Fort, which appears to be a product of the second half of the third century BC.[74] Few would dispute the fact that there are marked differences between the fortifications of the acropolis and those of this fort, differences that immediately suggest a different date. Indeed, the presence of ground-storey tower chambers, the projection of the corner towers, the use of a different tower shape, the different techniques employed in the construction of the curtains, and the obvious signs of speed and economy all suggest that the South Fort post-dates the acropolis circuit.

How are these building phases to be interpreted in the larger historical and chronological context of southern Arkadia? The prevailing opinion is still that proposed by Martin in the 1940s—namely, that both the early fourth-century BC acropolis circuit and the later third-century BC South Fort functioned as fortresses. The original acropolis, he believed, was built and garrisoned by Megalopolis and the Arkadian League as a stronghold to protect access to the plain of Megalopolis from the north.[75] Indeed, he argues that 'l'enceinte

[69] Winter (1971a: 213).
[70] Martin (1947–8: 128); Winter (1971a: 103, n. 8; 1971b: 414).
[71] Martin (1947–8: 137).   [72] Winter (1971a: 103, n. 8).
[73] Winter (1971b: 414).   [74] Martin (1947–8: 134).
[75] Martin (1947–8: 139).

gortynienne diffère à la fois de la simple acropole fortifiée et de l'enceinte de ville; elle est plutôt un camp dont le rôle est moins de protéger la cité que de défendre un passage et interdire l'accès de la plaine de Mégalopolis; elle est une pièce importante du système défensif de la capitale arcadienne'.[76] Martin also points to the fourth-century BC Arkadian League coins discovered on the acropolis, arguing that such a large number of them can be explained only by the occupation of league soldiers.[77] Of the later history of the acropolis, Martin maintains that the repair to the NNE indented trace can be attributed to the Macedonians, who, possibly under Demetrios Poliorkites, occupied the site as a garrison base in the early years of the third century BC.[78] While he makes it clear that he believes the acropolis was no longer functioning as a fort at the time the second southern fortress was constructed, the reasons behind its final decline and abandonment are not provided. Furthermore, Martin believed the remains of the later South Fort demonstrate that it had a similar function, but the reasons behind its inception and exactly who oversaw its construction are harder to narrow down. He offers several possibilities based on the increasing Aitolian presence in the area, including the notion that it was built by Megalopolis in order to defend itself against Aitolians intruders, or the possibility that it was built by the people of Gortys themselves to provide protection to their southern sanctuary.[79] In any event, it appears that the fort was conceived in Arkadia's turbulent time sometime during the second half of the third century BC.

There are, however, several significant problems with Martin's interpretation. Besides the fact that the fortified acropolis of Gortys is not different in scale or scope from other Arkadian examples, as Martin would have us believe, or the fact that there exists no evidence it ever served as a base for one of Demetrios' garrisons, the truth remains that the location of the South Fort is most impractical. Unless its ultimate purpose was to protect the adjacent sanctuary, would it not have been more practical (and economical) to have incorporated the summit of the acropolis? Not only is this the strongest part of the circuit, which would have been (based on its present preservation) easily supplemented, but, as mentioned, it is the summit of the acropolis that commanded the most accessible north–south route through the Gortys basin. Even if one was travelling north along the edge of the river, one could easily have circumvented the South Fort completely by going around the south-west and west sides of the acropolis. Finally, the presence of Arkadian League coins on the acropolis of a city that was a member of the Arkadian League should only come as a surprise if, as Pausanias tells us, Gortys did participate in the synoikism. Whether this decision was implemented, however, remains far from certain. Indeed, the abundance of fourth-century BC

---

[76] Martin (1947–8: 142–3).   [77] Martin (1947–8: 139).
[78] Martin (1947–8: 144–5).   [79] Martin (1947–8: 146).

remains discovered in the sanctuary and residential area north of the acropolis could be taken as evidence to the contrary: that some, or all, of the population of Gortys remained in their ancestral home.

Whether Gortys was a fort or fortified *polis*, it is still conceivable that the original fortifications were erected under the auspices of the Arkadian League, in order to protect the northern approach to Megalopolis, as Martin suggests.[80] Certainly, the northern access to the Lousios Gorge was commanded by the city of Teuthis, which, like Methyrdion and Theisoa (Karkalou), was apparently a dependent *polis* of Orchomenos.[81] Orchomenos' initial refusal to join the Arkadian League must have put it at odds with members of the league and may have inspired Megalopolis to ensure the safety of the northern approach from Orchomenos (via Theisoa (Karkalou) and Teuthis) by fortifying Gortys.

Additional problems with Martin's interpretation are based on the fact that, at present, a precise chronology for the NNE repair and the South Fort is lacking. It is, therefore, not inconceivable that both of these Hellenistic repairs are more or less contemporary. Indeed, Martin saw the influences of Macedonian engineering in both the fort and the NNE trace, but did not go so far as to link the two. The notion that the South Fort may be contemporaneous with the NNE trace and the rest of the acropolis has important repercussions and forms the foundation for a new interpretation of the remains—one based ultimately on the idea that there never was a South Fort. It is important to remember that the only evidence for the existence of the South Fort at all is the lack of a lower wall between Gates B and C of the acropolis, the slightest hint of a north-east wall making it appear independent, and a different construction technique. The strength of this evidence, however, is questionable. For example, the quarry north-west of the fort has obscured the trace of any remains that might have existed between Gate C and the South Fort. Furthermore, the remains of the north-east wall are so few that not only were they overlooked by every early traveller to the site, but may have actually been part of the original trace. Indeed, in the reconstruction of the original circuit (see Fig. C5.10), it is argued that the course of the original early fourth-century BC circuit actually embraced the area now occupied by the so-called South Fort, and, thus, the creation of the latter was actually a modification of the former. In this scenario, as was the case for the indented trace on the acropolis, the different construction technique here is interpreted as a later repair to the original circuit.

Martin admits that the original NNE indented trace needed repair, not because of the wear of time, but because it was violently destroyed.[82] If the walls of the South Fort are actually repairs (to the original circuit) that are contemporary with the repaired indented trace, is it possible that the same act

[80] Jost (1999: 228). [81] Paus. 8.27.4. [82] Martin (1947–8: 143).

of violence transpired in the south-eastern part of the circuit as in the NNE part of the acropolis? Is there any historical evidence to complement such an interpretation? Surprisingly, although such evidence exists, it is not associated with the remains in the published literature. In the early years of the Social War between the Aitolian League and the Achaean League, Elis, which had sided with the former, sent the generals Lykergus and Euripidas to wreak havoc among Achaian League cities in Arkadia. Polybius picks up the story, telling us that in 219 BC 'Lykurgus seized the Athenaeum of Megalopolis, and Euripidas followed up his former successes by taking Gortys'.[83] Here Polybius provides what is possibly the crucial link between the third-century BC repairs to the fortifications and the historical record. Finally, it should also be added that Martin's description of the masonry characteristic of these later repairs is very similar to the rubble masonry described by Loring as belonging to the rebuilding/repair of the walls at Megalopolis, which he (I think correctly) ascribes to 221 BC.[84] In this scenario, it is easy to imagine architects from nearby Megalopolis being employed to help repair the damaged sections of the walls at Gortys in a style and technique with which they were of course familiar, having repaired their own walls only a few years earlier.

In summary, the evidence suggests that the original fortification circuit at Gortys was constructed in the early fourth century BC, perhaps in the years around the synoikism of Megalopolis. Contrary to other interpretations, it is posited here that this original circuit enclosed the small plateau in the south-east occupied by the so-called South Fort, and that, as an independent unit, this fort never actually existed. After Gortys had been sacked in 219 BC and the Elians had withdrawn, repairs were required in several parts of the circuit, and are observable specifically in the NNE indented trace and the south-east part of this circuit. The haste and interest in economy demonstrated in these sections, as well as their resemblance to the *c.*221 BC walls of Megalopolis, accord well with this scenario. That is, as a member of the Achaian League still at war with the Aitolians, it would be crucial for Gortys to rebuild its circuit as quickly and cheaply as possible. Thus along the NNE and in the south-east, architects more or less followed the original course. Further to save time and money while giving an impression of strength when the circuit was viewed from the outside, architects decreased the width of the curtain in the south-east section and added a fake tower. Yet, as products of their time, these same architects incorporated the contemporary technology, including, for example, a highly developed form of the indented trace as well as ground-floor tower chambers.

[83] Polyb. 4.60.
[84] Cf. the descriptions by Loring (1892: 111) and Martin and Metzger (1940–1: 279).

BIBLIOGRAPHY

Polyb. 4.60; Paus. 8.27.4, 8.27.7, 8.28.1; Gell (1817: 105); Dodwell (1819: ii. 381–2); Leake (1830: ii. 23–5); Boblaye (1836: 161); Curtius (1851: i. 349–52); Rangabé (1857: 74–6, pl. VI, 2); Bursian (1862: ii. 233); Rochas d'Aiglun (1881: 73–4); Frazer (1898: iv. 307–11); Bolte (1912b); Martin and Metzger (1940–1: 280–6; 1942–3: 334–9); Scranton (1941: 162, 165, 170, 184, 186); Martin (1947–8); Metzger (1951: 130–3); Ginouvés (1955; 1956: 399–401); Reekmans (1955: 335–40; 1956: 401–6); Winter (1971a: 31, 96, 103, n. 8, 117, n. 35, 119, 122, 146–7, 167, n. 51, 212, 213, n. 15, 322; 1971b: 413–15, 423–4); Garlan (1974: 189, 192, 193, 196, 197, 199, 248, 342, 346, 362, 363); Moggi (1974: 91–2); Lawrence (1979: 138, 217, 221, 253, 307, 310, 346, 353, 366, 440, 454); Adam (1982: 179); Jost (1973: 247; 1985: 203–8; 1999: 197); Sarantakes (1993: 72–4); Papachatzis (1994: 296–9); Mee and Spawforth (2001: 281); Nielsen (2002: 562–3); Maher (2012a: 455–99; 2014).

6

Halous, Western Arkadia

LOCATION

Halous is located in western Arkadia on the north bank above the Ladon Lake. The acropolis comprises the summit and north-east side of a small spur attached by a narrow saddle to a larger mountain to the north-east (Fig. C6.1). Inhabitation was largely limited to the (unfortified) area of the saddle, north-east of the acropolis.

POLIS STATUS

Nielsen maintains that 'Halous deserves inclusion among the *poleis* of Arkadia only because it may have had a Delphic *theorodokos* in the late fifth/early fourth century BC'.[1] Although we cannot unequivocally confirm an independent *polis* status for Halous based on the attestation of a *theorodokos* alone,[2] such a conclusion may be reached on the basis of historical probability. Perlman, for example, maintains that, in half a century of employing the *theorodokoi* lists as political documents, 'not one of the hundreds of toponyms found in the lists has been securely identified as a community which was itself part of a larger state at the time of the list's compilation'.[3]

HISTORY

Nothing of the history of this small city is known. In fact, it is almost certain that, if not for a brief mention by Pausanias,[4] a few lines found inscribed on a

---

[1] Nielsen (2002: 555). For the inscription see *REG* 62, p. 6 l.10.   [2] Perlman (1995: 135).
[3] Perlman (1995: 116). The question of whether Halous was a dependent *polis* of Kleitor, as is often suggested or implied, is discussed under Local Topography. See also Part Two, Chapter 7.
[4] Paus. 8.25.2.

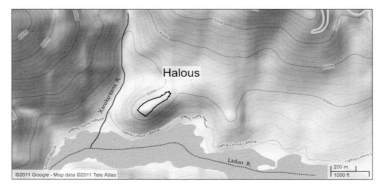

Fig. C6.1. Halous, topographical map showing line of walls and surrounding area. (© *2011 Google-Map data © 2011 Tele Atlas*)

block at Delphi,[5] and the work of one diligent German scholar,[6] the site of ancient Halous would remain all but unknown today.

LOCAL TOPOGRAPHY

The site of ancient Halous is located atop a small hill on the north side and at the western edge of the Ladon Lake (see Fig. C6.1).[7] This hill, rising 145 m from the Ladon below, comprises a southern spur of Mt Paliovouna, from which it is separated by a narrow saddle to the north-east.[8] From the summit, the slopes of the hill fall relatively steeply in all directions except on the north-east side opposite the saddle. While the Ladon River originally bordered the site to the south, the Xerokaritena Valley and its south-flowing stream flank the western side of the hill. Just east of the hill a small spur of similar dimensions radiates south from Mt Paliovouna towards the Ladon, completing the topographical envelopment of the site. Surrounded by steep mountains on almost every side, the amount of arable land in the valley is certainly limited. Today, most of this land is located at the east end of the valley, on and around the low peninsula where the modern village of Mouria stands.

---

[5] *REG* 62, p. 6 l.10.   [6] Meyer (1939a: 78–82).

[7] This lake is a modern reservoir and was created in the later twentieth century by the damning of Ladon River, approximately 2 km south-west of Halous. It supplies water, not electricity, to the prefecture and prevents flooding in the low-lying areas. The ancient course of the Ladon would presumably have followed the same one as the meandering lake, although obviously at a shallower depth.

[8] When Meyer visited the site, he estimated the lake to be 10 m deep surrounding the site (1939a: 79). The overall height of this hill in antiquity, therefore, would have been closer to 155 m above the original course of the river.

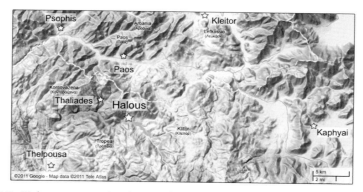

Fig. C6.2. Halous, topographical map of north-western Arkadia. (© *2011 Google-Map data © 2011 Tele Atlas*)

With the addition of the low-lying areas lining the original course of the river and now submerged beneath the lake, presumably this was the main area of agricultural production for the settlement.

Nestled in the eastern half of the Ladon River Valley, the site is surrounded by a formidable landscape. On the opposite shore, south of the site, the land rises from the Ladon sharply and to considerable heights. Similarly, the rugged bulk of Mt Paliovouna dominates the site to the north and west. It is only at the eastern end of the valley, near modern Mouria, that the terrain is negotiable. Such terrain must also have served to delineate the territories of the neighboring *poleis* (Fig. C6.2). Opposite the Xerokaritena Valley, the long north–south running crest of Mt Paliovouna probably formed the border between Halous and Thaliades. The eastern half of the same mountain would have served as the boundary with the territory of Paos to the north. Mt Vithoulas and Mt Drakovouni, parts of the large north–south running chain of mountains east of the Ladon Valley, would have marked the boundary with Kaphyai to the east. Finally, rising sharply on the south side of the Ladon River, immediately south-west of Halous, the bulk of Mt Konstantinos separated the site from the territory of Thelpousa.

There is a suggestion in some of the literature that the north side of the Ladon Valley (including Halous) actually comprised part of the territory of Kleitor.[9] The *Dictionary of Greek and Roman Geography*, for example, maintains that all the towns on the Ladon belong in Kleitorian territory.[10] Similarly,

---

[9] See Part Two, Chapter 7, under Local Topography. This issue is further confused by the fact that this part of the Ladon Lake falls under the modern municipality of Klitoras—not to be confused with the village of Kleitoria, which stands next to the ancient site of Kleitor.

[10] Smith (1873a: 193). It is conceivable that the authors may be referring to those settlements further to the north-east closer to the river's origin, which is near Kleitor. If that is the case, then those settlements probably did fall under the Kleitorian sphere of influence.

Fig. C6.3. Halous, the site (facing north). (© *Matthew Maher*)

the brief article on Halous in the *Realencyclopädie der Classischen Altertums-wissenschaft* also describes the site as being located in the territory of Kleitor.[11] Finally, even in the political map of Arkadia produced by Jost, the borders of Kleitor's influence extend all the way south to embrace what is today the Ladon Lake.[12] To the best of my knowledge, however, there is no evidence to suggest that the borders of Kleitor extended that far south. While Pausanias is clear about the boundaries of Kleitorian territory to the east and west,[13] nowhere does he mention those to the south. In the absence of any evidence, archaeological or literary, it can be assumed that Halous was a small, yet independent *polis* and not a dependent *polis* of Kleitor.

NATURAL DEFENCES

Natural defences are provided by the height offered by the acropolis, and the steep slopes on the southern and western sides of the site (Fig. C6.3). The river valley and surrounding mountains limit the approaches to the site from routes primarily from the east and south. The Ladon River flanks the site to the south, while a tributary, the Xerokaritena, flanks the entire west side of the acropolis.

FORTIFICATION TYPE

Acropolis type.[14] The circuit follows the contour of the hill, encircling the summit and extending down the north-east slope (Fig. C6.4).

---

[11] Bölte (1912a: 2286).   [12] Jost (1985: pl. 1).
[13] Paus. 8.23.9; 8.19.4.   [14] Jost (1999: 196).

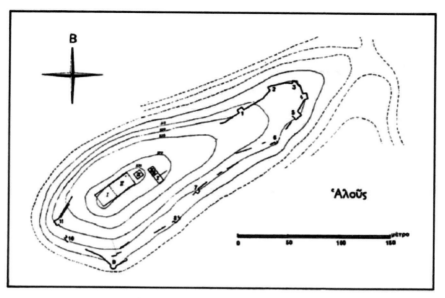

Fig. C6.4. Halous, plan of the site from Meyer (1939a: pl. 4).

PRESERVATION

The site is generally poorly preserved; parts of the long south-east side are moderately preserved. The long north-west stretch is completely obscured by vegetation. The total length of the circuit is *c.*640 m and encloses an area of *c.*1.7 ha.[15]

CONSTRUCTION

The superstructure was mudbrick (not preserved), while the stone foundations of the acropolis circuit were constructed in a coursed polygonal style (Fig. C6.5). The style varies considerably, ranging from large generally well-cut and well-fitted blocks to thin rectilinear-like slabs. Although the internal structure of the curtain is nowhere directly discernible, the mass of small stones visible in

[15] Meyer (1939a: 82). I would like to thank the 39th Ephorate of Prehistoric and Classical Antiquities for granting me a study permit to examine the remains of ancient Halous. Because much of the circuit was concealed by dense overgrowth, however, I was unable to make many useful measurements and had to rely instead on those made and published by Mayer (1939a: 78–82). Unless otherwise cited, all photographs and measurements are based on personal observation from my visits to the site in spring 2011.

places accumulated directly below the curtains strongly suggest that a core of packed rubble existed between the two faces. The thickness of the curtains is only 1.30 m.[16]

SUMMARY OF TACTICAL COMPONENTS

The acropolis circuit contains one semicircular (*c*.11 m diameter) and ten rectangular towers (*c*.5-6 m × 3 m), mostly regularly spaced at *c*.30–5 m intervals (see Fig. C6.4). No gates or posterns are preserved. A further complex of buildings that may have had a defensive function are located at the summit of the acropolis.

Towers

The fortification system at Halous includes at least eleven towers, all but one of which are rectangular in shape. With a few exceptions, the rectangular towers possess strikingly similar dimensions, with most measuring *c*.5–6 m in width and projecting *c*.3 m from the wall (see Fig. C6.5).[17] The towers do not appear to be bonded to the curtains. The towers also show regularity in their deployment, and most are spaced *c*.30–5 m apart except in the more vulnerable areas of the circuit, where the spacing is closer. Located at the southernmost point in

Fig. C6.5. Halous, polygonal masonry and rubble fill of Tower 5 (facing north-west). (© *Matthew Maher*)

---

[16] Meyer (1939a: 80). Presumably because of the dense overgrowth, Meyer was able to attain the thickness of the wall in only one place, specifically, in the section running north-east from the corner of Tower 11.

[17] All tower measurements taken from Meyer (1939a: 80).

the circuit is Tower 9, the only semicircular example at Halous. It projects 3.50 m from the surrounding curtains and has a radius of 5.70 m.

Gates

No gates or posterns are preserved.

COMMENTS

The final component of the city's defences is a complex of structures located within the circuit on the very summit of the hill. The principal building is a large rectangular structure with robust polygonal walls measuring 39.60 m long by 13.80 m wide.[18] Internally a transverse wall divides this building into two sections, measuring 17.10 m and 22.50 m in length (I and II respectively in Fig. C6.4).[19] Less than 5 m to the north-east of this structure is an isolated tower (III in Fig. C6.4). Measuring 7.30 by 6.0 m, the 0.65 m thick walls of this tower still stand to a height of 2 m.[20] Finally, a few metres lower and to the east of this tower is yet another tower-like edifice. Meyer describes this structure as being essentially comprised of two joined towers, each with walls 0.70 m thick and measuring 6 m in length with a width of 4.50 (IV and IVa in Fig. C6.4).[21] Axially aligned and attached to IV and IVa was another structure, measuring 9.80 m long (V in Fig. C6.4).[22] Meyer maintains that this complex of towers and buildings, taken together, represents a last line of defence, or, at the very least, served as an arsenal for the city's garrison.[23]

OVERALL DEFENSIVE PLANNING

The easiest way of gaining entrance to the acropolis at Halous today, as in antiquity, is by way of the gently sloping saddle located immediately north-east of the site. Because of its accessibility, proximity to the acropolis, and its relatively gentle terrain, this saddle remains a good candidate for the location of the main settlement at Halous. Alternatively, if people choose to clamber up

---

[18] Meyer (1939a: 80).   [19] Meyer (1939a: 80).
[20] Meyer (1939a: 80). The entrance to this tower was observed on its north-east side.
[21] Meyer (1939a: 80).   [22] Meyer (1939a: 80).
[23] Meyer (1939a: 80). This complex is discussed in greater detail under Overall Defensive Planning.

the steep south-east side of the hill, they will be immediately rewarded by a wealth of cultural material littering the slope at their feet.[24] It is this abundance of material that led Meyer to suppose that the lower city embraced both the upper slopes of the south-east side of the hill as well as the saddle to the north-east.[25] While the precise size of the main settlement will remain unknown without systematic archaeological survey or excavation, it is likely that 'Die Stadt ist also bedeutend größer als der Mauerring'.[26] If the residential area was smaller than the intramural area of the acropolis, we would, of course, expect to find the main settlement located within the acropolis walls.

A lower city surrounding the south-east and north-east sides, and within easy reach of a fortified acropolis, is a defensive strategy seen elsewhere in Arkadia.[27] As at those sites, the site chosen for the settlement of Halous demonstrates a conscious appreciation of the defensive advantages afforded by the immediate and peripheral topography of the area. Of the former, the hill is both easily defensible and accessible. Natural protection is provided by the Ladon River to the south and the Xerokaritena Valley and stream on the west, as these considerable obstacles have inherent defensive advantages. Furthermore, the mass of Mt Paliovouna to the north and the small spur stemming from it to the east of the site also ensured security from unwelcome advances towards the city from those directions. Moreover, the general position of Halous within the eastern part of the Ladon Valley also had its advantages.

Despite the fact that the damming of the Ladon has caused the water level to rise considerably, the main east–west artery through the valley in antiquity must have followed the general course of the river near the bottom of the valley. That the locals told Meyer of the existence of graves along the southern foot of the hill[28] suggests that, just as today, an ancient road might once have skirted this side of the site. Halous would have been very well positioned, therefore, to command such a route through the valley. Indeed, anyone gaining access to the eastern part of the Ladon Valley, whether from the direction of Paos and the Lopesi Valley to the north, from the direction of Kleitor in the north-east, from Kaphyai in the east, or from anywhere in central Arkadia to the south-east and south, would have had to pass by Halous. The fortuitous location of the hill, close to where the narrow western part of the Ladon Valley opens up, also ensured command of the route along the river from the west and the direction of Thaliades and Thelpousa. Finally,

---

[24] For example, although the surface vegetation was thick, I observed a plethora of roof tiles, several large pithoi fragments, and one identifiably Hellenistic black glazed echinus bowl fragment on this side of the hill.

[25] Meyer (1939a: 82).   [26] Meyer (1939a: 82).

[27] e.g., Nestane and Paos, Theisoa (at Karkalou), Dipaia, and perhaps also Kynaitha and Eutaia. For Kynaitha and Eutaia, see the Appendix.

[28] Meyer (1939a: 82).

the substantial height of the hill provided a considerable viewshed from which to observe an approach from any of these directions.

While the larger strategic decisions inherent in the relationship between the natural topography and the choice of site are clear, more subtle are the tactical considerations that functioned to make the site more defensible. The course of the acropolis enceinte was dictated by the contours and topography of the hill itself. As the trace was limited by the terrain in this way, the construction of substantial towers deployed at fairly regular intervals was necessary in order to safeguard all sides of the hill. Still, that some sides of the circuit were afforded greater protection suggests these parts were deemed more vulnerable than others. This is most apparent at the north-east part of the site, where not only is the largest tower in the system employed (Tower 5), but the distance separating the towers is the shortest. Such a concern is reasonable if the lower city was spread across the upper south-east slope and the north-east saddle. Such an array of closely spaced towers would have protected the most accessible route to the acropolis from all directions—protection both for citizens, if forced to retreat, and from any unwelcome company attempting to take the acropolis.

Although the inconsistent remains in certain sections of the circuit some-what constrain our understanding of the defensive planning envisioned by the architects of the fortification system at Halous, some deductions may be considered, however speculative.

Even though most of the circuit on the north-west side of the hill is no longer visible, from the patterns employed throughout the rest of the circuit it is reasonable to assume that it too would have included towers spaced at fairly regular intervals. We might also envision another semicircular tower north of the crest, where the wall radiating from Tower 11 meets that leaving Tower 1. The strategic placement of the semicircular Tower 9 in just such a junction on the south side ensured a 270° view. A strategic placement of a similarly shaped tower to the north, overlooking both the Xerokaritena Valley and the approach from the west, would have been equally advantageous.

If we apply the same line of reasoning employed for working out the probable location of the main settlement, it should follow that the main gate to the acropolis should be located nearby. A spot somewhere between Towers 6 and 7 immediately comes to mind. As alluded to above, the *c.*80 m distance between these two towers is the largest uninterrupted stretch in the circuit, and it is plausible that some defensive installation existed in this otherwise poorly preserved section.[29] A gate here would have met this requirement. Not only would it have been close to the settlement on the slopes immediately below and to the north-east, but an enemy approaching the gate from the saddle

---

[29] Surely placing a gate further west, between Towers 8 and 9, for example, would have been too far from the residential area of the settlement.

would have been compelled to advance (with his unshielded right side exposed) for some distance below the line of the wall.

Finally, it only remains to determine, if possible, the function(s) of the structures on the crest of the hill comprising the so-called acropolis complex. Lawrence appears to have no reservations about the function, asserting that the 'tall detached building [which] stood on the highest point of the acropolis of Halus in Arcadia... may, like the towers inside forts and camps, have been used chiefly for signaling'.[30] Perhaps that was one component, but such a set of structures must have had additional uses. Although independent of the main circuit, the complex referred to as I, II, and III on Meyer's plan does generally resemble the citadel of Alipheira and may have had a similar function.[31] Specifically, it is conceivable that it could have been both a barracks for soldiers on watch, as well as a last line of defence if the main circuit had been breached. In this interpretation, Tower III, built on the highest point on the site, would have been well situated to protect the citadel and at an appropriate elevation for signaling, as suggested by Lawrence. The structures labeled IV, IVa, and V on the plan are more problematic—not least because Meyer refers to them as 'Türme'.[32] Instead of three separate 'towers', which makes little sense in this context—especially placed less than 7 m away from Tower III—this complex is better suited as a single structure and is perhaps better understood as a utility building for the citadel and/or, as Meyer suggests, an arsenal for the storage and maintenance of weapons.[33]

CHRONOLOGICAL SUMMARY

From historical probability and architectural affinities, it would seem that the entire circuit surrounding the *polis* of Halous was probably constructed *c.*400–350 BC.

CHRONOLOGICAL ARGUMENTS

The Hellenistic pottery observed by Meyer[34] and corroborated by the author strongly suggests that the settlement of Halous, if not the fortifications, were in place by that time. Determining when the walls were constructed, however, is less obvious. By comparing the towers with analogous examples at Heraklea and Athens, Meyer believes the circuit at Halous was built sometime in the

---

[30] Lawrence (1979: 440).   [31] Cf. Fig. C2.5.   [32] Meyer (1939a: 81).
[33] Meyer (1939a: 81).   [34] Meyer (1939a: 82).

fourth century BC.[35] The cumulative evidence not only supports this date, but can also help narrow down the building period to a more specific chronological range within this century. For instance, coursed polygonal masonry, Scranton tells us, was 'particularly favoured'[36] in the western Peloponnese during the fourth century BC. Particularly significant here is that the surviving examples suggest that, by the late fourth or early third century BC, this style of masonry had all but run its course.[37] Although hardly indicative in their own right, the polygonal walls of Halous do fall into this category. Arguably more convincing, however, is the evidence provided by the layout of the circuit and its composite parts.

Winter calls attention to an interesting trend in Greek fortifications, noting that, during the later fourth century BC and the Hellenistic period on the Greek mainland, 'it is not uncommon to find the circuit of a city reduced in extent'.[38] Thus, as exemplified at Halous, fortification systems of these periods were often more compact and better provided with natural or artificial defences than had been the case in the fifth and earlier fourth centuries BC.[39] Furthermore, in response to the advances in siege warfare, at the end of the fifth century BC the regular and systematic use of towers became common features in Greek fortifications. By the second half of the fourth century BC, we know that artillery had found its true place as a defensive rather than an offensive weapon, and the mounting of these machines had become the most important function of towers.[40] In the first half of the century, however, before the common use of tension artillery and the invention of torsion machines, towers were often much smaller (that is, first generation). That the towers at Halous are frequent yet relatively small, and are deployed with spacing comparable to Stymphalos, Mantineia, and Alea, for example, suggests that they were built after the invention of artillery, but before its widespread use—that is, during the first half of the fourth century BC.

Finally, there is another interesting feature of the relationship between Tower 5 and the adjoining curtains: this tower is not bonded to the curtains behind. Construction of towers that stand independently from the curtain was largely a precautionary measure linked to advances in siege warfare. Certainly by the second quarter of the fourth century BC, 'when mining, rams, and artillery were all in common use, the inadvisability of bonding towers and curtains together would have been quite evident'.[41] For this reason, a lack of bonding between the towers and curtains points to a date no earlier than the late fifth century BC, or perhaps even the first half of the fourth century BC, and

---

[35] Meyer (1939a: 81)—a date corroborated in his opinion by the discovery of a sherd from a fourth-century BC black-glazed Attic cup.
[36] Scranton (1941: 51).   [37] Scranton (1941: 50).   [38] Winter (1971a: 114).
[39] Winter (1971a: 115).   [40] Winter (1971a: 156, 165, 167).
[41] Winter (1971a: 167, n. 51).

certainly does not necessarily indicate a Hellenistic date.[42] Ultimately, when the polygonal masonry, the systematic use of small, regularly spaced towers, and the example of an unbonded tower are all taken together, they represent a body of evidence that strongly suggests that the fortifications at ancient Halous were constructed in the first half of the fourth century BC.

BIBLIOGRAPHY

Paus. 8.25.2; Gell (1817: 121); Leake (1830: ii. 272; 1846: 228); Boblaye (1836: 156); Curtius (1851: 374); Frazer (1898: iv. 287); Bölte (1912a: 2286); Meyer (1939a: 78–82); Lawrence (1979: 440, n. 10); Jost (1985: 42, 45–6; 1999: 196); Papachatzis (1994: 276–7); Nielsen (2002: 555); Maher (2012a: 367–87).

[42] Winter (1971a: 167, n. 51).

7

Kleitor, Northern Arkadia

LOCATION

Located in northern Arkadia, the city of Kleitor can be found in the western part of basin defined by mountains on all sides (Fig. C7.1). The settlement is laid out on a generally flat plain between two rivers. The intramural area comprised the main area of inhabitation.

POLIS STATUS

The collective use of the city ethnic can be found employed both internally and externally.[1] The city began minting coins around the middle of the fifth century BC,[2] and an inscription from the early third century BC records a long list of the city's *proxenoi*.[3] Another inscription tells us a *theorodokos* from Argos resided at Kleitor in *c.*330 BC.[4] The city boasted two Olympic victors from the early fourth century BC.[5]

HISTORY

According to an Archaic dedication from Olympia observed and recorded by Pausanias, some time in the sixth century BC the citizens of Kleitor erected a statue of Zeus to whom a tithe was dedicated from the spoils taken 'from many cities [they had] reduced by force'.[6] Kleitor was a member of

---

[1] Attested internally on fifth-century BC coins (Head 1963: 446) and externally as implied by Xenophon (*Hell.* 5.4.36).

[2] Head (1963: 446).   [3] *IG* V.2 368.   [4] *SEG* xxiii. 189.II.22.

[5] *Olympionikai,* nos 395 and 406; for a more detailed catalogue of all the evidence, see Nielsen (2002: 560–2)

[6] Paus. 5.23.7.

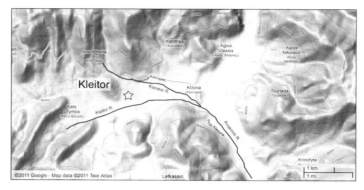

Fig. C7.1. Kleitor, topographical map of area. (© *2011 Google-Map data © 2011 Tele Atlas*)

the Peloponnesian League,[7] a leading member of the Arkadian League,[8] and, later, a member of the Achaian League.[9] In 379 BC, during the Theban war with Sparta, Kleitorian mercenaries fought alongside the forces of Kleomenes in the hostilities directed against Orchomenos.[10] Finally, when, during the Social War, Kleitor refused to abandon its alliance with the Achaian league, Aitolian forces besieged the city, but, upon 'meeting with a bold and determined resistance from the inhabitants',[11] the Aitolian army abandoned its attempt to take Kleitor.[12]

LOCAL TOPOGRAPHY

The ancient site of Kleitor stands on the flat plain at the western end of a small valley in north-central Arkadia (see Fig. C7.1).[13] The territory of Kleitor, encompassing an estimated 625 km², was considerably larger than that of its closest neighbours.[14] The immediate *chora* of the city, however, was comprised of the valley in which it was located. This valley is not particularly large,

---

[7] Xen. *Hell.* 5.4.36–7.   [8] *IG* V.2 1.52.   [9] Polyb. 4.19.
[10] Xen. *Hell.* 5.4.36. Jost (1999: 227) raises the interesting idea that it was the expansion policy of Orchomenos over Methydrion, Teuthis, and Thisoa (Karkalou) that might have been the cause of the war between Orchomenos and Kleitor.
[11] Polyb. 4.19.
[12] See Maher (2015b: 86–8) for the history of scholarship on the site.
[13] Today, the area is part of the prefecture of Achaia, not Arkadia. Much of the following geographical description appears in Maher (2015b: 88–90).
[14] This estimate is based on the map in Jost (1985: pl. 1), and includes the territories of Lousoi, Paos, Thaliades, and Halous. Such an estimate is probably too high, as it is not even certain whether these *poleis* were dependencies of Kleitor before the Roman period (Nielsen 2002: 560).

Fig. C7.2. Kleitor, topographical map of area and territory. (© *2011 Google-Map data © 2011 Tele Atlas*)

measuring *c*.6 km from east to west and 1.50 km north to south, and is surrounded on all sides by hills. While the hills to the south and west of the valley are relatively low, the hills bordering the north of the valley are more impressive, reaching heights of over 600 m above the plain. The lower slopes of Mt Chelmos, which rise steeply from the plain reaching heights of over 1000 m, define the east and north-east parts of the valley. East of the city, at the foot of this chain, the Kleitor Valley opens onto the Aroanios Valley, where the river flows south to meet the Ladon on its east–west course. The mountainous terrain defining the territory of Kleitor also served to separate it from that of the surrounding *poleis* (Fig. C7.2). The hills to the north and east marked the boundary between Kleitor and Kynaitha and Paos respectively, while those to the west separated Kleitor from Phenean territory.

Ancient Kleitor lies on the nearly completely flat plain at the western end of its valley, where, like ancient Stymphalos, the city occupies almost the complete width of available land. As such, it is separated by only *c*.250 m from the hills to the north, by less than 150 m from the eastern slope of Pantelemona Hill to the west, and, in places, by less than 150 m from the hills to the south. While to the west of the city, on the other side of Pantelemona, there is some arable land (*c*.100 ha), the majority of the farmland, some 500 ha, lies east of the city. Today, as in antiquity, these fields were supplied by two primary water sources: the Kleitor and the Karnesi Rivers (see Fig. C7.1). The former runs parallel to and just south of the city, and the latter in a north-west to south-east direction to the north and east of the city. These rivers meet just outside the south-east limit of the settlement before heading south-east to meet the Aroanios River.

Although there is little surviving evidence of the ancient road network traversing the territory of Kleitor, the topography does suggest a number of

Fig. C7.3. Kleitor, the site (facing north-east). (© *Matthew Maher*)

possibilities.[15] There must have been a road leading over the mountains from Pheneos to the Aroanios River Valley. Not only was this the route taken by Pausanias, but Gell observed 'traces of an ancient road' on his journey from Lykouria to Kleitor.[16] Where exactly on this route he noticed this road remains unclear, but somewhere in the Aroanios Valley seems as good a candidate as any, as this route provided the easiest means of communication between Kleitor and Pheneos, Kaphyai, and north-eastern Arkadia beyond. Furthermore, the identification of two of the city gates—one in the north-west and one in the west of the circuit—is also suggestive. While the former lies south of another narrow river valley, leading north towards ancient Kynaitha (modern Kalavryta), the latter was ideally positioned to provide access to the western end of the valley, and, ultimately, to the Ladon Valley, and the cities of Paos and Psophis to the south-west.[17]

NATURAL DEFENCES

The low heights offered by Kontra Hill on the south provide the site with its natural defences. The surrounding mountains limit the main approaches to the site to routes from the east and south-west (Fig. C7.3). The city is flanked on the north by the Karnesi River, on the south by the Kleitor River, and on the east by the bulk of Pantelemona Hill.

---

[15] See Pikoulas (1999c) for more detail about the road network and extra-urban defence installations.

[16] Gell (1817: 130).

[17] Jost (1985: 38) notes the strategic and communicative importance of these river valleys.

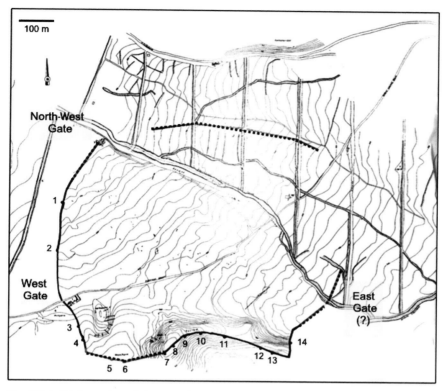

Fig. C7.4. Kleitor, plan of the site after Petritaki (2005: fig. 1). (© *Norwegian Institute in Athens*)

FORTIFICATION TYPE

Uneven type.[18] Although the vast majority of the extant circuit was constructed on flat terrain and encircled equally flat terrain, the southern sections of the wall engage a small rise (known as Kontra Hill) characterized by its two low conical peaks, each rising to a height of less than 20 m (Fig. C7.4). There was no formal acropolis.[19]

---

[18] Listed as a 'villes de plain' type by Jost (1999: 203).
[19] Jost (1999: 203). For a detailed description of the trace of the circuit, see Maher (2015b: 90–2).

PRESERVATION

The site is poorly preserved for the most part; traces of the east and south sides are visible. The north side has completely disappeared. The length of the total circuit is estimated to be *c*.2,500–3,000 m, with an intramural area of *c*.58 ha.[20]

CONSTRUCTION

The foundations of the walls are about 4.25–4.50 m thick throughout, and comprised of isodomic courses of trapezoidal blocks (Fig. C7.5).[21] All the curtain and tower foundations in the circuit once supported a mudbrick superstructure (not preserved). The curtain consists of an inner and outer facing of blocks with regularly spaced perpendicular courses of stone forming compartments within. Excavations have demonstrated that the fill largely consists of densely packed rubble.[22]

Fig. C7.5. Kleitor, trapezoidal masonry of the North-West Gate (facing north-east). (© *Matthew Maher*)

---

[20] Petritaki (1996: 88). This is an estimate, as the course of most of the northern stretch of the city wall is lost. Still, there appears to be no consensus on the size of the intramural area. Jost (1985: 40) and Winter (1989: 189, n. 2) suggest an area of 28 ha—a number apparently based on the belief that the missing northern part of the walls followed the modern course of the Karnesi River. Even Petritaki is not consistent, providing an area of 145 acres (= 58 ha) in one publication (1996: 88) and 1.90 km² (= 190 ha) in another (2005: 351). From the conjectured line of the northern wall on Petritaki's plan, however, the figure of 58 ha appears to be the most accurate.

[21] From a German Institute photograph, Scranton (1941: 171) classifies the walls of Kleitor as isodomic trapezoidal.

[22] Petritaki (2005: 351). Prior to the excavation, Winter (1989: 198) had argued the internal fill was probably comprised of solid blocks.

SUMMARY OF TACTICAL COMPONENTS

Fourteen towers, all semicircular (*c*.7.50–8.50 m in diameter), are preserved in the circuit, strategically, rather than regularly, spaced (see Fig. C7.4). Ten are located on the high ground in the south, and four along the east side. Two gates are attested on the east side, one a simple frontal opening type gate, the other a monumental gatecourt type. No posterns are preserved.

Towers

The southern section of the circuit can be traced for *c*.1.50 km, and has been found to contain fourteen towers. Regardless of their location in the circuit, all the towers are semicircular.[23] With an average diameter of 7.50–8.50 m, these towers project *c*.4 m from the adjacent curtains (Fig. C7.6).[24] Although their foundations are largely constructed in a manner similar to the socle of the curtains, they were built to stand independently of them.[25] These towers are strategically, rather than regularly spaced; ten are located on the high ground in the south, and four along the east side.

Gates

While there are no evidence for posterns in the surviving sections of the city wall, two and possibly three gates are attested.[26] The North-West Gate, aligned

Fig. C7.6. Kleitor, semicircular
Tower 8 (facing north-west).
(© *Matthew Maher*)

---

[23] See Winter (1971a: 193, n. 110).   [24] Winter (1989: 198).
[25] Petritaki (2005: 353, fig. 1).
[26] Interestingly, as noted by Petritaki (2005: 354–5), the locations of the two established gates are still traversed today by small rural roads.

Catalogue

Fig. C7.7. Kleitor, North-West Gate (facing east).
(© *Matthew Maher*)

Fig. C7.8. Kleitor, southern half of West Gate (facing north-east).
(© *Matthew Maher*)

on a north-west–south-east axis, appears from the plan to have been a simple frontal gate and had at least two different building phases (Fig. C7.7).[27]

Located some 600 m south of the North-West Gate, at the foot of Pantele-mona Hill, excavations have revealed the southern half of the West Gate (Fig. C7.8).[28] Oriented on an east–west axis, the West Gate was of the gatecourt

---

[27] Petritaki (2005: 354). It is unclear from the plan whether a tower flanked the left side of the opening, though I suspect that this is the case.
[28] The southern half of this gate is preserved, from which the form of the other half can be extrapolated (Petritaki 2005: 354).

type. Essentially a large rectangle, it was accessed externally by a small frontal opening in the wall, which in turn led to two separate courts.[29] The outer court was protected by a small semicircular protrusion on the south, on which defenders could mass, and was separated from the inner court by a small door.[30] Also on the south side, excavators found the remains of four column bases, suggesting a propylon-like entrance for pedestrians, as well as traces of a ramp for carts.[31] Like the North-West Gate, excavations have revealed at least two phases of construction on the West Gate.[32] Finally, the discovery of an ancient cemetery just outside the south-east part of the circuit, where the walls meet the bed of the Karnesi River, has been taken as evidence for the possible existence of a third gate in this area.[33]

COMMENTS

Winter proposes that the 'towers in the plain were generally *c*.35 m apart, but at times under 30 m—in any case more closely set than at either Mantineia or Orchomenos'.[34] This assessment, however, must be approached with caution, as there is an inherent problem with his evaluation. This problem derives from the fact that Winter employs a revised version of Papandreou's plan of the walls, which, in turn, is based on that of Le Bas and Reinach—both of which, unfortunately, are incorrect.[35] While Winter adjusts the inflated scale of the plan, he seems to follow the number and spacing of the towers portrayed. The most recent plan published by Petritaki, however, tells a decidedly different story.[36] For example, Tower 1 and Tower 2 are spaced *c*.160 m apart, with the former located *c*.220 m south of the North-West Gate and the latter *c*.180 m from the West Gate. Moreover, approximately 80 m from the West Gate is Tower 3 and Tower 4, themselves separated by 40 m. The towers on the eastern half of Kontra Hill are the only ones that show any regularity in their spacing, averaging between 35 and 45 m.

---

[29] Petritaki (2005:354).   [30] Petritaki (2005: 354).   [31] Petritaki (2005: 354).
[32] Petritaki (2005: 353–4).   [33] Petritaki (2005: 354–5).
[34] Winter (1989: 198). Even if the towers at Kleitor were spaced 30–5 m apart, Winter is wrong in his assertion that they are more closely set than those at Mantineia, which are spaced on average 25–6 m apart.
[35] Papandreou (1920: 113); Le Bas and Reinach (1888: pl. 34). For an even earlier yet accurate plan of Kleitor, see Leake (1830: ii. 258). On the problems with Papandreou's plan, see Meyer (1939a: 109–10) and Winter (1989: 189, n. 1). For a detailed assessment about the inconsistencies in the mapping of the fortifications of Kleitor over the centuries, see Maher (2015b).
[36] Petritaki (2005: fig. 1).

OVERALL DEFENSIVE PLANNING

The decisions to found the settlement at its present location and eventually to construct a sizeable fortification circuit were not made lightly nor arbitrarily. In fact, the valley, the location of the city within it, and the fortifications were individual elements, which, when taken together, operated to ensure the security of the inhabitants. The overall defensive planning that incorporated these elements was dictated largely by the strategic and tactical considerations that were both typical of the time and intrinsic to the natural topography of the Kleitor Valley.

The location of the valley itself played no small part in the history of the city, as it occupied a valuable strategic sector of Northern Arkadia.[37] Its location not only commanded an important north–south route between central Arkadia and Achaia and the coast, but also the eastern end of the Sireos River Valley— a significant east–west passage running the length of northern Arkadia between the Pheneos Valley and Elis. In order to complement the commercial and strategic importance of the valley, the city was ideally situated for controlling the traffic through the territory. Located towards the western end of the valley, occupying almost its entire breadth, the city was positioned so that traffic progressing along the most accessible routes from both Kynaitha to the north and Paos to the south-west would have had to pass through—or at least very near—the city itself. Although the immediate commercial and strategic benefits of this arrangement are evident, ultimately the defensive considerations were paramount. Accordingly, and as usual, it was the considerable natural defences immediately surrounding the site itself that must have been the decisive factors in the architects' evaluation and eventual choice of this location in which to build and fortify their city.

Foremost among the natural defences of the valley are the two rivers, the Kleitor and the Karnesi. The River Kleitor, originating in the south-west corner of the valley, skirts the southern part of the valley (and the ancient site) in a north-easterly direction (see Fig. C7.1). The Karnesi originates north-west of the site, near the modern village of Ano Klitoria, following a south-easterly course. The confluence of these two rivers is located less than half a kilometre from the south-east limits of the ancient settlement. Kleitor is well situated in the fork caused by the course of these two rivers. The course of the Kleitor River has altered little (if at all) from its course in antiquity, and must always have formed a natural defensive barrier on the south side of the city.

---

[37] Winter (1989: 198) maintains that the importance of this valley 'was responsible for its survival as a city down to the time of Pausanias and beyond'. Excavation and survey suggest that Kleitor remained an important trading centre throughout the Roman period, and the administrative nucleus probably moved east, to the site of the present village Kleitoria in the early Medieval period (Petritaki 1996: 88).

The ancient course of the Karnesi, on the other hand, presents more uncertainty. Although almost every published plan of the site shows the remains of the fortifications extending to the north of this river,[38] Winter maintains that the river 'must have coincided, more or less, with the line of the walls in the northeast sector of the city'.[39] The most recent work on the site, however, has traced much of the elusive northern part of the circuit, demonstrating not only that the city was larger than previously thought, but that in antiquity the course of the Karnesi River was further to the north.[40] Thus, although he had mistakenly judged the present course of the river to be the same as in antiquity, Winter was correct in his assertion that the fortifications must have coincided with the course of the river.

Nestled in the angle between these two rivers, Kleitor was provided with natural defences on its north, east, and south sides. Similar consideration of the defensive advantages inherent in the topography of the valley is also evident in other parts of the circuit. For example, although the west side of the city was devoid of any rivers, it was not devoid of natural defences. Here, the bulk of Pantelemona Hill, towering some 100 m above the city along its entire western flank, formed an effective natural obstruction in this direction.[41] The inclusion of the low Kontra Hill into the overall defensive scheme of the city was also strategically significant.

In their choice for the location of the site—one surrounded on all sides by hills and rivers—the town planners effectively exploited the natural topography of the valley to a considerable strategic advantage. We see in the extant fortifications and its constituent parts tactical considerations designed both to complement the natural strength of the site and to limit its weaknesses. On the west section of the circuit between the two gates, for example, we find only two towers (Towers 1 and 2). The relative lack of man-made defences along this stretch suggests the confidence inspired by the Pantelemona Hill in keeping enemies at a distance from the walls. The dimensions of this hill meant that any approach to the city from the west would be limited to a narrow stretch of land (*c.*400 m wide) defined by the southern slope of Pantelemona Hill and the north bank of the Kleitor River. Without the protection of a river or natural elevation, this section was the most vulnerable part of the circuit south of the

---

[38] The exception is Leake's plan (1830: ii. 258). Nonetheless, beyond where he thought the northern trace of the circuit wall was located, he did observe ancient remains in the 'the whole cultivated plain included between the river of Klitora and the river of Karnesi' (Leake 1830: ii. 258–9).

[39] Winter (1989: 198). The same opinion is implied by Leake (1846: 224). It is these arguments that may account for Winter's (and others') underestimation of the area of the intramural space (e.g., Meyer (1939a: 109–10; Jost 1985: 40; Winter 1989: 189).

[40] Petritaki (2005: 352–3).

[41] A hill of this elevation and proximity to the city not only formed an effective defensive barrier, but would also have been offensively advantageous if held by an enemy. In times of danger, therefore, control of this hill must have been of primary importance.

North-West Gate. It is with an aim to protect this approach, therefore, that the south-western and southern sections of the circuit were devoted.

In the short stretch of wall south of the West Gate, in the section immediately opposite this narrow western approach, there were two closely set semicircular towers. While Tower 3 was placed close enough to provide enfilading for the approach on the West Gate, and Tower 4 was in a position to cover a more southerly approach towards Kontra Hill, the semicircular shape of both towers also ensured 180° coverage of the open terrain immediately opposite them—that is, the 400 m wide stretch of land comprising any western approach. If an aggressor was so bold as to attempt to skirt these south-western defences and challenge Kontra Hill directly by sticking close to the banks of the Kleitor River, they would find themselves confronted by the most intimidating part of the city defences.[42] Indeed, the relationship between the topography of the site and the fortifications of Kleitor was at its most effective in the defences of Kontra Hill.

An approach from the west along the southern part of the city would first be met by two more semicircular towers (Towers 5 and 6). Artillery from these towers would have easily covered the short strip of land between the walls and the Kleitor River. To the north-west of these towers lies Kontra Hill, which, although rising to a height of less than 20 m, was tactically crucial to the southern defences of the city.

This hill, roughly crescent shaped, rises steeply to its highest point on its western end, before descending gradually towards the north-east and then the south-east. The fortifications follow the general contours of the hill and include five regularly spaced towers (Towers 7 to 11), followed by three more at the lower south-eastern section of the hill (Towers 12 to 14). As this hill rises almost directly from the north bank of the Kleitor River, there exists only the narrowest sliver of practicably traversable land between it and the river. Thus, anyone approaching from the west would be forced to navigate the bottleneck effect produced by the hill and its imposing artillery towers on one side and the river on the other.[43] Although this hill cannot be considered an acropolis in the normal sense, the advantage taken of the high ground in this part of the circuit suggests the defences of Kontra Hill were 'intended primarily to block assault from that quarter, while still controlling the route along the valley of the Kleitor river'.[44]

---

[42] It might seem strange at first glance that no tower was placed in the south-west corner of the circuit where the western wall meets the southern stretch. The theoretical 180° field of fire provided by the towers' semicircular shape, however, suggests that this area of the wall would have been sufficiently protected by both Tower 4 and Tower 5.

[43] This relationship between the natural topography and the fortifications is paralleled at the approach towards the Pheneos Gate at ancient Stymphalos.

[44] Winter (1989: 198).

The discussion of Kleitor's defensive planning has thus far been limited to the areas south of the modern course of the Karnesi River, where the surviving sections of the fortifications are known. Of the largely lost north and north-eastern sections of the circuit, I can only conjecture. It is certain, however, that these parts of the fortifications traversed level and open ground. If the original course of the Karnesi River did more or less follow the walls north and north-east of the city, we might expect to see the use of bridges and/or gates in a arrangement similar to that at Mantineia or Stymphalos. Moreover, as demonstrated at other Arkadian sites, the use of regularly spaced rectangular or semicircular towers in this area would be equally viable options. At Mantineia and Stymphalos, for example, we see rectangular towers protecting the open and flat areas beyond the fortifications. And from Psophis and Stymphalos it is clear that the use of semicircular or rectangular towers within the same circuit was not uncommon. Finally, whether predominantly rectangular or curvilinear towers were installed along the flat parts of the circuit, the chronology of the fortifications at Kleitor suggest the possibility that one or more large artillery bastions, characteristic of the Hellenistic period, may have enhanced this, now lost, part of the city defences.

CHRONOLOGICAL SUMMARY

Historical probability, external evidence, and architectural affinities all suggest that the fortifications of ancient Kleitor are among the youngest in Arkadia, having been constructed sometime in the late fourth or early third century BC.

CHRONOLOGICAL ARGUMENTS

In his brief survey of the fortifications of Kleitor published in 1989, Winter maintains that 'the walls of Kleitor are obviously quite different in concept from these of either Mantineia or Orchomenos'.[45] He is, of course, correct. Mantineia was a city almost twice the size of Kleitor, laid out completely on flat ground, and which employed predominately rectangular towers, while the fortifications of Orchomenos were limited to the acropolis of Kalpaki Hill, incorporated no open terrain, and were considerably shorter in overall length. The circuit of Kleitor, although largely laid out in the plain, did assimilate some high ground, contained only semicircular towers, and extended for a

---

[45] Winter (1989: 196).

considerable length. Still, it is difficult to understand how, in his attempt to establish a chronology of the walls based on these perceived differences, Winter reaches the conclusion that 'that the defensive system [of Kleitor] is much more sophisticated in design than anything at either Mantineia or Orchomenos'.[46] In fact, although the system at Kleitor demonstrates a conscientious defensive plan characterized by its efficient use of the natural topography, I would argue that there is nothing original nor especially sophisticated about it.[47]

For example, the use of rivers or streams as natural defensive boundaries have many regional parallels in Northern Arkadia, including at Stymphalos, Psophis, and Paos. Similarly, if the Karnesi River did originally flow immediately outside the northern and eastern walls of Kleitor, then its function as an outwork is analogous to the use of the Ophis at Mantineia. The incorporation of some elevated terrain in a circuit otherwise laid out over predominately flat and open ground is also the strategy employed at Stymphalos. The use of only circular towers throughout the circuit, moreover, can be seen in the remains of nearby Pheneos. As for the curtains, not only is the masonry used similar to that at Mantineia, but Winter himself admits that the curtains at Kleitor are 'about the same thickness as at Mantineia'.[48] Finally, even the gatecourt at Kleitor—the circuit's most distinctive feature—has parallels at Mantineia and Stymphalos. Owing to the archaeological data, the written sources, and appropriate comparanda, however, establishing a plausible chronology for the walls of Kleitor is not without hope.

We know from Polybius that, in 220/219 BC, the Aitolians carried out an unsuccessful siege of the city of Kleitor.[49] It is safe to assume, therefore, that the fortifications as they exist today were probably in place by that time. Although this account provides a convenient *terminus ante quem*, it does not answer the question of when the circuit was constructed. During the excavation of parts of the West Gate, Petritaki discovered two building phases, both of which were identified as belonging to the Hellenistic period.[50] Although admitting the difficulties she encountered in dating the earliest phase, using the principles of the typology and evolution of siege warfare, Petritaki tentatively dates the initial phase of construction to the late fourth century BC.[51] This date is fairly consistent with excavations of other parts of the curtain (and at least one tower), which again, she maintains belong to the Hellenistic period.[52]

---

[46] Winter (1989: 198).

[47] For arguments why this statement by Winter must have been the result of the problematic plan of the fortifications he employed, see Maher (2015b: 98–100).

[48] Winter (1989: 198).   [49] Polyb. 4.19.   [50] Petritaki (2005: 353–4).

[51] Petritaki (2005: 354).   [52] Petritaki (2005: 354).

Petritaki seems to follow the opinion of Winter, who is more specific in his analysis, stating that the towers of Kleitor are of the second-generation type and should not pre-date *c*.300 BC.[53] Although the problems of Winter's assessment of the tower spacing have been touched on already (and are discussed in detail elsewhere[54]), of those towers he did observe he correctly states that they are indeed larger than those of Mantineia and Orchomenos.[55] To add further weight to his argument for the existence of second-generation towers, Winter observed at 'the southeast angle…a large battery [12 m wide], perhaps of pentagonal plan'.[56] Unfortunately, he is no more specific as to its precise location, and no other published source mentions this installation. Nonetheless, although we may differ on the details, I think that Winter is essentially correct in his belief that the topography of the area indicates that the people of Kleitor relied on a fortification system that permitted extensive use of defensive artillery for their security.[57] Therefore, while it may be hard to imagine that the city remained unfortified throughout the Classical period, the available evidence suggests that the original circuit does belong to the Early Hellenistic period. More specifically, as it is consistent with the archeological, typological, and literary evidence, I would recommend a date sometime in the late fourth or early third century.

BIBLIOGRAPHY

Xen. *Hell.* 5.4.36-37; Polyb. 4.19; Strab. 8.8.2; Paus. 5.23.7, 8.21.1–4; Gell (1817: 130); Dodwell (1819: ii. 442–4); Leake (1830: ii. 257–9); Boblaye (1836: 156–7); Curtius (1851: i. 374–7); Bursian (1862: ii. 263–4); Le Bas and Reinach (1888: pl. 34); Frazer (1898: iv. 264–7); Hiller von Gaertringen and Lattermann (1911: 7–8); Papandreou (1920: 96–114); Meyer (1939a: 109–10); Scranton (1941: 171); Winter (1971a: 39, n. 90, 193, n. 110; 1989: 196–9; 1997: 260); Jost (1985: 38–46; 1999: 203); Petritaki (1987, 1988, 1989, 1991, 1992, 1993, 1996, 2005); Papachatzis (1994: 253–6); Nielsen (2002: 560-562); Maher (2012a: 240–62; 2015b).

[53] Winter (1989: 199). For the number and type of artillery machines these towers may have housed, see Winter (1997: 260).
[54] Maher (2015b: 98–100).
[55] Winter (1989: 199). Furthermore, the towers at Kleitor are also larger than the semicircular towers at both Stymphalos and Pheneos.
[56] Winter (1989: 198, n. 24). In a later article, Winter (1997: 260) says 'the structure at the SE angle of the circuit may have been an artillery battery, perhaps over 10.00 m. wide'.
[57] Winter (1989: 199).

8

Mantineia, Eastern Arkadia

LOCATION

The ancient city of Mantineia is located in eastern Arkadia near the eastern edge of a vast plain in a basin (with *katavothroi*) defined by mountains on all sides (Fig. C8.1). The settlement is situated on flat terrain and surrounded by a river. The intramural area comprised the main area of inhabitation.

POLIS STATUS

Mantineia was not only one of the five *megalai poleis* of ancient Arkadia described by Pseudo-Skylax; it is also arguably the one best historically documented.[1] As Mantineia was unquestionably a *polis* in the political sense, a comprehensive listing of the extensive evidence for such is wasted here.[2]

HISTORY

An artificial foundation, Mantineia was created by the political and physical synoikism of four or five small villages sometime in the late sixth or early fifth century BC.[3] Mantineia was a member of the Greek alliance against Persia, and in 480 BC contributed 500 hoplites at the Battle of Thermopylai.[4] Later, the city was a member of the Peloponnesian League,[5] but in 421 BC Mantineia defected from the League, entering instead into an alliance with Argos, Athens,

---

[1] Ps.-Skylax 44. The others being Stymphalos, Orchomenos, Tegea, and Heraia.
[2] For a comprehensive summary of all the evidence pointing to Mantineia's political status as a *polis*, see Nielsen (2002: 567–72).
[3] Strab. 8.3.2.
[4] Hdt. 7.202. Incidentally, the Mantineians arrived too late to participate at Plataia.
[5] Thuc. 5.29.2; Xen. *Hell.* 5.2.3.

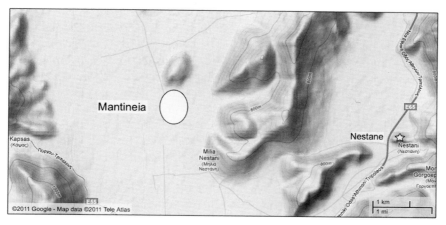

Fig. C8.1. Mantineia, topographical map of area. (© *2011 Google-Map data © 2011 Tele Atlas*)

and Elis.[6] After three years, the city was again brought into the Spartan fold following its defeat at the first Battle of Mantineia in 418 BC.[7] In 385 BC, the Spartans sacked the city by digging a trench around the city's mudbrick fortifications, into which they diverted the adjacent Ophis River. As the trench filled with water, the level rose and eventually undermined the mudbrick superstructure of the city's fortification.[8] The tearing-down of the walls and a forced dioikism of its inhabitants to their ancestral villages were among the conditions imposed on Mantineia by the Spartans.[9]

Following Sparta's defeat at Leuktra in 371 BC, the scattered Mantineians, perhaps with Theban assistance,[10] were synoikized again and returned to rebuild their city (and city walls) so recently destroyed by the Spartans.[11] Around the same time, the Arkadians were moving towards the foundation of the Confederacy, a process in which Mantineia performed a leading and instrumental role.[12] The same Mantineia would also play a major role in the

---

[6] Thuc. 5.29.1.

[7] Thuc. 5.81.1. For a detailed historical analysis of this, the largest land battle of the Peloponnesian War, see Kagan (2003: 228–50).

[8] Xen. *Hell.* 5.2.5.

[9] That is, they returned to the four or five *komai* that comprised the settlements that had participated in the original synoikism of the late Archaic/early Classical period. See Demand (1990: 67–9). Pausanias (8.8.9) maintains that the Spartans left a small part of the city inhabited.

[10] For the argument against Theban involvement in the second synoikism of Mantineia, see Demand (1990: 109–10).

[11] They also wisely diverted the course of the Ophis River from its previous one, passing through the city to a new course circumventing the city—and thus from a strategic liability into an additional measure of protection (Xen. *Hell.* 5.2.7).

[12] For a brief historical summary of the synoikism and the role played by Mantineia, see Maher (2015a: 17–18).

splitting of the Arkadian Confederacy just a few years later. In 362 BC, parts of Arkadia, with Mantineia at its head, jealous of the rising power of Megalopolis and Tegea, deserted the Arkadian League and joined in treaty with Athens and Sparta.[13] In response to Tegea's appeal to Thebes for support, Epaminondas advanced south and, with his Tegean-led Arkadians, Argive, Messenian, and Boeotian allies, took the field against the Spartans and their allied forces of Elis, Athens, and the Mantineia-led faction of Arkadians.[14] Although the Thebans were victorious in the second Battle of Mantineia, this battle, meant to decide the hegemony over the Peloponnese, resulted in 'even more confusion and disorder in Greece after the battle than before',[15] and ultimately paved the way for Macedonian conquest.

In the early years of the Hellenistic period, Mantineia, like Megalopolis, appears to have been the leading city of a diminished confederacy.[16] Soon after joining the Achaian League, the city fell for a short time into the hands of Kleomenes and the Spartans before being recovered by Aratos.[17] Finally, in 222 BC, the city revolted against Macedonian control and was destroyed by Antigonos III. Resettled by the Achaian League, an ally of Macedon in 221 BC, the city was renamed Antigoneia, a name that it retained until the second century AD.[18]

LOCAL TOPOGRAPHY

The *polis* of Mantineia is located approximately in the centre of its territory, which comprises the northern half of Arkadia's great eastern plain (see Fig. C8.1). In its entirety, this plain is roughly hourglass-shaped, with the narrow middle section representing the boundary between the plains of Tegea to the south and Mantineia to the north (Fig. C8.2).

The Mantineian plain, measuring *c.*13 km north to south and between 4 and 7 km east to west, is surrounded by mountains on three sides. Separating Mantineian territory from that of Orchomenos to the north was Mt Armenias and the low ridge called Anchisia.[19] The eastern limit of Mantineian territory was the plain of Nestane, which was separated from the main Mantineian plain by Mt Stravomyti and Mt Barberi. South of Nestane lies the small enclosed valley of Louka, which almost certainly represented the south-east

---

[13] Buckley (1996: :461); Woodhouse (1892: 3).   [14] Xen. *Hell.* 7.4.40.
[15] Xen. *Hell.* 7.5.27.   [16] Nielsen (2002: 572).   [17] Polyb. 4.8.4.
[18] Polyb. 2.58.4; Paus. 8.8.11. Mantineia was not ignored by the Romans. Augustus made repairs to public buildings, and Hadrian, besides restoring the city's original name, instituted a cult of Antinoos. The city continued to be inhabited into the sixth and seventh centuries AD (Mee and Spawforth 2001: 259).
[19] Paus. 8.12.8–9.

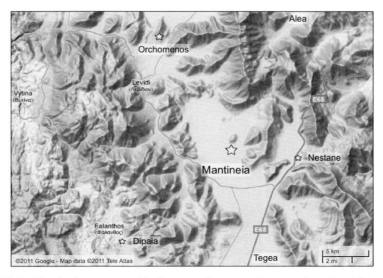

Fig. C8.2. Mantineia, topographical map of area and territories of neighbouring *poleis*. (© *2011 Google-Map data © 2011 Tele Atlas*)

extent of Mantineian territory.[20] The boundary with Tegea to the south was defined not by mountains, but by the narrowest part of the plain between Mt Krobriza and the hill of Mytika.[21] To the west, Mantineian territory extended certainly to the lower eastern slopes of Mt Menalo, though it probably extended as far west as ancient Helisson.[22] In short, the territory of Mantineia encompassed the plain of Nestane, the plain of Louka, and the plain of Mantineia, in which the *polis* itself was located. But the city of Mantineia was not the only community in its territory, and a number of other smaller settlements—including at least two dependent *poleis*—are attested to by Pausanias.[23]

---

[20] Hodkinson and Hodkinson (1981: 244).

[21] This narrow stretch of the plain is *c*.3 km wide east to west. Gell (1817: i. 141), Dodwell (1819: ii. 421), and Clark (1858: 136–7) all observed remnants in this area of what they believed to have been an ancient wall separating the territories of Mantineia and Tegea.

[22] For a summary of the arguments as to whether the territory also included the narrow north–south running Kapsia Valley, immediately west of the Mantineian plain and east of the Menalo Mountain range, see Hodkinson and Hodkinson (1981: 244–6).

[23] The *poleis* include Nestane and Helisson. While Helisson was not originally Mantineian, the city voluntarily became a dependent *polis* sometime during the first quarter of the fourth century BC (*SEG* xxxvii. 340; Nielsen 2002: 556). The other settlements mentioned by Pausanias include Maira (8.12.7), Melangia (8.6.4), and Ptolis (8.12.7). For the arguments on the disputed locations of Maira and Melangia, see Hodkinson and Hodkinson (1981: 248–50, 252). It is almost certain that Ptolis was located on Gourtsouli Hill, immediately north of Mantineia.

The Mantineians built and fortified their settlement in the flat plain, immediately south of Gourtsouli Hill, and roughly in the centre of the Mantineian plain. This plain contains not only a large amount of arable land, but also an ample supply of water to ensure its fertility.[24] There are three main streams. The first, originating above modern Pikerni in the north-east part of the plain, flows west into a series of three *katavothroi*.[25] The second is the infamous Ophis River, which originally flowed through the city but whose course was diverted to circumvent the town in 370 BC. This stream originates south of the city and ultimately ends in the *katavothroi* already mentioned. The third major tributary supplies water to the southern part of the plain. It originates near the modern town of Skopi and flows north-west until it reaches a *katavothros* on the south-west edge of the plain.

As Mantineia was a major *polis* located in the plain in the centre of an extremely large valley, we should expect its road network to be more complex than in those areas more confined by the mountainous topography characteristic of most of Arkadia.[26] Basing his calculations on the fact that the fortifications contain ten gates and employing the local itinerary of Pausanias, Fougères assumes there must have been a corresponding number of roads leading to the major *poleis* outside Mantineian territory.[27] From the topography of the valley (and Mantineia's position therein), and its relation to eastern Arkadian geography, we can confidently presume the existence of two major roads leading towards Tegea and Pallantion in the south,[28] one (or two) that skirted the Anchisia ridge north towards Orchomenos,[29] one that led towards the city and plain of Nestane from the Argolid (via the Prinus Pass) to the east,[30] one that ran north–south through the plain of Nestane towards the Klimax Pass in the direction of Nemea and Corinth in the north-east of the plain,[31] and at least one that led towards the Helisson Valley and Methydrion to the west.[32]

[24] Jost (1999: 202). Some might say there is, in fact, too much water. Many of the travellers describe sections of the plain as swamps or marshes in the nineteenth century. Today, drainage appears to be less of a problem, as evidenced by the growth of wheat almost everywhere. On the agricultural potential of the territory, see Hodkinson and Hodkinson (1981: 265–71).
[25] If the ruins near Pikerni are to be associated with ancient Melangia, as maintained by Hodkinson and Hodkinson (1981: 252), then this stream was the source of the Mantineian drinking water, as mentioned by Pausanias (8.6.4).
[26] On the traces of the ancient road network around Mantineia, see Pikoulas (1999a: 260–5, 274).
[27] Fougères (1898: 160–1). Leake (1846: 112) has his own opinions in this regard.
[28] Loring (1895: 82–3).   [29] Paus. 8.12.5–8.13.1; Loring (1895: 84–5).
[30] Paus. 8.6.4; Loring (1895: 80–1).
[31] Paus. 8.6.4; Loring (1895: 81–2); Pikoulas (1990–1c; 1995: 104–9, 288–90).
[32] Paus. 8.12.2; Loring (1895: 83–4).

Fig. C8.3. Mantineia, the site (facing north-east). (© *Matthew Maher*)

NATURAL DEFENCES

Gourtsouli Hill prevents a direct approach to the city from the north (Fig. C8.3). Essentially functioning as an outwork, the course of Ophis River was diverted to circumvent the circuit, and converted into a moat.[33] The post-370 BC city, therefore, was accessible only by bridges.[34] Otherwise, the site of Mantineia lies nearly in the centre of a flat, open plain largely devoid of natural defences.

FORTIFICATION TYPE

Horizontal type.[35] The circuit was laid out in an elliptical shape on what was, especially for Arkadia, nearly completely level ground (Fig. C8.4). There was no formal acropolis located within the intramural area.

---

[33] Xen. *Hell.* 5.2.7; Jost (1999: 202).

[34] In addition to the natural defences and its impressive fortification circuit, Mantineia was further safeguarded by no fewer than seven signal towers located along the periphery of its territory to monitor the main roads through and access points into its *chora*. On these extra-urban military installations, see Pikoulas (1984; 1990–1b; 1995: 244–51); Sarantakes (1993: 24–5); Topouzi et al. (2000, 2002); Maher and Mowat (forthcoming).

[35] Listed as a 'villes de plain' type by Jost (1999: 202–3).

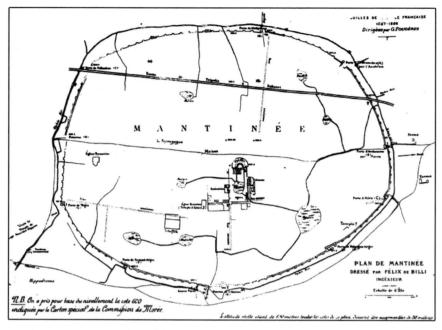

Fig. C8.4. Mantineia, plan of the site from Fougères (1898: pl. VIII). (© *G. Fougères*)

PRESERVATION

The site is well preserved for the most part; with the exception of some sections on the west, the stone foundations are preserved for nearly its entire extent. The total length of the circuit is 3.9 km and it encloses an area of 124 ha.[36]

CONSTRUCTION

The coursed limestone foundations of the walls are about 4.20–4.70 m thick throughout, and the greater part is comprised of isodomic trapezoidal blocks (Fig. C8.5);[37] the remaining minority is in the coursed polygonal style.[38] As the

---

[36] Fougères (1898: 140, 150, 151 ff.).   [37] Fougères (1898: 141); Scranton (1941: 90).

[38] I could not find the polygonal portions when I visited the site, although they were noted or observed by Leake (1830: i. 104), Curtius (1851: 236), Clark (1858: 134), Fougères (1898: 141), Frazer (1898: iv. 202), Scranton (1941: 57–9), and Winter (1989: 192). Hodkinson and Hodkinson (1981: 257) maintain that the polygonal section is located in the southern part of the circuit between Gates F and I.

Fig. C8.5. Mantineia, detail of section of south-east part of circuit (facing west). (© *Matthew Maher*)

trapezoidal sections were laid atop the polygonal sections of the curtains, it follows that they must be later.[39]

The stone socle is comprised of the standard three elements: an inner wall, an outer wall, and the fill in between. Every three or four metres, some of these blocks are laid perpendicularly to act as headers.[40] These headers helped to bind the wall to the earth and rubble fill that packed the space between the two faces.[41] All the curtain and tower foundations in the circuit once supported a mudbrick superstructure (not preserved).

SUMMARY OF TACTICAL COMPONENTS

The circuit contained 126 towers in total: 105 rectangular towers (*c.*6.50 m × 4.50–5 m) were regularly spaced (*c.*25 m) on the main curtains, and 20 circular towers were reserved exclusively for protecting the gateways (see Fig. C8.4); it also included one hexagonal tower. The circuit was furnished with ten gates; nine were overlap gates flanked by two semicircular towers, while one was of the gatecourt type. Some of the rectangular towers were provided with posterns. No posterns in the curtains are attested.

---

[39] The chronological implications of the differing masonry styles are addressed under Chronological Arguments.

[40] Fougères (1898: 141, 144).

[41] Both Leake (1830: i. 104) and Frazer (1898: iv. 202) claim to have observed mortar mixed in with the rubble fill. I could find no mention of this by Fougères and I suspect that Leake and Frazer were mistaken or observed later Roman additions/repairs.

Towers

The Mantineian circuit was provided with two basic types of towers—rectangular and circular—with each type performing a different function. There are 105 rectangular towers, 20 circular towers, and 1 hexagonal tower, for a total of 126.[42] The rectangular towers were placed predominately along the main curtains; the circular towers and hexagonal example were exclusively reserved for protecting the gateways.[43] The rectangular towers measured an average of 6.50 m to 6.60 m in width and projected between 4.50 m and 5.0 m from the curtains.[44] These towers were placed at fairly regular and close intervals, with an average of only 25 m to 26 m between each.[45] The stone socle of the rectangular towers was not bonded to the curtain and was comprised of a double row of blocks, with an average thickness of 1.60 m.[46] While each tower was provided with a ground-floor chamber that communicated with the city by a narrow opening in the curtain,[47] some were also provided with small posterns.[48]

Gates

The Mantineian circuit is furnished with ten gates, more or less regularly distributed around its perimeter. Nine of these gates are of the overlap variety (Gates B, C, D, E, F, G, H, I, K),[49] and one is of the gatecourt type (Gate A).[50] While the nine overlap gates are similar in form, their plans differ in detail (Fig. C8.6).

Gates B and D represent fairly standard examples of the overlap type gate, in which the narrow entrance (*c.*4.4–5 m wide)[51] is formed by two extended stretches of the curtain protected by circular towers on each side. Gate C closely resembles B and D, but, instead of flanking circular towers, it possesses one circular tower protecting the right side and a long rectangular bastion on the left. Gates F and K too combine different tower shapes. In the latter we find

---

[42] Fougères (1898: 150). The early travellers could not reach a consensus regarding the number of towers. Gell (1817: i. 141) noted 116 towers, Leake (1830: i. 104) 118, Ross (1841: i. 125) 129, and Curtius (1851: 237) 120.

[43] Because of this, the circular towers are discussed under Gates.

[44] Fougères (1898: 146).   [45] Fougères (1898: 143).   [46] Fougères (1898: 147).

[47] Fougères (1898: 147).   [48] Fougères (1898: 157–9).

[49] Scranton makes an interesting observation regarding the large number of overlap gates. He writes that the presence of so many overlapping gates in the curtains 'is an interesting example of a trace resembling the indented trace, but not using it as it was originally intended' (1941: 156).

[50] There is no Gate J. Gates E, H, and I have left no trace. For the arguments that they did indeed exist, see Fougères (1898: 155–6). On the discrepancies between the early travellers' descriptions of the gates, see Fougères (1890: 84–8).

[51] Lawrence (1979: 303).

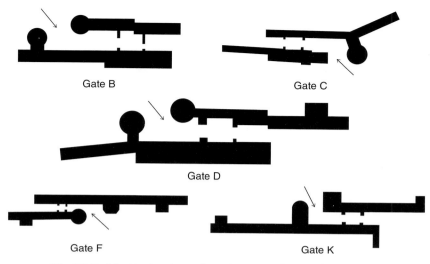

Fig. C8.6. Mantineia, plans of overlap gates. (© *Matthew Maher*)

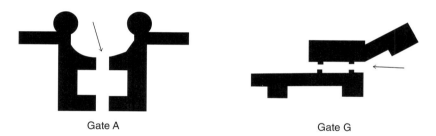

Fig. C8.7. Mantineia, plans of Gates A and G. (© *Matthew Maher*)

its entrance protected by both a rectangular tower and a semicircular example, while a circular and hexagonal tower guards the former. What these gates have in common is that the towers placed to the right of the entranceway in every case are curvilinear or hexagonal—that is, not rectangular. Their advantageous shape ensured the maximum field of fire necessary to cover an approach from any direction.[52] Moreover, the gates are all designed in a way that would force an enemy to turn left upon entry, thus exposing their unshielded right side to the internal wall. Gate A is unique among those of the Mantineia, as it is the circuit's only gatecourt type entrance (Fig. C8.7).[53]

The frontal entrance is preceded by a semicircular outer court flanked by two circular towers. In the centre of this court was a small door that led to another rectangular courtyard behind. This inner courtyard too was provided

---

[52] Fougères (1898: 152); Frazer (1898: iv. 203).   [53] Fougères (1898: 153).

with a small gate opposite the first.[54] The parallels between Gate A, the Arkadian Gate at Messene, as well as the Phlious Gate at Stymphalos are obvious and have been commented upon by others.[55]

COMMENTS

When Leake visited the site in the early nineteenth century, he was dismayed to discover next to the site 'a great number of serpents sleeping in the sun on the edge of the ditch under the walls'.[56] This ditch full of snakes, somewhat ironically, was what remained of the Ophis River.[57] In order to avoid the disaster imposed by the Spartans in 385 BC, when the Mantineians were rebuilding their city after Leuktra, they aimed to divert the river's original course through the city.[58] To achieve this, and to turn the river into part of the larger defensive system of the town, they proceeded to dig a ditch around the whole city into which the course of the river was turned. In this way, Mantineia 'affords a rare example of a moat...completely encircling a city'.[59]

OVERALL DEFENSIVE PLANNING

Located less than 1 km north of Mantineia stands Gourtsouli Hill. With a circumference only slightly smaller than the city itself, the hill rises 100 m from the surrounding plain. That this seemingly ideal natural acropolis was not incorporated into the defences of the city remains, as Leake observes, 'a curious fact in reference to the military engineering of the Greeks'.[60] This is a fact that concerned many of the early travellers to the site. Clark, for example, maintains that the reasons 'why the Mantineians abandoned the old and to all appearance more eligible site, and why they did not retain the old city for the Acropolis of the new, are questions we have no means of answering'.[61] It is Leake, however, who appeared most unsettled by this 'curious fact', and who expended a considerable amount of his Mantineian account on this very subject. Leake implies that cost was the main factor in the hill's exclusion

---

[54] As such courtyard gates are more typical of the Hellenistic period, Winter (1971a: 227) wonders if this rectangular court was contemporary with the rest of the structure, or was a latter addition.

[55] e.g., Fougères (1898: 153); Frazer (1898: iv. 204); Winter (1971a: 217); Gourley and Williams (2005: 232–3).

[56] Leake (1830: i. 105). [57] *Ophis* is Greek for 'snake'. [58] Xen. *Hell.* 5.2.7.

[59] Winter (1971a: 272). [60] Leake (1846: 382). [61] Clark (1858: 132).

from the larger city defences.[62] This would perhaps have been true if, as he suggests, the hill was fortified as a separate citadel.[63] Similarly, uprooting and moving the foundations of the original fortifications and moving the city slightly north to embrace the hill upon the city's refoundation in 370 BC, would also have been cost prohibitive. But these reasons do not explain why the hill was not included in the city's defences at the time the original circuit was constructed after the first synoikism. The simplest and most plausible reason, as suggested by Leake, was that because at the time of its original construction artillery had not been invented, and after the second synoikism it was still in its infancy and the hill was 'too distant to effect much injury with ancient missiles'.[64] In other words, besides being able to observe the activities of the inhabitants, the offensive advantages of an enemy holding the heights of Gourtsouli Hill would have been minimal before the widespread use of artillery.[65] Instead of incorporating the high ground, the underlying defensive principles employed by the Mantineians, implied by their choice of a site on completely open ground, would rely less on topography and more on tactics manifested in the man-made defences.

When the scattered Mantineians came together (again) from their ancestral villages to rebuild their city after Leuktra, they chose the same site on which the earlier city had stood.[66] Having learned the brutal lesson handed to them by the Spartans in 385 BC, the Mantineians immediately set to turn the topographical disadvantages of the site to their advantage—first by increasing the height of the stone socle of the fortification circuit, and, second, by turning the course of the Ophis River so it became a defence rather than a danger.[67] A higher stone socle not only increased the overall strength of the walls, but also eliminated the risk of its collapse by inundation. The defensive advantages of this moat are also twofold: as an outwork, it acted to keep enemies from easily reaching the walls, and, if an enemy did command the bridges and was able to cross the moat, it would find itself confined to a small strip of land between the walls and the water. From this unlucky position, offensive numbers would count for little and any attempt to retreat would be impeded by the moat.[68] Not satisfied with a higher socle and an impressive outwork, the Mantineians also introduced a number of tactical innovations to the towers and the gates—innovations 'foreshadowing those of the Hellenistic period'.[69]

[62] Leake (1846: 382).　　[63] Leake (1846: 382).　　[64] Leake (1846: 382).
[65] Fougères believes the reason they did not include this hill was politically motivated and the decision was promoted by Epaminondas. Specifically, he maintains that 'ces citadelles risquaient en revanche de compromettre l'ordre intérieur en offrant un repaire aux factieux de toutes sortes, aristocrates sans scrupules, ou démagogues aspirant à la tyrannie' (1898: 135).
[66] Fougères (1898: 132).　　[67] Xen. *Hell.* 5.2.7.
[68] The strip of land between the moat and the city walls is, on average, 20 to 25 m wide (Fougères 1898: 157).
[69] Winter (1971a: 240).

Fig. C8.8. Mantineia, plans of towers with and without posterns. (© *Matthew Maher*)

Because of its exposed position in the plain, Mantineia required defensive provisions be taken on all sides. Consequently, it is in the towers placed throughout the entirety of the circuit where innovation is most apparent. Relatively rare before the Hellenistic period was the introduction of posterns in the external flanks of towers (Fig. C8.8). At Mantineia, although many of the towers were provided with posterns, they are mostly grouped in the eastern part of the circuit.[70] Moreover, that these openings are usually only 1 m wide and always occur on the tower's right side indicates a military rather than a civilian function.

Directly and functionally related to these posterns were the ground-storey tower chambers, which again were rare before the time of Epaminondas and the Macedonians.[71] If an enemy managed to cross the moat, there was a real danger that they could bring rams or ladders against the fortifications. To prevent the enemy from reaching the walls, these posterns afforded defenders a close and safe position from which defensive sallies could be made. Furthermore, the tower's lower chamber, from which the postern was accessed, provided the defenders with a place to muster for the attack. As the time of greatest risk to the defending troops was the moment they emerged from the towers in a single file, the posterns were constructed on the tower's right side (that is, facing the field). Thus, as the defenders sallied forth from the postern, they presented their shielded left side to the enemy.[72]

One of the general tactics employed by Greek military architects is the placing of a tower to the right of gates where possible.[73] Fougères acknowledges this general rule, but notes that, in the gates of Mantineia, 'pareille précaution n'a pas été prise'.[74] Indeed, all the gates (except Gate A) are designed with the flanking towers on an attacker's left. There are several,

---

[70] Fougères (1898: 157). Fougères (1898: 159) also correctly points out that, because of the relatively small size of the posterns and the protection provided by flanking towers, there was little risk of an enemy breaking into the tower and the city through these openings.
[71] Winter (1971a: 162).   [72] Fougères (1898: 158); Winter (1971a: 240).
[73] Winter (1971a: 216).   [74] Fougères (1898: 159).

non-mutually exclusive motivations and advantages to this system. That each gate was covered by a second tower just outside the gate on the inner wall (that is, on the attacker's unshielded right) suggests that the main advantage of 'such gates lay in compelling the enemy to advance some distance below the line of the main wall'.[75] But how could they ensure that an attacker approached from the appropriate direction? As Mantineia was surrounded by a moat, access to the city required passage over bridges. I believe these bridges, which naturally appear to have been located in the vicinity of the gates, would have been purposely situated in a way that dictated the most defensibly advantageous routes towards the gates.[76] Placing the main gate tower on the attacker's left ensured that, if enemies did penetrate the outer court, they still had to fight their way through two doors and an inner court, all while their unshielded right side was exposed to the inner wall. At all the gates, this inner wall extended internally for a considerable distance, on which a large number of defenders could mass to repel any assault on the gates.

The resourceful conversion of the Ophis into a moat, the incorporation of ground-storey chambers and posterns into many of the towers, and the sheer number of close-set towers are all features 'typical of the new concept of "active" rather than "passive" defensive strategy that evolved between the end of the fifth and the middle of the fourth century'.[77] Also characteristic of this active strategy is the defensive use of heavy calibre artillery, which became common after the time of Philip II. In the circuits that pre-date this innovation, we might expect to see the later addition (or modification) of structures designed to house such weapons.[78] At Mantineia, however, no such towers were constructed. As Winter maintains, the small scale of the tower chambers at Mantineia (averaging $c.25$ m^2) could not have housed any heavy caliber artillery—torsion or non-torsion.[79] While they certainly would have possessed smaller calibre weapons, the heavy stone-throwers, 'of great potential value in such open terrain, would in most cases have been out of the question'.[80] Perhaps the Mantineians believed the inherent strength of their circuit was enough; that, even if enemy artillery set up at a distance caused a breach in the walls, the 'active' defences inherent in the outworks, gates, and towers would be sufficient to protect the inhabitants from incursion into the city itself. Ultimately, just as we may never definitively know why Gourtsouli Hill was not incorporated into the original circuit, so too the question of why the fortifications of Mantineia never adapted to the evolving conditions of

---

[75] Winter (1971a: 217). The same is the case for the gate at Nestane.

[76] Gell (1817: i. 141–2) observed remains of three bridges leading to the gates, but does not give their location nor specify to which gates he is referring. Curtius (1851: 237) too mentions the remains of bridges without providing their position relative to the city. Fougères (1898: 157) observed the remains of bridges in front of Gates B, C, H, and K.

[77] Winter (1989: 191). [78] e.g., ass witnessed at Stymphalos or Alea.

[79] Winter (1989: 191). [80] Winter (1989: 191).

Greek warfare and *poliorketics* of the later fourth century BC and Hellenistic period may never be answered. What is more certain, however, is that the refounding and fortification of Mantineia were probably tied to the larger political interests and defensive strategy of Epaminondas and Thebes. The second Mantineian synoikism, therefore, was not only aimed to reverse the misfortune of 385 BC, but was also part of a strategic plan both to frustrate and to curb any Spartan attempt to re-establish its hegemony in the Peloponnese. In addition to Messene, Megalopolis, and probably also Nestane, Alea, and Stymphalos,[81] Mantineia formed part of a network of cities whose geographic positions formed a continuous northern barrier around Lakonia.[82] Because this grand defensive strategy was instituted in the wake of the Battle of Leuktra, the fortifications of Mantineia are among a handful of circuits whose chronology can be confidently established.

CHRONOLOGICAL SUMMARY

The original circuit (fifth century BC) was built before 385 BC (in the coursed polygonal style); the walls were rebuilt on same course *c*.370 BC (in the trapezoidal style); these dates are based on historical probability, external evidence, and architectural affinities.

CHRONOLOGICAL ARGUMENTS

Thanks to the testimony of Xenophon, almost every published work with cause to mention the extant circuit of Mantineia is in agreement that its construction commenced at the time of the second synoikism in 370 BC.[83] As to their completion, Winter suggests that the work was probably finished in the early 360s BC—the haste necessitated by the city's total lack of natural defences.[84] As there is no indication that the circuit was ever subsequently modified, 370 BC serves as a convenient *terminus ante quem* for the extant remains. Determining a *terminus post quem*, however, is more complicated,

---

[81] Gourley and Williams (2005: 219, n. 10).

[82] For more on the role of these Arkadian cities as fortresses, especially Stymphalos and Alea, see Maher (2015a).

[83] Xen. *Hell.* 6.5.3–5. To my knowledge, the single exception is Rochas d'Aiglun (1881: 80), who puts their date at 320 BC. I suspect, however, that this is a typographical error, since he does correctly acknowledge that the circuit of Mantineia is contemporary with that of Messene and dates the latter to 370 BC (Rochas d'Aiglun 1881: 81).

[84] Winter (1989: 191, n. 3).

and we must return to the polygonal sections of the south and south-eastern curtains mentioned earlier. Basing his conclusions on stylistic grounds and the historical evidence, Scranton believes that the polygonal sections of the trace belong to the fifth century BC.[85] Furthermore, the low socle—resulting from the fact that only two or three courses in this style exist—adds weight, he maintains, to a pre-385 BC date.[86] Specifically, the inundation caused by Agesipolis and the melting of the mudbrick walls in 385 BC are compatible with the presence of such a low stone foundation.

Finally, although opposed by the Spartans, in 370 BC a number of Arkadian cities agreed to send both men and money to help Mantineia construct their walls—again, suggesting a certain hurriedness.[87] The use of a mudbrick wall atop a coursed trapezoidal socle for the fortifications of the post-Leuktra circuit was also a conscious and expedient choice and further testimony of the desire for a quickly built circuit.[88] Although construction in the polygonal style is generally more time-consuming than rectilinear masonry, and at first glance the sections at Mantineia in this style are perhaps best explained as belonging to the pre-385 BC circuit, caution is warranted. One of Winter's key criticisms of Scranton is the latter's failure to acknowledge that a circuit exhibiting more than one masonry style may 'simply indicate different "work-shops", or groups of masons, rather than different building periods'.[89] As Xenophon tells us that certain of Mantineia's Arkadian and Elian allies participated in the construction of the post-Leuktra circuit, Winter's evaluation may be especially applicable here.[90] Nonetheless, the aid donated by the Arkadian allies, the vulnerable location of the city, the materials and construction style employed, and the superimposition along the trace of the earlier circuit all suggest a desire for a quickly built circuit.[91] In this scenario, therefore, it is not implausible that, in the interests of time and expense, the polygonal parts of the fifth-century BC trace that had survived the Spartan siege of 385 BC were incorporated into the walls of the 370 BC circuit.

BIBLIOGRAPHY

Thuc. 5.29.1–2, 5.81.1; Xen. *Hell.* 5.2.1–11, 7.4.37–40, 7.5; Polyb. 2.58.4, 4.8.4; Paus. 8.8.4–8.12.9; Gell (1817: i. 141–2); Dodwell (1819: ii. 421–4); Leake

---

[85] Scranton (1941: 59). He adds that they may in fact date to the time of the first synoikism, which he dates to 472 BC.

[86] Scranton (1941: 59).   [87] Xen. *Hell.* 6.5.5.

[88] Winter (1971a: 73, n. 11, 86–7); Hodkinson and Hodkinson (1981: 258). Lawrence (1979: 420) refers to Mantineia as 'the last great city founded with a mudbrick wall'.

[89] Winter (1971a: 83).   [90] Xen. *Hell.* 6.5.5.

[91] For the similarities between the circuits of Mantineia, Stymphalos, and Alea, see Maher (2015a: 32–8).

(1830: i. 102–9; 1846: 111–12, 382); Boblaye (1836: 139–40); Ross (1841: i. 124–6); Curtius (1851: 235–42); Clark (1858: 132–7); Bursian (1862: ii. 209–13); Rochas d'Aiglun (1881: 80–1); Fougères (1890; 1898: 130–61); Loring (1895: 80–9); Frazer (1898: iv. 201–416); Scranton (1941: 57–9, 65, 90, 156–7, 163, 172); Marsden (1969: 148, 164); Howell (1970: 85–8); Winter (1971a: 30, n. 60, 30, n. 62, 31, n. 64, 33 and n. 68, 56, n. 6, 58, 71 and n. 4, 113, 115, n. 33, 119, n. 43, 123, n. 53, 240, 272–3; 1989: 189–92); Garlan (1974: 66, 77, 82, 151, n. 5, 178, 191, 192, 193, 196, 198, 362, 394); Lawrence (1979: 57, 120, 123, 178, 203, 206, 222, 280, 303, 319, 333–4, 337, 420); Hodkinson and Hodkinson (1981); Pikoulas (1984; 1995: 244–51; 1999a: 260–5, 274); Jost (1985: 122–41; 1999: 202–3); Demand (1990: 109–10); Sarantakes (1993: 20–5); Papachatzis (1994: 196–210); Topouzi et al. (2000, 2002); Neilsen (2002: 567–72); Maher (2012a: 147–71; 2015a: 1–18, 34–5, 37, 39–42); Maher and Mowat (forthcoming).

9

Megalopolis, Southern Arkadia

LOCATION

The remains of ancient Megalopolis can be found in southern Arkadia, located near the middle of a large plain in a basin defined by mountains on all sides (Fig. C9.1). The settlement is situated on broken terrain and is traversed by the Helisson River. The intramural area comprised the main area of inhabitation.

POLIS STATUS

The well-documented history of the site and its known *raison d'être* remove any doubt about its political and social status as a *polis*.[1]

HISTORY

In an attempt to limit any future Spartan aggression after their defeat at the Battle of Leuktra in 371 BC, a confederation of Arkadian cities was established and Mantineia and Megalopolis were synoikized as defensive consolidations under the guidance of the Theban general Epaminondas. While the people of Mantineia returned to the site from which they had been expelled by the Spartans in 385 BC, the foundation of Megalopolis between 371 and 367 BC,[2] was a totally artificial foundation. Hardly had Epaminondas finished his work when dissensions among the Arkadians broke out, as it appears that the

---

[1] If its name is not enough ('Megale *polis*'), a summary of the evidence for the settlement's *polis* status is provided by Nielsen (2002: 572).

[2] Pausanias (8.27.8) puts the date at 371/370 BC, while Diodorus (15.72) puts it later, under the year 368/367 BC. While the exact date of the foundation is uncertain, it is not critical for the present purposes. On this debate, see Hornblower (1990).

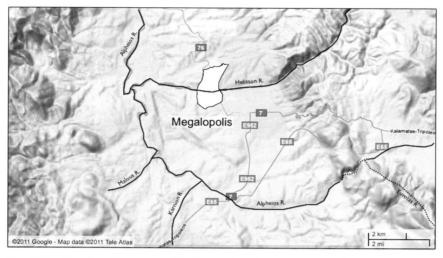

Fig. C9.1. Megalopolis, topographical map of the basin and city walls. (© *2011 Google-Map data © 2011 Tele Atlas*)

Theban association became distasteful to those who had originally promoted it.[3] Unable to reach a resolution, in 362 BC, a large section of Arkadia, with Mantineia at its head, jealous of the rising power of Megalopolis and Tegea, deserted the Arkadian League and joined in treaty with Athens and Sparta.[4] The resulting Battle of Mantineia, therefore, witnessed Arkadians fighting on opposite sides, and, although many of the synoikized towns took advantage of a clause in the peace that followed to desert Megalopolis, the Thebans compelled them to return.[5]

In 352 BC the Spartans invaded Megalopolitan territory.[6] Because Thebes had been weakened by the Sacred Wars, and an attempt to ally itself with Athens had failed, Megalopolis had few options but to approach Philip II of Macedon. Although no formal alliance was made, the connection with the Macedonian royal house was ever afterwards maintained. Thus, after the Battle of Chaironeia in 338 BC, Megalopolis became the stronghold of Macedonian influence in the Peloponnese, and, as Woodhouse maintains, 'by a strange fate, the city founded to ensure the liberty of Greece became one of the instruments of its complete enslavement'.[7]

When, in 331 BC, Agis III of Sparta rose against the Macedonian Antipater, Megalopolis was besieged and very nearly capitulated.[8] Shortly after, it appears

---

[3] Xen. *Hell.* 7.1.23–4.   [4] Xen. *Hell.* 7.4–5.   [5] Xen. *Hell.* 7.4–5.
[6] Paus. 8.27.10.   [7] Woodhouse (1892: 4).
[8] Pausanias (8.27.9) credits the North Wind with destroying the Spartan engines. The North Wind was duly honoured in consequence.

that Megalopolis sided with Kassander during the troubled times that followed Alexander's death, and the city was attacked (unsuccessfully) by his rival Polyperchon in 318 BC.[9] When Kassander refounded Thebes in 315 BC, the citizens of Megalopolis sent aid, and were thus able to return to Thebes the service that had been rendered to them half a century earlier.[10]

Megalopolis disappears from the historical record until the early third century BC, at which time the city is in the hands of its first tyrant, Aristodemos. During his rule, the Spartan King Akrotatos invaded the territory of Megalopolis but was killed in battle.[11] Some two generations later, Lydiades became the second tyrant of Megalopolis, but soon relinquished his position by resigning voluntarily.[12] In 234 BC, Lydiades brought Megalopolis into the Achaian League (of which it remained a member until 146 BC) and was made *strategos*.[13] In 227 BC Lydiades was killed and the Achaians were defeated by Kleomenes III in the Battle of Ladokeia staged just south of Megalopolis.[14] This defeat arguably paved the way for the fall of Megalopolis at the hands of its Spartan nemesis, which would come in 222 BC, when Kleomenes III finally seized Megalopolis.[15] While apparently most of the citizens escaped in safety to Messenia, those who remained were slaughtered, and the Spartans looted and destroyed the greater part of the city.[16] When the Achaians finally defeated Kleomenes at the Battle of Sellasia a year later, the Megalopolitan refugees returned home and began to rebuild their city.

Almost immediately, a dispute arose over the fortifications and the proposed size of the new city, with one group pushing to restore it to the size of the original intramural area, while the other favoured a contracted and more easily defendable circuit. In the end, perhaps owing to arbitration by Aratos, the former opinion seems to have held the day, and the city walls were rebuilt to their original scale.[17] Although these new walls were strong enough to repel the attack by the Spartan tyrant Nabis in 198 BC, they seemed to have quickly fallen into decay.[18] Indeed, a quarter century later, in 175 BC, Antiochus IV Epiphanes promised the citizens of Megalopolis that he would surround their city with a wall and delivered most of the money to defray the costs.[19] Under the Roman peace, the city's political *raison d'être* ceased to exist, and, although inscriptions reveal building activity by Roman patrons, even by Strabo's time the Great City had become a great desert.[20] A century later, things had

---

[9] Diod. 18.68.3, 18.69.3–18.72.1.   [10] Paus. 9.7.1
[11] Paus. 8.27.11; Plut. *Agis*, 3.   [12] Paus. 8.27.12.
[13] Polyb. 2.44; Plut. *Cleom* 6.7; *Arat*. 30.4–7.
[14] Paus 8.27.16; Polyb. 2.51.3, 2.55.2; Plut. *Cleom*. 6.1–7.   [15] Paus. 8.27.15.
[16] Polyb. 2.55.1–9, 61.2–62.12, 5.93.2; Liv. 38.34.7; Plut. *Cleom* 23–5, 26.2, 29.3; *Phil*. 5.1–5; Paus. 4.29.7–8, 7.7.4, 8.27.15–16, 8.28.7, 8.49.4.
[17] Polyb. 5.93.   [18] Plut. *Phil*. 13.1–2.   [19] Liv. 41.20.6.
[20] The oft-cited observation by an unknown Greek comic poet, reported second-hand by Strabo (8.8.1).

changed little, prompting Pausanias to note that Megalopolis lay 'mostly in ruins, shorn of all its beauty and ancient prosperity'.[21]

LOCAL TOPOGRAPHY

The plain of Megalopolis comprises the interior of a considerable basin, not unlike the great eastern plain of Arkadia (see Fig. C9.1).[22] Within the larger basin, the plain measures *c*.9 km north–south by 11 km east–west and is surrounded on all sides by mountains.[23] Occupying nearly the whole of southern Arkadia, the basin of Megalopolis shared borders with both Messenia (separated by Mt Lykaion) and Lakonia (by the Taygetos mountains) in the south-west and south-east respectively (Fig. C9.2).

The western limits of Mt Menalo formed the natural boundary in the north and north-west, while a long north-west running spur from Mt Tsimbarou marked the eastern limit and beginning of the Asean plain. If the territory of Megalopolis was actually comprised of all the communities mentioned by

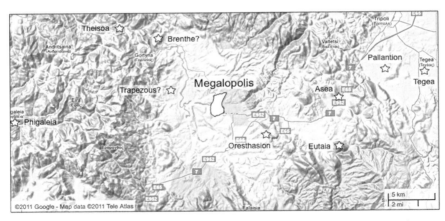

Fig. C9.2. Megalopolis, topographical map of southern Arkadia. (© *2011 Google-Map data © 2011 Tele Atlas*)

---

[21] Paus. 8.33.1.

[22] Perhaps it was thought that such terrain could better accommodate a large population than could the hills characteristic of the majority of Arkadian settlements.

[23] On the traces of the road network in the territory of Megalopolis, see Pikoulas (1999a: 272–96).

Pausanias,[24] then it would have measured 1,500 km^2.[25] Alternatively, if the reconstruction is based on Diodorus, then the territory of Megalopolis would have been considerably smaller.[26] The city itself, standing astride the Helisson River, occupied broken and uneven ground, which, wherever possible, the military architects employed to their defensive advantage.

The fertile Megalopolis plain was very well watered, being served primarily by the Alpheios and Helisson Rivers, but also by their numerous tributaries, as well as a number of seasonal streams. The Alpheios emerges from its subterraneous course from the Asea Valley, entering the Megalopolis basin southeast of the city near the modern village of Anemodouri (ancient Oresthasion). After a short south-westerly course, the Alpheios turns north-west and then north, moving along the western edge of the basin. As a number of small tributaries add their water to the Alpheios, it continues its northward path, eventually exiting the basin at modern Karitaina. The Helisson, on the other hand, originating in the Helisson Valley in central Arkadia, entered the Megalopolis basin on its east side. It then flowed almost due west, travelling directly through the city, before reaching its confluence with the Alpheios, *c.*3 km west of Megalopolis.

NATURAL DEFENCES

The height offered by the plateau north of the river and the steep slopes on its north and east side, and the hills in the south-west corner of the circuit, provide the site with natural defences. The eastern, western, and parts of the northern sides of the city (north of the Helisson River) are flanked by small tributaries.

FORTIFICATION TYPE

Uneven type.[27] North of the river, the circuit was laid out largely following the elevated contours of a small plateau, while south of the river, the walls engaged both low hills and flatter terrain (Fig. C9.3). There was no formal acropolis.

---

[24] Paus. 8.27.3–4.   [25] Roy et al. (1988: 179).
[26] Diod. 15.72.4.   [27] Listed as a 'villes de plain' type by Jost (1999: 200–1).

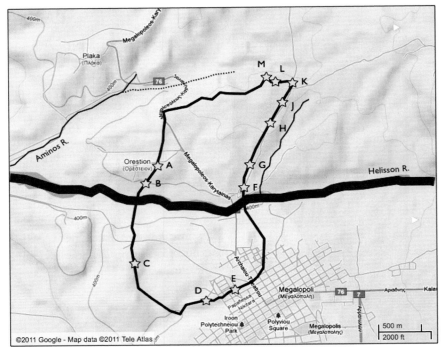

Fig. C9.3. Megalopolis, topographical map of fortifications showing excavated areas. (© *2011 Google-Map data © 2011 Tele Atlas*)

PRESERVATION

The site is extremely poorly preserved; nothing of the walls remains visible on the surface.[28] From the account by Polybius and a reconstruction by Loring, the total length of the circuit is estimated to have been 8.85 km.[29]

CONSTRUCTION

The foundations of the original walls excavated range between 2 m and 4.87 m in thickness, while the later walls are only *c.*1.20 m thick.[30] The original circuit

---

[28] Although I have visited the site on a number of occasions, the actual walls of Megalopolis are the only fortifications in the entirety of the present work that I did not observe first hand, having been told by archaeologists from the 39th Ephorate of Prehistoric and Classical Antiquities that nothing of the walls is visible on the surface today. Thus, what can be deduced concerning the course of the walls and architectural details is based almost entirely on the excavations conducted and published by Loring (1892: 106–21).

[29] Polyb. 9.21; Loring (1892: 114). [30] Loring (1892: 109–11).

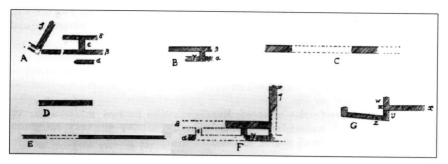

Fig. C9.4. Megalopolis, plans of the excavated sections of 'early' walls from Loring (1892: 108, fig. 1).

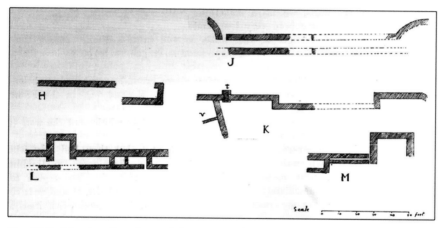

Fig. C9.5. Megalopolis, plans of the excavated sections of 'later' walls from Loring (1892: 108, fig. 1).

was constructed in a polygonal style (coursed or uncoursed is uncertain) (Fig. 9.4);[31] the later repairs to the wall were in the dry rubble style (Fig. 9.5).[32] The walls consist of the usual double facing of conglomerate and/or limestone blocks enclosing a core of rubble and packed earth.[33] Although these are not extant in all examples, it appears that the core was divided into compartments by perpendicular internal cross-walls placed at

---

[31] Loring (1892: 109).   [32] Loring (1892: 111).
[33] Loring (1892: 108). These building materials are seemingly used indiscriminately, although Loring (1892: 111) notes that the mixture of materials may suggest later repairs.

regular intervals of about 2 m.[34] The prohibitive costs for such a large circuit and the lack of stone blocks at the site suggest that all the curtain and tower foundations once supported a mudbrick superstructure (not preserved).

SUMMARY OF TACTICAL COMPONENTS

While the original circuit probably had hundreds of towers, only four have been uncovered, two rectangular (*c*.5 m × 3 m, and *c*.7.60 m × 4 m), and two semicircular (*c*.6 m in diameter), the latter spaced *c*.30 m apart. The circuit must have had at least eight gates (according to Pausanias), but none has been discovered. One possible postern (1.5 m wide) exists.

Towers

Excavations have established the existence of at least two rectangular and two semicircular towers, all of which have been dated to the later repair/rebuilding phase of the circuit (see sections L, J, and M on Fig. C9.5).[35] Overlooking the river valley from the eastern edge of the plateau, section J comprised two semicircular towers and the adjoining curtain.[36] From the published plan, these towers appear to have had a diameter of *c*.6 m, projected *c*.3 m from the curtain, and were spaced *c*.30 m apart. Above the steep slope on the northern edge of the plateau was the rectangular tower from section L. This tower appears to have been *c*.5 m wide and projected 3 m from the curtain. Just to the north-east of section L, section M is similarly located on the northern edge of the plateau. This section contained a rectangular tower measuring *c*.7.62 m wide and projecting *c*.4 m.

Gates

There is evidence of an entrance (*c*.1.5 m wide) in section K.[37] Its width and its location at the extreme north-east tip of the circuit suggest this entrance was a postern (see Fig. C9.5).

---

[34] Loring (1892: 108, 109).

[35] Both Loring's silence and the simplicity of the plan, however, remove any possibility of determining whether the towers were bonded to the curtains or had ground-storey chambers.

[36] The section letters A through M (the letter I was not employed) correspond to the twelve areas of the fortifications excavated by Loring.

[37] Loring (1892: 111).

COMMENTS

Many of the early travellers made two important oversights concerning the topography of Megalopolis. First, they failed fully to appreciate the incredible size of the intramural area defined by the fortifications; second, their accounts give the impression that the city was constructed more or less in the centre of a level plain.[38] There is little excuse for the first error, as Polybius himself tells us that the walls of Megalopolis measured fifty stades.[39] As Polybius was from Megalopolis, there is little reason to doubt his estimate of the size of his own city. Loring largely puts the blame for the second common misunderstanding directly at the feet of Leake.[40] When Leake observed that 'the difference of level in every part of the site of Megalopolis is very slight',[41] and compares it to the 'level situation for [the Mantineians'] new city',[42] the idea of a flat Megalopolis took root. Such an idea has a direct bearing on the fortifications, as it assumes, of course, that the city walls lacked any natural defences, which in turn implies that the architects trusted completely in the man-made defences alone to protect the city and its inhabitants. Loring very quickly dispels this idea, clarifying that, when contrasted with the mountains, the area 'is naturally called a "plain", [but] when looked at in detail [it] is really an accumulation of hills and valleys for the most part very well defined'.[43] The city itself, therefore, was not erected atop completely flat terrain, nor were the walls without natural defences.[44]

OVERALL DEFENSIVE PLANNING

It is well known that the synoikism of dozens of Arkadian *poleis* into one Mega-*polis* was largely a defensive policy, which, operating with Messene and Mantineia, was aimed at limiting future Spartan excursions northwards. Implicit in this consolidation, of course, is the strategy of strength in numbers; if the synoikism was to survive and succeed, such numbers had to be both accommodated and protected. In this way, the strategy inherent in the foundation of the city and the conception of its fortifications is inseparable from the political consolidation strategy as a whole. In other words, in order to function as a bulwark for the rest of Arkadia, Megalopolis had to be able to defend itself and its population. Although the paucity of remains and the

---

[38] Loring (1892: 107).   [39] Polyb. 9.21; 50 stades is equivalent to *c.*9.20 km.
[40] Loring (1892: 107).   [41] Leake (1830: ii. 40).   [42] Leake (1830: ii. 41).
[43] Loring (1892: 107).
[44] This idea is in no way contradictory to Kleomenes' statement (as recorded by Polybius) that Megalopolis was 'difficult to guard, owing to its great extent, and the sparseness of its inhabitants' (2.55.2).

largely conjectural course of many parts of the wall limit the amount of detail with which to explore the strategy, tactics, and defensive planning of the city, a general understanding is not beyond our reach.

It is clear that the misconception that Megalopolis was founded on flat terrain has promoted the idea that the location was poorly conceived and, by association, its fortifications were in some way inferior.[45] Roy, for example, maintains that 'its location and wall-circuit were not ideal for defence',[46] Winter, implies as much when he writes that Epaminondas did not 'show great interest in the natural strength for the federal capital of Megalopolis',[47] and Jost not only classifies the city as a 'villes de plaine' but also argues that 'ses qualités défensives intrinsèques sont presque nulles'.[48] On the contrary, as the city was founded in a location that cannot in any way be said to be flat, we see the course of the fortifications dictated by the natural strength of the topography. This strategy of exploiting the terrain to a defensive advantage is most evident north of the Helisson, where the course enjoys the advantages afforded by the northern and eastern edges of the plateau. Moreover, this plateau north of the river had the additional protection provided by several of the Helisson's small tributaries, which surrounded it on every side. Even south of the river, we see that the south-west corner of the circuit also incorporated the high ground wherever possible. It is uncertain where the Helisson itself fits into the larger defensive strategy, as the relationship between the river and the fortifications is not clear—not least of all because its original width is not known.[49] Clearly, whatever provisions were made, the architects did not fear a repeat of the disaster that befell the Mantineians at the hands of the Spartans in 385 BC. Ultimately, as nothing in the defence of a city was left to chance, that the site was chosen for the location of the Great City is evidence in itself that it was perceived as defensible.[50]

The overall defensive strategy implicit in the choice of site was complemented tactically by the walls themselves and their constituent parts. While we know that the circuit utilized both rectangular and semicircular-shaped towers strategically placed on the edge of the plateau, had at least one postern, and was comprised of mudbrick on a stone foundation, unfortunately, we know little else. Any analysis of the circuit's tactics, therefore, is restricted to

[45] See under Comments.
[46] Roy (2007: 294). Admittedly, there is still some truth in this statement when its location is compared to other Arkadian settlements.
[47] Winter (1971a: 33).   [48] Jost (1999: 201).
[49] Loring (1892: 113) correctly notes that, 'had it been…even half or a quarter as wide, as it is now, it would (one would think) have been as prejudicial to any adequate defence [with] two great breaches in the wall…one on the eastern and one on the western side of the city'.
[50] Indeed, the size of the plain ensured that they were not without options. Just 3 km to the west, for example, they could have chosen to build their city at the confluence of the Helisson and Alpheios, where the water would have provided a natural defence on two sides in the seemingly typical Arkadian settlement pattern.

generalization and analogy. Still, by employing such appropriate Arkadian comparanda as the contemporary circuits at Mantineia and Stymphalos—with the former probably, and the later possibly, having been built under the direction of Epaminondas—we are well positioned to make plausible deductions. For example, the attested tower spacing of *c.*30 m between Megalopolis' semicircular towers is consistent with those of Mantineia and Stymphalos, as is the use of both rectangular and semicircular-shaped examples. We might imagine, therefore, a restored vision of the Megalopolis fortifications to include more or less regularly spaced towers of either shape, distributed throughout the circuit. Moreover, although no gates survive, we know from the routes described by Pausanias that it once had eight gates,[51] some of which, like Mantineia and Stymphalos, must have been overlap types. Yet these two systems also contained monumental entranceways, which would certainly not have been out of place in the fortifications surrounding the Great City of Arkadia.

CHRONOLOGICAL SUMMARY

The historical sources leave little doubt that the original circuit was built with the assistance of Thebes and coincided with the foundation of the Arkadian League in the years around 370 BC. While this circuit was constructed in the polygonal style, at least parts of the walls were repaired/rebuilt on same course *c.*221 BC, employing the dry rubble style of masonry. The chronologies of construction for these two major phases are based on historical probability, external evidence, and architectural affinities.

CHRONOLOGICAL ARGUMENTS

Establishing a chronology for the walls of Megalopolis is a straightforward task that presents few difficulties, compared to the majority of cases encountered thus far. First, however, as it has a direct bearing on the chronology, we must return to the assumption already presented, that the later walls commented upon by Polybius followed the same course as the original circuit. Loring argues that this must be the case, since 'in no single instance have late remains been found in positions parallel, or nearly so, with the earlier ones; all the remains, of whatever date they may be, fall naturally, not into two lines, but

---

[51] On the routes to/from Megalopolis, see Jost (1973); Pikoulas (1988a: 198–227; 1999a).

into one'.[52] Furthermore, Polybius himself hints that when the walls were rebuilt in *c.*221 BC, after having been destroyed by Kleomenes the year before, it was possible they were erected along the same lines as the original circuit.[53] Although it could be argued that a smaller later circuit would be easier to man and defend, it is equally true that, because of the inherent natural strength the topography provided to the reconstructed trace of the original circuit, its course would not be readily abandoned if at all possible. Finally, as noted by Roy, 'it [is] unlikely that the choice of an extensive wall-circuit was an ill-considered mistake…[since] Megalopolis several times held out against direct attacks, including sieges, before it was destroyed by Kleomenes'.[54] If the idea of a single course with at least two different chronological phases can be accepted, it remains only to assign dates to these periods.

Few would disagree that the first circuit was erected with the foundation of the city, sometime between 371 and 367 BC. Walls of this first and earliest date are represented by the excavated sections A–G (see Fig. C9.4). If Loring is correct, there is only one other clear building phase—represented by sections H–M (see Fig. C9.5).

In truth, this later group could represent repairs to the wall at any time between *c.*370 BC up to and including the repairs made with the money provided by Antiochus IV Epiphanes in 175 BC. Nonetheless, the most likely historical event necessitating the rebuilding of the fortifications of Megalopolis is the sack of the city by Kleomenes in 222 BC. It follows, therefore, that the walls were probably rebuilt upon the return of the Megalopolitan refugees in the wake of Kleomenes' defeat at the Battle of Sellasia in 221 BC.[55] Even if Kleomenes failed to raze the fortifications completely—as attested by the survival of the earlier sections A–G—this second building phase must have been extensive. The similarities demonstrated between these five later sections suggest that they were conceived as part of the same chronological phase.

BIBLIOGRAPHY

Xen. *Hell.* 7.1.23–4, 7.4–5; Polyb. 2.44, 2.51.3, 2.55.1–9, 5.93, 61.2–62.12; Diod 5.72, 18.68.3, 18.69.3–18.72.1; Liv. 38.34.7, 41.20.6; Plut. *Agis*, 3; *Cleom* 6.1–7, 23–5, 26.2, 29; *Arat.* 30.4–7; *Phil.* 5.1–5, 13.1–2; Paus. 4.29.7–8, 7.7.4, 8.27, 8.28.7, 8.33.1, 8.49.4, 9.7.1; Gell (1817: 97); Dodwell (1819: ii. 370–8); Leake (1830: ii. 28–42); Boblaye (1836: 167–8); Ross (1841: i. 74–84); Curtius (1851: i. 282–9); Rangabé (1857: 95–103); Bursian (1862: ii. 244–50); Welcker (1865: 263–4); Loring (1892); Woodhouse (1892); Bury (1898); Frazer (1898:

---

[52] Loring (1892: 112).   [53] Polyb. 5.93.
[54] Roy (2007: 294); see under History.   [55] Loring (1892: 115).

iv. 317–52); Winter (1971a: 31, n. 64, 33, 52, n. 14, 56, n. 6, 59, 112, n. 25, 113, 118, 273, n. 14); Jost (1973; 1985: 221–34; 1999: 201–2); Garlan (1974: 20, n. 3, 82, 193, 198, 206, 217, 233, 236, 243, 252, 254, 362, 373); Moggi (1974); Lawrence (1979: 60, 120, 122, 154, 423, 452); Roy et al. (1988); Pikoulas (1988a: 198–227; 1999a: 272–96); Demand (1990: 111–19); Hornblower (1990); Sarantakes (1993: 113–18); Papachatzis (1994: 290–5, 309–20); Nielsen (2002: 572–6); Corso (2005); Roy (2005, 2007); Lauter (2005); Maher (2012a: 499–520).

10

Nestane, Eastern Arkadia

LOCATION

The fortified acropolis of ancient Nestane is located in eastern Arkadia, about 7.5 km due east of Mantineia, on a small rocky hill, immediately north-west of the modern eponymous village (Fig. C10.1). The remains are to be found in the south-east corner of a basin (with *katavothroi*) defined by mountains on all sides. The acropolis comprises the summit of a small spur attached by a narrow saddle to a larger mountain to the east. Inhabitation was largely limited to the (unfortified) area of the saddle, east of the acropolis.

POLIS STATUS

The settlement of ancient Nestane appears to have been a dependency of Mantineia that reached *polis* status after 385 BC.[1] While Nielsen admits that the substantiation for this conclusion rest solely in the existence of the city ethnic, there is another important piece of evidence from which a *polis* status for Nestane may be inferred.[2] Briefly, an inscription, believed to date between *c.*385 and 370 BC, records an agreement by which the citizens of Helisson are willingly made citizens of Mantineia, with the *polis* of Helisson accordingly becoming a dependant of Mantineia.[3] This decree, Nielsen maintains, supports 'that the same was true of Nestane and the other *komai* situated in the Mantinike'.[4]

---

[1] Hodkinson and Hodkinson (1981: 246–8); Nielsen (1996b: 66–7; 2002: 578).
[2] Nielsen (1996b: 66). The city ethnic is mentioned by both Ephorus (*FGH* 70 F 234) and Theopompus (*FGH* 115 F 175).
[3] *SEG* xxxvii. 340; xxxviii. 351; xix. 392; xl. 371. See Nielsen (1996b: 67–70).
[4] Nielsen (1996b: 70). Xenophon (*Hell.* 5.2.7) mentions four *komai* in the territory of Mantineia, while Strabo (8.3.2) mentions five. It is almost certain that Nestane was one of these settlements.

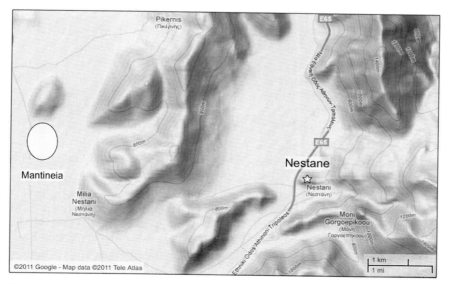

Fig. C10.1. Nestane, topographical map of the site and territory. (© *2011 Google-Map data © 2011 Tele Atlas*)

HISTORY

What is known of the history of Nestane relates primarily to its relationship with Mantineia. When the people of Mantineia were expelled from their city by the Spartans in 385 BC, they returned to their ancestral villages, including perhaps Nestane.[5] It may be reasonable to assume that not only was there an earlier settlement on the later site of Nestane, but that the site was occupied between 385 and *c*.370 BC before Mantineia was refounded.[6] Pottery found from the Classical and Hellenistic periods implies that the site continued to be inhabited after the second Mantineian synoikism.[7] The construction of the fortification circuit also suggests occupation at the site at least in the second half of the fourth century BC. Without systematic excavation, however, the history of Nestane after 370 BC remains largely unknown.

[5] Xen. *Hell.* 5.2.7.; i.e., they returned to the four or five *komai* that comprised the settlements that had participated in the original synoikism of the late Archaic/early Classical period. See Demand (1990: 67–9).

[6] Hodkinson and Hodkinson (1981: 264) caution that, because of the paucity of archaeological evidence, it cannot be assumed that settlement at Nestane ceased with the original synoikism of Mantineia, and there may have been activity at the site prior to 385 BC. Howell (1970: 87) reported Neolithic and Bronze Age pottery on the site.

[7] Howell (1970: 87); Jost (1999: 224).

LOCAL TOPOGRAPHY

The fortified acropolis of ancient Nestane is located on the low rocky Paniyir-istra Hill that commands the small plain of Nestane to the north as well as two narrow passes to the south-west: the more northern one leading to the Mantineian plain, the other, separated by Mt Stravomyti, led towards the plain of Tegea (see Fig. C10.1).[8] The small *chora* of Nestane is surrounded by mountains on all sides.[9] It is separated from the territory of Alea to the north by Mt Artemesio; from the territory proper of Mantineia to the west by Mt Barberi; while the Artemision Mountain range forms the boundary with the Argolid on the east and Tegea to the south.

The small hill of Paniyiristra, on which lie the extant remains of the site, measures approximately 160 m east–west by 100 m north–south. It rises *c.*90 m from the surrounding plain, and is relatively flat at its highest point. On the south, west, and north sides, the hill falls precipitously away to the plain below, while its east side is connected to the Artemision mountains by a narrow saddle some 350 m long.[10] Although in the early part of the twentieth century the hill was treeless and comparatively barren, by the early twenty-first century a variety of weeds, tall grasses, Aleppo pines, and wild flowers had somewhat obscured much of the ancient remains.[11] North of the settlement lies the plain of Nestane, which, oriented north–south, is *c.*7 km long by 2.5 km wide. Pausanias tells us that this plain was known in antiquity as the *Argon Pedion* or 'Fallow Plain' since 'the rainwater coming down into it from the mountains prevents the plain from being tilled; nothing indeed could prevent it from being a lake, were it not that the water disappears into a chasm in the earth'.[12] This *katavothros* has been located in the south-east corner of the plain, just north of the base of Paniyiristra Hill.[13] Besides the seasonal streams, the settlement also procured water from a number of mountain springs—most

---

[8] The passes from the Argolid into the plain of Nestane and relevant road network are addressed under Summary of Tactical Components.

[9] Although for convenience I refer to the 'territory' of Nestane, it is important to keep in mind that the territory of Nestane, as a dependent *polis* of Mantineia, is ultimately inseparable from the territory of Mantineia.

[10] As Pausanias makes it clear that the settlement was not in the plain, and as the hill itself is too small to accommodate even a modest population, this saddle linking the acropolis to the bulk of the mountains to the east is the best candidate for the location of the ancient settlement (Hodkinson and Hodkinson 1981: 247).

[11] Cf. with photos of the barren site published by Lattermann (1913: 407–8, abb. 5), which present a stark contrast to conditions in the early twenty-first century. A low modern cement/block safety wall, which runs around the south and west part of the hill, is another relatively recent addition.

[12] Paus. 8.7.1.

[13] Curtius (1851: i. 245); Fougères (1898: 92); Hodkinson and Hodkinson (1981: 243, fig. 2).

Fig. C10.2. Nestane, the site (facing north-west). (© *Matthew Maher*)

famously, the spring of Philip mentioned by Pausanias found in the modern village on the saddle, east of the acropolis.[14]

NATURAL DEFENCES

The height offered by the acropolis, and the steep and rocky slopes on its south, west, and northern sides, provide the site's natural defences (Fig. C10.2). The natural defences on these sides of the hill were apparently deemed sufficient, as they remained unfortified. The surrounding mountains largely limit the approaches to the site to routes from the west and north. There is a pass above Nestane leading from Argos mentioned by Pausainas.[15] The seasonal lake/marsh (emptied by the *katavothros* immediately north of the hill) would have inundated much of the plain to the north, limiting the approach from that direction.

FORTIFICATION TYPE

Acropolis type.[16] Following the general contours of the hill, the fortifications are limited to the eastern side only (Fig. C10.3).

---

[14] Paus. 8.7.4; Hodkinson and Hodkinson (1981: 247).
[15] Pausanias (8.6.4) calls this the Prinos Pass. The other pass leading from the Argolid and mentioned by Pausanias, the Klimax Pass, is located *c*.6 km due north of Nestane above and to the east of the modern village of Sanga.
[16] Jost (1999: 196).

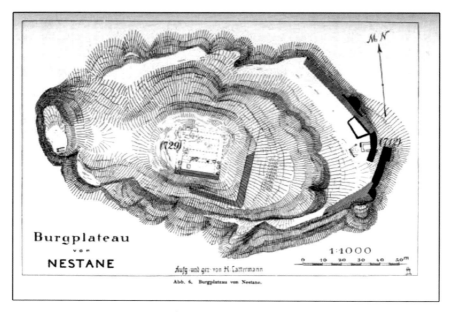

Fig. C10.3. Nestane, plan of site from Lattermann (1913: abb. 6).

PRESERVATION

The extant sections of the fortifications on the east side of the hill are well preserved for the most part, with the exception of some sections of curtain on either side of the gate. The exterior of the south curtain shows signs of weakness, and a large crack in its north-east corner is apparent.[17]

CONSTRUCTION

The superstructure was mudbrick (not preserved), while the stone foundations of the acropolis circuit are best described as predominately coursed polygonal with occasional trapezoidal and rectangular blocks (Fig. C10.4).[18]

---

[17] To prevent further damage, a large wooden scaffold has been erected on the south side of the south curtain.

[18] This description for the masonry is not irreconcilable with Scranton's classification (1941: 175), where, although he lists the walls of Nestane among other examples of irregular ashlar, he notes that they are 'perhaps rather irregular trapezoidal'.

Fig. C10.4. Nestane, north curtain exterior (facing west). (© *Matthew Maher*)

The foundations measure 3.20–3.87 m in thickness and survive in places to a height of 3.10 m.[19]

SUMMARY OF TACTICAL COMPONENTS

The acropolis circuit contains two semicircular towers (*c.*8–9 m in diameter), and two rectangular towers (6.90 m × 4.40 m, and 6.81 m × 3.25 m) at either end of the circuit's only (overlap) gate (see Fig. C10.3).

Towers

The acropolis circuit is comprised of north and south curtains, each stretch housing a semicircular tower (*c.*8–9 m in diameter), with their terminal ends coming together to form the corridor of an overlap gate. At the end of each section of curtain are two rectangular towers (6.90 m × 4.40 m and 6.81 m × 3.25), which represent the east and west sides of the gate's corridor (Fig. C10.5).

[19] I would like to thank the 39th Ephorate of Prehistoric and Classical Antiquities for granting me a study permit to examine the remains of ancient Nestane. Unless otherwise cited, all photographs and measurements are based on personal observation from my visit to the site in autumn 2009 and summer 2015.

Fig. C10.5. Nestane, the gate (facing south). (© *Matthew Maher*)

Gate

The acropolis of Nestane contains only a single overlap gate and no posterns. The gate, formed by the overlapping stretches of curtains, is oriented north–south and the passageway is preserved for a length of *c.*10 m (see Figs C10.3 and C10.5). About halfway down the east side is a flat stone on the ground abutting the curtain with a circular cutting (dia. 14 cm) to receive the axle for a door.[20] Also on its east side, the courses in the curtain decrease in number (from north to south) corresponding to the slight rise in the passageway as one enters, so that the final three courses of blocks at the southern terminus of this curtain rest directly on a bedrock outcrop. At this spot, the width of the passageway is 2.69 m, only slightly narrower than the opposite end, which measures 2.86 m in width.

COMMENTS

While several scholars have attempted to reconcile the limited visible remains on the hill with one or another of the temples mentioned by Pausanias, what is important here is that 'whether the hill was a sanctuary area or not would not have precluded its use as a village citadel, for which it was eminently suited'.[21] The location of the fortifications on the east side of the hill, facing the narrow saddle, provides further support that this is where the main settlement was

---

[20] For a sketch of this cutting, see Lattermann (1913: 412, abb. 7) and, on its mechanics, see Lawrence (1979: 253).

[21] Hodkinson and Hodkinson (1981: 247).

probably located.[22] It should be mentioned also that the date for the walls, the style of masonry, the location of the site, and Nestane's political relationship with Mantineia all raise the possibility that the fortified acropolis at Nestane may have served as a fort (that is, housed a standing garrison) in the larger defensive network protecting the chora of Mantineia.[23]

OVERALL DEFENSIVE PLANNING

Both the topography and geographical location made Paniyiristra Hill a well-chosen setting for the acropolis of Nestane. Rising 90 m on the edge of a plain, this hill comprised the highest point of a small east–west running spur that was linked to its main mass by a narrow saddle on which the ancient settlement probably stood. The topography of the hill, characterized by precipitous slopes on all sides but the east, not only eliminated the need for fortification works in these areas, but provided a defendable height that was easily accessible from the adjacent settlement.[24] Still, the fortification works on the east do suggest an uncertainty concerning the inherent defensibility of this side of the hill and the need to safeguard the only point of access to the otherwise secure acropolis.

As an acropolis-type circuit, it is not surprising to find that the main purpose of Nestane's fortifications was the protection of both the gate and the main approach. The position of the semicircular tower on the north curtain strongly suggests that access to the gate was from this direction (see Fig. C10.3). As this tower barely covers the gate, its position so far north can be explained only if the path leading to the gate ran in front it. Not only would this tower command a 180° range of fire, but advancing from this direction would ensure that the right, unshielded side of anyone approaching was presented to it. Indeed, it was the location of a road rather than that of the tower that enabled the defenders to employ the natural features of the site to its greatest advantage.[25]

The position of the rectangular tower, on the other hand, shows that its defensive role in the circuit was more straightforward. Located firmly at the

---

[22] By the early twenty-first century, much of this ridge had been obscured by houses, a school, and a cemetery.

[23] i.e., it served both as a fortified refuge for the people of Nestane and as a garrisoned fort. On the possible role of Nestane as a fort in the larger defensive network of Mantineia, see Maher and Mowat (forthcoming).

[24] Accessibility for the citizenry would have been especially important if the citadel did house the Sanctuary of Demeter mentioned by Pausanias (8.8.1), as maintained by Lattermann (1913: 415–16) and Hodkinson and Hodkinson (1981: 247).

[25] Winter (1971a: 216).

opening of the gate, this tower was undoubtedly meant to safeguard entry into the citadel itself. Still, its advantageous location also meant that it could provide cover for the main approach from its northern side, while its eastern side could guard approaches from south of the acropolis. Placing the gate's flanking tower on the approach's left side rather than the right suggests that this latter function must have been considered important. The necessity for vigilance and protection from the south is also implied by the form and position of the other semicircular tower. According to Lattermann's plan, this tower is placed at the point where the southern curtain changes direction towards the south-west.[26] Although of no use in protecting the northern approach or the gate itself, its curvilinear form ensured a 180° view of the area north-east to south-west of the acropolis.

These tactical elements of the circuit on the east, constructed to complement the natural defences of the rest of the hill, provide some clues to the larger strategic concerns of Nestane, and, ultimately, the *polis* to which it was a dependant, Mantineia. On one hand, this acropolis functioned as a citadel, perhaps even a sanctuary, for the *polis* of Nestane; on the other, it appears to have functioned as a kind of fortress to guard the passes from the Argolid and the roads from Tegea.[27] Pausanias records two mountain passes leading into the Mantinike from the Argolid: the passes of Klimax and Prinos,[28] the former issuing in the northern part of the plain of Nestane, the latter, just east of the modern village of Nestane. Paniyiristra Hill was certainly selected for its capacity to observe both. It is likely, moreover, that the route traversed by the modern Korinthos–Tripoli highway along the east side of the plain of Nestane was also a major thoroughfare linking Arkadia to Argos[29] and the Corinthia beyond. This road, passing through the territory of Nestane, continued south, linking the Mantinike with the territory of Tegea—their long-standing regional adversary. Besides being ideally positioned to observe routes from the Argolid, Nestane was also conveniently situated to monitor the movements of its southern neighbours.[30] The semicircular tower on the south curtain of Nestane's acropolis, therefore, while ineffectively placed to guard the gate itself, is, on the other hand, well suited to protect approaches from the south. Finally, the remains of a rectangular signal tower located on Stravomyti Hill directly opposite Paniyiristra Hill is further 'evidence of Mantineian vigilance in this region of their territory'.[31]

---

[26] Lattermann (1913: 409–10, abb. 6).
[27] Cf. with the early and astute observations of Clark (1858: 129–30). For arguments why the acropolis at Nestane may have housed a Mantineian or local garrison, see Maher and Mowat (forthcoming).
[28] Paus. 8.6.4.   [29] Jost (1999: 196).
[30] Here, of course, including the Spartans as well as the Tegeans.
[31] Hodkinson and Hodkinson (1981: 247). For more on this signal tower and others in the area, see Maher and Mowat (forthcoming).

CHRONOLOGICAL SUMMARY

Taken together, the historical probability, external evidence, and architectural affinities all suggest a date of *c.*370–350 BC for the entirety of this small circuit.

CHRONOLOGICAL ARGUMENTS

Although over the years, several scholars and travellers have drawn parallels between the fortifications of Nestane and the great circuits of Mycenae and Tiryns, the walls of Nestane's acropolis are undoubtedly not relics of the Late Bronze Age.[32] Instead, this perceived similarity owes more to the effective and common design of Classical and Hellenistic period gates that had simply been 'anticipated by the military engineers of the Bronze Age'.[33] Instead of looking for Bronze Age parallels, Lattermann more appropriately compares the fortifications of Nestane with those of the rebuilt Mantineia, and concludes that both are contemporaneous and date to *c.*370 BC.[34] Such a date corresponds well with the historical and archaeological evidence. The fragments of Ephorus and Theopompus,[35] which mention Nestane, have been dated by Jacoby to the Arkadian resurgence after Leuktra in 371 BC,[36] and the period of 346–328 BC[37] respectively. These references probably demonstrate that Nestane was inhabited at least in the second third of the fourth century BC.[38] Nor is such a date contradicted by the composition of the fortifications themselves or the styles of masonry employed. The Hodkinsons note the differing styles of masonry in the walls, and assume that they denote not different chronological periods, but the 'simultaneous work of different masons'.[39] In this I think they must be correct for the simple reason that, to function at all effectively as a defendable gate, then both curtains had to have been built contemporaneously. From

---

[32] For example, 'the resemblance of Nestane to Tiryns and Mycenae in natural situation, in the style of its fortifications, and in the appearance of artificial leveling at the top of the hill' (Frazer 1898: iv. 200); and '[at Nestane] there is a gateway defended like that at Mycenae by a projecting wall' (Clark 1858: 128). Hope Simpson and Dickinson (1979: 79) too maintain that parts of the circuit resemble Cyclopean work from the Late Bronze Age.

[33] Winter (1971a: 210). Winter specifically cites the gate at Nestane as an example of this trend.

[34] Lattermann (1913: 414).

[35] Ephorus (*FGH* 70 F 234); Theopompus (*FGH* 115 F 175).

[36] *FGH* ii C 27, 103.   [37] *FGH* ii B 31.

[38] As noted by Hodkinson and Hodkinson (1981: 248), this evidence accords well with the sherds discovered by Howell (1970: 87).

[39] Hodkinson and Hodkinson (1981: 247). This idea finds support by Winter (1989: 195), who notes that 'differences in masonry style often occur, for a variety of reasons, in contemporary portions of a single circuit and do not necessarily indicate a difference in date'. See also Winter (1971a: 82–4).

the history, known archaeology, composition, and masonry styles, the fortifications appear to have been constructed in a single period, most likely between *c*.370 and 350 BC, in connection with the second synoikism of Mantineia.[40]

BIBLIOGRAPHY

Ephorus (*FGH* 70 F 234); Theopompus (*FGH* 115 F 175); Paus. 8.7.1–4; Leake (1830: iii. 54; 1846: 378–9); Boblaye (1836: 141); Ross (1841: 132); Curtius (1851: i. 245); Clark (1858: 128–30); Loring (1895: 81); Fougères (1898: 92–3); Frazer (1898: iv. 199–200); Lattermann (1913); Scranton (1941: 175); Howell (1970: 87); Winter (1971a: 52, n. 14, 216, 193, n. 110); Lawrence (1979: 176, 178, 253); Hope Simpson and Dickinson (1979: 79); Hodkinson and Hodkinson (1981); Jost (1985: 14, 123, 140–2; 1999: 196); Sarantakes (1993: 26); Papachatzis (1994: 191–5); Nielsen (2002: 578); Maher (2012a: 132–47); Maher and Mowat (forthcoming).

[40] Lawrence (1979: 178) too maintains that 'a site so appropriate for guarding the frontier is likely to have been exploited soon after the refounding of Mantineia in 371'.

11

Orchomenos, Eastern Arkadia

LOCATION

Rising above the modern village that shares its name, the site of ancient Orchomenos is located about 5 km north of the town of Levidi in eastern Arkadia (Fig. C11.1).[1] The acropolis comprises the summit of a small hill, located between two large plains, and attached by a low and narrow saddle to a larger mountain to the west. Inhabitation was largely limited to the (unfortified) area below the acropolis on the south and south-east slopes of the hill.[2]

POLIS STATUS

Tradition holds that the city of Orchomenos was among the five great *poleis* of ancient Arkadia,[3] and, with its foundation assigned to an eponymous son of Lykaion[4] and its mention in Homer's 'Catalogue of Ships', also one of the oldest.[5]

HISTORY

Herodotus tells us that 120 Orchomenian hoplites participated in the Battle of Thermopylai and 600 soldiers were present at Plataia in the following year.[6] During the Peloponnesian War, Orchomenos was an ally of Sparta and a member of the Peloponnesian League.[7] In 418 BC Athenians and their Argive

---

[1] The modern village of Orchomenos was formerly Kalpaki.   [2] Jost (1999: 198).
[3] Ps.-Skylax 44.   [4] Paus. 8.3.3.
[5] Hom. *Il.* 2.605–8. The identity of Orchomenos as a *polis* is unquestionable. A comprehensive list of this evidence is supplied in Nielsen (2002: 578–81).
[6] Hdt. 7.202, 9.28.4.   [7] Xen. *Hell.* 5.4.37.

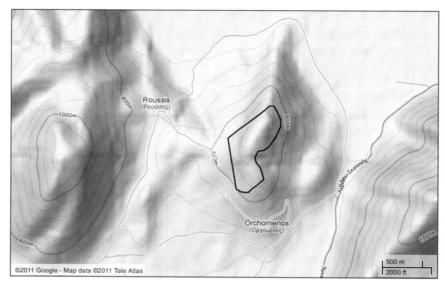

Fig. C11.1. Orchomenos, topographical map of Kalpaki Hill and fortification trace. (© *2011 Google-Map data © 2011 Tele Atlas*)

allies laid siege to Orchomenos in the hopes of emancipating a group of Mantineian hostages placed and held there by the Spartans.[8] The citizens of Orchomenos were 'alarmed at the weakness of their wall and the numbers of the enemy, and at the risk they ran of perishing before relief arrived, capitulated'.[9] After this defeat, Orchomenos joined the alliance between Athens, Argos, Elis, and Mantineia.[10] Orchomenos was at war with Kleitor in 378/377 BC, though none of the details is known.[11]

Having initially refused to join the Arkadian League owing to its animosity towards Mantineia,[12] Orchomenos allied with Sparta and Phlious in the years following Leuktra. In 370 BC, Xenophon records that the Mantineians 'made an expedition against the Orchomenians [but] they came off very badly from their attack upon the city wall'.[13] Despite their initial misgivings, Orchomenos did eventually join the Arkadian League.[14] Prior to the synoikism of Megalopolis, Orchomenos was still very active politically and appears to have been at the head of an organization that included the dependent *poleis* of

---

[8] Thuc. 5.61.4; Diod. 12.79.2.   [9] Thuc. 5.61.5.

[10] Thuc. 5.61.5. By 418 BC, therefore, Orchomenos possessed some form of fortification circuit—but whether it encircled the whole settlement or only the acropolis is unclear. This is addressed in more detail under Chronological Arguments.

[11] Xen. *Hell.* 5.4.36.   [12] Xen. *Hell.* 6.5.11.

[13] Xen. *Hell.* 6.5.13. This valuable, if brief, mention of the walls is significant for it shows that in 370 BC the city was fortified and defensible.

[14] *IG* V.2 1.46. Probably in the 360s BC (Nielsen 2002: 581).

Methydrion, Teuthis, and Theisoa (Karkalou).[15] It remains unclear exactly how this organization functioned and 'whether any of these minor *poleis* were conceived of as situated within Orchomenian territory'.[16] Although the political importance of Orchomenos diminished after the foundation of Megalopolis, because of its advantageous location and topographical situation the city frequently attracted the attention of the major Macedonian powers during the Hellenistic period.

During the struggle for power between Kassander and Polyperchon, the former took Orchomenos in 315 BC and installed a garrison.[17] A few years later, the city was again attacked, this time by Demetrios Poliorketes. In 303 BC, after the sack and resettlement of Sikyon, Demetrios advanced into Arkadia with eyes on Orchomenos.[18] When the commander of the garrison refused to yield the city, Demetrios 'brought up engines of war, overthrew the walls, and took the city by storm'.[19] As paralleled at Mantineia, in 229 BC, soon after joining the Achaian League, Orchomenos was attacked by Kleomenes of Sparta.[20] In 223 BC, however, Antigonos III retook the city by force from a garrison loyal to Kleomenes.[21] Having taken the city, instead of returning it to Achaian control, Antigonos installed a garrison and stored his siege equipment there. Polybius reasons this was because the city was too important strategically to return control of it to the Greeks, as it guarded an important route into the Peloponnesian interior.[22] After the death of Antigonos, however, the city appears to have once again reverted to the Achaians.[23]

LOCAL TOPOGRAPHY

The remains of the settlement are centred on the top of Kalpaki Hill which, rising *c.*230 m, separates the plain of Levidi in the south from the plain of Kandyla in the north-east (Fig. C11.2).[24]

---

[15] 'ἐκ δὲ τῶν συντελούντων ἐς Ὀρχομενὸν Θεισόα Μεθύδριον Τεῦθις' (Paus. 8.27.4). Pausanias is referring to the site of Theisoa located near modern Karkalou; not to be confused with the other Arkadian Theisoa situated on Lavda Hill in western Arkadia.

[16] Nielsen (2002: 579). We do know that both the population and the territories of these dependent *poleis* may have been transferred to Megalopolis during the synoikism of 370 BC (Paus. 8.27.4).

[17] Diodoros (19.63.5) explains that Kassander was admitted into the city by citizens who were hostile to the son of Polyperchon, which suggests that Orchomenos itself may have been spared a siege.

[18] Diod. 20.103.5. [19] Diod. 20.103.5. [20] Polyb. 2.46.

[21] Polyb., 2.54. [22] Polyb. 4.6. [23] In 199 BC (Livy 32.5).

[24] Both of these plains were in Orchomenian territory. There is a third plain, north-west of Kalpaki Hill, which is the territory of Kaphyai. See the Appendix for more on Kaphyai.

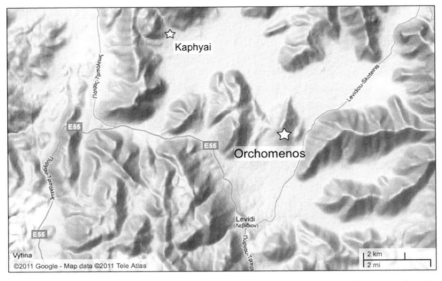

Fig. C11.2. Orchomenos, topographical map of site and territory. (© *2011 Google-Map data © 2011 Tele Atlas*)

The southern plain, roughly 4 km by 4.5 km, is defined by and separated from the territory of Mantineia by the Trachy Mountains to the east and south-east, and by the Anchisia ridge to the south.[25] The western edge of this plain is defined by the foothills of Mt Menalo, separating Orchomenian territory from that of Methydrion, Theisoa (Karkalou), and Helisson beyond. The northern limit of the southern plain and the south-western edge of the north-eastern plain is represented by Kalpaki Hill—the site of the *polis* itself. This north-eastern plain, *c.*5 km by 3 km, is limited on the north by Oligirtos, which forms a natural barrier between Orchomenos and the *poleis* of Pheneos and Stymphalos. While a spur from the Trachy Mountains formed the southern limit of the plain, to the east the bulk of this mountain chain separated the *chora* of Orchomenos from the territory of Alea. Finally, although there is no natural boundary between the Kandyla plain and the plain of Kaphyai to the west, the border between the two *poleis* probably lay somewhere immediately to the north or north-east of Kalpaki Hill.[26]

---

[25] Paus. 8.12.8–9.
[26] Hiller von Gaertringen and Lattermann (1911: 19) maintain that a river formed the boundary between the two plains, and ultimately the two *poleis*.

With low wetland basins surrounded on all sides by mountains, the topo-graphical situation of Orchomenos, as noted by Jost, 'présente une structure analogue à celle de tous les États de l'Est arcadien'.[27] And, like the other eastern Arkadian states, the drainage of excess water always appears to have been a concern. As noted by several visitors to the area, the copious springs at the foot of Mt Trachy east of the city, as well as the rainwater and seasonal springs, all contribute to the marshy condition in parts of the two plains.[28] Although flooding was a concern even in Pausanias' time, the problem went back much further, as evidenced by the discovery of artificial Bronze Age constructions for drainage and for the redirection of rivers.[29] Despite this dam, located east of the city in the narrow pass connecting the two plains, even in Frazer's time, 'throughout the winter and as late as the end of May this part of the plain [was] still an impassable swamp'.[30] Today, however, owing to the construction of a large canal running the length of the Kaphyai Valley into the northern Orchomenian plain, the swamp has all but disappeared, leaving behind numerous tracts of arable land.

The site of ancient Orchomenos is located on Kalpaki Hill. Although the hill itself is generally oval in shape (with its main axis oriented north–south), the southern half of the hill incorporated in the fortifications is comprised of a wide, roughly sickle-shaped ridge (see Fig. C11.1). While lofty and steep in places—especially the eastern half—this hill possesses no precipitous gradi-ents. The eastern slope of the hill is separated from the Trachy Mountains by a narrow defile, less than 500 m wide. On the western side, Kalpaki Hill is joined by a small saddle to an adjacent hill. The city of Orchomenos, consequently, occupied a strong and advantageous position, from which it was able to command not only the plains comprising its *chora*, but also what must have been several major Arkadian roads. For example, the valley of Orchomenos controlled access to central Arkadia from Achaia via Pheneos in the north and from the Corinthia via Stymphalos in the north-east.[31] Internally, Orchome-nos stood between Kleitor and Mantineia (and Tegea beyond) and between Alea (and the Argolid) and the *poleis* of central Arkadia. In this light, the attention the city received from the major powers during the Hellenistic period because of its advantageous location is hardly surprising.

[27] Jost (1985: 113).
[28] Rangabé (1857: 115); Frazer (1898: iv. 224); Hiller von Gaertringen and Lattermann (1911: 19); Jost (1985: 114).
[29] The northern plain, Pausanias (8.13.4) writes, 'is very considerable in extent, but the greater part of it is a lake'. See also the Hellenic Ministry of Culture (2007b).
[30] Frazer (1898: iv. 224).
[31] For remains of the road network in the territory of Orchomenos, see Pikoulas (1999a: 265–72).

Fig. C11.3. Orchomenos, the site (facing east). (© *Matthew Maher*)

NATURAL DEFENCES

The height offered by the acropolis, and its steep eastern slope, provide the site with its natural defences (Fig. C11.3). Its position in relation to the surrounding mountains largely limits the approaches to the site to routes from the north and south. The east side of the hill is flanked by a small, but fast-flowing stream.

FORTIFICATION TYPE

Acropolis type.[32] Enclosing the summit of the hill, the L-shaped circuit was laid out largely around its peak and down its southern half, where it follows the general contours of the hill (Fig. C11.4).

PRESERVATION

The site is generally poorly preserved; while there are some visible remains of the southern part of the circuit, most of the circuit is covered by dense overgrowth. The walls run for a length of 2.30 km and enclose an area of *c.*20 ha.[33]

---

[32] Listed as a 'ville mixtes' type by Jost (1999: 198–9).
[33] Hiller von Gaertringen and Lattermann (1911: 28); Nielsen (2002: 580).

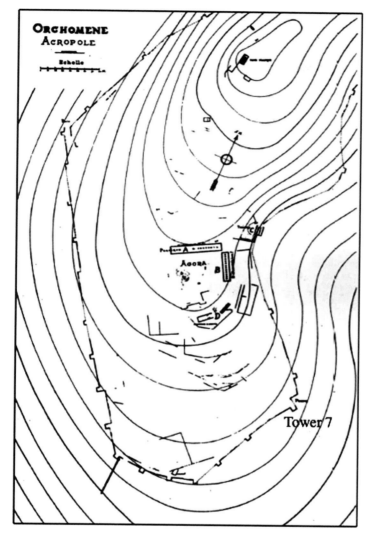

Fig. C11.4. Orchomenos, plan of site from Blum and Plassart (1914: pl. III).

CONSTRUCTION

The foundations of the walls range between 2 m and *c*.4 m in thickness,[34] and were constructed in an isodomic trapezoidal style (Fig. C11.5).[35] Frazer

---

[34] Hiller von Gaertringen and Lattermann (1911: 20, 28).
[35] While this is the same classification provided by Scranton (1941: 171), early travellers to the site rarely agreed in their terminology regarding the masonry. For example, Dodwell (1819: ii.

Catalogue

Fig. C11.5. Orchomenos, exterior front of Tower 7 (facing north-west). (© *Matthew Maher*)

observed a stretch of the curtains' socle that survived to a height of *c.*2.30 m.[36] All the curtain and tower foundations in the circuit once supported a mud-brick superstructure (not preserved).

SUMMARY OF TACTICAL COMPONENTS

The acropolis circuit contains twenty-nine towers, all rectangular and meas-uring *c.*6.50 m by 4 m (see Fig. C11.4). There are remains of a large tower/bastion on the highest point of the hill. The circuit possessed at least two gates, one of which appears to be an overlap type. No posterns are attested.

Towers

The acropolis circuit of Orchomenos contains at least twenty-nine rectangular towers.[37] These towers, distributed fairly regularly throughout the circuit, are on average 6.50 m wide across the front and extend some 4 m from the walls

426) maintains the walls resemble a 'rough Tirynthian style'; similarly, Curtius (1851: 220) observed that 'das Gemäuer hat an manchen Punkten den Charakter eines tirynthischen Cyklopenbaus'. Leake (1830: iii. 101) says the walls of Orchomenos have the 'appearances of a remote antiquity'; Frazer (1898: iv. 225) that they were coursed and 'on the whole quadrangular'; and Borrelli (1976: 653) maintains that the whole wall was of polygonal masonry. Winter (1989: 192–6) skirts the subject completely by discussing the chronology of the circuit without once referring to the specific masonry style(s).

[36] Frazer (1898: iv. 226),
[37] This number is derived from the plan by Blum and Plassart (1914: pl. III). Hiller von Gaertringen and Lattermann (1911: 30) put the total number of towers at thirty.

Fig. C11.6. Orchomenos, Medieval
bastion with earlier Greek
foundations (facing east).
(© *Matthew Maher*)

(see Fig. C11.5).[38] It appears that the towers in the steeper northern and eastern parts of the hill are generally smaller and more widely spaced than those located in the western and southern parts of the circuit, where the gradient of the hill is gentler.[39] Although it was not a part of the general acropolis circuit, the remains of a sizeable tower can be found isolated on the highest point of the summit. The use of small stones, and reused roof tiles and brick, bonded together by the liberal use of mortar, initially suggests a Late Roman or medieval date for the structure. As observed by Rangabé, however, although the superstructure of this tower is certainly of a later date, it is 'reposant sur des fondations helléniques'.[40] Indeed, the original foundations of the structure are still clearly visible today (Fig. C11.6).

Gates

The acropolis circuit contained at least two gates.[41] One is located on the west corner of the circuit, at the point across from the adjacent saddle where the wall turns north-east and rises up the hill. This gate appears to be of the overlap type flanked by a protecting tower on the attacker's left.[42] The location

---

[38] Measurements and tower labels are after Hiller von Gaertringen and Lattermann (1911: 28). As the 39th Ephorate of Prehistoric and Classical Antiquities was working on the site, I was not granted a study permit for Orchomenos. Unless otherwise cited, all photographs are based on personal observation from my visits to the site in autumn 2009 and winter 2010.

[39] Winter (1997: 259–60) believes the towers were both too small and too early to have housed stone-throwing artillery.

[40] Rangabé (1857: 115).   [41] Hiller von Gaertringen and Lattermann (1911: 20).

[42] I could observe no trace of the gate when I visited the site. The description is based on the plan alone.

of the second gate is less clear, and is described by Hiller von Gaertringen and Lattermann only as being in the south-east corner, at the end of the shortest path to the village of Kalpaki below.[43] If that path is the same as the one that exists today, then the likeliest candidate for this gate is the area immediately north of Tower 7, where the southern curtain turns north. There is no evidence of posterns.

COMMENTS

Immediately south-west of Orchomenos on the lower slopes of Mount Trachy is a conspicuous horseshoe-shaped cutting of significant dimensions. This depression represents a likely candidate for the source from which the lime-stone blocks for the socle were quarried.

OVERALL DEFENSIVE PLANNING

The overall defensive strategy inherent in the choice of Kalpaki Hill for a fortified acropolis is obvious. Its geographic location not only ensured command of the two well-watered plains comprising its *chora*, but was also ideally situated to dominate the network of major roads that undoubtedly traversed its territory.[44] Moreover, both the roads and the plains were safeguarded by the unparalleled viewshed afforded by the lofty heights of this hill. Besides its valuable elevation, the topography of the hill itself—with relatively steep terrain on three sides—contributes significantly to its natural defensibility. The fortification circuit both complemented the advantageous topography of the site and enhanced its already strong position by providing security to the more vulnerable southern part of the hill. Although by its very nature as an acropolis-type circuit this fortified hill would have functioned as a place of refuge during times of danger, that it enclosed the city's agora, theatre, and at least one temple demonstrates that it was also the monumental civic centre of Orchomenos.[45] That the fortified acropolis be easily accessible to the citizens, yet readily defendable against enemies, was, therefore, a primary and crucial strategic concern.

The layout of the fortification and the placement of its constituent parts reflect an attempt to compensate for the inherent weaknesses of the

---

[43] Hiller von Gaertringen and Lattermann (1911: 20).   [44] Jost (1999: 198).
[45] Although the enclosed area was considerable, to date no evidence of an urban settlement has been discovered on the acropolis.

site—specifically, the comparably low-lying southern and western parts of the hill. Indeed, the topography of the hill was such that, if an attack was to be launched on the walls of Orchomenos, it would be from either (or both) of these directions. The western part of the hill was especially vulnerable, as it was accessible by an adjacent saddle (see Figs C11.1 and C11.3). Although narrow, the elevation of this strip of land, if held by an enemy, represented a threat to the security of the western side of the circuit. Accordingly, we see on the west side not only the longest stretch of the circuit, but the greatest concentration of towers (see Fig. C11.4).[46] Furthermore, instead of following the contour of the hill and extending the walls westwards in a shallow but level arc, the architects constructed this stretch of wall in a straight line. Consequently, like a flattened arch, the middle of this wall rises up the slopes with its point of greatest elevation, located roughly in the middle of the stretch, *c.*20 m higher than its terminal ends. In the southern section of the circuit, we see the same compensation but manifested in a different arrangement. While the west half of this section follows the convex contour of that part of the hill, the eastern portion (just north-east of the theatre) of the southern trace exhibits the opposite pattern. Here, the wall changes to follow a concave course up the hillside. Such a course not only added *c.*10 m in elevation at the middle of the wall, but its inward curve afforded all four of its towers a field of fire in which to defend an approach from this direction. Finally, the stretch of wall extending from the south-west tower, and, if the plan is to be believed, what appears to be a similar one continuing from near the south-east tower, were further measures of protection to safeguard both the lower city and the citizens' access to their acropolis.

CHRONOLOGICAL SUMMARY

From historical probability, external evidence, and architectural affinities, it would appear that the fortifications of Orchomenos were probably constructed *c.*375–325 BC.

CHRONOLOGICAL ARGUMENTS

Establishing a chronology for the fortifications at Orchomenos is complicated by both the preservation of the remains and their recorded history during the

---

[46] One-third of all the towers in the entire circuit are located along the western side.

Classical and Hellenistic periods, and it is not surprising that scholars have been unable to reach a consensus on an exact date.[47] At the same time, however, employing these two elements is essential in any attempt to date the walls. What we do know, from the historical sources, can be briefly summarized. In 418 BC, Orchomenos possessed a walled city (or acropolis) but the fortifications were deemed inadequate by its inhabitants.[48] In 370 BC, the Mantineians were repelled by the fortifications at Orchomenos, so the circuit must have been stronger and more defensible than previously.[49] In 315 BC, Kassander took the city, having been admitted without an attack on the walls.[50] In 303 BC, Demetrios demolished part of the circuit and took the city by force.[51] Finally, in 223 BC, Antigonos took the city from a garrison loyal to Kleomenes.[52] From these scattered historical references and the remains themselves, several authorities maintain that a reliable chronological history of the walls can be ascertained.

Martin argues that this evidence suggests three chronological phases of construction for the Orchomenian circuit. Briefly, that the city possessed very weak defences in 419 BC; that the fortifications were improved as part of Spartan policy between c.380 and 370 BC; and that, following Demetrios' siege and the resultant capitulation, the city walls were repaired and strengthened sometime in the early third century BC.[53] Moreover, he felt that these chronological phases are consistent with the extant remains of the wall, in which he perceived different periods of construction.[54] Of course, the main weakness of this argument, as pointed out by Winter, is 'that differences in masonry style often occur, for a variety of reasons, in contemporary portions of a single circuit and do not necessarily indicate a difference in date'.[55] Meyer, on the other hand, is perhaps on firmer ground in arguing that the absence of early remains within the enclosed area of hill is evidence that the fifth-century BC settlement was, in fact, located at the foot of the hill.[56] For this reason, Meyer maintains that the extant walls of acropolis belong to one phase—built c.360–350 BC when the city was moved higher up the hill for reasons of security.[57] Although Meyer's placement of the fifth-century city at the foot of the hill is reconcilable with the recorded account of the inhabitants' concern for the weakness of their walls in 418 BC,[58] it does not explain the events of 370 BC.

---

[47] Winter (1989: 194).   [48] Thuc. 5.61.4; Diod. 12.79.2.   [49] Xen. *Hell.* 6.5.13.
[50] Diod. 19.63.5.   [51] Diod. 20.103.5.   [52] Polyb. 2.54.
[53] Martin (1944: 109–13). For a summary and critique of Martin's argument, see Winter (1989: 194–6).
[54] Martin (1944: 114).   [55] Winter (1989: 195). See also Winter (1971a: 82–4).
[56] Meyer (1939b: 893)—i.e., in roughly the same location as the modern village of Orchomenos.
[57] Meyer (1939b: 892). For a summary and critique of Meyer's argument, see Winter (1989: 194–5).
[58] i.e., if Orchomenos had a fortified acropolis in 418 BC, then their concern 'would have been incomprehensible, especially in terms of fifth-century siegecraft' (Winter 1989: 195).

Specifically, if the city was not properly fortified until *c*.360–350 BC, how could the fortifications have been successful in holding back the Mantineians, who, Xenophon records, 'came off very badly from their attack upon the city wall'[59] in 370 BC?

It is Winter who makes the strongest (albeit not entirely convincing) argument concerning the date of the Orchomenian circuit. Subscribing to Meyer's opinion about the location of the fifth-century BC town, Winter proceeds to argue the reasons for a fourth-century BC date for the hilltop circuit. As the towers are generally too small to have housed heavier calibre torsion machines, he is undoubtedly correct in his assertion that the fortifications are 'more typical of the period before the general use of defensive artillery'.[60] Furthermore, although he notes some similarities between the tower dimensions and spacing of the southern half of the circuit and those of Mantineia, he maintains that the system at Orchomenos 'seems to be somewhat later than that of Mantineia'.[61] To answer the obvious question of how much later, Winter attempts to narrow the date down further by incorporating the evidence provided by the other architectural elements of the intramural area. For example, because the theatre was provided with a *proskenion* from the very beginning, Winter believes it is unlikely to be earlier than *c*.300 BC.[62] He also points to the 'Hellenistic appearance of the agora and the overall town-plan'[63] as suggestive of a late Classical or early Hellenistic date.

Winter is again certainly right in his assertion that, once the hilltop had been chosen for the site, then the walls would have been built as quickly as possible. He adds that, after the walls had been constructed, then 'it would of course have been necessary to construct new private houses and public buildings [and last, to build] "embellishments" such as the theatre'.[64] When the system of the walls and the intramural architecture are taken together, Winter proposes that, following the conception of the town plan *c*.350 BC, the 'city walls, agora and other public buildings, and theatre, [were] built in that order over the next 40–50 years'.[65]

While the logic behind such an argument is sound, it is not without its flaws. Not least of all is Winter's suggestion of a town plan and private houses. Unless he is speaking abstractly—in the sense that every town has a plan—attempting to reconcile the scanty remains of the site with any semblance of an organized schematic is an exercise in futility. With the exception of the buildings of the agora, there are no hints (orthogonal outlines or otherwise) to suggest a conceived town plan for Orchomenos. Moreover, as already mentioned, there is no evidence at all of private houses within the intramural area. This immediately suggests that the residential area of the settlement

---

[59] Xen. *Hell.* 6.5.13. [60] Winter (1989: 195). [61] Winter (1989: 194).
[62] Winter (1989: 196). [63] Winter (1989: 196). [64] Winter (1989: 196).
[65] Winter (1989: 196).

remained at the foot of the hill—where it had been in the fifth century BC, where it was when Pausanias visited the site in the second century AD, and where it remains today.

The fact that the theatre was not built until *c.*300 BC means little in the context of a functioning acropolis and means even less when employed as a chronological marker for the dates of the wall. In other words, I do not doubt Winter's assertion that the theatre was built after the walls, but that in no way negates the use of the hill as a refuge at any time before that, walled or not. His argument that the walls must have preceded the construction of the agora is not inconceivable. Still, suggesting a late-fourth-century BC date for its construction because it has a Hellenistic appearance is less conceivable. The agora at Megalopolis, for example, is truly of the Ionic form and considerably more Hellenistic in its appearance than that of Orchomenos. But the layout of the agora at Megalopolis was likely to have been conceived with the foundation of the city, planned in *c.*370 BC, even if the main buildings were not constructed until around the middle of the century.[66]

Returning to the fortifications, Winter states that 'the Orchomenian system should probably be dated not earlier than 350 BC nor later than *c.*325 BC'.[67] While the evidence outlined here is given for why the walls should be later than 350 BC, Winter does not provide any reasons why the walls cannot be earlier than that date. Besides mentioning that the walls of Mantineia and Orchomenos cannot be as close in date as Meyer suggested, and that the system at Orchomenos is hardly more advanced than that of Mantineia, Winter does not entertain the idea that the walls of Orchomenos may pre-date 350 BC. Again we have to return to the words of Xenophon and the role the fortifications played in repelling the Mantineians in 370 BC. This documentation presents three chronological scenarios concerning the *terminus post quem* for the fortifications of Orchomenos: the Mantineians were unsuccessful because (1) the 'weak' walls of the lower city of 418 BC were strengthened sometime before 370 BC; (2) the walls of the acropolis were thrown up *c.*380–370 BC, as Martin suggests; or (3) the acropolis was fortified *c.*350–325 BC, as Winter maintains. The first scenario seems the most unlikely. If the defences of the lower city existed and were sufficient to repel an enemy in 370 BC, why then abandon them and build a completely new circuit on the acropolis?[68] Ultimately I believe that the answer lies in the combination of the second and third options. Winter presents an accurate analysis of the general character of wall and makes a strong case for their existence in the third quarter of the fourth century BC. Nonetheless, there is nothing about the Orchomenian system that would preclude a date in the 370s BC for its construction. Furthermore, the

---

[66] On the excavations of the agora of Megalopolis, see Richards (1892).

[67] Winter (1989: 195).

[68] Moreover, they would probably have left some trace in the archaeological record.

existence of a fortified and defensible system before 370 BC is also reconcilable with the account of Xenophon. In the end, therefore, I would push Winter's date for the construction of the fortifications in their present form back a quarter of a century to *c.*375–325 BC.

BIBLIOGRAPHY

Hom. *Il.* 2.605–8; Ps.-Skylax 44; Hdt. 7.202, 9.28.4; Thuc. 5.61.4–5; Xen. *Hell.* 5.4.36., 5.4.36, 6.5.11–17, 6.5.29; Polyb. 2.46, 2.54, 4.6; Diod. 12.79.2, 19.63.5, 20.103.5; Strab. 8.8.2; Livy 32.5; Paus. 8.3.3, 8.13.1–6, 8.27.4; Gell (1817: 144–5); Dodwell (1819: ii. 426); Cramer (1828: iii. 306–7); Leake (1830: iii. 100–2); Boblaye (1836: 148–50); Curtius (1851: i. 219–21); Rangabé (1857: 115–17); Bursian (1862: ii. 203–6); Frazer (1898: iv. 224–6); Hiller von Gaertringen and Lattermann (1911: 18–29); Blum and Plassart (1914); Meyer (1939b); Scranton (1941: 171); Martin (1944: 107–14); Howell (1970: 82–3); Winter (1971a: 31, n. 64, 32, n. 65, 33, n. 68, 52, n. 14, 193, n. 108; 1989: 192–6; 1997: 259–60); Garlan (1974: 125, 127, n. 3, 148, 179); Borrelli (1976); Lawrence (1979: 123, 124, 178); Jost (1985: 113–22; 1999: 198–9); Sarantakes (1993: 26–9); Papachatzis (1994: 222–30); Pikoulas (1999a: 265–72); Neilsen (2002: 578–81); Maher (2012a: 172–92).

12

Paos, Northern Arkadia

LOCATION

Paos is located in northern Arkadia on the north bank above the Lopesi/Sireos River (Fig. C12.1). The acropolis comprises the summit of a small spur attached by a narrow saddle to a larger mountain to the north. Inhabitation was probably largely limited to the (unfortified) area in the small hollow east of the acropolis.

POLIS STATUS

The evidence available suggests that ancient Paos was regarded as a *polis* in the Classical and Hellenistic periods, if not earlier.[1] Substantiation for such a claim apparently resides first and foremost in the testimony of Herodotus. He describes how, in the early sixth century BC, among the suitors to the daughter of Kleisthenes (tyrant of Sikyon) was a man named Laphanes, who was from the 'Παίου πόλιος'.[2] Another central piece of evidence supporting the community's *polis* status comes from Delphi, where an inscription discovered reveals that a Delphic *theorodokos* resided in Paos sometime in the late third century BC.[3]

HISTORY

Besides Herodotus, Pausanias represents the only other ancient source that mentions Paos at all. Unfortunately, both tell us almost nothing concerning

---

[1] Nielsen (2002: 582–3, 549, n. 2) has no doubts about this, placing Paos among those Arkadian communities whose identification as a *polis* he considers to be a certainty.

[2] Hdt. 6.127.3. Meyer (1942: 2400) maintains that, for the city to boast a suitor for the hand of Kleisthenes' daughter, then in the Classical period it must have been wealthy and important and its territory must have been large and fertile.

[3] Plassart (1921: ii. 72).

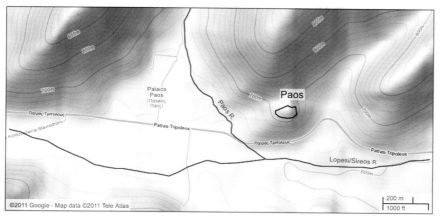

Fig. C12.1. Paos, topographical map of site and territory. (© *2011 Google-Map data © 2011 Tele Atlas*)

the history of this small *polis*. We are left to wonder whether Paos was a member of the Peloponnesian League or the later Arkadian Confederacy. The city's relationship with the Achaian League is equally unknown. It lies roughly halfway between Psophis and Kleitor—the former attacked by Philip V, the latter by the Aitolians—so it would be very interesting to learn of the allegiances and alliances of this small Arkadian settlement within the larger picture of the Social War and late-third-century BC Hellenistic politics in general. The one point that can be established, based on Pausanias' narrative, is that, around the middle of the second century AD, Paos lay within the territory of Kleitor.[4]

LOCAL TOPOGRAPHY

The ancient site of Paos is located 10 km south-east of Psophis, on a small fortified hilltop on the northern side of the narrow Lopesi Valley (see Fig. C12.1). The hill itself rises *c.*120 m from the valley below and is the southernmost spur of the larger Mt Trifia, from which it is separated by a narrow saddle. The small plateau at the crest of the hill representing the actual intramural area measures only *c.*100 by 150 m; within the walls is a small circular knoll measuring 65 by 34 m.[5] Directly below this plateau, the hill slopes away relatively evenly and gently on the east, west, and south. To the north, the

---

[4] Paus. 8.23.9.   [5] Papandreou (1920: 125).

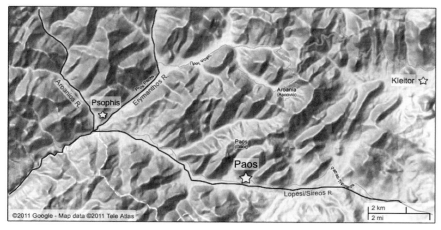

Fig. C12.2. Paos, topographical map of site and surrounding territories. (© *2011 Google-Map data © 2011 Tele Atlas*)

slope is somewhat steeper and after only a few metres is immediately met by a narrow saddle in the shape of a steep-sided concavity, less than 100 m long and only *c*.50 m wide.

The site commanded the convergence of two major rivers (Fig. C12.2). Originating at the head of the ravine immediately north-west of the site is the River Paos. This river flows south-east along the foot of the mountain before turning east, where it skirts the southern flank of the site on its way towards the eastern end of the Lopesi Valley and the plain beyond. The other river is the Lopesi/Sireos River, which runs south-east down the Lopesi Valley from its junction with the Erymanthos and Aroanios at Psophis. The confluence of the Paos and Lopesi/Sireos Rivers is located at the base of the south-west corner of the site. Nestled between these two rivers and the hills to the north is a roughly diamond-shaped plain, measuring *c*.900 by 700 m. This plain is now bisected by the Patras–Tripoli road, with just the southern half given over to farming, as its northern half is completely covered by the modern village of Neos Paos. This well-watered area in the widest part of the Lopesi Valley must have been the primary source of cultivation for the ancient settlement.

With its location along a narrow river valley instead of in a natural basin surrounded by mountains, the position of ancient Paos—not unlike Psophis— does not follow the typical pattern observed by most of the other northern and eastern Arkadian settlements. Consequently, attempting to determine the natural (and presumably political) boundaries of this *polis* is not a straightforward task. Certainly the mass of Mt Trifia to the north and north- east- separated Paos from the territory of Kleitor; similarly, the bulk of

Fig. C12.3. Paos, the site (facing east). (© *Matthew Maher*)

Mt Aphrodisio and the subsidiary chains on the south-west and south must have served to divide the territory of Paos from that of Thelpousa and Halous. With no significant natural boundaries, the extent of Paos' territory to the east and west is less certain. As the *polis* situated closest to the plain at the east end of the Lopesi Valley, it is conceivable that this narrow swathe of land and the small radiating valleys were indeed controlled by Paos. To the west, perhaps the narrowest part of the Lopesi Valley (at modern Ag. Georgios), nearly halfway between Paos and Psophis, represented the limits of the respective territories.

NATURAL DEFENCES

The height offered by the acropolis and the steep slope on its southern side give the location of Paos its natural defences (Fig. C12.3). The river valley and surrounding mountains limit the approaches to the site for the routes from the east and west. The Lopesi/Sireos River flanks the hill to the south, while one of its tributaries, the Paos River, flanks the site to the west.

FORTIFICATION TYPE

Acropolis type.[6] The circuit follows the contour of the hill, encircling the summit (Fig. C12.4).

---

[6] Jost (1999: 195).

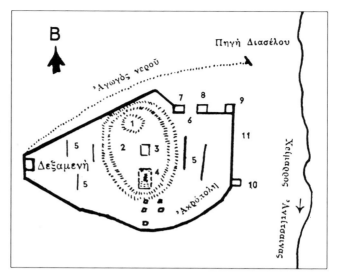

Fig. C12.4. Paos, plan of the site from Papachatzis (1994: 269).

PRESERVATION

The site is generally poorly preserved; parts of the east side are moderately preserved, while most of the other sides are obscured by vegetation and modern terracing. The total length of the circuit is 516 m,[7] enclosing an intramural area of c.2–3 ha. Isolated sections of curtain in the eastern part of the circuit still stand to a height of c.3 m high in places.

CONSTRUCTION

The superstructure was mudbrick (not preserved), while the stone foundations of the acropolis circuit were constructed (seemingly indiscriminately) in both a coursed and an uncoursed polygonal style (Fig. C12.5).[8]

---

[7] Papandreou (1920: 122).
[8] Papandreou (1920: 123); Meyer (1939a: 83; 1942: 2399). Gell (1817: 123) too observed that 'this fortress has very curious remains of masonry'.

Fig. C12.5. Paos, eastern side of circuit (facing west). (© *Matthew Maher*)

SUMMARY OF TACTICAL COMPONENTS

The acropolis circuit contains four rectangular towers (of various sizes), strategically rather than regularly spaced, as well as one simple frontal opening type gate (see Fig. C12.4).

Towers

The circuit at Paos contains four rectangular towers, all concentrated in the east and north-east parts of the circuit.[9] Tower 10, located at the junction between the eastern and southern sections of the trace, is the largest of the four towers, measuring 3.90 m wide and extending *c.*7 m from the adjacent curtains. Just over 50 m north of this tower, at the north-east corner of the circuit, is Tower 9. Measuring 4.30 m wide and projecting 3.85 m, this tower is the smallest in the circuit. To the west of Tower 9 are the final two examples, Towers 8 and 7. These towers have identical dimensions, with their north sides measuring 4.40 m and their lateral sides 6.80 m. That these two towers are identical is not altogether surprising, as they are part of the same gate complex.

---

[9] Neither the gate nor any of the towers was visible on my visit to Paos in March 2011. All the measurements provided here, therefore, are from Papandreou (1920: 124). Tower numbers correspond to those on Fig. C12.4.

Gates

There is evidence for only a single gate and no posterns. The gate is a simple
frontal opening type with a narrow (*c.*3 m) north–south-oriented opening
defined on the east and west by the long lateral sides of flanking rectangular
towers (Towers 7 and 8).

OVERALL DEFENSIVE PLANNING

As in every other fortified Arkadian site, there is nothing random in the
relationship between the choice of site and the corresponding overall defensive
planning and strategy at ancient Paos. Located on the edge of a plain, on the
tip of a spur that extended from the flank of a mountain and linked to its main
mass by a narrow saddle, the acropolis of Paos was ideally positioned for its
function as both a refuge in times of danger and a safe and expedient place
from which to command its territory. From its relatively modest height on the
north side of the valley, this hill—distinguished by both its accessibility and its
inherent natural strength—was also afforded an advantageous viewshed to
oversee traffic moving from all approachable directions.[10] This is a significant
point, as the Lopesi Valley was the main east–west artery of north-west
Arkadia, not only linking Paos to Psophis and Kleitor, but also serving to
link Arkadia with Elis and Achaia.

Shielded largely by the bulk of Mt Trifia to the north, the fortified hill was
provided with further natural defences in the form of two rivers circumventing
its base (see Fig. C12.1). Originating in the valley north-west of the site and
providing protection along the west side of the hill is the River Paos. This river
is met by the Lopesi/Sireos River at the base of the south-west corner of the
site. After this confluence, the united rivers, continuing their journey east
down the Lopesi Valley, inadvertently offer their protection to the southern
flank of the hill. In this way, the acropolis of Paos was provided with natural
defences on the north, west, and south sides of the hill. Only the east side of the
hill was denied any apparent natural topographical advantages—an observation not lost on the military engineers who constructed the small circuit on
its peak.

The fortification circuit of Paos is best understood in relation to the natural
topography of the hill. Like most acropolis-type sites, not only does its trace
follow precisely the contours of the hill, but it was constructed specifically to
enhance the natural strength of the site while at the same time to compensate

[10] Jost (1999: 195).

for inherent weaknesses. That the walls generally follow the shape of the hill is clear enough: the southern wall curves to follow the general elevation contour on that side of the hill, while the long north-west section follows the ridge running north-east–south-west at the crest of the hill. It is on these two sides where the absence of any tower is most conspicuous. Certainly the steep slopes found on the north-east and south sides, as well as the two rivers at their base, were deemed sufficient protection. It is the east and north-east sections of the circuit—areas devoid of any substantial natural defences—where the tactical additions reflecting defensive concerns are most apparent.

The positioning of all the circuit's towers as well as of its only gate here indicates that the north-east and eastern part of the system represented the defensive focus of the acropolis. It is no coincidence that Tower 10, the largest in the circuit, is found where the east curtain meets the southern stretch of wall. From its position it was well placed to dominate any approach from the east and the south-east. Its relatively long flanks (*c.*7 m) would have ensured maximum coverage against any attacker that managed to reach the curtains. Further to the north is Tower 9, which, although smaller, could equally safeguard against any unwarranted approach from the east or north-east. With its eastern wall representing essentially an extension of the eastern curtain, however, it is clear that the primary focus of this tower's attention— and those to the west—was defence of the gate from the direction of the saddle, located some 30 m below and to the north of the circuit.[11]

As the most easily accessible part of the hill, this saddle represents the most likely point of entrance to the acropolis itself, and it is not surprising, there-fore, to find a gate facing this direction.[12] In the same way, as the most easily accessible point, it is also not surprising to find the densest concentration of towers immediately opposite. Indeed, the construction of three north-facing towers along a stretch of wall only 40 m in length is confirmation of the fact that Towers 7, 8, and 9 were designed to command access to the gate and protect against an attack launched from the saddle. The defence of the north-east part of the circuit was enhanced by the oblique stretch of wall branching from the north-west corner of Tower 7 to meet the long north wall of the circuit. This arrangement, providing a *c.*16 m long curtain set at a 45° angle to the left of the gate, would have provided defenders with a further platform from which to fire missiles upon an enemy's unshielded right side as it approached the gate.[13]

---

[11] Papandreou (1920: 122).

[12] The placing of a gate to give access from a narrow saddle is also a tactic employed in the circuit at Nestane.

[13] The oblique course of the wall emanating from Tower 7 created, in effect, a small concavity in front of the gate—an arrangement similar to Gate B at Gortys and also that proposed for the north-east gate at Psophis.

CHRONOLOGICAL SUMMARY

Late fifth or early fourth century BC (?), based on historical probability and architectural affinities.

CHRONOLOGICAL ARGUMENTS

Even if Paos had a *polis* identity by the early sixth century BC, as suggested by Herodotus,[14] it does not necessarily follow that the settlement was fortified at that time. As ancient Paos remains all but invisible in the historical record, any attempt to assign a rough chronology to the acropolis fortifications must rely almost exclusively on the meagre remains themselves. An approximate date can be considered only after the construction methods and the tactical components of the circuit are evaluated within the framework of evolving Greek warfare and through appropriate comparanda.

Scranton's comprehensive survey of the masonry of Greek fortifications reports that the polygonal style has its origins in the fifth century BC and that specifically Peloponnesian examples—both coursed and uncoursed—are rare after the late fourth and the beginning of the third century BC.[15] Meyer arrived at a similar conclusion independently, admitting that, although the walls may date to the early Hellenistic period, he doubts that the circuit can be older than the fourth century BC.[16] While the line of reasoning behind Meyer's chronological opinion remains unstated, it is unlikely he took the larger tactical components of the acropolis trace into consideration. If, for example, he did take into account the form and distribution of the towers, the gate, and the curtains, he might instead have proposed a slightly earlier date—one that perhaps pre-dates the widespread use of artillery.

In a circuit spanning just over 500 m in length, the construction of only four towers is telling and suggests that, where possible, the architects relied almost exclusively on the natural defences afforded by the topography itself. This situation accords well with Winter's description of fifth-century BC systems in which towers were employed sparingly and unsystematically, and usually only where special precautions were required—in areas easily accessible to attackers, such as at gates, angles, or where the wall stood on a gentle slope.[17] Moreover, in these systems, as at Paos, simple jogs or short returns and long stretches of unflanked curtain were still frequent.[18] Besides their limited deployment, one of the most observable features in the circuit is the relatively small size of the towers employed. Averaging a modest *c*.4 by 7 m, the four

---

[14] Hdt. 6.127.3. [15] Scranton (1941: 50, 55, 69). [16] Meyer (1942: 2399).
[17] Winter (1971a: 154, 160). [18] Winter (1971a: 154).

towers at Paos are similar in dimension to those towers at Psophis, Mantineia, and Orchomenos, for example, which seem to be products of the late fifth to early fourth centuries BC.

Unfortunately, the form and location of the gate and the apparent absence of posterns in the circuit are not as chronologically informative. While, in general, the use of posterns was less common in earlier circuits—when defenders still relied on the strength of their walls before the widespread use of artillery—their absence at Paos does not necessarily designate an early date for the walls. In an acropolis circuit already sufficiently protected by the topography of the hill on three sides, such tactical features would have been ultimately unnecessary during any stage in the evolution of ancient Greek siege warfare. As a simple opening, logically situated at the only accessible part of the acropolis, the single gate offers little evidence as to the date of the circuit as a whole. This gate, moreover, is fairly typical and at Paos it follows the general pattern outlined by Winter where 'the line of the wall was more often than not determined by...natural features, and the gates were subsequently placed where they would be under cover of projecting salients or angles'.[19] While the flanking towers and the additional measure of swinging the western wall sharply outward to a point some distance from the gate created an area for enfilading on an enemy's unshielded right side, it adds little to the chronological question.

Every fortification circuit is, of course, more than a sum of its parts. Yet, it is placing the parts into the appropriate archaeological and historical contexts that gets us closer to the chronological truth. Both the style of masonry and the limited use of relatively small towers immediately suggest that the circuit of Paos was constructed before the widespread use of artillery. Yet the apparent 'old-fashioned' nature of the system may instead reflect its isolation, its function as an acropolis refuge, and/or the topography of the hill on which it was built. In other words, the lack of towers on all sides but the north-east and the conservative use of polygonal masonry may still have been appropriate tactical decisions in a time when siege warfare had displaced the traditional pitched hoplite battle. Certainly, the construction of a large cistern at the west end of the acropolis served by a 230 m long aqueduct originating outside the walls suggests a defensive concern in the unlikely event of a siege.[20] Until a systematic excavation sheds further light, however, based purely on the remains themselves, a date of late fifth to early fourth century BC for the construction of the circuit is the most inclusive for all the evidence available.

---

[19] Winter (1971a: 212).
[20] On this cistern see Papandreou (1920: 122). Whether this cistern is contemporaneous with the circuit, however, is unclear.

BIBLIOGRAPHY

Hdt. 6.127.3; Paus. 8.23.9; Gell (1817: 123); Leake (1830: ii. 249; 1846: 221); Boblaye (1836: 157); Curtius (1851: i. 379–80); Bursian (1862: ii. 263–4); Frazer (1898: iv. 281); Papandreou (1920: 121–9); Meyer (1939a: 83; 1942); Jost (1985: 25, 42, 43, 45; 1999: 195); Pritchett (1989: 20–1); Papachatzis (1994: 269–70); Nielsen (2002: 549, n. 2, 582–3); Maher (2012a: 291–307).

13

Pheneos, Northern Arkadia

LOCATION

Pheneos is located in northern Arkadia in the northern part of basin (with *katavothroi*) defined by mountains on all sides (Fig. C13.1). The site comprises a small acropolis with a citadel at its highest point. It is likely that inhabitation was largely limited to the lower city in the plain directly south of the acropolis.

POLIS STATUS

Although no Archaic or Classical period sources specifically identify Pheneos as a *polis*, few would doubt its identity as such.[1] In the fifth century BC, the settlement began striking its own coinage bearing the city ethnic[2] and dedicated a statue of Hermes at Olympia in the city's name.[3] In the fourth century BC, the city could boast an Olympic victor,[4] an Argive *theorodokos*,[5] and a citizen who was granted Argive *proxenia*.[6]

HISTORY

As is the case with so many minor Arkadian *poleis*, Pheneos is infrequently mentioned in the surviving historical accounts.[7] When the ancient historians and geographers did have cause to refer to the settlement, it was usually in

---

[1] Polybius (2.52) provides the earliest surviving written reference to Pheneos as being a *polis*. For a comprehensive inventory of the evidence, see Nielsen (2002: 585–6).

[2] Head (1963: 452).   [3] Paus. 5.27.8.

[4] Neolaidas of Pheneos (*Olympionikai* no. 380).   [5] Nielsen (2002: 586).

[6] *SEG* xxx. 356.

[7] See Giannakopoulos et al. (2012: 51–2) for more detail on Pheneos' mythological and historical past.

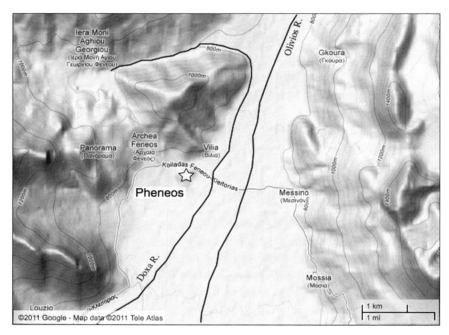

Fig. C13.1. Pheneos, topographical map of site and territory. (© *2011 Google-Map data © 2011 Tele Atlas*)

regard to one of two factors: its proximity to the River Styx or its capture by Kleomenes in his struggles against the Achaian League in 225 BC.[8] Despite its strategic location on a major route between Arkadia and Achaia, between the time of Pausanias and the visit by Leake and Dodwell, 'the little valley [of Pheneos] has been without an historian'.[9]

LOCAL TOPOGRAPHY

The acropolis of ancient Pheneos comprises a conical, crescent-shaped hill, situated on the northern edge of a large plain[10] (see Fig. C13.1). The hill itself is relatively small and unassuming, measuring 450 m by 350 m and rising from the plain to a height of only *c.*60 m. The height of the hill is not uniform, but

---

[8] e.g., Polyb. 2.52; Liv. 28.7.16; Plut. *Arat.* 39.3; Plut. *Cleom.* 17.3.
[9] Baker-Penoyre (1902: 236).
[10] For a detailed description of the topography of Pheneos, see Tausend and Tausend (2014: 19–20) and Giannakopoulos et al. (2012: 51).

distributed differently over three sections.[11] The highest part (the citadel) is located in the centre of the crescent (the north-west part of hill), with the lower areas to the south and east.[12]

The citadel in the north-west part of the hill is comprised of a rounded knoll, which is considerably higher than the flatter and lower eastern section. This eastern section of the acropolis, on the other hand, is comprised of a flat plateau, longer than it is wide, and is oriented east–west.[13] The hill slopes gradually on its south sides, as well as on the north-east. The slopes around the high north-west section are fairly precipitous and may have been a separately fortified citadel. Overall, the small size of the hill suggests that this was the acropolis only and that the lower city of Pheneos was located at its base. Although no remains of the lower city have been discovered, its approximate location can be inferred with some certainty.

The acropolis of Pheneos is separated from the hills to the north by a narrow plain about 300 m wide, which could accommodate a small settlement. Placing the lower city in this area, however, is unlikely. Not only would the high ground to the north negate any defensive advantage afforded by a fortified acropolis, but a lower city to the north would not even have been visible from the southern part of the hill. In this case, the middle and highest part of the hill would have blocked any visual communication between the city and the southern part of the hill, defeating the purpose of a fortified acropolis. Furthermore, until recently the only excavated structure at Pheneos—a sanctuary to Asklepios—is located at the south-eastern foot of the acropolis. It is difficult to comprehend why a sanctuary here would be placed at the extreme opposite end of the settlement. Instead, the location of this sanctuary and the topography of the hill itself suggest that the lower city was south of the acropolis. In this scenario, the sanctuary is firmly included in the settlement and all parts of the city would be visible from all parts of the acropolis. Finally, the ascent to the acropolis is most easily accomplished from the south, where the terrain is less steep—an important consideration for the defensive needs of a population with a fortified acropolis.

The territory of Pheneos is considerable, by some estimates encompassing as much as 345 km².[14] The bulk of this territory is comprised of the large

---

[11] Howell (1970: 97) refers to these sections as three different hills.

[12] The highest section of the hill is fairly steep on all sides (especially to the north and west) and, while it is not precipitous, it is the only part of the acropolis that is in any way reconcilable with Pausanias' description (8.14.4).

[13] Although Clark (1858: 318) maintains that the eastern section of the hill was artificially terraced, it is not clear if this is true.

[14] As noted by Nielsen (2002: 585), this figure includes the territory of Nonakris to the north-west, which is thought to have been a dependent *polis* of Pheneos. For Nonakris, see the Appendix.

Fig. C13.2. Pheneos, topographical map of site and surrounding territories. (© *2011 Google-Map data © 2011 Tele Atlas*)

plain located south of the city, the maximum dimensions of which measure approximately 14 km north to south by 8 km east to west (Fig. C13.2).[15]

The plain of Pheneos represents the epitome of the Arkadian Valley basin. It is defined by three of the largest mountains in the Peloponnese, which, with their subsidiary ranges, also serve as the boundaries between Pheneos and the territories of the surrounding *poleis* and regions. Mt Kylene and its foothills on the east and north-east separate Pheneos from the territory of Stymphalos; Mt Oligyrtos on the south from that of Orchomenos and Kaphyai;[16] and Mt Chelmos to the west from that of Kleitor and to the north from that of Achaia.

The other characteristic of the typical Arkadian basin is the drainage of water by *katavothroi*. Indeed, as in many Arkadian valleys, Pheneos had to contend with an excess rather than a deficiency of water. As well as seasonal streams formed by melting snow and rain, the main sources of water are the Olvios River (called in antiquity the Aroanios) and the Doxas River (see Fig. C13.1). These rivers originate north of the valley and proceed in a south-westerly direction before emptying into a *katavothros* on the south-west edge of the plain.[17] A third stream, smaller than those already mentioned, originating near ancient Kaphyai, enters the southern part of the plain through the Guioza gorge, before reaching another *katavothros* on the south-east edge of the plain, opposite the modern village of Achladies.[18] In the 2,000 years of

[15] Baker-Penoyre (1902: 228) quite correctly describes the shape of the plain as resembling a 'miniature African continent'.

[16] Giannakopoulos et al. (2012: 51). On the road between Orchomenos and Pheneos, see Tausend (1998c); on the other roads servicing the valley of Pheneos, see Tausend and Tausend (2014: 19–20).

[17] Tausend and Tausend (2014: 19). This river continues underground and is believed to be the source of the Ladon River (Baker-Penoyre 1902: 230–1).

[18] Although the underground course of this stream is uncertain, Baker-Penoyre (1902: 231) maintains that it may be linked to the larger hydraulic system of Lake Stymphalos.

recorded history—and almost certainly longer—all these water sources were responsible at different times and in different ways for the alteration from lake to plain in the Pheneos Valley.[19] During much of the nineteenth century, for example, the acropolis of Pheneos was surrounded by water, resembling 'a peninsula jutting into the lake'.[20] At the end of the century Frazer tells us that the lake surrounding the acropolis had disappeared, having formed around the south-east *katavothros* at the extreme southern end of the valley.[21] Finally, only a few short years later, on a visit in 1901, Baker-Penoyre observed that the lake was nearly gone.[22] At the time of writing, although some of the lower areas of the plain are seasonally marshy, the lake has not returned.[23]

NATURAL DEFENCES

The height offered by the acropolis and the surrounding mountains limit the approaches to the site to routes from the north and south (Fig. C13.3). The Doxas and Olivios Rivers flank the eastern and southern side of the site.

Fig. C13.3. Pheneos, the site (facing south-west). (© *Matthew Maher*)

[19] Tausend and Tausend (2014: 19).
[20] Frazer (1898: iv. 235). See also Boblaye (1836: 153); Curtius (1851: i. 191); Clark (1858: 318); Rangabé (1857: 56).
[21] Frazer (1898: iv. 235); Tausend and Tausend (2014: 19).
[22] Baker-Penoyre (1902: 228).
[23] Tausend and Tausend (2014: 19). This was still the case when I visited the site in the spring of 2010, as well as in the summers of 2013, 2014, and 2015.

FORTIFICATION TYPE

Acropolis type. Much of the circuit survives *in situ* along the north edge of the hill (Fig. C13.4). The length of the total circuit is estimated to have been 1.5–2 km in length.[24] A separately fortified citadel might have covered part of the acropolis in the north-west (the highest point of the hill). Although it remains uncertain whether or not the lower city was fortified, it seems that this was the case.[25] Not only would this be analogous to the situation at nearby Stymphalos and Kleitor, but the remains of some fifty scattered blocks have been found at the base of the hill encircling it to the east, south, and west.[26]

PRESERVATION

The stone foundations of the acropolis circuit are fairly well preserved on the eastern end of the northern side of the hill, where they have been exposed by recent excavations. Nothing is known of a lower city circuit.

CONSTRUCTION

The foundations of the surviving acropolis wall and its towers were constructed in a coursed polygonal style in which, owing to the fine coursing and shaping of the blocks, it appears that several sections tend more towards coursed trapezoidal than polygonal (Fig. C13.5).[27] The lime-stone curtains are 3.20 m thick and comprised of an inner and outer face of blocks between which a mix of rubble was added for strength and cohesion (Fig C13.6).[28] Occasional header courses run through the width of the curtain to form compartments. The stone foundations of all the curtains and towers in the circuit probably once supported a mudbrick superstructure (not preserved).

---

[24] Kissas et al. (2014: 139).   [25] Kissas (2013: 145).
[26] Kissas et al. (2014: 139, fig. 7); Tausend and Tausend (2014: 27).
[27] Scranton (1941: 166) too lists the walls of Pheneos as coursed polygonal.
[28] Giannakopoulos et al. (2012: 56, 58, 60, 61); Kissas (2013: 144); Kissas et al. (2014: 134); Tausend and Tausend (2014: 27).

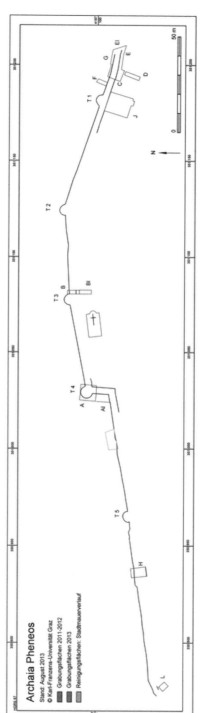

Fig. C13.4. Pheneos, plan of the site from Kissas et al. (2014: 134, fig. 2). (© *Institut für Archäologie der Universität Graz*)

Fig. C13.5. Pheneos, polygonal masonry of curtain between Towers 1 and 2 (facing south). (© *Matthew Maher*)

Fig. C13.6. Pheneos, rubble core of curtain between Towers 1 and 2 (facing west). (© *Matthew Maher*)

SUMMARY OF TACTICAL COMPONENTS

The exposed section of the hill's circuit contains four semicircular towers (5.5 m diameter) and one nearly round tower (5.9 m diameter) irregularly spaced between 47 and 60 m (see Fig. C13.4). There is no clear evidence of gates or posterns among the remains.

Towers

The surviving northern section of the acropolis circuit contains four nearly identical semicircular-shaped towers (Towers 1, 2, 3, 5), each with a diameter of 5.50 and projecting 2.90 m from the wall.[29] Located approximately in the centre of the surviving section, where the circuit makes a short southward jog or short return in the curtain, is another curvilinear tower. Comprising three-quarters of a circle, Tower 4 (5.90 m diameter) more closely resembles a round tower than a semicircular one.[30] All the towers appear to be bonded to the curtains,[31] and, as they are spaced 47 to 60 m apart,[32] they are strategically rather than regularly spaced. The excavators have suggested that a sixth tower should be sought somewhere at the western extremity of the northern trace.[33] On the highest part of the acropolis, in what might have been the citadel, sections of a rectangular structure were discovered.[34] While the date of this structure is not certain, Kissas maintains it is 'most probably a Medieval tower'.[35]

Gates

No gates or posterns are attested.

Citadel

Several years of cleaning operations along the highest point of the hill in the north-west have revealed the traces of numerous sections of walls, as well as terraces, and quarried areas (Fig. C13.7).[36] Although not continuous, isolated sections of wall are visible following the contours near the base along the southern half of the acropolis at a fairly uniform elevation.[37] Further work and excavation are required to confirm this point, but these remains are suggestive of the existence of a separately fortified citadel atop the acropolis summit.[38]

---

[29] Kissas (2013: 144); Tausend and Tausend (2014: 26). Tower numbers are taken from the plan in Kissas et al. (2014: 134, fig. 2).

[30] Giannakopoulos et al. (2012: 54).

[31] Kissas et al. (2014: 134); Tausend and Tausend (2014: 26).

[32] Kissas et al. (2014: 134).   [33] Kissas et al. (2014: 139).

[34] Giannakopoulos et al. (2012: 61).

[35] Kissas (2013: 145). This view is echoed by Giannakopoulos et al. (2012: 61).

[36] Kissas (2013: 145); Kissas et al. (2014: 151).

[37] Giannakopoulos et al. (2012: 61–2); Kissas (2013: 145).

[38] Kissas et al. (2014: 151). For a plan of this area showing the structures in question, see Giannakopoulos et al. (2012: 63, fig. 13).

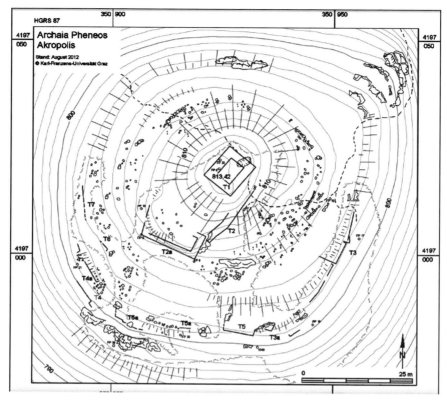

Fig. C13.7. Pheneos, plan of the citadel from Kissas et al. (2014: 152, fig. 17). (© *Institut für Archäologie der Universität Graz*)

COMMENTS

Prior to the excavation of parts of the fortification circuit at Pheneos, I had speculated on a number of points based on the visible remains themselves— the only evidence available at the time. Although the results from the subsequent excavations (and publication) are not at odds with all the previous conjecture, some of the arguments have since proven to be incorrect. For instance, earlier I had supposed the existence of two rectangular towers in the area west of Tower 4.[39] Recent excavations, however, have clearly demonstrated that the remains of these structures are built against the city walls and thus are not contemporary with the original circuit.[40] Nor is it certain whether these

---

[39] Maher (2012a: 206, 211, 212).   [40] Kissas et al. (2014: 137).

structures were towers at all. Finally, my original proposed chronology for the walls of *c.*400–350 BC has proven to be too early,[41] as the archaeological evidence now suggests this date should be pushed back to the years after *c.*345 BC.[42]

OVERALL DEFENSIVE PLANNING

Geographically, the small hill of Pheneos is one of the few locations in the valley suitable for a natural acropolis. As the plain is bordered on all sides by rather steep slopes, few other candidates immediately suggest themselves. Although today several villages line the eastern edge of the plain on the lower slopes of Mt Kylene, since most of these lie in the narrow north-east corridor leading towards Achaia, they are poorly positioned to command the bulk of the great plain to the south. Despite the relatively diminutive nature of the hill itself, the Phenean acropolis is both appropriately located and practically fashioned for defensive use.

Located at the edge of the plain, the site was defensible without being too high or inaccessible, and was close enough to protect the arable land in its territory.[43] Moreover, the decision to position the site in the northern part of the plain was a choice reflecting larger strategic considerations. For example, where access to the valley from the east, south, and west was made difficult by three of Arkadia's great mountains, an approach from the north was considerably easier.[44] Like the acropolis of Alea, the Phenean stronghold is ideally positioned precisely at the point where a narrow corridor opens into the larger plain. Such a location ensured control of the former and command of the latter. Furthermore, Pausanias observed a large channel running across the plain, south of the city, which he estimated to be around 9 km long and some 9 m deep.[45] Although its primary purpose was to reduce the excess water that has plagued the valley throughout its history, the defensive possibilities of such a construction cannot be understated. As a defensive outwork, a canal of such dimensions would certainly add another element of defence to the city, especially in impeding an enemy's approach from the south.

---

[41] Maher (2012a: 211–13).   [42] Kissas et al. (2014: 140 and n. 16).

[43] For isolated towers and defensive outposts throughout the territory, see Tausend (1998a; 1999b), Tausend and Tausend (2014: 23–5).

[44] For traces of the road network in the territory of Pheneos, see Pikoulas (1999a: 297–8).

[45] Paus. 8.14.3. No trace of this canal exists today. In the early nineteenth century, however, Leake (1830: iii. 151–2) echoes the observation of Gell (1817: 151) that this canal was by then 'a road conducted upon a magnificent mound'. Perhaps this mound was the result of centuries of dredging and piling of silt from the canal.

A review of the literature suggests it was not the scanty ruins of the ancient acropolis, but the undersized stature of the hill itself, that struck most of the ancient travellers as especially noteworthy. Nonetheless, the topography of the hill is fairly well suited for a defendable acropolis. Whether parts of the site were left unfortified, as maintained by Pausanias, or whether parts of the circuit encompassed the entire area, the heights it afforded (supplemented by strategically placed artillery towers) were sufficient to meet the defensive demands inherent in its purpose. From the acropolis of Pheneos, not only was almost all the territory visible, but the towers of the extant fortifications ensured that the hill was well equipped to meet any deficiencies caused by its relatively short stature.

Although there are apparently no posterns in the surviving section, both the course of the walls and the choice of tower shape certainly reflect a concern for keeping the enemy at a distance from the walls. While the topography of the north side of the hill would have permitted a straight, east–west-oriented, course for the fortifications, the military architects opted for asymmetrical arrangement, deciding instead to lay out the walls with an obtuse and right angle. In this way, the semicircular Tower 2 (see Fig. C13.4) is more favourably positioned to provide artillery fire to safeguard the approaches on the flanking section of walls—a tactic that would have been unachievable if the eastern half of the circuit was straight and did not possess the shallow angle that it does. Similarly, the 90° angle separating the so-called eastern and western sections of the fortifications also provided the towers with a greater field of fire with which to guard against any hostile approaches. That is, setting the western stretch back (*c.*10 m to the south) created an open area to the north that could receive additional coverage by the circular Tower 4—again, a tactic that would have been unattainable with a straight course of walls and less efficient with rectangular towers.[46] In short, the tactical modification of the trace guaranteed that both Tower 4 and Tower 2 were in a position to add further defensive support to the western trace and its approaches. Finally, although only a fraction of the fortifications is under discussion here, the tactical and strategic approaches they utilize are probably not unique to the cleared area of the northern circuit, but representative also of the parts of the circuit that are no longer (or not yet) visible.

[46] As no gate was discovered in the area of this jog (an otherwise obvious location for such a candidate), Kissas et al. (2014: 134) suggest this deviation in the wall's course might have been to avoid the existence of an earlier sanctuary. Still, I would argue that defence concerns and the wish to respect the boundaries of an existing *temenos* are not mutually exclusive. See also Kissas (2013: 145).

CHRONOLOGICAL SUMMARY

Historical probability, the external evidence, and known architectural affinities, all suggest that the small circuit of Pheneos was built *c.*345–300 BC.

CHRONOLOGICAL ARGUMENTS

Owing to the recent excavations at the site, the fortifications of Pheneos can now be added to the small but growing list of Arkadian examples whose date, facilitated by hard archaeological data, can be more confidently established. During the excavation of the curtain just east of Tower 3, excavators discovered a bronze Sikyon coin, an issue dating to between *c.*345 and 320 BC.[47] As this coin was found in a stratified context in the foundation trench, it provides a fairly secure *terminus post quem* of 345 BC for the construction of the city wall. As for the latest possible date for the construction of the city walls, the excavators suggest a *terminus ante quem* of around 300 BC.[48] This invaluable stratified archaeological evidence recommending a chronological range of *c.*345–300 BC is corroborated by both historical probability and the style of the fortifications themselves.[49]

The excavators have suggested that the historical catalyst for the construction of the walls of Pheneos was the Macedonian campaign in the Peloponnese under Antipater in 331/330 BC.[50] In that year, with Alexander and his army deep in the heart of the Persian Empire, Thrace rose up in rebellion against the Macedonians, and King Agis III of Sparta saw his chance to do the same in the south.[51] When Antipater heard of the events in the south, he quickly came to terms with the Thracians before leading his army to Megalopolis to confront the Spartan-led rebels.[52] In the battle that followed, the so-called Battle of Megalopolis, the Spartans and their Peloponnesian allies were defeated by the

---

[47] Kissas et al. (2014: 140 and n. 16); Tausend and Tausend (2014: 28).

[48] Kissas (2013: 145); Kissas et al. (2014: 140). Tausend and Tausend (2014: 30) believe that the extra urban military installations are probably contemporary with the city walls, and thus the whole defensive system of the Pheneos was conceived at a single time.

[49] Tausend and Tausend (2014: 28) maintain that the small size of the towers suggests they should date to the time before the widespread use of torsion artillery (*c.*320 BC).

[50] Kissas et al. (2014: 140); Tausend and Tausend (2014: 30–47).

[51] Diod. 17.62.4–6.

[52] Diod. 17.63.1. Alexander had no intention of returning from Asia to help Antipater, and according to Plutarch (*Ages.* 15.4), when he heard of his regent's battle with Agis, he said 'it would seem, my men, that while we were conquering Darius here, there has been a battle of mice there in Arkadia'.

forces of Antipater, and Agis III himself was killed.[53] In short, the excavators maintain that after the Macedonian victory, as punishment for Arkadian participation in the rebellion, Pheneos was fortified and subsequently occupied by a Macedonian garrison in order to check future insurgencies in the region.[54] Not only was this a practice that has other Macedonian parallels (and one that conveyed a very strong political message), but, as the excavators correctly argue, the costs of constructing the fortifications would have been but a fraction of the 3,000 talents sent to Antipater by Alexander for the 'mouse-war' campaign.[55] Thus, a date during the second half of the fourth century BC accords well with the evidence outlined here.

BIBLIOGRAPHY

Polyb. 2.52; Liv. 28.7.16; Strab. 8.8.2; Plut. *Arat.* 39.3; *Cleom.* 17.3; Paus. 5.27.8, 8.14–8.15.8; Gell (1817: 151–2); Dodwell (1819: ii. 437–8); Leake (1830: iii. 117, iii. 135–53); Boblaye (1836: 153); Curtius (1851: i. 190–1); Rangabé (1857: 56–8); Clark (1858: 318); Bursian (1862: ii. 200); Frazer (1898: iv. 235–6); Baker-Penoyre (1902); Bölte (1938: 1963–80); Scranton (1941: 166); Daux (1959: 625); Protonotariou-Deilaki (1961–2, 1965); Howell (1970: 97); Winter (1971a: 34); Jost (1985: 27–37); Papachatzis (1994: 232–5); Erath (1999); Tausend (1998a, 1998b, 1998c, 1999a, 1999b, forthcoming); Pikoulas (1999a: 297–8); Nielsen (2002: 585–6); Kissas (2011, 2013); Giannakopoulos et al. (2012); Maher (2012A: 193–213); Kissas et al. (2014); Tausend and Tausend (2014).

---

[53] Diod. 17.63.1–4. For a detailed biography of Agis III and the so called Battle of Megalopolis, see Badian (1967).
[54] Tausend and Tausend (2014: 45–7); Kissas et al. (2014: 140).
[55] Ar. *An.* 3.16.10; Tausend and Tausend (2014: 47); Kissas et al. (2014: 140).

14

Phigaleia, Western Arkadia

LOCATION

The site comprises a considerable plateau on the north bank of the Neda River in western Arkadia (Fig. C14.1). The plateau is nowhere uniform or flat, but generally slopes down from north to south. The acropolis is situated at the summit of the plateau. Inhabitation was limited to the intramural area.

POLIS STATUS

Phigaleia—or Phialia as it was alternatively referred to on coins and inscriptions—was undeniably a *polis* in the political and social sense of the word.[1] Phigaleia was listed as a *polis* in the political sense in accounts of the Delphic *naopoioi* (in *c*.360s BC), which tell of the city's collective donation of money for the construction of the new temple.[2] While this same inscription represents the external and collective use of the city ethnic, the individual use of the city ethnic is provided by Herodotus.[3] Furthermore, an inscription discovered reveals that a citizen of Phigaleia was appointed *proxenos* by the Aitolian League (*c*.270 BC).[4] Surviving records indicate that citizens of Phigaleia attained Olympic victories as early as the sixth century as well as in the fourth century BC.[5]

---

[1] For detailed account of all the evidence for the settlement's polis status, see Nielsen (2002: 586–8).
[2] *CID* II 4.III.1 and 45; see also Diod. 15.40.1–2 for use of the term *polis* in a political sense.
[3] Hdt. 6.83.2.   [4] *IG* IX.1² 13.19.
[5] *Olympionikai* (nos 95, 99, 102, 392).

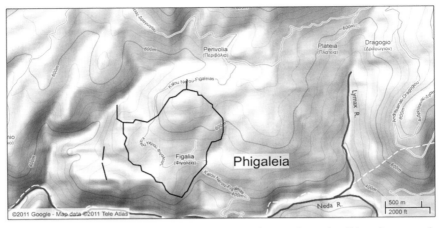

Fig. C14.1. Phigaleia, topographical map of site (showing line of walls) and surrounding area. (© *2011 Google-Map data* © *2011 Tele Atlas*)

HISTORY

Located in the south-west corner of Arkadia, close to the frontiers of Messenia and Triphylia, Phigaleia was often—willingly or unwillingly—drawn into the larger conflicts of the area. In 659 BC, as a result of its frequent aid to the insurgent Messenians, a Spartan army besieged and then occupied the city of Phigaleia.[6] The Phigaleian refugees then sought the advice of the Oracle at Delphi, who told the exiles that they could recapture their city only with the help of 100 men from Oresthasion.[7] The soldiers of Phigaleia, with the help of their fellow Arkadians from Oresthasion, eventually met the Spartan forces, fulfilled the prophecy, and retook their city.[8] The animosity with Sparta would continue, and the people of Phigaleia would witness the attack and occupation of their city several more times in the fifth century, between 421 to *c.*414 BC, and again during *c.*401–395 BC.[9] Finally, in 375 BC the city expelled a pro-Lakedaimonian faction from their city, whereupon the exiles, after taking possession of nearby Heraia, made excursions against Phigaleia before retreating to Sparta.[10] Nielsen assumes that Phigalia was a member of Arkadian League, and, prior to this, at some point also of the Peloponnesian League.[11]

In the third century BC, like many Arkadian *poleis*, Phigaleia was embroiled in the wars between the Aitolian and Achaian Leagues. As a member of the former, in 222 BC Phigaleia was used as a base for Aitolian mercenary troops,

---

[6] Paus. 8.39.3.   [7] Paus. 8.39.4.   [8] Paus. 8.39.5.
[9] Cooper (1976: 703).   [10] Diod. 15.40.
[11] Nielsen (1996b: 87, 92, 94–5; 2002: 588).

from which raids were conducted into the territory of Messenia.[12] Before long, however, 'the people of Phigalia, hearing of what had taken place in Triphylia, and disliking the alliance with the Aitolians, rose in arms and seized [their city]'.[13] When the Aitolian mercenaries had been driven away, the citizens delivered themselves and their city to the forces of Philip and became members of the Achaian League.[14] Because the site of Phigaleia has never been excavated, very little is known of its subsequent history. Surface material and chance finds from the Roman period and later, however, suggest that, although the site went into decline in late antiquity, it has more or less remained continuously occupied.[15]

LOCAL TOPOGRAPHY

Ancient Phigaleia is situated in the south-west corner of Arkadia, close to the borders of Triphylia and Messenia (Fig. C14.2).[16] This part of Arkadia is distinguished from the rest by its especially inhospitable topography, notable

Fig. C14.2. Phigaleia, topographical map of southwest Arkadia. (© *2011 Google-Map data © 2011 Tele Atlas*)

[12] Polyb. 4.3.   [13] Polyb. 4.79.

[14] While Cooper (1976: 703) asserts Phigaleia was a member of the Achaian League, Nielsen (2002: 588) maintains membership can be assumed but not explicitly attested. Cooper is certainly correct, however, as Achaian League coins bearing the name 'ΑΧΑΙΩΝ ΦΙΓΑΛΕΩΝ' and 'ΦΙΑΛΕΩΝ' (c.208 BC) are known (Gardner 1963: 15; Head 1963: 418).

[15] Cooper (1976: 703).

[16] The ancient site of Phigaleia is now a part of the region of modern Messenia.

for its relative lack of open plains or arable land. Instead, it is characterized by a number of river valleys, radiating in all directions, and carved into the otherwise all-pervasive and steep mountainous terrain.

Meyer is certainly not exaggerating with his claim that Phigaleia possesses the most extreme mountain location of all the cities of ancient Arkadia.[17] The ruggedness of the terrain around Phigaleia is largely the result of three factors: the neighbouring mountains, the uneven terrain of the site itself, and the two sources of water surrounding and defining it (see Fig. C14.1). The most conspicuous natural feature of the site is the Neda River Valley. Bounding the site to the south and south-west, this precipitous gorge is of tremendous depth, falling over 100 m from the Phigaleian plateau to the river below. Furthermore, approximately 2 km east of the city flows a tributary of the Neda still known by its ancient name, the Lymax. This river, originating near the modern village of Dragogio, flows south down a narrow valley, joining the Neda south-east of Phigaleia.

Frazer observed that that the 'other sides [of the city are] surrounded by a semicircle of mountains'.[18] Pausanias too reports that Phigaleia is enclosed by mountains: specifically, 'it has Kotilion on the left, and another mountain projecting on the right, Mount Elaion. Kotilion is just five miles from the city; there is a place there called Bassai'.[19] According to Pausanias' orientation, if Mt Kotilion lies to the north-east of the site—identified, of course, by the great temple—then Mt Elaion must be located south and south-west of the city, on the opposite side of the Neda River.[20] These boundaries, as well as others, correspond to the territory of Phigaleia, estimated to cover *c*.125 km². Mt. Kotilion probably represented the eastern limit of the territory—and the boundary with the Messenian *polis* of Eira—while the north slope of Mt Elaion formed the southern extent of Phigaleian land.[21] To the west, the Yervitsa Valley (just west of modern Stomio) represented the border with Triphylia, and, to the north, the chain of hills collectively known as Mt Mintha separated Phigaleian territory from that of Alipheira.[22]

Surrounded by these natural features is the city itself. As noted by Pausanias, the site resembles a plateau that is 'mostly precipitous and high in the air'.[23] While this plateau is defined on the south and west by the deep valley of the Neda and on the east by the Lymax, the northern part of the site is defined by a tall hill, representing the city's acropolis.[24] The southern half of this hill, which actually comprises the majority of the intramural space, slopes to the south. Although the north-west corner of the site includes a separate and

---

[17] Meyer (1938: 2068). The feeling of remoteness and desolation inherent in the area's topography is a recurring theme in the travel narratives of the nineteenth century; e.g., see Curtius (1851: i. 318–19); Bursian (1862: ii. 251); Boblaye (1836: 165); Frazer (1898: iv. 390).
[18] Frazer (1898: iv. 390).   [19] Paus. 8.39.7.   [20] Jost (1985: 83).
[21] A point strengthened by Jost's discovery (1985: 83) of a Phigaleian sanctuary here.
[22] Jost (1985: 83).   [23] Paus. 8.39.5.   [24] Jost (1999: 200).

Fig. C14.3. Phigaleia, the site (facing south). (© *Matthew Maher*)

smaller hill, overall, the plateau of Phigaleia slopes from the acropolis toward the Neda to the south (see the North-West Rise on Fig. C14.3).[25] The only part of the city where the terrain exhibits a regularity approaching the horizontal is in the south-east, where the modern village stands.[26]

NATURAL DEFENCES

The height offered by the acropolis, and the steep slope on its southern side, provide ready natural defences (Fig. C14.3). The river valley and surrounding mountains would have limited the main approaches to the city gates to routes from the east and west. The Neda River and its precipitous slope flank the hill to the south, while one of its tributaries, the Lymax River, flanks the site to the east.

FORTIFICATION TYPE

Uneven type.[27] The circuit generally follows the contours of the hill, especially the eastern section (Fig. C14.4).[28] The westernmost section embraces a small

---

[25] The north half of the site, comprised of the immediate southern slope of the acropolis, is the steepest part. While the southern half of the intramural area is certainly not flat, the slope is gentler.

[26] Modern Phigaleia, formerly the village of Paulitza.

[27] Listed as a 'ville mixtes' type by Jost (1999: 200–1).

[28] Pausanias (8.39.5) writes: 'Phigaleia lies on high land that is for the most part precipitous, and the walls are built on the cliffs. But on the top the hill is level and flat.'

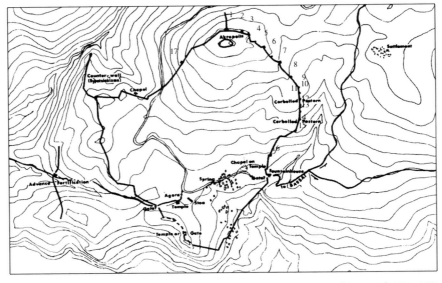

Fig. C14.4. Phigaleia, topographical plan of site from Cooper and Myers (1981: 127, fig. 4). (©*Journal of Field Archaeology*)

rise (that is, the North-West Rise in Fig. C14.3). These fortifications are often cited as a common example of the *Geländemauer* type of circuit, in which the walls followed a path around the settlement taking advantage of topography and enclosing a much larger area than was inhabited, 'not the frame into which the city was fitted'.[29]

PRESERVATION

The site is relatively well preserved, especially the north and eastern sections, although most of the trace has survived enough to define the general outline.[30] The total length of the wall is *c.*4.5 km, and the total intramural area is estimated to be *c.*195 ha.[31]

[29] Wycherley (1962: 39).
[30] The outline of the circuit was observed in nearly its entirety by Gell (1817: 79), Leake (1830: i. 495), Boblaye (1836: 165), Curtius (1851: i. 320), Rangabé (1857: 85), Clark (1858: 254), Bursian (1862: ii. 251), Wyse (1865: ii. 19), and Frazer (1898: iv. 390).
[31] Cooper and Myers (1981: 124).

Fig. C14.5. Phigaleia, curtain
showing polygonal masonry
(facing west). (© *Matthew Maher*)

CONSTRUCTION

The foundations of the acropolis walls and towers were constructed in
a predominantly coursed polygonal style (Fig. C14.5).[32] The height of the
remains suggests that they probably once existed to the level of the wall-
walk, above which, the upper tower chambers would then have been raised in
mudbrick and/or timber.[33] These curtains consist of the typical inner and
outer parallel faces filled with loose stones, rubble, and presumably earth. The
average thickness of the curtains varies slightly in places, but in general has
been measured to between 2.10 and 3 m.[34]

SUMMARY OF TACTICAL COMPONENTS

The city wall contained seventeen towers, all but one of which are located in
the north-east part of the circuit (see Fig. C14.4). Rectangular and semicircular

[32] Rangabé (1857: 85); Clark (1858: 254); Frazer (1898: iv. 390); Meyer (1938: 2070); Scranton
(1941: 109, 164); Adam (1982: 180). These same accounts also accept that the polygonal masonry
is not uniform throughout, but is, in places, closer to an isodomic quadrangular style in
appearance. Whether the polygonal style tended towards irregular ashlar, as held by Scranton
(1941: 109, 175), or trapezoidal, as maintained by Adam (1982: 180), the inconsistent mix of style
is still clearly visible in the early twenty-first century in different parts of the circuit.
[33] Frazer (1898: iv. 390) observed the curtains still standing to over 6 m, while Cooper (1976:
703) maintains that they stand to heights of 10 m in some areas. The southern section of the city
walls is the poorest preserved, so much so that, until the most recent survey by Cooper and
Myers (1981), it was believed that no wall even existed here since the 'steep slopes of the Neda
gorge made protection from the flank unnecessary' (p. 128).
[34] Curtius (1851: i. 320); Rangabé (1857: 85); Frazer (1898: iv. 390); Meyer (1938: 2070);
Adam (1982: 180).

towers are employed indiscriminately. Two corbelled posterns are attested. No gates have been identified, but the location of at least two has been plausibly suggested. Traces of both a *hypoteichismata* and *proteichismata* are preserved.

Towers

The fortification circuit contains seventeen towers (nine rectangular, seven semicircular, one round) in total, strategically rather than regularly spaced.[35] While one rectangular tower is located on the north-west slope of the acropolis hill, every other example can be found on the east side of the site, in the stretch of wall running from the acropolis to the East Gate. With the exception of one tower (Tower 3, measuring 8 × 10 m), the rectangular towers are all *c*.5 m wide and project 4 m from the curtain. The towers along the eastern section are the most regular in terms of their spacing and dimensions. Arranged along this *c*.300 m long stretch of wall are Towers 9–15, all of which are semicircular (*c*.7 m diameter) and are regularly spaced (*c*.35 m). Unique on the north-east side of the circuit is the round Tower 4 (Fig. C14.6). Leake explains: 'on the northern side the wall is flanked with quadrangular towers and in the midst of them it [i.e., Tower 4] forms in one place a salient angle terminating in a round tower.'[36]

Gates

The circuit contained at least one gate, but perhaps as many as three. Of the city's three possible gates, the location of the East Gate is the only one

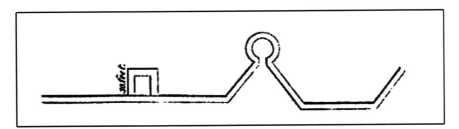

Fig. C14.6. Phigaleia, schematic drawing of Tower 4 from Leake (1830: i. 496).

---

[35] Every visitor to the site has noted the presence of several towers in the circuit, 'some square, some round' (Clark 1858: 254), yet nowhere is it explicitly stated exactly how many towers exist, nor exactly which are square and which are round. The total number of seventeen is based on satellite imagery, personal observation, and the rough plan published by Cooper and Myers (1981: 127, fig. 4). Note: the tower numbers provided on Fig. C14.4 are added for convenience here and are not on the original published plan.

[36] Leake (1830: i. 496).

generally accepted.[37] The location (or even existence) of the other two gates is far less certain. Both Curtius and Adam, for example, mention the survival of a gate somewhere in the south-west part of the circuit.[38] On the most recent published plan of the site, however, the possible location of two gates—both in the south-west part of the circuit—is provided.[39] Two posterns are attested in the eastern section of the circuit, both of which are notable for their simple stepped corbelling architecture.[40] These posterns, placed approximately 150 m apart, were prudently positioned on the left side of Tower 11 and Tower 14. Such an arrangement ensured that these towers were in a position to provide protection to the unshielded right side of any defenders who sallied forth from the safety of the walls.[41]

COMMENTS

It appears that both *hypoteichismata* (cross-walls) and *proteichismata* (out-walls) were also employed as part of the larger defensive system at Phigaleia.[42] *Hypoteichismata* have been identified radiating from two different parts of the main circuit. The first can be seen stretching due north for *c.*30–40 m from Tower 1 in the centre of the northern trace.[43] The second example is much longer and better preserved. It is found in the north-west extending for *c.*165 m from the westernmost part of the circuit (Fig. C14.7). Standing 'at the edge of a steep precipice...[t]his section of the wall skirts the top of a razorback knoll that bisects the slopes of a gorge'.[44] Finally, the *proteichismata* discovered runs north–south, spanning a small ravine approximately 150 m west of the main circuit.[45] This outwall contains a large gate roughly in its centre, at the narrowest and deepest part of the ravine.[46]

The crown of the acropolis was fortified separately by a small elliptical circuit, measuring *c.*70 m east–west by 40 m north–south. The diminutive size and haphazard arrangement of the blocks suggest that this is a later, probably

[37] Like the West Gate at Kleitor, the site of this gate is still traversed by a modern road.
[38] Curtius (1851: i. 321); Adam (1982: 180).
[39] Cooper and Myers (1981: 127, fig. 4) demonstrate their uncertainty by placing a question mark at the proposed location of one of these gates and labelling the other as 'Temple or Gate'.
[40] See Adam (1982: 181) for a photograph of one of the corbelled posterns.
[41] Adam (1982: 180).   [42] Jost (1999: 201).
[43] Cooper and Myers (1981: 128).
[44] Cooper and Myers (1981: 130). A comparison between Cooper and Myers's plan (Fig. C14.4) with the satellite image of this north-west cross-wall shows the former to be incorrect. Instead of curving to the north-east, the photograph shows that the wall actually curves slightly to the north-west.
[45] Cooper and Myers (1981: 132).   [46] Cooper and Myers (1981: 132).

Fig. C14.7. Phigaleia, satellite image of north-west cross-wall. (© *2011 Google-Map data © 2011 Tele Atlas*)

medieval addition—a point on which nearly all the early travellers as well as modern scholars agree[47]—and thus it merits no further mention here.

OVERALL DEFENSIVE PLANNING

As an archetypical example of the *Geländemauer* type of circuit, we see at Phigaleia an intricate relationship between the fortification circuit and the topography in which it was constructed. Characteristic of this system is how the walls were raised around the settlement with little regard to the layout or dimensions of the city, but focused instead on including and utilizing as many natural defensive barriers as possible. This is precisely the pattern employed by the trace at Phigaleia (see Fig. C14.4). With approximately 4.5 km of walls, military architects went to great lengths—literally and figuratively—to ensure that the main circuit employed all the defensive advantages afforded by the terrain.

Thus, we see the west and south sides of the city standing on a small plateau, which was both defined and protected by the Neda River Valley. Even though the defences offered by the steep slopes of this gorge were already considerable on these sides, they were amplified by the erection of the city walls atop their perimeters. We see a similar pattern in the trace of the eastern fortifications, which descending south from the acropolis stand on the heights of a narrow

---

[47] e.g., Boblaye (1836: 165); Curtius (1851: i. 321); Frazer (1898: iv. 390); Jost (1999: 200). Leake (1830: i. 495–6) and Lawrence (1979: 441) seem to be the only ones willing to entertain the notion that the separately walled acropolis is ancient.

ridge. Further protection is given to this section by a narrow ravine lying directly below and to the east. Similar to the south and west sides, any foray made against the city from the east would require negotiating a steep slope before even reaching the walls. While the plateau on which the city stood is defined and protected on the west, south, and east sides by narrow valleys, the north too was not without its own natural defences. The northern part of the circuit embraces the site's highest elevation and retains all the inherent defensive advantages thereof.

While certainly effective, the course of the city wall, itself dictated by the rugged topography of the site, could not offer absolute protection. Indeed, even as most of the circuit was arranged best to exploit the terrain to a defensive advantage, unfortunately not all of the landscape was completely obliging. Consequently, some areas of the circuit were provided with additional defences—not only to balance the shortcomings perceptible in the terrain, but also, as will be demonstrated, as a calculated means of directing and regulating the main approaches to the city. These tactical supplements are most obvious on the north-east, east, and west sides of the circuit, where it is not coincidental that the main gates of the city are also found.

The defences on the east and north-east side of the city are arguably the most intimidating in the entire circuit. It is on these sides where both posterns and all but one of the circuit's identified towers are located. Without a doubt, the deployment of sixteen towers over a distance of *c*.800 m demonstrates a real concern for the defence of these sectors. The question remains, however, why the greater part of the city's defences should be concentrated in this quarter of the fortifications. The answer can be found in the surrounding topography and involves two separate but related concerns. The first relates specifically to the north-east section (between Towers 1 to 8). This stretch of wall is located directly opposite a narrow saddle—linking the Phigaleian acropolis with the hills to the east—and, thus, the only practical approach from the north and north-east (Fig. C14.8).

The existence of a counter-wall here, radiating north and perpendicular to the northern trace, is telling. The orientation of this wall would not only keep enemies at a distance if they planned to circumvent the northern defences, but its position parallel to and facing the saddle—the only conceivable position from which siege engines and artillery could be brought against the city— provided another platform for defensive enfilading.

The well-fortified eastern section (between Towers 9 and 15), on the other hand, is a reaction to the second concern: namely, to protect the approach to the East Gate from the north. Access to this gate from the north was possible by way of the lower slopes of the saddle and down the narrow ravine to the east of the circuit (see Fig. C14.8). By taking this route, moreover, it would have been possible essentially to avoid the north-east section of wall and thus enter the head of the ravine generally unimpeded. The eastern fortifications and

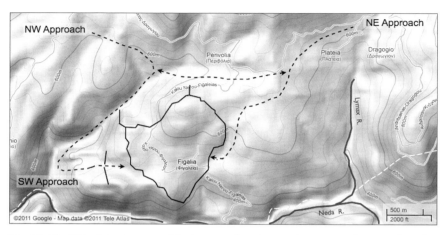

Fig. C14.8. Phigaleia, topographical map showing main approaches to the city.
(*© 2011 Google-Map data © 2011 Tele Atlas*)

their seven regularly and closely spaced towers were crucial, therefore, for
providing flanking protection against any unwelcome approaches to the city's
main gate from the north.

An equal concern for the defence of the west side of the city and its
approach is demonstrated by the exploitation of the topography and the
addition of both *hypoteichismata* and *proteichismata*.[48] The incorporation
into the circuit of the highest hills along steep edges of the plateau in the
north-west and south-west not only ensured the maximum viewshed, but also
largely obstructed any approach from these directions. Yet the city could still
be approached from the ravine defining the north-west side of the plateau and
from the west, along a narrow ravine leading up from the Neda Valley.
Consequently, we find *hypoteichismata* and *proteichismata* constructed to
guarantee command of these routes (see Fig. C14.8). In the north-west, one
of these counter-walls was erected leading from the westernmost part of the
circuit in a small arc down to the valley floor. That this arc opens towards the
north-east suggests it was designed to command the approach from that
direction. Traffic from the north-east, therefore, would be forced to circumvent the west side of the city at a safe (and easily observable) distance along the
valley floor until it joined the narrow ravine leading up from the Neda Valley.
This narrow passage is defined by the north-west edge of the plateau and
a small hill to the south-west of the city. Whether directly from the Neda
Valley to the west or by way of the valley to the north-west, this small ravine

---

[48] Jost (1999: 201).

represented the only feasible approach to the western side of the city. Accordingly, *hypoteichismata* were built at the entrance of this passage, separated by a small opening or gateway. Since this opening still corresponds to the modern route to the Neda Valley, which was presumably the ancient route as well, the main function of this wall must have been to reinforce the main access to the city.[49]

When taken together, the *hypoteichismata* and *proteichismata* on the west side of the city, as well as the powerful defences characteristic of the north-east and eastern part of the circuit, are essentially different parts of the same system—a system that, with the help of the natural terrain, was designed not only to protect the approaches to the city, but actively to manipulate them. With this system, the military architects ensured that not only the terrain, but the fortifications themselves, would dictate the main approaches to the city and its gates. The rough and inconsistent topography of the area limited the number of routes to the city to those coming from the south-west, north-west, and the north-east (see Fig. C14.8). The *hypoteichismata* and *proteichismata* made certain that anyone approaching the West Gate from a south-west or north-west direction was forced to follow a single route. Similarly, a combination of the topography and the positioning of the eastern and north-eastern parts of the circuit limited access to the East Gate to a single route—one flanked by the most imposing part of the circuit.

CHRONOLOGICAL SUMMARY

Constructed *c*.425–375 BC, the fortifications of Phigaleia are among the earliest to appear in Arkadia. This chronological range was established using historical probability, external evidence, and architectural affinities.

CHRONOLOGICAL ARGUMENTS

Most of the early travellers who visited Phigaleia were content simply to classify the fortifications as 'cyclopic',[50] 'ancien',[51] or being from 'remote antiquity'.[52] Obviously, as noted by Meyer, such cautious and indefinite descriptions are not very helpful and get us no closer to narrowing down a precise chronology.[53] It was around the middle of the nineteenth century, however, when Clark became the first visitor to Phigaleia to propose a specific

---

[49] Cooper and Myers (1981: 132).   [50] Wyse (1865: ii. 20).
[51] Rangabé (1857: 85).   [52] Leake (1830: i. 495).   [53] Meyer (1938: 2070).

date for the fortification circuit. From his limited understanding of the construction, he maintains that 'rude masonry [is] of an order intermediate between the polygonal and the Hellenic and may perhaps date from the seventh century BC'.[54] Far from being based solely on his grasp of the masonry—as his statement would imply—the date recommended by Clark must have been influenced by his interpretation of Pausanias. Pausanias tells us that in 659 BC, as a result of the frequent Phigaleian aid to the rebellious Messenians, 'the Lakedaimonians . . . invaded Phigalia . . . and sat down to besiege the city. When the walls were in danger of capture the Phigaleians ran away.'[55]

Even if Pausanias' historical account is accurate, it is likely that he is describing an earlier, smaller, and more simple circuit—one that is no longer visible today nor even necessarily in the same general area as the present circuit. Certainly this would explain why it was so promptly and easily taken by the Spartans at a time before any significant advances existed in the field of Greek siege warfare. Ultimately, however, for no other reasons than the sheer size and tactical complexity of the fortification system as it exists today, a seventh-century BC date seems much too early. This is the consensus among modern scholars, who would instead place the construction of the city walls at Phigaleia in the Classical or Hellenistic period. Still, as is often the case, even within this more restricted temporal frame, there is little agreement, and there are four general arguments: that the walls are from the fifth century BC, from the fourth century BC, from a mixture of the fifth and fourth centuries BC, or belong to the Hellenistic period.

Scranton describes the Phigaleian walls as regular polygonal with irregular ashlar, which he dates to about 450 BC.[56] Yet it would appear that he never actually visited the site and instead formed his opinion from a photograph.[57] Regardless, he tells us that this date is 'based on no specific external evidence, but on the general probabilities of the historical background viewed in relation to the sequence of periods seen in the masonry at the site'.[58] Scranton is alone in his claim for an exclusively fifth-century BC date. Proponents for an early fourth-century BC date are equally sparse and include only Winter and Lawrence. It should be noted, however, that Lawrence's trust in an early fourth century BC date is misleading, as it is based on spurious evidence. Specifically, it is derived from comparing the overlap gate in the separately fortified Phigaleian acropolis to those early fourth-century BC examples at both Mantineia and Stymphalos.[59] As the walls of this acropolis are almost certainly medieval,[60] such a comparison—and the date derived from it—is irrelevant. While admitting that 'the walls of Phigaleia cannot be securely dated on

---

[54] Clark (1858: 254).   [55] Paus. 8.39.3.   [56] Scranton (1941: 109).
[57] Scranton (1941: 164, 174).   [58] Scranton (1941: 159).
[59] Lawrence (1979: 441).   [60] See under Comments.

external grounds',[61] Winter nonetheless argues for a fourth century BC date. The crux of his argument rests on the similarity in the size and general character of the Phigaleian circuit compared to that at Messene. As the fortifications of the latter were almost certainly constructed in the wake of the Battle of Leuktra, Winter believes Scranton's date is a century too early. Thus, even though 'the walls of Phigaleia have a slightly less developed appearance than those of Messene',[62] Winter finds it difficult to date them later than *c.*375–350 BC.

Several early travellers to the site took certain elements of the fortifications—including different masonry styles and/or tower arrangements—as proof of more than one phase of construction. Leake, for example, believed that the towers on the north-east and east sides of the circuit 'were added at a later age to the original enclosure which probably had few or perhaps not any towers'.[63] Similarly, from the different masonry employed, Curtius maintains 'dass man mit gutem Grunde verschiedene Zeiten der Erbauung annehmen kann'.[64] Still, it was Boblaye who was the first to assign a date to the two different building phases, writing that the Phigaleian circuit is 'un beau modèle de l'architecture militaire des Grecs au tems de la guerre du Péloponnèse; leur construction moins régulière que celle des remparts de Messène montre des restaurations qu'on peut attribuer à l'époque de ces derniers'.[65] More recently, both Meyer as well as Cooper are of the same general opinion: that, while parts of the circuit may date from as early as the fifth century BC, some time around the middle of the fourth century BC portions of the circuit were rebuilt with the addition of square and circular towers.[66]

Finally, and at the opposite end of the chronological spectrum, is the argument of Kirsten and Kraiker, who maintain that the fortifications of Phigaleia date exclusively to the Hellenistic period.[67] Although their argument is also based on a comparison with Messene, it differs from those just outlined. Specifically, because nearly the whole valley is enclosed within the circuit at Messene, they believe the site to be a typical example of a Hellenistic period *Fluchtburg* or refuge site. Consequently, if the Phigaleian circuit is similar to that of Messene, and if their Hellenistic date for Messene is accepted, it follows, therefore, that Phigaleia must also be Hellenistic.[68] As most scholars, however, do not in fact accept a Hellenistic date for the construction of the Messenian fortifications, then a Hellenistic date for the walls of Phigaleia is also unlikely. Winter removes any final doubt, suggesting that 'in specific details (frequency of towers and posterns, size of towers, use of open roof-platforms, as well as of crenellations rather than solid screenwalls, little

---

[61] Winter (1971a: 111, n. 23).   [62] Winter (1971a: 111, n. 23).
[63] Leake (1830: i. 497).   [64] Curtius (1851: i. 320).   [65] Boblaye (1836: 165).
[66] Meyer (1938: 2070); Cooper (1976: 703).   [67] Kirsten and Kraiker (1967: 422).
[68] Kirsten and Kraiker (1967: 422).

provision for artillery) Messene and Phigaleia are the very antithesis of Hellenistic [fortifications]'.[69]

Having dismissed an Archaic period date as too early and a Hellenistic date as too late, by process of elimination it is left to determine, if possible, whether the walls belong to one building phase in the fourth century BC or whether they are a product of the fifth century BC and modified in the fourth century BC. Without excavation, however, such an attempt is ultimately wasted, not only because most of the composite elements of the Phigaleian circuit refused to be compartmentalized neatly into distinct chronological periods, but also because the chronological distinctions themselves are largely subjective. In other words, the masonry employed, the trace of the walls (that is, the *Gelände-mauer*-type circuit), and the size, type, and distribution of towers at Phigaleia would not be out of place in either the late-fifth- or early fourth-century BC Peloponnese. Even if the posterns and the outworks (*hypoteichismata* and *proteichismata*) are generally characteristic of fourth-century BC systems, there is no way of knowing whether they are contemporary with the main circuit.

Most scholars do agree on one point—namely, that the length of the circuit suggests that the considerable intramural area at Phigaleia could never have been completely occupied and, thus, the site is best understood as a *Fluchtburg* or refuge site.[70] The one apparent exception is Lawrence, who, while agreeing that the intramural space was greater than the immediate needs of the population, maintains that the 'local resources were certainly inadequate to build the strong walls of Phigaleia'.[71] Consequently, instead of a functioning *polis*, 'only as a border fortress for all Arcadia can the wall have been worth its cost, of which presumably every confederate state bore a share'.[72] Lawrence is justifiably alone in his assertion. On the other hand, Kirsten and Kraiker, as mentioned, would put the walls of Messene (and by comparison, those of Phigaleia) in a Hellenistic period context. While noting the similarities with Messene, Winter believes that 'on account of its location Phigaleia was suffi-ciently involved in the power-politics of the early and mid-fourth [century] to have made the building of such a refuge just as desirable during that period as in Hellenistic times'.[73] Indeed, similar to many other Arcadian *poleis*, the Phigaleians had a troubled relationship with Sparta in the fifth and early fourth

[69] Winter (1971a: 112, n. 23).
[70] Curtius (1851: i. 321); Rangabé (1857: 85); Meyer (1938: 2069); Kirsten and Kraiker (1967: 422); Winter (1971a: 111–12 and n. 23); Lawrence (1979: 117–18); Jost (1999: 200).
[71] Lawrence (1979: 117). One might argue that the same 'local resources' were certainly adequate to build the Temple of Apollo at Bassai.
[72] Lawrence (1979: 118). 'Presumably' is the key word here, as there is no external evidence to suggest that Phigaleia functioned as an Arkadian border fort. Indeed, the evidence clearly demonstrates that Phigaleia was a *polis* in the accepted and conventional use of the term. Lawrence's scenario would make Phigaleia unique not only among Arkadian settlements but, to the best of my knowledge, in the entire Peloponnese.
[73] Kirsten and Kraiker (1967: 422); Winter (1971a: 112, n. 23).

century BC.[74] Winter is certainly correct, therefore, that the construction of such a circuit would have been appropriate before the Hellenistic period.

Whether constructed in the late fifth century BC, the early fourth century BC, or during a time spanning these periods, the *Geländemauer*-type circuit and its function as refuge site are intelligible only if the circuit was constructed in a single phase.[75] Certainly, in the absence of a fortified acropolis or citadel, the different approaches available towards the city would have made a partially fortified area essentially worthless. The circuit is effective only because it embraces all the plateau and its highest points, leaving no advantageous terrain outside the system. Furthermore, as has already been explored,[76] the relationship between the topography and the circuit actively limited the approaches to the city to essentially two directions. Thus, despite the considerable size of the circuit, the approaches would have been difficult and predictable, so that a minimal number of defenders would have been required at any given point. In this way, 'the disadvantages of an extended perimeter were therefore balanced by the far smaller number of men required in each sector'.[77] Whether the posterns, the outworks, or some (or all) of the towers were added to the circuit at a slightly later date can be confirmed only by archaeological excavation. Until then, however, the available evidence suggests that, on the whole, it is reasonable to suppose that the Phigaleian circuit was constructed sometime in the late fifth to early fourth centuries (*c.*425–375 BC).[78]

BIBLIOGRAPHY

Hdt. 6.83.2; Polyb. 4.3, 4.79; Diod. 15.40; Paus. 8.39–42; Gell (1817: 79–80); Leake (1830: i. 490–7); Boblaye (1836: 165); Ross (1841: 97–9); Curtius (1851: i. 318–24); Rangabé (1857: 84–9, pl. VII); Clark (1858: 254–5); Bursian (1862: ii. 250–4); Welcker (1865: 272–5); Wyse (1865: ii. 18–225); Frazer (1898: iv. 390–1); Scranton (1941: 109, 164, 175); Winter (1971a: 31 and n. 65, 39, n. 90, 111–12 and n. 23, 158 and n. 26, 222, n. 42, 253); Cooper (1972, 1976); Lawrence (1979: 117–18, 248, 379, 441, 444); Cooper and Myers (1981); Adam (1982: 180); Jost (1985: 82–98; 1999: 200–1); Papachatzis (1994: 351–60); Nielsen (2002: 586–8); Maher (2012a: 338–67).

---

[74] See under History.

[75] The different masonry styles may indicate that different teams of masons were working at the same time in order to complete the lengthily circuit as quickly as possible. See Winter (1971a: 82–4; 1989: 195).

[76] See under Overall Defensive Planning.   [77] Winter (1971a: 112).

[78] While acknowledging the difficulty in trying to date the walls of Phigaleia, Jost (1999: 201) too advocates a fifth- or early fourth-century date for their construction.

15

Psophis, Northern Arkadia

LOCATION

Psophis is located in northern Arkadia along the north bank of the confluence of Aroanios and Erymanthos Rivers (Fig. C15.1). The site comprises the summit and south-western slope of a small spur attached by a narrow saddle to a larger mountain to the north. Inhabitation was largely limited to the intramural area.

POLIS STATUS

While Polybius is the first written source to refer explicitly to the city as a *polis*, there are other clues that suggest the city's identity as a *polis* can be traced back to at least the Classical, if not the Archaic, period.[1] At Olympia, an inscribed shield dedicated collectively by Psophis has been discovered and dated to the sixth century BC.[2] This suggests a military activity of some sort in the Archaic period, and may be related to the statue of Zeus at Olympia, described by Pausanias 'as dedicated by the Psophidians for a success in war'.[3] In the fifth century BC, we know Psophis began striking its own coinage bearing the city ethnic.[4] Pausanias mentions a sculptural group at Olympia, which he thought represented *proxenoi* of Psophis from Elis.[5] Finally, a Delphic *theorodokos* resided in Psophis in the late third century BC.[6]

---

[1] Polyb. 4.70.3–4. For stray archaic finds on the site, see Jost (1985: 57).
[2] *SEG* xxiv. 299.   [3] Paus. 5.24.2; Nielsen (2002: 589–90).
[4] Head (1963: 453).
[5] Paus. 6.16.7; Nielsen (2002: 590). Pausanias gives no hints as to the date of this sculptural group.
[6] Plassart (1921: ii. 120 ff.).

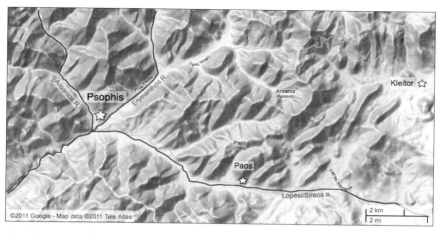

Fig. C15.1. Psophis, topographical map of site and surrounding area. (© *2011 Google-Map data © 2011 Tele Atlas*)

HISTORY

Besides the sixth-century BC military activity suggested by the shield found at Olympia,[7] we know exceedingly little about the history of this small city during the Archaic and Classical periods. Psophis is not mentioned as part of any larger organization, political or otherwise, during these periods, and it is unclear whether Psophis was a member of the Peloponnesian or Arkadian Leagues.[8] At the time of the Social War, Psophis was in the possession of a garrison from Elis.[9] As Philip V had entered into an alliance with the Achaian League against the people of Elis and Aitolia, in the winter of 219/218 BC, a Macedonian and Achaian army marched on Psophis. Polybius records that Philip 'stationed his men, who had ladders at three different spots, and divided the other Macedonians among these three parties ... and began the assault on the walls at once'.[10] Despite the formidable defences of the town, after a brief resistance the Elian soldiers fled to the acropolis, which soon capitulated as well. After the successful siege, Philip left a garrison of Achaians to guard the city while the Psophidians themselves 'received back the possession of the town'.[11] Although most of the monuments described by Pausanias were in

---

[7] *SEG* xxiv. 299. [8] Nielsen (2002: 589).
[9] Polyb. 4.70–2. [10] Polyb. 4.71.
[11] Polyb. 4.72. As Polybius' account concerns both the topography of the town and its fortifications, it will be addressed in more detail under Overall Defensive Plannng and Chronological Arguments.

ruins by the time he visited, his mention of locals in his account suggests at least some continued occupation of the site.

LOCAL TOPOGRAPHY

Psophis was bestowed with natural topographical advantages that were practically unparalleled by the situation of any other Arkadian *polis*.[12] Focusing on the two major rivers flanking the site (the Aroanios and Erymanthos), Polybius provides a colourful and accurate description of the landscape.[13] The Aroanios flows in a south-easterly direction past the west side of the city where it meets the Erymanthos.[14] The Erymanthos flows to the south-west and flanks the eastern and southern parts of the city.[15] These rivers converge about 100 m south of the site, where they are united with a third stream, the Lopesi or Sireos River (see Fig. C15.1).[16]

The city of Psophis was not only ideally located in the angle between these rivers, it also included the fortified hill mentioned by Polybius.[17] This hill rises steeply between the two rivers, though less so on the east. Although roughly conical in shape, this hill, rising c.70–80 m above the surrounding city, contains a sharp rocky crest that extends to the peak in a north-easterly direction from the Aroanios River Valley. The lower south-western part of this ridge is separated from the highest part of the summit to the north by a narrow saddle. The fortifications embraced this ridge and its spurs for most of its northern course—a stretch comprising about half the total length of the circuit. The other half of the circuit was laid out just north of the Erymanthos. The fortifications thus enveloped and defined the settlement, which occupied the whole south-east side of the hill. Finally, immediately opposite and parallel to the south-east side of the site, on the other side of the Erymanthos, is a small

[12] Leake (1830: ii. 241) writes, 'among the remarkable positions with which Greece abounds, and which seem to have been intended by Nature for the strong holds of small republics, Psophis is one of the most distinguished for strength and singularity of site'.

[13] Polyb. 4.70.

[14] The modern name of the Aroanios River is recorded as the Nousaïtiko River by Papandreou (1920: 130) and Jost (1985: 53) and as the Poretse or Germoutsani by Frazer (1898: iv. 282).

[15] The Erymanthos' modern incarnation is the Livartsino River. Petropoulos (2005) inexplicably mixes up the Erymanthos and the Aroanios Rivers, placing the former on the west and the latter on the east. Perhaps he is following the plan in Papandreou (1920: 130), which is also mislabelled. Meyer (1959: 1422) and Pritchett (1989: 3) dispute Papandreou's interpretation of Polybius and his reversal of these two rivers.

[16] As Frazer (1898: iv. 282) reminds us, it is 'from these three rivers the place takes its modern name of Tripotamo, or "Three Rivers"'. The modern village of Tripotama is located south-east of the site, while just north of the ancient Psophis can be found the small village of Psofis.

[17] Polyb. 4.71.

crescent-shaped ridge from which it is likely that Philip's army launched their assault on the city in 219/218 BC.[18]

Although today the site and modern village of Psophis fall within the Prefecture of Achaia, in the past, wavering allegiances aside, Psophis and its territory were part of Arkadia (see Fig. C15.1). Moreover, as the north-western most Arkadian *polis*, Psophis shared a border with both Achaia to the north and Elis to the west.[19] Within Arkadia itself, to the east was the *polis* of Paos—separated by only a chain of small hills and accompanying valleys—while to the south of Psophis the bulk of Mt Aphrodisio represented its border with the *polis* of Thelpousa.[20] With the exception of some very narrow tracts of land west of the city adjacent to the Aroanios, the majority of the arable land is to be found south-east of the city in the Lopesi River Valley. Exactly how much of this land belonged to Psophis is not clear, but it must have controlled the valley at least to the proximity of the city of Paos, located some 8 km to the east. The total territory of Psophis, however, is estimated to have comprised *c.*280 km².[21]

NATURAL DEFENCES

The height offered by the acropolis, and the steep slope on its north-western and north-eastern side (Fig. C15.2). The river valleys and surrounding mountains limit the approaches to the city to routes from the north-east, north-west, and south. The Aroanios and Erymanthos Rivers flank the city to the west and east respectively.

FORTIFICATION TYPE

Uneven type.[22] While estimates on the enclosed area of the walls differ,[23] from the summit the circuit descends to surround the lower terrain between the two

---

[18] For a detailed account of the siege of Philip and the topography of the site, see Pritchett (1989: 22–8).

[19] The site of Phigaleia is now a part of the modern region of Achaia. Incidentally, the modern village of Tripotamia is the point where the regions of Arkadia, Achaia, and Ilia still converge today.

[20] On his way from Psophis to Thelpousa, Pausanias (8.25.1) observed near the Ladon River a boundary stone on which was recorded in Archaic script: 'The boundary between Psophis and Thelpousa.'

[21] Nielsen (2002: 589).   [22] Listed as a 'ville mixtes' type by Jost (1999: 199).

[23] Meyer (1959: 1424), for example, suggests an enclosed area of 80 ha, while Petropoulos (2005: 364), presumably following Papandreou (1920: 138), maintains (an incredible) 800 acres (= 324 ha). Both estimates are certainly too large, and the area is more likely to be closer to around 40 ha.

Fig. C15.2. Psophis, the site
(facing east). (© *Matthew Maher*)

rivers, generally following the contours of the hill. Thus the walls both
enclosed a relatively flat, low-lying section of terrain as well as integrated an
acropolis of considerable bulk (Fig. C15.3).

PRESERVATION

The site is moderately well preserved, especially the northern and parts of the
southern section. For the most part, the long south-west stretch of the circuit is
not preserved.

CONSTRUCTION

The foundations of the walls were constructed in a predominately isodomic
trapezoidal style,[24] although sections of the wall in the north-east part of the
circuit combine polygonal with the trapezoidal (Fig. C15.4); the polygonal
sections may be a later repair.[25]

The only observable pseudo-isodomic courses are limited to the lowest courses
of the towers in the northern stretch of walls.[26] The curtains were constructed

---

[24] Scranton (1941: 171). Bisbee (1937: 530) describes the masonry at Psophis as 'nearly
rectangular polygonal . . . also called the semipolygonal, pseudo-polygonal, or quasi-polygonal'.
[25] Petropoulos (2005: 365).
[26] See Scranton (1941: 174). It remains uncertain, therefore, whether true pseudo-isodomic
exists at the site, or whether the longer, narrower blocks were employed instead only in the
construction of the towers' foundations.

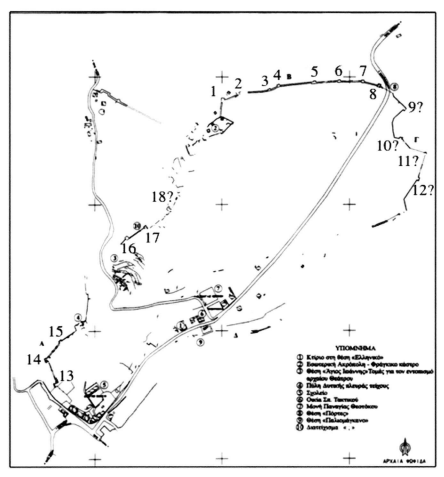

Fig. C15.3. Psophis, plan of the site from Petropoulos (2005: fig. 1). (© *Norwegian Institute in Athens*)

Fig. C15.4. Psophis, northern curtain (facing south-east). (© *Matthew Maher*)

Fig. C15.5. Psophis, northern curtain showing interior composition (facing east). (© *Matthew Maher*)

with parallel faces of blocks, with an average width of some 2.50 m,[27] and filled with rubble and presumably earth (Fig. C15.5). The blocks were laid horizontally in the usual manner, and there is no evidence that stretchers were employed. All the curtain and tower foundations in the circuit once supported a mudbrick superstructure (not preserved).

SUMMARY OF TACTICAL COMPONENTS

The city wall contained thirteen rectangular towers (possibly as many as eighteen, including one semicircular example), strategically rather than regularly spaced (see Fig. C15.3). No gates or posterns have been confidently identified. It remains uncertain whether the separately fortified citadel is medieval.

Towers

The fortification circuit of Psophis appears to contain at least thirteen towers, but perhaps as many as eighteen. In his brief publication, Petropoulos does not provide the dimensions of any of the towers. The towers are certainly relatively small, and, from personal observation, I would estimate them to be on average 5–6 m across the front and extending 3 or 4 m from the curtains.[28] Although

---

[27] Petropoulos (2005: 365).

[28] The numbers labelling the towers on Fig. C15.3 are provided by me for convenience and do not appear on the original plan. Those numbers with question marks denote those that appear to be towers on Petropoulos' plan but are not referenced otherwise in his text.

regular in places, the spacing of these towers is generally inconsistent, and therefore best described as being strategically spaced.[29] The circuit may have contained at least one semicircular tower, as Bursian claims to have witnessed in the early 1860s.[30] Although his description of its exact location is somewhat imprecise, it is clear enough that it stood in the south-western corner of the ancient city, in the area now completely covered by the modern village.[31]

Gates

Of the city gates that provided access to the ancient city, we know considerably less than the other elements of the fortifications. Only two candidates have been proposed, the evidence for both of which is far from conclusive. Papandreou maintains that the city's main East Gate was located just south-east of Tower 8, in the area where the modern road passes through this end of the site.[32] Meyer, on the other hand, puts the eastern gate slightly below, or south-east of the modern road.[33] Finally, while acknowledging the existence of a gate somewhere in this area, Petropoulos does not provide any information pertaining to its precise location.[34] He is equally vague concerning details about his team's discovery of a second gate in the western part of the city. The remains of this gate—predicted by both Meyer and Pritchett and apparently confirmed in the 2001 investigations—lie just north-east of Tower 15.[35] Besides mentioning the discovery of a second gate and referring the reader to its location on the plan, however, Petropoulos mentions nothing of its form, orientation, or architectural details.[36] Even on the ground, what Petropoulos refers to as the Western Gate could easily be interpreted as a well-preserved stretch of curtain wall.[37] Until further evidence is provided and rationale is offered, ultimately, we can at best cautiously assume the probably existence of a gate in this section of the circuit.

---

[29] It is only in the spacing between Towers 5 and 6, 6 and 7, and 7 and 8 that any kind of regularity appears, as these are separated by 50 m, 50 m, and 40 m respectively.

[30] Bursian (1862: ii. 261).

[31] This is the only attested example of a curvilinear tower at Psophis, and Bursian's observation is often cited by others. Frazer (1898: iv. 282), while not explicitly confirming the existence of the circular tower, does enigmatically hint that the walls 'are defended by towers, *mostly* square' (emphasis added). A circular-shaped tower here, in presumably the southernmost part of the circuit, would be very practical, as it could better command and observe the point where all three of the city's rivers meet.

[32] Papandreou (1920: 130).   [33] Meyer (1959: 1423).

[34] Petropoulos (2005: 365).   [35] Meyer (1959: 1423); Pritchett (1989: 25).

[36] Petropoulos (2005: 365).

[37] So conspicuous is this section—incredibly well preserved and standing to a height of 4 m— that this 'gate' was in fact mistaken by Meyer (1959: 1423) for a piece of the curtain.

COMMENTS

On the acropolis of the site stands the ruins of a small Frankish citadel, and the question remains whether it overlies an earlier enclosure that was more or less contemporary with the rest of the circuit.[38] Leake was the first to address this question and admitted that '[while] there was probably a citadel on the summit...[he] could not trace the enclosure of it'.[39] A century and a half later, Pritchett similarly failed to find traces of an earlier circuit, and was resigned to the fact that, although 'one sees sections of walls in various parts of the site, [there is] no obvious line of an inner acropolis wall'.[40] Finally, while also recognizing the fact that the Frankish constructions have either destroyed or masked the earlier enclosure, Petropoulos is hopeful that future investigations of the site by the Ephoreia of Byzantine Antiquities will shed more light on the matter.[41]

OVERALL DEFENSIVE PLANNING

The defensive advantages apparent in the Psophidians' choice of site for the location of their city are many. Geographically, not only did the site command major strategic (not to mention commercial) routes between north-western Arkadia and both Achaia in the north and Elis to the west, but topographically the site itself effectively enhanced the inherent natural defensive strengths of its position with the addition of complementary defensive architecture. Certainly these advantages were not lost on Polybius, whose description of the site remains as succinct as it is precise when he writes 'defended on three sides by...streams; while the fourth, or northern, side is commanded by a hill, which has been fortified, and serves as a convenient and efficient citadel'.[42] Such advantages were, of course, not the product of chance, but the vision of military architects who consciously exploited the topography in order to maximize the defensive potential of the site.

Polybius' description of the site underlies the primary defensive strategy in which the natural topography was engaged, where possible, to make the site defensible. First and foremost in this regard were the Erymanthos and Aroanios Rivers, which provided a safeguard to the south-east and west sides

[38] Polybius (4.7.11) refers to the acropolis, but does not mention whether it was separately fortified or not. I was unable to investigate the remains here, as the whole acropolis was fenced off and closed to visitors.
[39] Leake (1830: ii. 242).   [40] Pritchett (1989: 28).   [41] Petropoulos (2005: 367).
[42] Polyb. 4.70. It is not clear whether the fortified northern part of the hill to which he refers was the northern part of the city wall or a separately fortified citadel.

of the city respectively. While the use of rivers as natural outworks was not uncommon in Arkadian defensive planning, at Psophis—unlike at Stymphalos or Kleitor, for example—the beds carved by these rivers (especially the Aroanios) were relatively deep and wide. As these rivers chiselled their way through the landscape over millennia, they not only left behind steep-sided riverbeds, but actually carved out a plateau, on the edges of which the fortifications could be employed to a greater advantage. An enemy would first have to navigate the rivers—which were still 'clear rapid streams'[43] in Frazer's day—and then scale their steep banks before even reaching the walls[44]—the whole time under the watchful eyes (and presumably missile fire) of the defenders. Besides offering protection against flooding and im- proved lines of sight, the main advantage of placing the circuit above the rivers on the edges of the plateau is that it provided no space at the base of the walls for enemy infantry to muster and launch a concentrated attack.

The strategic relationship between the topography of the site and the layout of the circuit is also evident in the incorporation of the high ground in the northern part of the settlement. Indeed, what made this hill such a 'convenient and efficient acropolis'[45] was both its natural character and how the fortifica- tions were positioned to intensify its already considerable defensive dispos- ition (Fig. C15.6).

The numerous defensive advantages of incorporating high ground in the circuit are obvious, and the point need not be repeated in more detail here. What is important to note, however, is the specific advantages inherent in the position and course of the northern wall. Although the sloping east–west ridge

Fig. C15.6. Psophis, northern fortification wall (facing south). (© *Matthew Maher*)

---

[43] Frazer (1898: iv. 282).

[44] Even Polybius (4.70) could not fail to notice the steep riverbeds whose 'waters have worn out for themselves by slow degrees, in the course of ages.'

[45] Polyb. 4.70.

on which this stretch of wall lies seems almost impossibly well suited for its purpose, the choice of laying out the wall here was only one of two options. At first glance, the other ridge, less than 100 m to the south and issuing immediately from the eastern limits of the acropolis, would seem an equally feasible option. In choosing the former ridge, however, the Psophidian military architects clearly demonstrated excellent foresight. If, for example, the southern ridge had been chosen as the site for the northern curtain, not only would the intramural space of the city itself have been reduced by some 25 per cent, but, more importantly, it would have left the other ridge, its adjacent saddle, and the high ground north of the city outside the circuit. Such a scenario would conceivably have made the north part of the circuit susceptible to an attack, especially if the enemy was in possession of this high ground. Although such a scenario is hypothetical and ultimately academic, since in the end the walls were built on the northernmost ridge, the tactical components of the circuit themselves do reflect a concern for perceived vulnerable spots in the trace.

While it may seem remarkable that Towers 1–4—a third of the total confidently attested examples in the circuit—exhibit the closest spacing and are densely grouped along a stretch spanning less than 150 m, when this is considered in the context of the surrounding topography, such a tactical consideration is easily understood. For these towers seem to have held a single purpose: to observe and safeguard against any unwelcome advance from the narrow saddle linking the acropolis to the hills to the north (see Fig. C15.6). Not only was this saddle vulnerable because of its proximity to the acropolis (less than 50 m), but, because it straddled an east–west running ravine, it could be approached from either the north-west or the north-east via the Aroanios and Erymanthos Valleys respectively. The same concern for the more vulnerable parts of the trace, reflected in the tactical arrangement of the circuit's components, can also be seen in other parts of the city.

As the northern section of the city wall left the protection of the heights and descended eastward towards the Erymanthos, it was inevitable that it would have to negotiate the open and the gently sloping ground between the terminus of the northern ridge and the river (section Γ on Fig. C15.3). In this area, where the topography of the site was frustratingly uncooperative for the larger defensive concerns, the military architects offered a practical solution. Not only are Towers 7 and 8 more closely spaced as the circuit approaches the flatter ground,[46] but, instead of making a straight run towards the river, the curtain was constructed in the shape of a large concave semicircle anchored between Tower 9 and Tower 11. Indeed, that this curvilinear section is the

[46] From the observed pattern of grouping towers close together in vulnerable sections, it is not inconceivable that a tower once existed between Towers 8 and 9 but was destroyed in the construction of the modern road. Certainly leaving an unprotected stretch of *c*.80 m between Towers 8 and 9 seems less probable.

only part of the extant circuit as a whole that does not follow a course dictated by the topography of the site suggests a conscious decision—certainly one with a perceived defensive advantage. Such an advantage, similar to that of a formal gatecourt, lies in the principle that attackers attempting to storm this section would be drawn in only to find themselves assaulted by enfilading from both flanks. Furthermore, the proposed location of Tower 10 as extending out slightly in the centre of this concave stretch further strengthens the efficiency of this principle. Situating Tower 10 in the centre of the larger concave section— essentially creating two smaller concave sections—potentially doubled the amount of defensive flanking fire on each stretch of curtain without losing direct frontal power while at the same time reducing the distance these missiles would have to travel. Finally, this arrangement ensured that, whether from Tower 9 or 10, the unshielded right side of enemy infantry would always be exposed to defenders.

Despite the earlier claim by Papandreou that the eastern gate was located east of Tower 8 in the vicinity of the modern road,[47] from the defensive considerations already outlined,[48] it is more likely that the eastern gate should be sought somewhere in this concave section of the circuit. True, construction of the modern road has obliterated all traces of the fortifications, and we cannot be certain, but the amount of rock cut away to make the road was considerable, as evidenced by the scar left behind (Fig. C15.7).

From the height of the bedrock visible on either side of the road and the surviving curtain atop, it appears that in antiquity the eastern end of the northern ridge must have extended across what is today the level of the modern road. Again, while it is not impossible that an area here was quarried

Fig. C15.7. Psophis, northern curtain and cutting of modern road (facing south-west). (© *Matthew Maher*)

[47] Papandreou (1920: 130).
[48] See under Summary of Tactical Components, under Gates.

in the past to make the terrain suitable for a gate, it is more likely that the eastern gate should be sought on terrain more appropriate to its function.

The concave section immediately suggests itself.[49] In this scenario, all traffic moving south-west down the Erymanthos Valley would be funnelled into the concavity by a narrow (*c*.150 m), relatively flat stretch of land between the eastern limit of the northern ridge and the west bank of the river itself. As the stretch of curtain immediately south of Tower 11 lies mere metres from the west bank, this concavity can be the only terminus of a road (and, therefore, a gate) to Psophis from the Erymanthos Valley.[50]

While enough of the south-western and western sections of the circuit survive to observe that it follows the edge of the plateau above the Aroanios with fairly regularly spaced towers—as may be expected with the consistent terrain—we know considerably less about the south-eastern section of the city wall (section Δ on Fig. C15.3). Of this area, Lawrence, somewhat paradoxically, writes that 'no towers seem to have existed in the flat valley between, where the wall, now lost, must have been perfectly accessible'.[51] If true, such an arrangement would fly in the face not only of the pattern witnessed at Psophis and most other fortified sites, but also of common sense. Certainly, should we not expect to find towers precisely at those vulnerable points that were perfectly accessible?[52] As the south-west part of the circuit, similarly laid out on the relatively flat terrain on the edge of the river, was fortified by a number of regularly spaced towers, it is feasible to suppose that this now lost section along the south-east contained a similar arrangement. Otherwise, we are left to believe that a *c*.1 km stretch of curtain wall was constructed without towers— an arrangement, to the best of my knowledge, unparalleled at any other fortified Arkadian city.

CHRONOLOGICAL SUMMARY

The original circuit (trapezoidal) was built late fifth or early fourth century BC, with a possible repair phase (polygonal intrusions) dated to the late third

[49] Polybius (4.71) does mention the defenders left through 'a gate in the upper part of the town' to meet the forces of Philip. As Philip attacked from the Erymanthos side of the circuit, a gate in the area of the concave section—which stands at a higher elevation than would have stood the now lost trace along the river—would satisfy Polybius' placement of it in the 'upper part of the town'.
[50] Admittedly, it is possible that a gate (or gates) existed somewhere further to the south (section Δ on Fig. C15.3) and was accessible only by bridge(s). Indeed Polybius (4.71) does mention that Philip 'led his army over the bridge across the Erymanthos'.
[51] Lawrence (1979: 478). Despite the fact that Polybius (4.70) states that the position of Psophis 'renders the city secure and difficult of approach'.
[52] In any case, the south-east part of the circuit was not that accessible, as any approach would first require crossing and then climbing the steep banks of the Erymanthos.

century BC—based on historical probability, external evidence, and architectural affinities.

CHRONOLOGICAL ARGUMENTS

As Philip V and his Achaian League allies marched on Psophis in the winter of 219/218 BC, discerning the mood of the Elian soldiers holed up within its walls can only be guesswork. Were they confident the city's strong position and formidable fortifications would protect them in the end? Or, after hearing of the failed Aitolian attack on Kleitor days earlier, news that no doubt reached Psophis before the combined Macedonian and Achaian army, did they feel their chances of survival were more indeterminate? We shall probably never know. What we do know, however, is that, after their arrival, Philip's forces 'began the assault on the walls at once',[53] and the town was quickly surrendered. Thanks to Polybius' description, it is safe to say that the fortifications of Psophis were in place before 219/218 BC. But can we determine when the fortifications were built? Is there enough evidence? Petropoulos is doubtful. He maintains that not enough evidence has surfaced from the excavations to determine a definitive chronology of its construction.[54] Moreover, he is also hesitant to rely on similarities to other Arkadian fortifications—a method he feels is not always safe.[55] Such reservations notwithstanding, and even if a chronology cannot be established definitively, certainly enough circumstantial evidence exists to provide an approximate date for the construction of the Psophidian circuit.

Assuming that the examples of pseudo-isodomic should instead be better understood as part of the foundation of some of the towers and not a distinct masonry style characteristic of all of the circuit, we are left to deal with the isodomic style that predominates at the site and presumably represents the first phase of construction. Scranton maintains that walls exhibiting blocks characterized as isodomic trapezoidal with quarry face surface treatment should be dated to *c.*425–375 BC.[56] While the shortcomings of stylistic dating have already been discussed,[57] the date provided by Scranton provides—at the very least—a good starting point from which to examine the other elements of the Psophidian fortifications.

The dimensions, distribution, and structure of the towers can tell us much in this regard. The relatively modest dimensions of the towers (*c.*5–6 × 3–4 m) noted by Lawrence as being 'quite small'[58] immediately suggest that they were not originally designed to house artillery—or at least machines of any

---

[53] Polyb. 4.71.   [54] Petropoulos (2005: 366).   [55] Petropoulos (2005: 366).
[56] Scranton (1941: 85).   [57] See Part One, Chapter 2.   [58] Lawrence (1979: 478).

significant size—and should pre-date the widespread use of defensive artillery beginning in the first quarter of the fourth century BC. Moreover, the fact that the small towers were neither used sparingly nor limited to only the perceived vulnerable parts of the extant sections is indicative of a late-fifth-century BC date. Basing his conclusions on numerous comparanda in his studies, Winter maintains that 'towers were used sparingly (and as a rule unsystematically employed) until about 450 BC, whereas from the time of the Peloponnesian War onward, they became a common feature'.[59] Finally, while the extremely overgrown and patchy remains leave us to wonder whether these towers had ground-storey chambers, were bonded to the curtain, or possessed posterns in the back of the towers, the construction of some of the towers is informative. For example, the curtain between Towers 16 and 17, as well as that between Towers 6 and 7, were not built continuously with the back of these towers. Instead we see an alternative arrangement whereby the curtain stretches between the front corner of the tower and the back corner of the adjacent one. This practice of aligning the front of the tower with the outer face of the curtain, giving the impression that the tower extends inwards, 'is rare after the fifth century'.[60]

The construction and layout of the curtain are equally informative. While admitting that the thickness of walls as a chronological marker is problematic, Winter maintains that, as a general rule, the thickest city walls are those of the mid-fourth century BC onwards.[61] With an average width of only around 2.50 m, the relatively thin curtains at Psophis do not fit the pattern of later circuits. Indeed, the lack of thick curtains suggests they were constructed before the widespread use of artillery, at a time when defenders still relied on the strength of their walls alone. Similarly, we may assign the lack of posterns at Psophis to the same accepted wisdom of the time. Certainly, by the fourth century BC, posterns became increasingly common, as 'city-walls lost much of their efficacy owing to the vast improvements in siege-equipment',[62] and, although there may exist some examples as early as the fifth century BC, normally the use of posterns is less common in the earlier circuits where defenders still relied on the strength of their walls.[63] As a final point, it should be noted that the structure of the curtains themselves also fits the usual late-fifth- or early fourth-century BC arrangement. Not only is the fill of earth, rubble, and masses of unworked stones consistent with other fifth-century BC examples, but the binding of the fill was achieved not with headers—typical of the fourth century BC and onwards—but simply by leaving the inner faces of the curtain blocks in the rough state in which they were quarried.[64]

While admittedly far from conclusive, the evidence outlined does recommend a late-fifth- or early fourth-century BC date for the original phase of

---

[59] Winter (1971a: 160).   [60] Lawrence (1979: 380).   [61] Winter (1971a: 134–5).
[62] Lawrence (1979: 338).   [63] Winter (1971a: 235).   [64] Winter (1971a: 135).

Fig. C15.8. Psophis, north-east section showing mixture of trapezoidal and polygonal masonry (facing north-west). (© *Matthew Maher*)

construction for the Psophidian circuit. Perhaps most significant is the lack of any identifiable features that can be clearly attributed to the middle fourth century BC or later. Even if an early date for these fortifications is accepted, it remains to be explained why this system did not keep pace with advances in offensive siege warfare. In other words, why did the inhabitants of Psophis retain for almost two centuries what must have seemed an obsolete system, when other cities in Arkadia went to great lengths to upgrade their defences, as technological innovations had tipped the balance in favour of the aggressor? Lawrence provides an intriguing answer and one especially appropriate to Psophis, suggesting that the early enceintes of some 'minor cities were left almost intact because the strength of their position compensated for anti-quated designs'.[65] Of course the siege by Philip and the Achaians shattered such self-assurance, demonstrating that cities possessing even the strongest of natural defences were not impervious to the advanced siege warfare of the Hellenistic period. Such is the advantage afforded by hindsight. Perhaps after the Elians had been expelled and the Psophidians once again took control of their city, the inhabitants went to work repairing the damages caused during the siege. It is possible that a second phase of construction, as mentioned, represented by the combined pseudo-isodomic trapezoidal and polygonal sections in the northern part of the city along the Erymanthos, is evidence of such repair (Figure C15.8).

   Despite the reservations of Petropoulos about trying to assign a concrete chronology to the fortifications at Psophis, attempting to ascertain an approximate date, based on the available evidence, is certainly not beyond the realm of possibility. True, many of his reservations lie in the fact that he is

---

[65] Lawrence (1979: 377). Such an outdated and unfamiliar circuit may explain why Polybius (4.70) considered the fortifications to be of 'unusual construction'.

waiting until the excavated material has been analysed. Until such material is published, however, it is reasonable to propose that the fortifications at Psophis, as originally alluded to by Scranton, were probably constructed in the late fifth or early fourth century BC, with a possible repair phase dated to the late third century BC. It remains to be seen in the future whether the excavated material will confirm this chronology, or whether a new one will be proposed.

BIBLIOGRAPHY

Polyb. 4.70.7–10, 71.3–4, 71.3.8–11, 72.5; Paus. 8.24; Gell (1817: 122); Leake (1830: ii. 240–50, pl. 1); Boblaye (1836: 158); Curtius (1851: i. 385–90, pl. 8); Bursian (1862: ii. 260–2); Welcker (1865: i. 290–4); Wyse (1865: ii. 161–70); Frazer (1898: iv. 282–3); Hiller von Gaertringen and Lattermann (1911: 7); Papandreou (1920: 130–46); Bisbee (1937: 530, 532, 534); Scranton (1941: 171, 174); Meyer (1959: 1421–8); Winter (1971a: 32, 35, n. 75, 39, n. 90); McAlister (1976); Lawrence (1979: 62–3, 129, 478); Jost (1985: 53–60; 1999: 199); Pritchett (1989: 22–8); Papachatzis (1994: 270–5); Nielsen (2002: 588–90); Petropoulos (2005); Maher (2012a: 262–91).

16

Stymphalos, Northern Arkadia

LOCATION

The *polis* of Stymphalos is located in a narrow mountain valley in northern Arkadia, on the north shore of Limni Stymfalia (Fig. C16.1). The remains lie on the northern edge of a basin (with *katavothroi*) defined by mountains on all sides. The city was laid out over largely flat terrain but also possessed an acropolis in the form of a small spur extending into the plain to the east. Inhabitation was limited to the intramural area.

POLIS STATUS

Stymphalos is listed among the five *megalai poleis* of ancient Arkadia mentioned by Pseudo-Skylax[1] and was a member of the Peloponnesian, Arkadian, and Achaian Leagues.[2] As is the case with Mantineia, Megalopolis, and Orchomenos, Stymphalos' political status as a *polis* is certain.[3]

HISTORY

The present remains on the site belong to an artificial foundation of the early fourth century BC. The location of the earlier Archaic and Classic period settlement, the one mentioned by Homer and Pindar, remains unknown.[4] Thus,

---

[1] Ps.-Skylax 44.

[2] Membership in the Peloponnesian League is assumed (Nielsen 1996b: 87). Membership in the Arkadian League is demonstrated by Xenophon (*Hell.* 7.3.1), and in the Achaian League by Polybius (2.55, 4.68).

[3] See Nielsen (2002: 590–2) for a summary of the evidence for Stymphalos' *polis* status.

[4] Hom. *Il.* 2.608; Pind. *Ol.* 6.99. Pausanias (8.22.1) confirms that Stymphalos 'was originally founded on another site, and not on that of the modern city'. Somewhere in the western end of the valley, near modern Lafka, is the best candidate for the location of the earlier settlement (Gourley, pers. comm.).

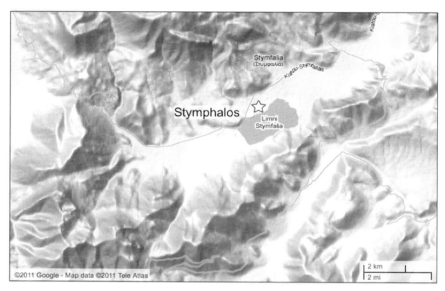

Fig. C16.1. Stymphalos, topographical map of site and territory. (© *2011 Google-Map data © 2011 Tele Atlas*)

despite the importance of this small Arkadian *polis*, little of its history is known prior to the early fourth century, when in 392 and again in 371/369 BC, the Athenian general 'Iphikrates and his troops invaded many districts of Arkadia, where they plundered and made attacks upon the walled towns'.[5] That Stymphalos was probably one of those 'walled towns' is supported by the testimony of Strabo, who provides a more detailed account of the Athenians' unsuccessful siege of Stymphalos. Strabo tells us that, having made little progress in the siege of the city itself, Iphikrates attempted to block the adjacent lake's sinkhole (*katavothros*) with a number of sponges.[6] Although Iphikrates was unsuccessful, presumably his intention was to cause the level of the lake to rise in the hopes that the rising water would eventually undermine the city's mudbrick fornications. These accounts are of particular importance for our understanding of the history of the city and its fortifications, as they suggest that the city was both in its current location and walled by 371/369 BC if not earlier.[7]

Stymphalos again enters the historical record in 315 BC, when the city was captured in a night attack by Apollonides, one of Kassander's generals.[8] This

---

[5] Xen. *Hell.* 4.4.16.   [6] Strab. 8.8.4.

[7] As noted by Gourley and Williams (2005: 219), such a tactic is reminiscent of the stratagem employed by the Spartans on the walls of Mantineia in 385 BC. Moreover, they accurately point to the fact that it 'seems a "chicken-and-egg" argument to consider whether Iphikrates tried this tactic in 392 BC, which suggested it to the Spartans in 385 BC, or vice versa' (Gourley and Williams 2005: 219, n. 11).

[8] Diod. 19.63.1–2.

event is significant to the history of the fortifications, as the archaeological evidence suggests it is associated with the late-fourth-century BC destruction layer discovered in the Acropolis Bastion.[9] Moreover, the subsequent rebuilding and enlargement of both the Bastion and the West Wall Tower have been linked to this event and the resulting presence of a Macedonian garrison in the city.[10] What little is known about Stymphalos in the Hellenistic period comes largely from the archaeological excavations of the site,[11] and, in this regard, the most important discovery was the large-scale abandonment of the site in the mid-second century BC and its partial resettlement in the late first century BC.[12]

LOCAL TOPOGRAPHY

Located at the crossroads of Arkadia, Achaia, the Argolid, and the Sikyonia, the city of Stymphalos controlled a valley of considerable strategic importance (Fig. C16.2).[13]

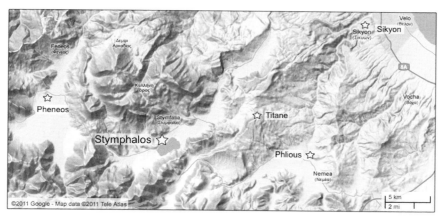

Fig. C16.2. Stymphalos, topographical map of site and surrounding territories. (© *2011 Google-Map data © 2011 Tele Atlas*)

[9] Williams et al. (1998: 313).

[10] Gourley and Williams (2005: 249). Both the attack by Iphikrates and Apollonides preserved in the ancient sources will play an important role in determining the chronology of the Stymphalian circuit and are discussed in greater detail under Chronological Arguments.

[11] For a summary of the history of scholarship and archaeological work at Stymphalos, see Maher (2012b: 113–14; 2015a: 19–21).

[12] Williams et al. (2002: 136). The discovery of a Roman coin (minted in 149 BC) of a type usually associated with the Roman army in Greece may suggest that, as a member of the Achaian League, Stymphalos suffered a fate similar to that which befell Corinth in 146 BC (Williams et al. 2002: 136 and n. 4).

[13] Stymphalos now belongs to the modern region of Corinthia.

Characteristic of north-eastern Arkadian geography, the Stymphalian Valley (or basin), *c.*13 km long and averaging 2 km in width, is sharply delineated by the surrounding mountains. Dividing Stymphalian territory from that of Alea and Phlious are Mt Ghidhomandra and Mt Stavaetos, located on the south and south-east of the valley respectively. In the south-west lies the bulk of Mt Oligyrtos, which separates the valley from Orchomenos and Kaphyai, while, to the west and north-west, Mt Mavro-vouni and Mt Gherondio mark the border between Stymphalos and the territory of Pheneos. Finally, dominating the valley on the north, and forming the border with Achaia, is Mt Kylene and its two highest peaks, Ziria and Mikri Ziria.[14]

The most conspicuous feature of the Stymphalian basin is Lake Stimfalia. Located immediately south of the ancient city, this lake (or, more accurately, a marsh) occupies nearly the complete width of the valley. Although the limits of the lake have varied over time, often alternating between two extremes—inundating parts of the lower city or drying up completely—it is certainly much larger today than in antiquity.[15] The lake is fed both by springs located on the slopes of Kylene north-east of the ancient city, and by a seasonal river originating north-west of the site.[16] Drainage of the lake is facilitated by a *katavothros* located on its south-west shore.[17] The settlement is situated on the north shore of the lake immediately south of the modern hamlet of Kionia. Although the majority of the site was laid out over a flat area, it did incorporate a small acropolis in the south-west part of the city. Measuring some 600 m by 230 m, the acropolis is a narrow triangular spur stemming from a low hill west of the city. It rises relatively gently from the plain below on all sides but the south-west, where there is a precipitous slope elevated 50 m above the lake.[18]

As the city and lake occupied roughly the centre of the basin, any traffic across Stymphalian territory would be compelled by the geography to pass through (or very close to) the city itself (see Fig. C16.1). Today, as in antiquity, there are three primary entrances into the valley, which represent the best candidates for the location of the ancient road network.[19] Two of these passes

---

[14] The exact eastern limit of Stymphalian territory—and south-western limit of Sikyon territory—is uncertain (Gourley and Williams 2005: 221). On the border with Sikyon, see Lolos (2011: 25–6).

[15] In the late nineteenth century, many of the natural outlets of the lake were sealed, creating a larger reservoir for an aqueduct to Corinth (Gourley and Williams 2005: 220, n. 13).

[16] Gourley and Williams (2005: 220–1).

[17] The Erasinos River near Argos is said to originate from the lake via this sinkhole. See Hdt. 6.76.1; Paus. 8.22.3; Strab. 8.8.3.

[18] Williams (1983: 196).

[19] The so-called Wolfsglen Pass, located above modern Lafka in the south-western part of the valley, may also have been an important road in antiquity. Although Gourley and Williams (2005: 219, n. 10)—echoing the sentiments of Frazer (1898: iv. 269)—state that this pass is

are traversed by the modern Stymfalias–Kiatou road—one via the north-east edge of the plain, the other through the Gherondio Mountains towards Pheneos. While the latter almost certainly follows an ancient route—this was the road taken by Pausanias[20]—evidence suggests that the former was also part of the ancient road network. This route represents the most obvious course to the coast and Sikyon, and interestingly, in the early 1800s, Dodwell apparently observed traces of the ancient road, running east–west just north of the city.[21] The third artery in and out of the valley was located in the pass above the south-east edge of the lake. Although modern quarrying has obliterated any trace of an ancient road, there are clues that suggest one existed here in the past. Not only is it easily traversable, but during his travels Gell observed that 'the pass between the mountain and the lake had also been fortified by two walls'.[22] That the pass here warranted rural defences suggests the existence of a main road at some point in the area's history. Finally, the only other tangible survival of the ancient road network is a small ramp leading from the lake to the Acropolis Gate, located outside and north-west of the city's main gate. This path, however, sheds little light on the larger road network of the valley as it could have been accessed by any of the roads mentioned.[23]

NATURAL DEFENCES

The height offered by the acropolis, and the precipitous slope on its south and south-west sides, offer the site its natural defences (Fig. C16.3). Spring-fed streams flank the east side of the city, while the lake covers the entire breadth of the city on the south. The lake and south slope of the acropolis create a natural bottleneck upon approach to the city from the south-west. The lowest slopes of Mt Kylene protect the site to the north.

'relatively easy to negotiate', I did not find this to be the case when I used the pass in May 2010 en route from Orchomenos. For more information about this pass, see also Plutarch (*Kleomenes* 26.3); Leake (1830: iii. 107–8); Meyer (1939a: 29–30); Curtius (1851: i. 208); Frazer (1898: iv. 230); Pritchett (1989: 12–17).

[20] Paus. 8.22.1.
[21] Dodwell (1819: ii. 434). This may have been the same road, now covered by the asphalt of the modern road, mentioned by Pikoulas (1999a: 297, no. 48).
[22] Gell (1823: 384). For more detail on this wall as well as contributions from other early modern travel writers at Stymphalos, see Maher (2012b).
[23] Pikoulas (1999a: 296–7, no. 47).

Fig. C16.3. Stymphalos, the site from across the lake (facing north east). (© *Matthew Maher*)

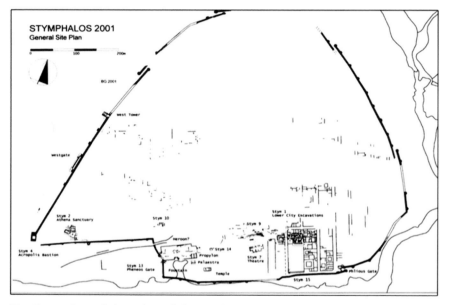

Fig. C16.4. Stymphalos, plan of the site from Gourley and Williams (2005: fig. 1). (© *Hector Williams and Ben Gourley*)

FORTIFICATION TYPE

Uneven type.[24] From the acropolis, the circuit descends to the north and to the east to surround the flat area comprising the lower city (Fig. C16.4).[25]

---

[24] Listed as a 'ville mixtes' type by Jost (1999: 199–200).
[25] For a more detailed discussion of the course of the wall and its constituent parts, see Maher (2015a: 22–7).

PRESERVATION

The walls and towers on the acropolis and western side of the city are fairly well preserved, but almost nothing of the northern and eastern sections exists above ground.[26] The circuit is *c*.2.5 km long and enclosed an intramural area of *c*.30 ha.

CONSTRUCTION

The foundations of the walls have an average width ranging between 2.50 m and 4.50 m,[27] and were constructed in a predominately polygonal style.[28] Excavation of the southern acropolis section has revealed that the stone socle is comprised of an inner and outer face of 'rough polygonal blocks'.[29] Header blocks were found distributed at fairly regular intervals in order to bond the faces with the earth and rubble core.[30] All the curtain and tower foundations in the circuit once supported a mudbrick superstructure (not preserved).

SUMMARY OF TACTICAL COMPONENTS

The city wall contained one hexagonal tower, six identical rectangular towers (*c*.6.50 × 2.50 m), one large rectangular tower (*c*.15 × 9 m), and 26 semicircular (*c*.6.35 m in diameter), regularly spaced throughout the circuit (see Fig. C16.4). There is one large rectangular bastion (21 m × 11 m) at the highest point on the acropolis. The circuit possessed seven gates, four of which were of the overlap type, one was a ramp gate, one was a simple frontal opening type, and one was a gatecourt type. Only one postern has been found. Remains in front of the western part of the circuit may have represented an outwork (that is, the 'West Wall Structure').

---

[26] Much of the eastern trace of the wall, including several of its towers, can be seen in satellite images in the form of parch marks.

[27] Gourley and Williams (2005: 222).

[28] Basing his comments on a photograph, Scranton (1941: 166) classifies the walls of Stymphalos as rubble with a tendency towards polygonal. This classification, however, is not reconcilable with any of the fortifications' extant remains. The only masonry on the whole site (which would have been visible before he published his work) that might fit this classification is the retaining wall supporting the south side of the ramp gate leading to the acropolis.

[29] Gourley and Williams (2005: 223).   [30] Gourley and Williams (2005: 223).

Towers

All seven of the city's rectangular towers are found exclusively on the north-east stretch of the circuit, regularly spaced at *c.*30 m intervals. Six of these towers are identical, measuring *c.*6.50 m by 6.50 m and projecting *c.*2.50 m from the wall,[31] while the seventh, the West Wall Tower, is considerably larger. The foundations of this rectangular tower (3 m thick) measure 15 m in length by 9 m in width, and survive for its entire height of three courses (Fig. C16.5).[32] Excavation of the West Wall Tower exposed the foundations of

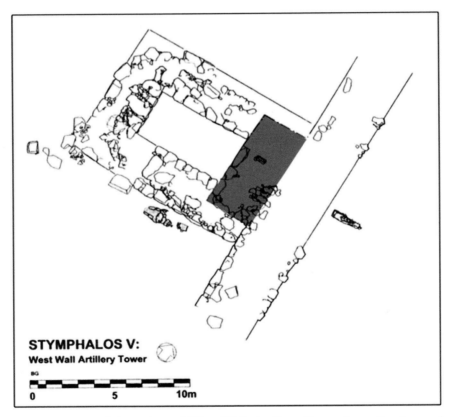

Fig. C16.5. Stymphalos, plan of West Wall Artillery Tower from Gourley and Williams (2005: fig. 14). (© *Hector Williams and Ben Gourley*)

[31] Gourley and Williams (2005: 241).

[32] Excavation of the tower in 2005, supervised by the author, showed that the lowest course of the foundations was built directly onto the bedrock, which had been carefully cut to receive it.

an earlier rectangular tower (the grey rectangle on Fig. C16.5), similar in size to the others.[33]

The semicircular towers are much more frequent, and twenty examples can be found regularly spaced along the lower eastern and southern sections of the trace. These towers are comparable in size to their rectangular counterparts, averaging 6.35 m in diameter and projecting 2.50 m from the curtain.[34] A further six regularly spaced semicircular towers are found on the southern side of the acropolis, which are about half the size of the towers elsewhere on the circuit.[35]

In addition to the West Wall Tower, the circuit at Stymphalos contained two other modified artillery installations, the Hexagonal Tower and the Acropolis Bastion. The Hexagonal Tower was initially believed to have been part of the original circuit, but excavation has demonstrated the presence of an earlier, semicircular tower, bonded to the curtain behind.[36] At 6.55 m wide, presenting five sides 4.0 m in length and 1.10 m thick, and projecting 5.90 m south from the adjacent curtain, this tower is considerably larger than the three semicircular towers situated on either side of it.[37] On the highest point of the acropolis and westernmost part of the circuit lie the foundations of the Acropolis Bastion, still standing to a height of 3 m in places (Fig. C16.6).[38] Excavation has demonstrated that the Acropolis Bastion, measuring 21 m by 11 m with walls 3 m thick, had replaced an earlier smaller rectangular tower, the remains of which were encapsulated by the later structure.[39] Excavations

Fig. C16.6. Stymphalos, north-west corner of Acropolis Bastion (facing south-east). (© *Matthew Maher*)

---

[33] A hoard of coins of the fourth and early third centuries BC was found in this tower and represents the most conclusive evidence for the date of its subsequent modification (Gourley and Williams 2005: 250).

[34] Gourley and Williams (2005: 243).   [35] Gourley and Williams (2005: 243).
[36] Gourley and Williams (2005: 245).   [37] Gourley and Williams (2005: 245–6).
[38] Gourley and Williams (2005: 247).   [39] Gourley and Williams (2005: 246).

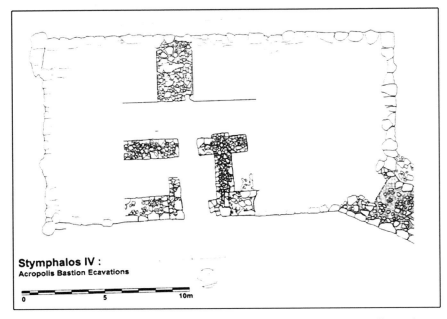

Fig. C16.7. Stymphalos, plan of Acropolis Bastion from Gourley and Williams (2005: fig. 13). (© *Hector Williams and Ben Gourley*)

also revealed an interior divided into several small rooms with a staircase providing access to the upper levels (Fig. C16.7).[40]

Gates

Seven gates are attested to at Stymphalos, four of which are of the overlap type and appear to belong to the original phase of construction: the West, North-West, North-East, and East Gates (see Fig. C16.4). All four contain a *c*.20 m long corridor formed by overlapping sections of the curtains and are protected both by a tower outside the approach and by a circular tower at the start of the corridor (on the attacker's left). Both the West and North-West gates contain a second circular tower protecting the intramural end of the corridor.[41] The circuit's only postern is located on the south curtain just outside the entrance to the North-West Gate. The Acropolis Gate, another feature probably belonging

---

[40] Gourley and Williams (2005: 246).
[41] Fig. 3.4 shows a 3D reconstruction of the West Gate.

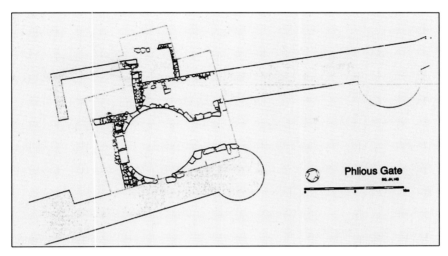

Fig. C16.8. Stymphalos, plan of Phlious Gate from Gourley and Williams (2005: fig. 7). (© *Hector Williams and Ben Gourley*)

to the original circuit,[42] is a simple frontal gate, accessed by a ramp, with an opening about 5 m wide.[43] This gate was not provided with any towers or additional protection and is the only one in the circuit not located on the flat plain. The Phlious Gate, located in the extreme south-east of the city, is an example of the gatecourt type (see Fig . C16.8).[44] Excavation has determined that this gate had been modified, having replaced an earlier simple overlap type gate.[45] This modification had been performed by constricting the corridor to 3 m in width at either end with the addition of a circular courtyard, *c.*7 m in diameter in the space between.[46]

The final gate of the circuit is the Pheneos Gate (Fig. C16.9). This gate, oriented east–west and comprised of a simple opening in the western stretch of wall, provided access to the lower city on the southern side of the acropolis. With the exception of a circular tower located some 20 m to the north, little in the way of defensive concern was given to the Pheneos Gate.[47]

[42] Although Gourley and Williams (2005: 239–40) do not provide a date for this gate, its form and, more importantly, its location suggest it was built at the same time as the general circuit.

[43] Gourley and Williams (2005: 240).

[44] Fig. 3.3 shows a 3D reconstruction of the Phlious Gate.

[45] Gourley and Williams (2005: 232).

[46] The original circular tower flanking the right of the corridor was maintained in the new arrangement (Gourley and Williams 2005: 233).

[47] Like the Acropolis Gate and ramp, it must have been felt that both the acropolis fortifications on the north and the lake to the south were sufficient to repel any unwanted approach from the west.

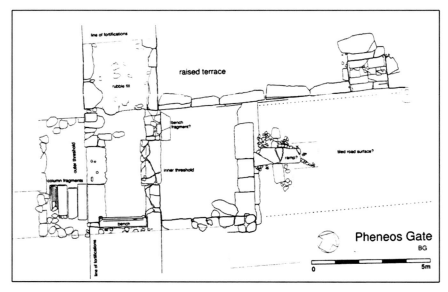

Fig. C16.9. Stymphalos, plan of Pheneos Gate from Gourley and Williams (2005: fig. 9). (© *Hector Williams and Ben Gourley*)

COMMENTS

The incredible size of the West Wall Tower and its strong foundations suggest it would have housed a battery of artillery, and its location and orientation reflect a concern for protecting the open and flat ground west of the city.[48] Such a concern is also manifested in the final addition to the circuit, the West Wall Structure, located 130 m south of the West Wall Tower (see Fig. C16.4).[49] This enigmatic structure is represented on the ground by 'a [50 m long] wall about a metre wide running about 2 m in front of the line of the west wall'.[50] Originally these remains were thought to correspond to later repairs, but it is now held that they may be better explained as a possible emplacement for a battery of artillery.[51] Although such an interpretation is speculative, an outwork in this location is completely in keeping with both the appearance of the

---

[48] Gourley and Williams (2005: 250–1).
[49] For more on this enigmatic structure, see Maher (2015a: 27).
[50] Gourley and Williams (2005: 253).
[51] Gourley and Williams (2005: 253, n. 52) maintain that a similar structure can be found on the acropolis of Alea. They are not specific as to exactly where on the acropolis such a structure is to be found, and I cannot find evidence (on the ground or from the plan) that suggests the existence of such an emplacement. I am left to guess that they are referring to the stretch of wall running north-west from Tower 15 towards the gate of the citadel. Although artillery certainly could have been placed atop this stretch, it is different from Stymphalos, however, in that it is a proper curtain wall and not a separate outwork.

extant remains and the larger defensive considerations given to this area of the Stymphalian circuit.

OVERALL DEFENSIVE PLANNING

The city of Stymphalos was provided with a number of natural defences, and, as noted by Gourley and Williams, 'we must assume that its very form and its position in the valley were largely dictated by defensive considerations'.[52] Indeed, not only was Stymphalos' position in the valley ideally suited for controlling the traffic through the territory, but the considerable natural defences immediately surrounding the site itself must have been decisive factors in the architects' evaluation and eventual choice of this location. Specifically, it was the hydraulic features of the valley—of so much interest to the early travellers—that, when combined, were responsible for providing a natural defence on three sides of the ancient city. It was only the western side of the city, devoid of natural defences, that could be threatened by a conventional land-based attack—an arrangement that accounts for the substantial defences in this part of the circuit.

In antiquity, a seasonal river, originating above the modern hamlet of Kionia and running parallel to, and just north of, the city, would have provided an effective natural boundary in this direction.[53] Furthermore, as the lower slopes of Mt Kylene can be found creeping into the valley just 300 m north of the city, they too would have acted as a natural boundary, providing additional protection to the northern part of the city. On the east side of the city, springs located to the north-west of the site formed a small river flowing south to the lake. This river, traces of which can still be seen today, ran almost parallel to the east side of the circuit, and, like the stream to the north, would have prevented access to this part of the city.[54] The last, but certainly not least, natural defence is the eponymous lake protecting the entire south flank of the city of Stymphalos. Although the lake is certainly much larger today than in antiquity, at the time the original circuit was in place it must have covered at least the length of the lower city.

This southern section of the city was unquestionably the best defended; not only because it contained the greatest number of towers, but more importantly because here the circuit was laid out to complement the natural topography in a way that is unparalleled with any other section of the circuit. While the lake

---

[52] Gourley and Williams (2005: 220).   [53] Gourley and Williams (2005: 220–1).
[54] Gourley and Williams (2005: 220). Like at Mantineia, perhaps on the north and east sides of the city bounded by these watercourses, we may suppose the existence of bridges leading towards the gates.

would have provided significant protection to the whole south side of the city, additional measures were employed to ensure the city's safety, characterized by the modification of both the Phlious Gate and the Hexagonal Tower. Sometime in the late fourth or early third century BC, the Phlious Gate was modified from a simple overlap gate into the more stalwart gatecourt that exists today.[55] The same defensive concerns that prompted this modification were also responsible for changes to the south trace of the circuit atop the acropolis.

This section of the wall with its original seven semicircular towers commanding one of the main approaches to the city must have been tactically important from the beginning. Even before the construction of the Hexagonal Tower, anyone approaching the Pheneos Gate would have experienced a bottleneck effect produced by a narrowing of the corridor caused by the rising acropolis and its array of towers on the left, and by the expanse of the lake to the right. As the Pheneos Gate itself had very little in the way of defensive architecture, it was crucial that any attackers be stopped before they reached it. Accordingly, again in the late fourth or early third century BC, military architects added further elements of defence for this approach, the Hexagonal Tower and the Acropolis Bastion.

The orientation of the Acropolis Bastion, with its broadest side facing to the west, suggests that, although it was in the position to protect some of the flat ground north of the acropolis, its primary purpose was to guard an approach from the west and south-west.[56] Similarly, the Hexagonal Tower was also intended primarily to guard this same approach. Its shape provided a greater field of fire than a simple rectangular one, and, at twice the size of the surrounding semicircular ones, would certainly have been able to house a greater number of larger machines. Not only would its placement in the middle of the trace and its five sides have provided effective coverage of the approach below, but also coverage of the Pheneos Gate itself, which was 'directly in line with the eastern oblique face of the tower'.[57] Taken together, the fortifications in this area, complemented by the topography, guaranteed that any unfriendly move towards the Pheneos Gate would have been incredibly intimidating, and a completely impractical offensive option.

Finally, the complex relationship between the natural topography and the fortifications is also observable in the western part of the city circuit. The flat area north of the acropolis is the only section of the city not provided with some form of natural defence. Accordingly, the overall security of the system is compensated in this area by an increased reliance on the composite parts of the circuit—that is, the deployment of towers. Significant in this regard are the two later additions to the circuit, the West Wall Tower and the West Wall

[55] Gourley and Williams (2005: 233).   [56] Gourley and Williams (2005: 251).
[57] Gourley and Williams (2005: 246).

Structure. Like the Hexagonal Tower on the acropolis, the placement of the West Wall Tower in the middle of the stretch of wall alludes to its primary function—namely, to command and dominate both the area immediately in front, and the adjacent curtains. As noted by Gourley and Williams, its 'projecting rectangular plan suits this requirement and provides the possibility of defending the frontal approaches to the wall, and also laterally along the line of the curtains in both directions'.[58] Importantly, because of its location and alignment, the West Wall Tower would also have been able to provide lateral fire to the north towards the entrance corridor of the West Gate. Providing additional coverage of the flat ground to the west was the West Wall Structure. If the remains of this structure have been interpreted correctly, and it does indeed represent an artillery platform, it only further reinforces the defensive significance of this part of the circuit.[59] As the flanking artillery from the West Wall Tower may not have been able to cover all of the curtain to the south towards the lower slope of the acropolis, perhaps this section was perceived as a weak spot in the circuit.[60] The West Wall Structure was probably part of the same building programme of the late fourth or early third century BC that witnessed the modifications of the other prominent defensive installations on the circuit.

CHRONOLOGICAL SUMMARY

The original circuit was laid out in the early fourth century BC; modifications were made to several towers (that is, the Acropolis Bastion, West Wall Tower, Hexagonal Tower) and gates (Phlious Gate and possibly the Pheneos Gate) in the late fourth or early third century BC—based on historical probability, external evidence, and architectural affinities.

CHRONOLOGICAL ARGUMENTS

As evidenced by the considerable summary already outlined, we have at our disposal an appreciable amount of detail regarding the fortifications of ancient Stymphalos. Owing to the careful excavation and detailed study, discerning a

[58] Gourley and Williams (2005: 251).　　[59] Gourley and Williams (2005: 253).
[60] The discovered damage to the original Acropolis Bastion notwithstanding, it is not inconceivable that this was the actual spot where Apollonides' forces breached the city in 315 BC. Such a scenario would fit both the chronology of the West Wall Structure and the belief that such a structure was subsequently essential to the security of the western trace.

chronology for the walls of Stymphalos presents very little trouble compared to many of the circuits under discussion in the present study. Although some earlier material (coins, pottery, sculpture, and so on) has come to light during the three decades of investigation at the site, the preponderance of the architectural evidence suggests that the city of Stymphalos was developed at its current location during the first half of the fourth century BC.[61] At that time, the settlement was laid out on a grid plan and fortified by an extensive circuit of walls, towers, and gates. The specific date of the refoundation may be narrowed down to around 371/369 BC, as Strabo's and Xenophon's account of Iphikrates' failed siege would suggest. Moreover, the similarities in the building material, layout, and constituent parts between the fortifications of Stymphalos and those of Mantineia also point to a date of *c*.371/370 BC. At that time, the scattered Mantineians, possibly with Theban aid, returned to rebuild their city (and city walls) destroyed by the Spartans in 385 BC. If Stymphalos was also associated with the network of Arkadian cities established to limit Spartan influence in the Peloponnese, as held by Gourley and Williams,[62] then a date during the first third of the fourth century BC for the refoundation of Stymphalos would not be implausible.[63]

Whether it was the new offensive threat imposed by the recently invented torsion catapult or the successful siege of the city by Apollonides in 315 BC— or, most likely, a combination of both—the archaeological evidence suggests that, sometime in the late fourth or early third century BC, the fortifications of Stymphalos underwent a second phase of construction. The best chronological evidence for this phase comes from the West Wall Tower, where, in 1999, excavations revealed a hoard of coins dating to the fourth and early third centuries BC.[64] These coins serve to date not only the modification of the West Wall Tower, but also the rebuilding of the other additions already mentioned.[65] Furthermore, the stratigraphy and associated ceramic deposits from the Phlious Gate, the Hexagonal Tower, and the Acropolis Bastion all further corroborate a late fourth- or early third-century BC date for their subsequent modifications.[66] Finally, the very form and nature of these modified structures themselves, exemplifying a very active defensive outlook, all point to the late fourth/early third century BC—a time when artillery was beginning to find its true place as a defensive, rather than offensive, weapon.

---

[61] Gourley and Williams (2005: 233).   [62] Gourley and Williams (2005: 219, n. 10).

[63] For a more detailed argument on why Stymphalos was probably part of the same defensive system envisioned with the foundations of Megalopolis and Mantineia around 370 BC, see Maher (2015a: 32–5, 39–40).

[64] The latest issued are those of Demetrios Poliorketes (Gourley and Williams 2005: 250).

[65] Gourley and Williams (2005: 250).

[66] Williams et al. (1997: 66); Gourley and Williams (2005: 232, 249).

BIBLIOGRAPHY

Hom. *Il.* 2.608; Pind. *Ol.* 6.99; Ps.-Skylax 44; Xen. *Hell.* 4.4.16, 7.3.1; Polyb. 2.55, 4.68; Diod. 19.63.1–2; Strab. 8.8.2, 8.8.4; Paus. 8.22; Gell (1817: i. 168); Dodwell (1819: ii. 432–5); Cramer (1828: iii. 308–14); Leake (1830: iii. 108–15); Boblaye (1836: 147–8); Curtius (1851: i. 202–7, pl. IV); Rangabé (1857: 1227, pl. XII); Clark (1858: 319–23); Bursian (1862: ii. 194–8); Frazer (1898: iv. 268–75); Hiller von Gaertringen (1915); Orlandos (1924, 1925, 1926, 1927, 1928, 1929, 1930); Scranton (1941: 166); Howell (1970: 97–8); Winter (1971a: 34); Lawrence (1979: 331, 334); Williams (1983, 1984, 1985); Jost (1985: 99–106; 1999: 199–200); Pritchett (1989: 12–17); Papahatzis (1994: 257–64); Williams and Cronkite-Price (1995); Williams (1996); Williams et al. (1997, 1998, 2002); Pikoulas (1999a: 296–7); Nielsen (2002: 590–2); Gourley and Williams (2005); Maher (2012a: 213–39; 2012b; 2015a: 19–27, 32–5, 39–42; forthcoming); Tsiogas (2013); Schaus (2014).

17

Teuthis, Central Arkadia

LOCATION

The city of ancient Teuthis is located in central Arkadia, on the east bank above the Lousios/Gortynios River and beneath the modern village of Dhimitsana (Fig. C17.1). The acropolis comprises the summit of a small spur attached by a narrow saddle to a larger mountain to the south-east. Inhabitation appears to have been both in the intramural area and on the adjacent saddle.

POLIS STATUS

Pausanias includes Teuthis, Methydrion, and Theisoa (Karkalou) in his list of those settlements voted to participate in the synoikism of Megalopolis, and adds that these three cities belonged to Orchomenos.[1] Implicit in this passage is that, before the foundation of Megalopolis, Orchomenos was at the head of an organization—described by the phrase συντελείν ἐς—which included Teuthis.[2] Pausanias also explicitly (if retroactively) refers to Teuthis as a *polis*. He writes: 'of the other cities [πόλεων] I have mentioned, some are altogether deserted in our time, some [i.e., τῶν πόλεων] are held by the people of Megalopolis as villages, namely . . . Teuthis.'[3]

HISTORY

Almost nothing of the history of this small city is known. Besides the fact that Teuthis belonged to an organization headed by Orchomenos and was voted to

---

[1] 'ἐκ δὲ τῶν συντελούντων ἐς Ὀρχομενὸν Θεισόα Μεθύδριον Τεῦθις' (Paus. 8.27.4).

[2] Nielsen (2002: 596) maintains that, even if it remains unclear exactly how this organization functioned, because the other communities in this group (Methydrion and Theisoa) 'were probably *poleis* . . . by analogy, [we] may class Teuthis as a possible *polis*'. This is the main criterion for Teuthis' inclusion in Nielsen's inventory of Arkadian *poleis*.

[3] Paus. 8.27.7.

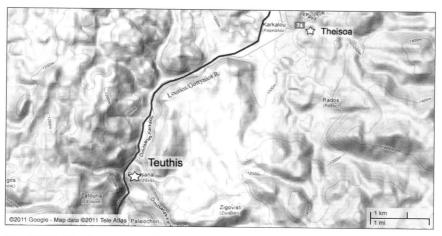

Fig. C17.1. Teuthis, topographical map of area. (© *2011 Google-Map data* © *2011 Tele Atlas*)

participate in the synoikism of Megalopolis, we know extremely little about the political history of this city. It is not even certain if the decision to join Megalopolis was ever implemented,[4] since Pikoulas believes the site was never abandoned.[5] Because they were voted to participate, however, it may be assumed that Teuthis was a member of the Arkadian League—again, whether they joined immediately at the League's conception, or whether they enrolled when Orchomenos too finally joined, is also uncertain.[6] Similarly, although we do not know when Teuthis became a member of the later Achaian League, the discovery of coins issued by the League bearing the city's name leaves little doubt that the city was a member at some point.[7] We know nothing of the site's history in the centuries that followed, until it re-emerges in Pausanias' account, which describes Teuthis as a village of Megalopolis.[8]

LOCAL TOPOGRAPHY

The topography of central Arkadia is unquestionably the most unforgiving of the entire region. Dominated by the mountains and foothills of the Ghortiniaka, Menalo, and Western Menalo ranges, central Arkadia is—almost without exception—set apart by the extremely severe terrain and general absence of

---

[4] Nielsen (2002: 579).   [5] Pikoulas (1986: 120).
[6] Probably in the 360s BC (Nielsen 2002: 581).
[7] Head (1963: 418).   [8] Paus. 8.27.7.

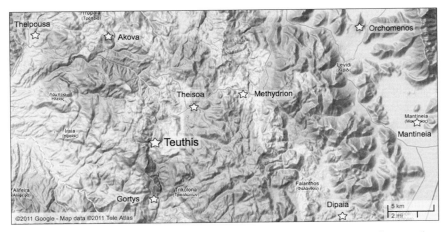

Fig. C17.2. Teuthis, topographical map of central Arkadia. (© *2011 Google-Map data* © *2011 Tele Atlas*)

plains, basins, or wide/flat valleys characteristic of all the other parts of Arkadia.[9] The location of the ancient city of Teuthis is no different, and, occupying a small conical hill on the east bank of the Lousios/Gortynios River, the site is entrenched in and completely dominated by its rugged surroundings (see Fig. C17.1). Although, it remains unclear whether Teuthis was ultimately 'conceived of as [being] situated within Orchomenian territory',[10] it must have had its own *chora*, with borders defined by the natural topography of the area (Fig. C17.2).

The Lousios Gorge, for example, must have served such a purpose. With Teuthis located at its northern end and Gortys at its southern, the boundary must have been somewhere in this gorge, even if the precise spot is indeterminate. To the west, the Lousios/Gortynios River itself and/or the mountains opposite would probably have marked where the territories of Teuthis and Heraia met. Similarly, the Ghortiniaka mountain range north-west of the site separated the territory of Thelpousa from that of Teuthis. Finally, in the northeast, the closest *polis* to Teuthis was Theisoa (Karkalou)—the two separated by the plateau-like mountain flanking the east (and, as it turns east, the south) side of the Lousios/Gortynios River.

Separated by a narrow saddle, the small conical hill comprising the site is actually the westernmost spur of this plateau-like mountain, itself the westernmost outcrop radiating from the bulk of Western Menalo. The river

---

[9] The relatively wide and flat expanse of the Helisson River Valley (north-west of modern Tripolis) is arguably the only exception.

[10] Nielsen (2002: 579).

changes its southern course here slightly, sweeping 'in a semicircle at the bottom of a deep gully round the western part of the town'.[11] On the north-east side, the site is dominated by the hill of Profitis Ilias, from which it is separated by a small stream in a narrow ravine. Thus, with the river flanking the south-west, west, and north-west sides, and the stream and ravine to the north-east, the hill of Teuthis is actually a promontory jutting into the Lousios Gorge. While the slopes along the river's west bank immediately north and south of the site are extremely precipitous, they are considerably less steep directly opposite the river to the west. Like Gortys, therefore, Teuthis stands across from a narrow east–west running ravine, which comprises one of but a handful of places in the gorge where a river crossing is possible.[12] As the river flows in a southern direction towards the Alpheios, naturally the site of Teuthis stands at a higher elevation than other sites to the south.[13]

The slopes of the hill itself, meeting at the summit 220 m above the river, are fairly uniform on all sides except the west. While the north and south slopes are more regular, the west side presents a precipitous—near vertical—drop to the river below. On the south-east the hill slopes gradually to where it meets the saddle. At only *c.*200 m long and less than *c.*100 m wide, this saddle links the hill of Teuthis with a second, slightly higher peak to the south-east. Although today the houses of Dhimitsana spread from the main hill across the saddle and up the lower slopes of the second hill, it appears that for the most part the ancient settlement was restricted to the main hill and the north-west end of the saddle.

NATURAL DEFENCES

The height offered by the acropolis, and the steep slopes on its north-western, western, and south-western sides, provide the site with its natural defences (Fig. C17.3). The river valley and local topography limit the approaches to the site to routes from the north and south. The Lousios/Gortynios River flanks the hill to the west and south-west, while one of its tributaries flanks the site to the north, north-east, and east.

---

[11] Frazer (1898: iv. 312).

[12] It is not a coincidence that today the major road linking central and western Arkadia crosses the Lousios/Gortynios at this point.

[13] As observed by Curtius (1851: i. 352), to the south the hill offers 'eine schöne Fernsicht... [und] man das enge Flussthal entlang über die Ebene von Megalopolis bis auf den hinter Leondari aufsteigenden Taygetos sehen kann'.

Fig. C17.3. Teuthis, modern Dhimitsana (facing south). (© *Matthew Maher*)

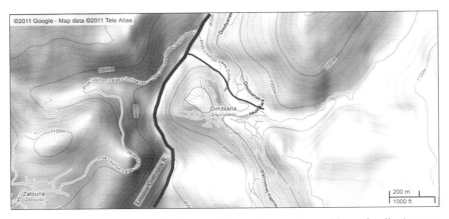

Fig. C17.4. Teuthis, topographical map of site and reconstructed line of walls. (© *2011 Google-Map data © 2011 Tele Atlas*)

FORTIFICATION TYPE

Acropolis type.[14] The circuit follows the contour of the hill, encircling the summit (Fig. C17.4).

PRESERVATION

The site is poorly preserved; remains of the circuit are limited to only nine isolated fragments located among the buildings of the modern village of Dhimitsana (Fig. C17.5).

---

[14] Jost (1999: 196).

Fig. C17.5. Teuthis, plan of modern Dhimitsana showing location of the preserved sections of the fortifications from Pikoulas (1986: 104, map 3). (© *1986 Yannis Pikoulas, Horos*)

CONSTRUCTION

The stone foundations of the acropolis circuit were constructed predominantly in a coursed trapezoidal style (Fig. C17.6),[15] with one (possibly earlier) section in

---

[15] Pikoulas (1986: 113) describes them simply as trapezoidal, while Scranton (1941: 169) classifies these walls as irregular trapezoidal verging on irregular ashlar. While the blocks do tend towards ashlar, they are clearly laid in more or less regular courses of differing heights (i.e., closer to pseudo-isodomic than irregular).

Fig. C17.6. Teuthis, irregular trapezoidal masonry from wall section B4 (facing south). (© *Matthew Maher*)

a rough polygonal or dry rubble style.[16] The superstructure was mudbrick (not preserved). The maximum widths of the curtains range from 1.40 m to 2.30 m,[17] but it is uncertain whether the surviving sections represent one of originally two faces or whether they stood alone.

SUMMARY OF TACTICAL COMPONENTS

Only two rectangular towers (*c.*6.50 m × 6 m) are preserved from the circuit. No gates or posterns survive.

Towers

Only sections of two rectangular towers survive from the acropolis circuit of Teuthis, Tower B4 and Tower Γ1.[18] Picturesquely incorporated into the courtyard of a modern house, Tower B4 is arguably the best preserved of all the extant fortification fragments (Fig. C17.7).

Still, although the foundations survive to their original height (3.30 m), only one external corner and two sides are preserved. Consequently, it is difficult to determine which side—the one facing the north-east (6.0 m long) or the one facing the south-east (6.50 m long)—was the front and which was the flank.[19]

---

[16] Pikoulas (1986: 113). The chronological implications of the different masonry styles are discussed under Chronological Arguments.

[17] Pikoulas (1986: 105–10).

[18] Tower and curtain letters are from the plan in Pikoulas (1986: 104, fig. 3).

[19] Pikoulas (1986: 106, 109).

Fig. C17.7. Teuthis, Tower B4
(facing west). (© *Matthew Maher*)

Complicating matters is the fact that a tower could have been advantageously oriented here to face either the approach from the ravine on the north-east side or the saddle to the south-east. Completely enclosing the small chapel of Ag. Nikolaos, about 35 m south-west of Tower B4, is the other attested example, Tower Γ1. With dimensions similar to those of Tower B, this tower measures 6 m by 6.40 m and is oriented almost due east to overlook the saddle below.[20]

COMMENTS

A proper interpretation of Pausanias is crucial for identifying the location of the ancient site. Although his statement that Teuthis stands 'just across the border from Theisoa'[21] is seemingly unambiguous, it has been used to shape the arguments for two main candidates for the site's location. The first contends that ancient Teuthis should be associated with the remains called Akova, near modern Ghalatas; the second, that Teuthis actually lies beneath the village of Dhimitsana (see Fig. C17.2). While it appears that Gell was the first to subscribe to the belief that Akova was the site in question, he was not alone in this opinion.[22] The idea that Teuthis stood at the site of Dhimitsana was also first proposed in the early nineteenth century, this time by Leake.[23] The Akova argument, seemingly solely a product of the nineteenth century,

[20] Pikoulas (1986: 110–11).
[21] Paus. 8.28.4. He is referring to Theisoa at modern Karkalou, not to be confused with Theisoa at Lavda.
[22] Gell (1817: 118–19); Ross (1841: 114); Boblaye (1836: 151–2); Curtius (1851: i. 354); Smith (1873b: 1133).
[23] Leake (1830: ii. 63).

steadily lost ground to the case for Dhimitsana, which is recognized today by most as the location for Teuthis best fitting Pausanias' description.[24]

Briefly, in his account of the main sites along the Lousios/Gortynios River, Pausanias describes Teuthis after Gortys but before Theisoa (Karkalou); the order of this narrative suggests that Teuthis should lie between the two. Moreover, while it is not inconceivable that Akova could be described as 'just across the border from Theisoa',[25] not only is Dhimitsana considerably closer to Theisoa—better fitting this description—but Akova is too far from Megalopolis for Pausanias to have included it in his description of the route north from it. In other words, if Teuthis really was at Akova, he would have probably included it in his description of Heraia or Thelpousa, as it is considerably closer to both of these. Finally, although the distance from Orchomenos to both Akova and Dhimitsana is equally considerable, the proximity of the latter to both Theisoa and Methydrion—the other *poleis* in the organization headed by Orchomenos—suggests a geographic (as well as political) relationship and that ancient Teuthis should be sought beneath modern Dhimitsana.

OVERALL DEFENSIVE PLANNING

Occupying 'a more or less isolated bluff or crag rising above a deep river-gorge, with some gently shelving land within reach of the summit',[26] the remains at Dhimitsana represent a good example of the acropolis type of fortified mountain settlement.[27] As always, strategic considerations were instrumental in the choice of site, and, for Teuthis, Pikoulas suggests that the main factors responsible for attracting almost continuous occupation from at least the middle Bronze Age were its geographic position and the natural defensibility of the hill.[28] Besides being situated at a strategic crossroads between central Arkadia and both western and southern Arkadia (a point that is expanded upon later in this section), its geographic location provided the necessary provisions for economic self-sustainability. From contemporary practices, it is clear that the fertile terraces and limited arable land can support cereals, vegetables, olives, and fruit trees (citrus, cherry, walnut, and so on), while the surrounding mountains and hillsides are more than suitable for pastoralism.[29]

---

[24] e.g., Rangabé (1857: 72); Bursian (1862: ii. 232); Hiller von Gaertringen and Lattermann (1911: 37–40); Howell (1970: 100); Jost (1985: 212; 1999: 196); Pikoulas (1986); Nielsen (2002: 596–7). Not everyone is convinced, however, and both Frazer (1898: iv. 312) and Levi (1971: 444, n. 211), for example, remain undecided.

[25] Paus. 8.28.4.   [26] Winter (1971a: 32).   [27] Jost (1999: 196).

[28] Pikoulas (1986: 100).   [29] Pikoulas (1986: 100).

It was the defensibility of the hill, however, that was probably the most important factor behind the choice of site. The topography of the hill and surrounding features provided considerable defensive advantages in almost every direction. The west side of the hill not only enjoyed the protection provided by its high and precipitous slopes, but also the added protection of the Lousios/Gortynios River below. Likewise, although the slope is more gradual, the north-east side of the hill also had the advantage of a ravine and watercourse. As demonstrated with several other Arkadian sites (for example, Halous, Paos, Dipaia), the preference for a site that embraces the spur of a mountain and is protected by water on at least two sides was not uncommon.

Even though Teuthis possessed considerable natural defences, the inhabitants did not put their trust in the heights and steep slopes provided by the hill alone; nor did they trust completely to the impregnability of the walls. Instead, we see the compromise of a fortification circuit erected that both complements the natural defensibility of the hill and compensates for its inherent weaknesses. Unfortunately, as is the case with the walls of Megalopolis, the paucity of remains and the conjectural course of the circuit restrict what can be offered concerning the tactics and general defensive planning envisioned at Teuthis to generalization and analogy. That being said, by combining the archaeological and historical data with what can be plausibly inferred from such evidence, a general understanding is attainable.

Without excluding the possibility of semicircular-shaped towers, the remains of B4 and Γ1, for example, show that the circuit employed at least rectangular towers. Moreover, their near identical dimensions establish the possibility that the circuit may have once contained a number of similarly sized towers deployed throughout. The spacing and location of the towers are also informative. Indeed, separated by *c.*35 m, B4 and Γ1 occupy the south-east part of the circuit overlooking the saddle. As the most practical point from which to launch a concentrated attack, the saddle is easily the most vulnerable part of the hill's topography. If these two towers were placed 35 m apart at such an important part of the circuit, it is unlikely that it was thought necessary to space any of the other towers more closely in the less vulnerable parts. We may infer, therefore, that, excluding provisions for a gate, *c.*35 m represents the minimum distance that any of the towers were spaced.

In his survey of the site, Pikoulas discovered no traces of any of the city's gates. Still, from its geographical location, the identification of at least two ancient cemeteries, and the topography of the hill itself, it can be safely assumed that the circuit possessed at least one gate in the south-east and possibly another in the north-east part of the circuit (Fig. C17.8).[30]

---

[30] Pikoulas (1986: 113, 115).

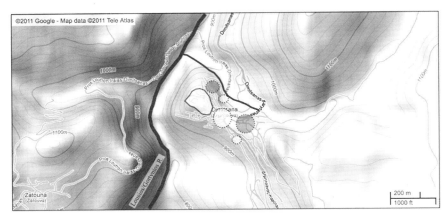

Fig. C17.8. Teuthis, topographical map of site showing reconstructed line of the city walls (solid black line), ancient cemeteries (dark grey), and areas of ancient habitation (light grey) after Pikoulas (1986: 101, map 1). (© *2011 Google-Map data* © *2011 Tele Atlas/1986 Yannis Pikoulas, Horos*)

The possible existence of a gate in the north-east somewhere south of section A is suggested by both the presence of a cemetery and the accessibility of the terrain on this part of the hill. It is probable that the road from this gate would have more or less followed the same route of the modern roads from Dhimitsana north to Orchomenos and west towards Heraia.[31] The other gate almost certainly stood in the south-east corner of the circuit directly facing the saddle below.[32] Not only was a second ancient cemetery located at the south-east end of the saddle, but any road from the south could practically reach the walls only via the saddle. This road would likewise have followed roughly the same course as a modern road, this time the road south towards Gortys and Megalopolis. Finally, as Pikoulas discovered evidence of extramural activity/habitation on the north-eastern end of the saddle, it follows that the intra-mural area must been accessible from that direction.[33]

From Pausanias we know that, sometime before the foundation of Megalopolis, Teuthis, Theisoa (Karkalou), and Methydrion were the minor *poleis* comprising a political organization headed by Orchomenos.[34] Unfortunately, Pausanias tells us nothing of how this organization functioned. What is certain, however, is that, together, these three closely spaced minor *poleis* (and thus, Orchomenos) commanded the main route across central Arkadia, between the top of the

[31] Pikoulas (1986: 113).
[32] The location of Towers B4 and Γ1 invites the possibility that one of them may have been part of this south-east gate (Pikoulas 1986: 113).
[33] This seems to have been the standard practice, since the only gates in the circuits of Nestane, Paos, and Halous are all oriented to face the adjacent saddle.
[34] Paus. 8.27.4.

Helisson Valley and the Lousios Gorge (see Fig. C17.2).[35] Indeed, similar to Epaminondas' defensive arrangement of Messene, Megalopolis, and Mantineia, the locations of Teuthis, Theisoa (Karkalou), and Methydrion also form a south-west–north-east-oriented barrier, but through the heart of central Arkadia. This was an important route for Orchomenos, one that ensured it access to western Arkadia, and, more importantly, to southern Arkadia without having to pass through the territory of Mantineia. Whether Orchomenos' control of this artery was primarily defensive or economic is uncertain. If the latter, it was well conceived, since any practical approach towards Orchomenos from north-west, west, or south-west Arkadia would have necessitated the use of at least some part of the road between Teuthis and Methydrion. Finally, Orchomenos' larger interests aside, an alliance between Teuthis and nearby Theisoa (Karkalou) and Methydrion was a defensive strategy beneficial for all involved.

CHRONOLOGICAL SUMMARY

It appears that the walls of Teuthis were constructed *c.*370–200 BC. While such a range is not ideal, it is derived from combining historical probability with external evidence and regional architectural affinities.

CHRONOLOGICAL ARGUMENTS

An attempt to establish a reliable chronology for a fortification system would ideally draw upon the form and style of the walls themselves, all the available archaeological evidence from the site, as well as its recorded history. Unfortunately, however, not only is Teuthis essentially invisible historically, but the archaeological evidence—ceramics found suggest continuous occupation of the site since the Middle Bronze Age[36]—paints a chronological picture with a brush too broad to be of any practical consequence. With little support provided by the external evidence, therefore, we are left with no choice but to turn to the meagre remains of the walls themselves to facilitate the chronological question. The character of these remains requires that, although not ideal, establishing a tentative date for the walls of Teuthis must rely almost exclusively on stylistic dating.

[35] Jost (1999: 196). From Teuthis it is only 8 km to Theisoa, it is only 12 km from there to Methydrion, and then 24 km separate Methydrion from Orchomenos.
[36] Howell (1970: 100).

As already identified, the style of masonry employed in the vast majority of the extant curtains is irregular trapezoidal. The large, roughly worked stones employed in the one exception, section Δ, are better described as comprising a dry rubble or rough polygonal style arrangement. Basing his comments on these differing styles and historical probability, Pikoulas suggests two building phases. While its use in a Mycenaean fortification of the hill cannot be ruled out, the earliest wall, represented by section Δ, probably belongs to the late Archaic period.[37] The remaining eight sections (A, B1–B4, Γ1, Γ2, and E) were constructed in the same period, which, in his opinion, was undoubtedly the Hellenistic period.[38] Pikoulas admits, however, the difficulties in attempting to narrow down the precise date and offers several possibilities based on historical probability: perhaps the walls of Teuthis were built during the second half of the fourth century BC by Megalopolis; or possibly during the second half of the third century BC when Megalopolis joined the Achaian League and Arkadia became the theatre of continuous conflict; or, finally, conceivably with the weakening of Megalopolis in the later third or early second century BC, when many of its villages gained their 'independence' and joined the Achaian League.[39] Like Hiller von Gaertringen and Lattermann before him, Pikoulas seems to find the last scenario most probable.[40] Yet could the walls of Teuthis be earlier than the Hellenistic period?

In the mid-nineteenth century Curtius observed that the masonry style 'erinnert an die Zeit des Epaminondas'.[41] Indeed, in his survey of different masonry styles employed in Greek fortifications throughout the Mediterranean, although Scranton discovered that the use of 'irregular trapezoidal work covers a period too long to be of any practical significance',[42] it was a style employed from the early fifth century until the early fourth century BC. The walls of Teuthis, however, are not that different from the early fourth-century BC walls of nearby Gortys, and the notion that they could be contemporary cannot be completely dismissed. What of historical probability? Can Pikoulas's list of historical events/periods that may have triggered the construction of Teuthis' walls be supplemented? Although admittedly speculative, two scenarios immediately suggest themselves, both surrounding the synoikism of Megalopolis *c*.370 BC. If around that time, for example, Teuthis did join the Arkadian League, thus leaving the συντελέια headed by Orchomenos (who

---

[37] Pikoulas (1986: 113) describes section Δ as comprised of large, roughly worked stones that have been arranged without a specific plan, thus almost resembling a rubble wall. This is probably the same wall (or at least style) observed by Frazer (1898: iv. 312), who notes the walls are 'polygonal at the west end of the ridge. The blocks ... are enormous.'

[38] Pikoulas (1986: 114). Pikoulas (1986: 112) maintains that the earlier section Δ was incorporated into the later circuit.

[39] Pikoulas (1986: 113).

[40] Hiller von Gaertringen and Lattermann (1911: 26); Pikoulas (1986: 113).

[41] Curtius (1851: i. 353).   [42] Scranton (1941: 98).

refused to join the Arkadian League), it is not inconceivable that Megalopolis would have wanted to secure its northern border—as at Gortys—by fortifying the city of Teuthis. Alternatively, if the decision to participate in the synoikism was not implemented, and/or Teuthis remained in the συντελέια, then perhaps the decision to fortify the city was made by Orchomenos as a response to Megalopolis' fortification of Gortys—located only a few kilometres away at the southern end of the Lousios Gorge—in order to preserve Orchomenos' control of central Arkadia.

Unfortunately, as already demonstrated, the evidence at our disposal does not permit a precise chronology for the erection of the walls at Teuthis. Pikoulas may be correct and the earlier section Δ may, in fact, belong to the late Archaic period. Conceivably, it could also belong to the Classical period. Indeed, there is nothing in the extant remains that is exclusively and demonstrably fourth or third century BC. In the end, therefore, no matter how unsatisfactory, it remains that, based on the predominate masonry style and the guesswork of historical probability, the circuit could have been constructed any time between *c.*370 and *c.*200 BC.

BIBLIOGRAPHY

Paus. 8.27.4, 8.27.8, 8.28.4–6; Gell (1817: 118–19); Leake (1830: ii. 63); Ross (1841: 114); Boblaye (1836: 151–2); Curtius (1851: i. 354); Rangabé (1857: 72); Bursian (1862: ii. 232); Smith (1873b: 1133); Frazer (1898: iv. 312); Hiller von Gaertringen and Lattermann (1911: 37–40); Scranton (1941: 169); Howell (1970: 100); Winter (1971a: 32). Levi (1971: 444, n. 211); Jost (1985: 212; 1999: 196); Pikoulas (1986); Sarantakes (1993: 70–2); Papachatzis (1994: 301–5); Nielsen (2002: 596–7); Maher (2012a: 521–41).

18

Theisoa (Karkalou), Central Arkadia

LOCATION

Located in central Arkadia, Theisoa sits on the eastern edge of a small plain and at the western terminus of a narrow valley above the modern village of Karkalou (Fig. C18.1). The acropolis comprises the summit of a relatively flat hill attached by a narrow saddle to a larger mountain to the south-east. Inhabitation appears to have been largely limited to the (unfortified) area on the adjacent saddle.

POLIS STATUS

Pausanias retroactively refers to the settlement of Theisoa as a *polis* twice,[1] and three inscriptions furnish further support for this notion. A late-third/early second-century BC inscription found *in situ* contains the city's only surviving public decrees.[2] It refers to Theisoa itself as a *polis* in the political sense, it employs the city ethnic (that is, internal collective use), it refers to a grant of *proxenia* by the city, and a grant of citizenship.[3] Furthermore, a fourth-century BC inscription discovered at Delphi, employing the external individual use of the city ethnic, attests to a grant of *proxenia* to a 'Theisoan Arkadian'.[4] A final inscription, again from Delphi, adds support for a *polis* status by establishing that a Delphic *theorodokos* resided in Theisoa sometime in the late third century BC.[5]

---

[1] Paus. 8.27.4; 8.27.7.   [2] *IG* V.2 510–11.

[3] See Nielsen (2002: 599–600) for comprehensive summary of the evidence.

[4] *SEG* xiv. 455. On this inscription, see Bousquet (1954: 432–3). Although Roy (1972b: 78) maintains that it is 'more likely that he belonged to the more northerly Thisoa' (i.e., Theisoa at Karkalou), there is no way of determining to which Theisoa this inscription refers, and the possibility that the Theisoan man could equally have come from one of the two settlements of that name must be entertained. For more on this argument, see Part Two, Chapter 19.

[5] Plassart (1921: 15, III.5).

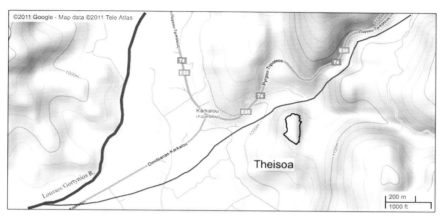

Fig. C18.1. Theisoa (Karkalou), topographical map of site showing approximate line of fortifications. (© *2011 Google-Map data © 2011 Tele Atlas*)

HISTORY

Before the foundation of Megalopolis, Theisoa, like Teuthis and Methydrion, was a member of the συντελέια headed by Orchomenos.[6] Whether the decision was implemented or not, Theisoa was voted to participate in the synoikism of Megalopolis, and thus the city's membership in the Arkadian League can be inferred.[7] Inscriptions found at the site and at Delphi suggest that the city existed and continued to function as a *polis* at least until the late third century BC,[8] and Achaian League coins may suggest the city was a member by *c*.194 BC.[9] By the mid-second century CE, Pausanias tells us that Theisoa was no longer a *polis*, but a dependent village of Megalopolis.[10]

LOCAL TOPOGRAPHY

Not only does the site of Theisoa occupy the middle of central Arkadia, but its location also corresponds roughly to the geographic centre of the entire Peloponnese. The hill of Theisoa lies on the same road linking Teuthis to Methydrion, 8 km from the former and 11 km from the latter (see Fig. C17.2).

---

[6] Paus 8.27.4. [7] Paus 8.27.4; Nielsen (2002: 599).
[8] *IG* V.2 510–11; *SEG* xiv. 455; Plassart (1921: 15, III.5).
[9] Head (1963: 418) lists Theisoan coins among those minted by the Achaian League (194 BC), but does not mention to which Theisoa (at Lavda or Karkalou) they refer.
[10] Paus 8.27.7.

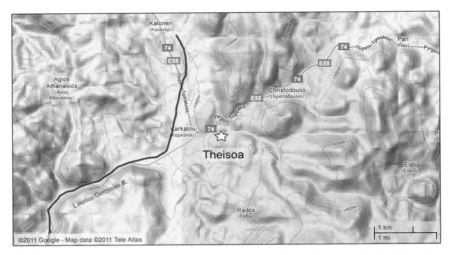

Fig. C18.2. Theisoa (Karkalou), topographical map of area. (© *2011 Google-Map data* © *2011 Tele Atlas*)

Like so much of the region, the site is dominated by the surrounding mountains, specifically the northern foothills of Western Menalo, which surround the site to the south, east, and north, and the Ghortiniaka Mountain,s which envelope the area north-west, west, and south-west of the site. Separating the bulk of these two great mountain chains are two narrow valleys and a plain through which flows the Lousios/Gortynios River (Fig. C18.2). Originating just north of the site—near modern Kaloneri, as its name and Pausanias suggest[11]—the river flows due south through a narrow valley where it meets the small plain west of Theisoa Hill. The river then adopts a south-west course, travelling down the western side of the plain, before exiting through a narrow valley as it makes its way to Teuthis, Gortys, and, eventually, to confluence with the Alpheios.

Unlike most *poleis* of central Arkadia, Theisoa commanded an area of relatively flat terrain. This small plain, measuring *c.*3.5 km (north–south) by 2.5 km (east–west), comprised the majority of arable land and would certainly have been the most important part of the city's larger territory. The western edge of the plain, where the narrow Lousios/Gortynios River Valley begins its descent towards Teuthis, probably represented the western boundary of the city's territory. The road east to Methydrion stood in the depression where the north-western slopes of Mt Madhara meets the southern slope of Mt Korifes. We might imagine the eastern limits of Theisoa's territory to lie somewhere along this road, perhaps at Mt Madhara.[12] The territorial boundaries to the north and south are harder to determine, as there are no other major *poleis* in these directions for a

---

[11] Paus. 8.28.3.   [12] Jost (1985: 212).

considerable distance. It is possible that the Ghortiniaka Mountains to the north-west divided Theisoa's territory from Thelpousa, Mt Korifes represented its north-east border with Torthenion, and the bulk of Western Menalo formed its border with Helisson and the *poleis* of the Helisson River Valley.[13]

The hill of Theisoa itself comprises a small north–south-oriented spur emanating from Mt Xerovouni, a northern peak of Western Menalo (see Fig. C18.1). It rises *c.*75 m above the plain to the west, measures *c.*160 m by 70 m, and is attached to the larger mountain to the south-east by a flat and narrow saddle. Although all the hill's slopes are covered today by a thick forest of pine trees, only the north and west sides can be said to be precipitous. The east and south sides of the hill, on the other hand, present a more gentle and rolling descent. Besides being extremely steep, the northern slope was further protected by a small, but fast-flowing stream originating north-east of the site and following the same course towards Theisoa as the road from Methydrion. The top of the hill itself is free of trees and relatively flat—sloping away slightly in all directions from the summit in the middle.

NATURAL DEFENCES

The height offered by the acropolis, and the precipitous slopes on its western and north sides, provide natural defences (Figure C18.3). The river valley and local topography limit the approaches to the site to routes from the west and north-east. A narrow but fast-moving tributary of the Helisson River flanks the hill to the north.

Fig. C18.3. Theisoa (Karkalou), the site (facing south). (© *Matthew Maher*)

[13] On the settlements of Thelpousa, Torthenion, and Helisson, see the Appendix.

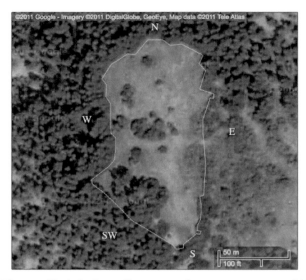

Fig. C18.4. Theisoa (Karkalou), satellite image showing reconstructed line of fortifications. (© *2011 Google-Map data © 2011 Tele Atlas*)

FORTIFICATION TYPE

Acropolis type.[14] The circuit follows the contours of the hill, encircling the summit (Fig. 18.4).

PRESERVATION

The site is poorly preserved; remains of the circuit are limited to a few courses of isolated sections of curtains and towers and to a few blocks strewn around the edge of the hilltop.

CONSTRUCTION

The stone foundations of the acropolis circuit, averaging *c.*2 m in thickness, were constructed predominantly in a coursed trapezoidal style (Fig. C18.5).[15] The superstructure was mudbrick (not preserved).

---

[14] Jost (1999: 197).
[15] Hiller von Gaertringen and Lattermann (1911: 38). Scranton (1941: 185) includes the walls of Theisoa among his examples of dry rubble masonry.

Fig. C18.5. Theisoa (Karkalou), North-East Tower showing trapezoidal masonry (facing north-west). (© *Matthew Maher*)

SUMMARY OF TACTICAL COMPONENTS

Parts of three rectangular towers are preserved, strategically rather than regularly spaced. The circuit also possessed one small ramp gate. No posterns are attested.

Towers

The remains of the Theisoan circuit include parts of three rectangular towers, which appear to be strategically spaced (Fig. C18.6).

The South Tower occupies the southernmost part of the circuit and is preserved to a height of 1.08 m.[16] It possesses a ground-floor chamber, accessible from the intramural area by a *c.*1 m wide opening near its north-east corner (Fig. C18.7). This tower measures *c.*8 m wide with flanks *c.*8.50 m long, and the western side of the tower projects *c.*4.25 m from the curtain, while the eastern flank projects only *c.*2.50 m.[17] The walls of this tower are 1.45 m thick and are comprised of two faces of blocks with a core of rubble and small stones.[18]

Although what is known about the North-East Tower comes largely from the published plan,[19] several things are clear.[20] Most obvious is that, like

---

[16] Hiller von Gaertringen and Lattermann (1911: 38).
[17] Hiller von Gaertringen and Lattermann (1911: 38).
[18] Hiller von Gaertringen and Lattermann (1911: 38). Presumably the curtains and towers throughout the circuit were similarly constructed.
[19] Hiller von Gaertringen and Lattermann (1911: 39, fig. 13).
[20] In their report, Hiller von Gaertringen and Lattermann (1911: 38) provide very little information about the North-East Tower, save that it 'ist noch mehrere Schichten hoch trefflich erhalten'.

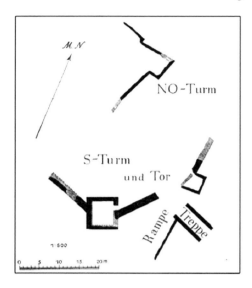

Fig. C18.6. Theisoa (Karkalou), plans of South Tower, gate, and North-East Tower on acropolis from Hiller von Gaertringen and Lattermann (1911: 8, abb. 13).

Fig. C18.7. Theisoa (Karkalou), South Tower (facing north-west). (© *Matthew Maher*)

Tower 2 from the so-called South Fort at Gortys, without an interior, this tower is better described as a pseudo-tower or bastion. Generally rectangular in shape, this tower presents three faces of differing lengths—that is, *c.*3 m to the south, 6.50 m to the east, and 9 m to the north (see Fig. C18.5). The last extant tower in the circuit protected the east side of the gate. It measures *c.*5.50 m on its south side, *c.*5 m on its east, and projects only 3 m from the curtain to the north. This tower appears to have had a ground-storey chamber, accessed by a small opening in its north-west corner.

Fig. C18.8. Theisoa (Karkalou), showing approximate limits of stairs leading up to gate (facing west). (© *Matthew Maher*)

Gates

Although the curtain leading east from the South Tower disappears after *c.*11.50 m, the presence of a ramp, stairs, and another tower immediately opposite suggests that it would have terminated at a gate (Fig. C18.8). Here, as succinctly described by Lawrence, 'a stair led straight up the hill, whereas the cart-road ascended aslant, passing to the right of [the South] tower and continuing on a ramp till both routes met at a gateway, and turned leftwards into it'.[21] Even without the converging stairs and ramp, the discovery of a lintel stone and pillars establishes without a doubt the presence of a gate.[22] The stairs, oriented east–west, survive for a length of *c.*9.5 m and are *c.*5.50 m wide, while only one side of the ramp, oriented north–south, survives for a length of *c.*12 m. The width of the actual gate opening does not survive.

COMMENTS

The discovery of an *in situ* decree bearing the name 'Θισοαιοι' has removed any doubt that the central Arkadian city of Theisoa—not to be confused with the other city of the same name at Lavda—occupied a small hill above the modern village of Karkalou.[23] This identification was a twentieth-century accomplishment, and, although the remains of the hill apparently eluded every nineteenth-century traveller in the area, it was assumed by most of

---

[21] Lawrence (1979: 308).   [22] Hiller von Gaertringen and Lattermann (1911: 38).
[23] *IG* V.2 510–11. The other Theisoa, described by Pausanias (8.38.9) as north of Mt Lykaion, is addressed in Part Two, Chapter 19.

them that ancient Theisoa must lie somewhere near Karkalou.[24] Pausanias provides the support for this belief, writing that Teuthis lies 'just across the border from Theisoa', and that the Gortynios River 'has its source in Theisoa, which borders on Methydrion'.[25] Because the city stood both in the vicinity of Methydrion and near the source of the Gortynios/Lousios River, Boblaye correctly determined that, although its ruins were not yet visible, they 'doivent se retrouver dans la plaine au-dessous de Rhado près du moulin et du képhalovrysi de Karkalou, à 6 kilomètres des ruines de Méthydrium'.[26]

OVERALL DEFENSIVE PLANNING

Although the extant remnants of Theisoa's 'ruined little enceinte'[27] are few and far between, they can still shed light on a number of defensive objectives that were envisioned with the circuit's conception, including the strategic choice of site and the tactical use of the system's composite parts. In adition to the advantages provided by its height, the hill was very well chosen for the site of Theisoa's acropolis. Not only did it command a small plain—otherwise rare for a central Arkadian *polis*—but both the geographical location and the topography of the hill were ideal for a functioning acropolis. Geographically located in the heart of the Peloponnese, Theisoa was strategically situated both astride the main road linking western and eastern Arkadia (like Teuthis), as well as at the terminal end of one of the major routes linking the central portion to northern and north-western Arkadia. The Lousios/Gortynios River and its tributaries ensured the area was well watered, while both the plain on the west and the low foothills to the east offered a significant amount of arable land suitable for agriculture and pastoralism.

Provided with a number of considerable natural defences, the hill itself was also well suited for its function as an acropolis. As demonstrated, the choice of fortifying a hill that is comprised of a spur, separated from the bulk of a mountain by a narrow saddle, was a common prerequisite for many Arkadian sites. It provided elevated terrain, both large enough for habitation and close enough for retreat to the acropolis in times of danger. That being said, while the exact location of the lower city is not certain, the arrangements at similar sites[28] would indicate that Hiller von Gaertringen and Lattermann, as well as Jost, are probably correct in their contention that the main area of habitation

---

[24] Leake (1830: ii. 316); Boblaye (1836: 151); Rangabé (1857: 70). The exceptions are Ross (1841: 115) and Curtius (1851: i. 354), who thought the remains at Dhimitsana belonged not to Teuthis, but to ancient Theisoa.
[25] Paus. 8.28.3–4.   [26] Boblaye (1836: 151).   [27] Lawrence (1979: 308).
[28] e.g., Nestane, Halous, Teuthis, and Paos.

did indeed cover this saddle east of the acropolis.[29] Concerning the natural
defences, the north and west sides of the hill are extremely steep and difficult
to scale. The north side of the hill had two additional measures of natural
protection: a small but rapid stream running across its base and the hills rising
from its opposite bank. These elements, as well as the precipitous north and
west slopes, would all but have guaranteed that any attack launched on the city
would not have come from either of those directions. Conversely, the east and
south sides of the hill possessed no discernible natural advantages and relied
instead almost exclusively on the tactical advantages afforded by the man-
made defences.

The trace of the fortifications around the edge of the hill as well as the form
and location of its tactical components clearly reflect the inherent topography
of the hill, and they work both to amplify the natural strength of the hill's steep
north and west slopes, while at the same time compensating for the natural
weakness of the terrain on the east and south sides. The South Tower was
strategically positioned where the acropolis was arguably most vulnerable—
opposite the saddle and next to the Ramp Gate. A concern for protecting both
the saddle and the gate is reflected in the tower's size and orientation.
Measuring *c.*8 m wide with flanks *c.*8.50 m long, the South Tower is not
only the largest surviving tower, but also probably the largest tower to have
existed in the original circuit. Its position here, in the southernmost part of the
circuit, and its orientation indicate careful and cautious consideration. It is not
a coincidence that it presents its main face to the saddle and the lower part of
the ramp to the south; nor that the acute angles formed by the attached
curtains allow a greater than 180° viewshed; nor that this viewshed includes
coverage of the south-west curtain west of the tower, and both the upper ramp
and gate to the east. The location and orientation of the Ramp Gate demonstrate similar consideration, but the gate and approach are really intelligible
only when the South Tower is viewed as part of the same system.

That the South Tower should be understood as part of the larger gate system
is not surprising when one considers it lies only *c.*12.50 m away and its south-
west corner was positioned to cover both the ramp and the gate. Besides the
South Tower, however, the gate was provided with another tower. Although
smaller than the South Tower, this one was equally well positioned, as the
architects ensured that its longest side faced south in order directly to overlook
the ramp as well as the top of the stairs. Not only did the position of this tower
guarantee that an enemy would be forced to expose its unshielded right side
upon approach, but its proximity to the South Tower ensured that the same
enemy could find itself vulnerable to enfilading from the left also. The ramp
and the stairs were crucial to this tactic, as they dictated the actual approach

---

[29] Hiller von Gaertringen and Lattermann (1911: 25); Jost (1985: 212; 1999: 197).

by compelling people to advance to the gate between these two towers. Even though the South Tower and Ramp Gate were designed primarily to safeguard the approach from the vulnerable saddle to the south, we see in the orientation of the gate's smaller tower a concern for protecting the east side of the acropolis.

The east side was among the most vulnerable parts of the acropolis. Whereas the north and west sides of the hill are especially precipitous, the east side had no natural defensive advantages. It does not have a steep slope or rapid stream, or even exposed bedrock, but instead consists of a moderate to gentle slope that opened up onto the adjacent low and rolling hills. While the placement of the gate opposite the adjacent saddle was common for its practicality, if nothing else, its precise location at Theisoa, both across from the saddle and at the point where the circuit swings north, was a tactical—not to mention economical—decision. From this position, the tower immediately flanking the gate was well sited to protect the approach from its south flank, while protecting the vulnerable east side from its north and east faces. The North-East Tower plays a similar role, although one, it seems, devoted entirely to the protection of the exposed east side of the acropolis.

From a consideration of the concern exhibited for the east side as demonstrated by the position and orientations of the gate tower and the North-East Tower, it is safe to assume that other towers must have existed on this side between the two. Although none is visible today, a century ago Hiller von Gaertringen and Lattermann cryptically noted that, besides the North-East Tower, 'Sonst sind lauern und Türme stark zerstört'.[30] Approximately 110 m stand between the North-East Tower and the gate tower. Thus, if we take an average of around 30 m—a common tower spacing at other Arkadian sites— the east side could have accommodated at least another three towers, regularly spaced between the two extant examples, bringing the total to five on the east side. We might imagine a similar deployment of regularly spaced towers along the south-west side, which, although possessing slopes steeper than on the east, cannot be said to be precipitous. While this is admittedly conjectural, the need to protect the exposed east side, and, to a lesser extent, the south-west side, make such a reconstruction neither irresponsible nor implausible.

Because of the poor preservation of the remains, establishing other perceived defensive concerns and reconstructing tactical considerations also rely on analogy as well as the understanding that the walls reflect the natural topography of the hill. It is reasonable to suppose, then, that the circuit possessed only the one gate. The east side is the only other part of the circuit towards which the approach could practically facilitate another gate. Yet piercing the curtain with an opening here would be a further defensive liability

---

[30] Hiller von Gaertringen and Lattermann (1911: 38).

in what is already the most vulnerable part of the circuit. Indeed, while it is not impossible that the east or south-west sides were provided with a postern or two, certainly a single gate, close to and facing the main area of inhabitation (that is, the saddle), would have been sufficient as the safest way to satisfy the circuit's function as an acropolis—a place of refuge to which the populace need retreat only in times of danger. Finally, if the *c.*2 m thick walls attested for the curtains attached to the South Tower, and the *c.*1.50 m thick curtain attached to the gate tower, are taken as representing the more or less average thickness for the rest of the circuit walls, it is immediately clear that, when allowance is made for the parapet, the remaining width devoted to the wall-walk would have been quite insufficient. Thus, as Winter suggests for Gortys, we might imagine the walls of the Theisoan acropolis to have been provided with wooden scaffolding, or *ikria*, to increase the width of the *parodos*.[31]

CHRONOLOGICAL SUMMARY

Historical probability and shared architectural affinities suggest that the fortification circuit of Theisoa was erected sometime in the third century BC (perhaps the second half).

CHRONOLOGICAL ARGUMENTS

Attempting to determine a reliable chronology for the fortifications at Theisoa presents the same difficulties as those encountered concerning the walls of Teuthis. Although there is a greater quantity of both external and internal evidence than for Teuthis, the fact remains that what evidence we do possess sheds little light on the chronological question. The epigraphical evidence, for example, while instrumental in establishing ancient Theisoa as a *polis*, is of little use in attempting to date the walls. That these texts range in date from the fourth century BC to the late third/early second century BC provides only a *terminus post* and *terminus ante quem* for the settlement's *polis* status, but perhaps, by association, also the likeliest chronological range for the construction of the fortifications. Although Theisoa was chosen to participate in the synoikism of Megalopolis, it is not even certain whether the decision was implemented. Furthermore, attempting to narrow down a more specific date is complicated by the fact that the same historical catalysts provided by Pikoulas

---

[31] Winter (1971a: 147).

for the construction of the walls of Teuthis apply also to Theisoa.[32] This in itself is not surprising, as these two *poleis* are separated by only 8 km, both were part of the same συντελεία headed by Orchomenos, and both were members of the Arkadian League and, later, of the Achaian League. The internal evidence provided by the archaeological record and the walls themselves is only slightly more obliging.

Unfortunately, the limited excavation conducted by Oikonomos at Theisoa in the very early twentieth century—focusing largely on a temple on the summit—offers no direct chronological insight about the fortifications. Still, it is important to note that the oldest remains that he discovered, as related in his brief report, are from the third century BC.[33] Concerning the walls themselves, although there is nothing in the extant remains that speaks exclusively to any time between the fourth or late third century BC (like Teuthis), there are elements that, when taken together, do tend to support a later date along this chronological spectrum. Indeed, while the ground-storey chambers in the towers (common after the time of Epaminondas) and the presence of a ramp gate (based on analogous examples from Stymphalos and Asea) may point to a date from the early or middle fourth century BC, other elements of the fortifications resemble more closely the late-third-century BC features from Gortys. Although the South Tower presents three instead of four faces to the field, the projection of this tower and the wide viewshed provided by the acute angles of the attached curtains closely resemble the arrangement of the corner towers from the so-called South Fort. The considerable size of the South Tower, 8 m by 8.50 m, also suggests it belongs to the period after the widespread use of defensive artillery. Furthermore, the way the South Tower stands independently from the curtain—with its back projecting into the intramural area—is particularly reminiscent of the construction of Tower 4, again from the South Fort at Gortys. Moreover, with the absence of an internal structure, we see in the North-East Tower at Theisoa what is essentially a pseudo-tower or bastion—one with an equivalent in Tower 2 from Gortys's South Fort. Finally, the thin curtains in the Theisoan circuit find few parallels in Arkadia, save for the walls of the South Fort.

Lawrence confidently asserts that the fortifications of Theisoa 'may be either a third-century fort of the Achaean League or a refuge built by the Arcadian inhabitants when they regained independence after 194'.[34] Certainly the Achaian League may have played a role (political or economic) in the construction of the Theisoan circuit, but the epigraphical evidence suggests that

[32] Pikoulas (1986: 113). For Teuthis, see Part Two, Chapter 17, under Chronological Arguments.
[33] Oikonomos (1911–12: 243).
[34] Lawrence (1979: 308). Jost (1999: 197), perhaps after Lawrence, also maintains the site might have been used to house a garrison.

Theisoa was a *polis* at least until the late third century BC, and not a fort or simple place of refuge. Yet Lawrence's belief in a third-century BC date does seem essentially correct. The parallels between the fortifications of Theisoa with the South Fort at Gortys, which almost certainly dates to the late third century BC, are compelling.[35] Ultimately, therefore, while the evidence cannot completely exclude the possibility of a later-fourth-century BC date, on the whole it suggests that in all probability the walls of Theisoa were erected some time in the third century BC, most likely during its second half.

BIBLIOGRAPHY

Paus 8.28.4–6; Leake (1830: ii. 316); Boblaye (1836: 151); Ross (1841: 115); Curtius (1851: i. 354); Rangabé (1857: 70); Oikonomos (1910–11); Hiller von Gaertringen and Lattermann (1911: 37–8); Meyer (1936a); Scranton (1941: 185); Head (1963: 418); Roy (1972b: 78); Lawrence (1979: 38, 482); Jost (1985: 210–12; 1999: 197); Papachatzis (1994: 300); Nielsen (2002: 599–600); Maher (2012a: 541–62).

[35] For Gortys, see Part Two, Chapter 5, under Chronological Arguments.

19

Theisoa (Lavda), Western Arkadia

LOCATION

Theisoa is located in western Arkadia, on the south bank of the Alpheios River (Fig. C19.1). The site occupies the summit of an isolated cone-shaped hill. Inhabitation appears to have been largely limited to the intramural area.

POLIS STATUS

Pausanias mentions Theisoa (πρὸς Λυκαίῳ) twice as a *polis* in the urban or political sense: first, he includes it among those settlements that participated in the synoikism of Megalopolis;[1] second, he maintains that, although in his day Theisoa was a village (κώμη), he is sure it was once a πόλις.[2] A fourth-century BC inscription discovered on a dedication at Delphi was made by a 'Theisoan Arkadian', who was a Delphic *proxenos*.[3] A late-fourth- or early third-century BC inscription from the site's citadel preserves the names and privileges provided to several Argive *theorodokoi* when they came to Theisoa to announce the celebrations for Hera at the Argive Heraion and for Zeus at his temple in Nemea.[4]

HISTORY

Regrettably, we know next to nothing about the history of Theisoa. Although Theisoa was listed among those cities that participated in the synoikism of

---

[1] Paus. 8.27.4.   [2] Paus. 8.38.3.

[3] *SEG* xiv. 455. On this inscription, see Bousquet (1954: 432–3). On the argument as to which Theisoa this inscription refers, see Roy (1972b: 78) and Part Two, Chapter 18.

[4] Goester et al. (2009: 200–1); Mattern (2010).

Fig. C19.1. Theisoa (Lavda), topographical map of area. (© *2011 Google-Map data* © *2011 Tele Atlas*)

Megalopolis,[5] it is not certain that such a decision was ever implemented. Sometime between the fourth century BC and Pausanias' visit in the second half of the second century AD, Theisoa was reduced from a *polis* to a village.[6]

LOCAL TOPOGRAPHY

The site of ancient Theisoa sits atop Lavda Hill on the south bank of the Alpheios River (Fig. C19.2). This hill rises on all sides from a small plateau, itself defined on the north and east by the deep Alpheios Valley, on the south by the lower northern slope of Mt Lykaion, and on the west by the Mylaon River Valley.[7] Standing where the north side of the plateau meets the lower slopes of Lavda Hill, between 280 and 360 m above the Alpheios River, is the modern village of Theisoa.[8] Lavda itself rises a further *c*.200 m above the uppermost part of the village, some 577 m above the Alpheios, and 757 m above sea level. Although generally conical in shape, the hill is not really uniform, as the gradients of the slopes vary considerably.

The summit of the hill is relatively flat at the 720 m contour, only sloping gently from north to south.[9] Not all of the summit is level, and approximately the middle third of the intramural area is occupied by a 20 m rise. From the summit to the modern village the northern slope of Lavda is very steep, dropping 77 m over an aerial distance of 100 m.[10] By comparison, the same

---

[5] Paus. 8.27.4.   [6] Paus. 8.38.3.
[7] On some maps, the Mylaon River is also called the Arkoudoremma River.
[8] Feije (1994: 49). Formerly the village of Lavda. The name was changed in 1915.
[9] It is this contour that the fortification circuit generally follows.
[10] Feije (1994: 55).

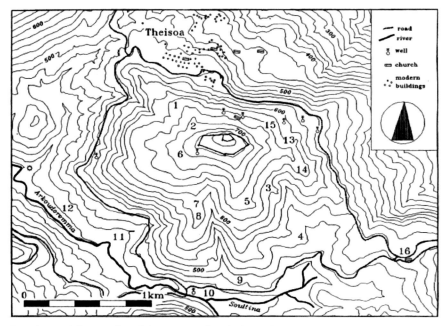

Fig. C19.2. Theisoa (Lavda), topographical plan of Lavda hill from Feije (1994: 53, fig. 3). (© *J. J. Feije*)

drop of 77 m on the western and southern sides of the hill is spread over a distance of 350 m and 250 m respectively.[11] Like the southern side, the slope on the eastern face of the hill to the plateau is also fairly gentle. Both the north and east sides of the plateau, however, become considerably steeper upon their descent towards the Alpheios. Indeed, if we consider that, while the north slope falls *c.*600 m from the summit of Lavda to the bed of the Alpheios, on the southern side one has only to descend 300 m to reach the bottom of the hill and the bed of the Soultina River, Feije is correct in his claim that 'the northern side of Lavda is also its protective back side'.[12]

    The heights afforded by Lavda Hill and its especially formidable north slope represent only a fraction of the advantageous features afforded by the topography of the area. Such advantages were complemented by other natural features that also served to provide protection—especially to the more vulnerable west, south, and east sides of the hill. The deep V-shaped profile of the Alpheios Valley would have provided a considerable natural barrier on the north, north-east, and east sides of Theisoa. The west and south-west sides of the hill were similarly confined by the Mylaon and Soultina Rivers. Consequently, it was only the north-west part of the hill that was not protected by a

---

[11] Feije (1994: 55, 57).   [12] Feije (1994: 57).

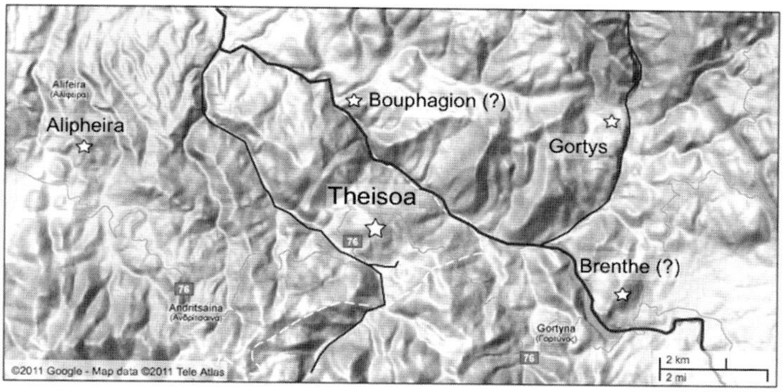

Fig. C19.3. Theisoa (Lavda), topographical map of site and surrounding territories. (© 2011 Google-Map data © 2011 Tele Atlas)

watercourse at its base. Furthermore, the landscape provided Lavda with further natural defences in the form of four remarkably similar-sized hills surrounding the site on every side. Some are isolated, like the hill of Kalogria (941 m) on the opposite side of the Alpheios to the north-east, and the hill of Matesi (834 m) north-west of the site; while others are foothills of Mt Lykaion, such as Tsouka (872 m) and Chelmos (789 m) on the south-west and southeast respectively. ¹³

These same topographical features served to define and separate the site from the surrounding *poleis* and settlements (Fig. C19.3). Matesi Hill and the north-west ridge of Kalogria must have represented the boundary between the territories of Theisoa and Bouphagon, ¹⁴ while the same Matesi and the Mylaon River Valley on its west side probably served as the border to Alipheiran territory. To the north-east, Kalogria Hill and the confluence of the Alpheios and Lousios Rivers stood between Theisoa and Gortys, whereas the Alpheios south of this confluence served to divide the territory of Brenthe from Theisoa. ¹⁵ Although these features served generally to delineate the territory of Theisoa from the surrounding settlements, the actual amount of arable land in the territory would have been considerably smaller than the total area within these boundaries would suggest. Indeed, as most of the territory is actually comprised of rugged hills and deep valleys, agriculture would have been largely limited to the slopes of Lavda Hill and the valley to the south between Chelmos and Tsouka Hills. ¹⁶

these slopes supported figs, olives, vines, tobacco, and certain nuts (Feije 1994: 55).

Feije (1994: 57).
See Appendix for information about Bouphagon.
See Appendix for information about Brenthe.

Although the modern villagers apparently gave up agriculture completely in 1991, on their first visit to the site in the late 1970s, Dutch researchers not only observed various crops being cultivated on the slopes, but were told by locals that, in the first half of the twentieth century.

Fig. C19.4. Theisoa (Lavda),
Lavda hill (facing west).
(© *Matthew Maher*)

NATURAL DEFENCES

The height offered by the acropolis and the steep slope on its northern side
provide the area with a natural defence (Fig. C19.4). The Alpheios River flanks
the hill to the north and east, while two of its tributaries, the Soultina and Mylaon
Rivers, flank the site to the south and south-west respectively.

FORTIFICATION TYPE

Acropolis type.[17] Roughly trapezoidal in shape, the circuit follows the contours of the hill, encircling the summit. There is a separately fortified citadel on
the highest point of the hill (Fig. C19.5).

PRESERVATION

Theisoa is moderately well preserved; most of the west and north sides of the
circuit, including parts of the citadel, survive. Most of the south and south-east
sides are no longer visible. Part of the north-east wall survives to a height of
3.20 m,[18] the north wall to 2 m,[19] and the south wall to 2.80 m.[20] The walls of
the citadel, although slightly higher, also survive to comparable heights: its
west wall rises to 4 m,[21] and the south to a height of just 3 m.[22] The circuit runs
for a total length of c.835 m.[23]

[17] Jost (1999: 196).   [18] Feije (1994: 74).   [19] Feije (1994: 76).
[20] Feije (1994: 67).   [21] Feije (1994: 79).   [22] Feije (1994: 81).
[23] Feije (1994: 61).

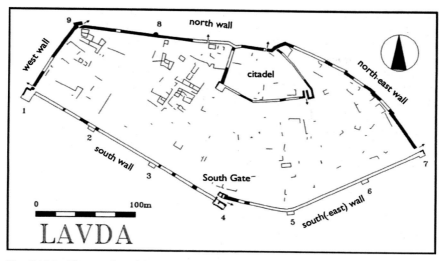

Fig. C19.5. Theisoa (Lavda), plan of site after Feije (1994: 58, fig. 5). (© *J. J. Feije*)

CONSTRUCTION

The vast majority of the circuit and citadel walls, ranging from 1.30 to 3 m in thickness,[24] were constructed in courses (or rough courses) of polygonal blocks (Fig. C19.6).[25]

Between the outer and inner faces, the core itself consisted of packed rubble and earth.[26] Although some blocks were laid inward as headers at fairly regular intervals (about every 2 or 3 m) to increase the bonding strength between the faces and the core, nowhere do they extend the width of the curtains to form compartments.[27] Three of the towers exhibit drafted edges. The superstructure was mudbrick (not preserved).

---

[24] Feije (1994: 62, 67, 74, 76).
[25] The one exception is the south wall of the citadel in the surviving section east of the tower. Although this wall too is largely comprised of polygonal blocks (with some trapezoidal), here they were clearly laid in courses with better care and with cleaner joints. The predominately roughly coursed polygonal style interspersed with some areas that are better and more clearly coursed matches well with Frazer's description (1898: iv. 388) of a style that is 'a sort of compromise between the quadrangular and the polygonal, but elsewhere . . . is almost completely quadrangular'. The blocks comprising the curtains are of limestone quarried directly from the bedrock of the hill.
[26] Feije (1994: 62).   [27] Feije (1994: 62).

Fig. C19.6. Theisoa (Lavda), west curtain wall showing coursed polygonal masonry (facing south-east). (© *Matthew Maher*)

SUMMARY OF TACTICAL COMPONENTS

The main circuit possessed one semicircular and eight rectangular towers regularly spaced at c.60–70 m, perhaps as many as three gates, no fewer than three posterns, as well as an indented trace (see Fig. C19.5). The citadel contained one large rectangular tower and was accessed from the lower city by a small axial-type gate.

Towers

Not including the separately fortified citadel, the fortifications of Theisoa were equipped with one semicircular tower and eight rectangular ones. Seven of the rectangular towers (Towers 1–7) are located on the south part of the circuit, while the eighth (Tower 9) is located in the north-west corner. Over half of these examples (Towers 2, 3, 5, 6, 7) uniformly measure 6.65 m in width and project 3.50 m from the wall.[28] The rest of the towers are considerably larger. Tower 1 is easily the largest at Theisoa, measuring 12.50 m in length by 9.60 m in width,[29] while Tower 4 is c.9.40 m in length and c.6.50 m in width.[30] Tower 9 measures 7.20 m across the front, projects 2.90 m on the west, and has an eastern flank 4.20 m in length.[31] Tower 9 is set apart from the others, not only because it is set at an oblique angle, but because it is the only example with a postern in the flank (Fig. C19.7).

---

[28] Feije (1994: 66).   [29] Feije (1994: 66).

[30] Feije (1994: 66). Like Towers 1 and 7, Tower 4 too seems to have drafted edges, at least on its north-east corner.

[31] Goester et. al. (1981: 655); Feije (1994: 76). Further details of Towers 8 and 9 await the publication of their recent excavation.

Fig. C19.7. Theisoa (Lavda),
Tower 9 (facing north-west).
(© *Matthew Maher*)

Fig. C19.8. Theisoa (Lavda), semicircular
Tower 8 (facing west). (© *Matthew Maher*)

Finally, Tower 8 is the only semicircular example at Theisoa (Fig. C19.8). Located in the middle of the north wall, it has a diameter of 5.20 m and projects 2.55 m from the curtain.[32]

---

[32] Feije (1994: 76). Although Leake (1830: ii. 19) was told by a 'Lavdhiote peasant . . . that [it] was once a windmill', he believes it was instead 'a signal tower'. Presumably basing his conclusions on Leake's account, Curtius (1851: i. 359) too is of the opinion that the tower was a signal tower built in the medieval period. While unique in the circuit and even 'slightly eccentric' (Feije 1994: 76), this tower appears to have been contemporary with the rest of the enceinte.

Fig. C19.9. Theisoa (Lavda), West Gate and north-west side of Tower 1 (facing south-west), with the opening marked with an arrow. (© *Matthew Maher*)

Gates

At the westernmost point in the system stands the so-called West Gate (Fig. C19.9). Its poorly preserved state reveals only a narrow passage, about 1.75 m in width.[33] Feije maintains that the West Gate is an example of an axial or frontal opening type of passage (that is, Winter's Type I).[34] Yet surely such a relatively small opening, conveniently placed to the left of a large tower, is better classified as a postern.[35]

A postern here would not have been unprecedented, as the circuit contained at least three others. All three of these posterns are found in the north wall of the circuit. One (1.70 m wide) is found in the flank of Tower 9, one (1.30 m wide) led through the shared north wall of the citadel/circuit wall,[36] and the other is *c*.60 m to the west, cut through the bedrock ridge. Located at the easternmost point in the circuit is the East Gate, which is comprised of a single narrow opening (*c*.5 m wide) flanked on the south by a large tower (Tower 7).[37] Again, whether the East and West Gates were true gates or large well-guarded posterns may ultimately be a matter of semantics. The South Gate, however, leaves no doubt as to its primary function. This gate is the only monumental example at Theisoa (see Fig. C19.5).[38] As an example of the overlap type, we see the south-east–north-west-oriented opening framed on the south by the

---

[33] Feije (1994: 64).   [34] Winter (1971a: 209, 222); Feije (1994: 64).

[35] This seems to have been the opinion after the initial reconnaissance of the site, since, in their description of the trace, Goester et. al. (1981: 655) describe this opening as a simple door.

[36] Feije (1994: 75).

[37] Feije (1994: 72) maintains that, like the West Gate, the East Gate is also an example of the frontal opening type.

[38] As deduced by Frazer (1898: iv. 387) over a century ago, from the nature of the terrain, 'the chief approach to the town would seem to have been from the south'. It is not surprising, therefore, that this is precisely where the main city gate is to be found.

Fig. C19.10. Theisoa (Lavda), south-west citadel wall (facing south-east); note: the knoll (*right*) is the highest point on the hill on which stood the south-west citadel tower. (© *Matthew Maher*)

projecting Tower 4 and on the north by the south wall curtain. The entrance passage narrows from *c.*5.50 m wide on the exterior, to *c.*4 m in front of the spur walls, to a width of only *c.*2.50 m between the spur walls.[39]

Citadel

Covering an area of approximately 85 m east–west by 50 m north–south, 'the walled area is oblong and comes to a point on the east side, roughly repeating the outline of the acropolis which shows the same form, protracted and ending in a point on the east side'.[40] Like the main circuit, the citadel was provided with a postern, one large tower (and possibly a second), and a gateway. The citadel's largest tower was placed at its south-west corner atop a small plateau and at the highest point on the whole hill (Fig. C19.10).

This tower projects *c.*3.75 m from the west citadel wall and appears to have been roughly square in shape, with sides measuring *c.*7.65 m.[41] Approximately 100 m east of this tower at the south-east end of the citadel was the only entrance to the complex. The passage, 2.40 m wide and *c.*7 m long, is oriented north-south and protected on its east side by what appears to have been another tower (Fig. C19.11).[42] This south-east tower, measuring *c.*9 m long by 6.50 m wide, like its counterpart on the south-west, has drafted edges.

[39] Feije (1994: 69).   [40] Feije (1994: 61).
[41] Feije (1994: 79).   [42] Feije (1994: 83).

Fig. C19.11. Theisoa (Lavda), citadel gateway (marked with arrow) and corner of south-east citadel tower (facing north). (© *Matthew Maher*)

COMMENTS

From the East Gate, the north-east wall follows an indented trace, ascending the slope towards the summit in a north-west direction for *c*.165 m. As an indented trace, the line is broken by a series of three small jogs or returns in the curtain, which turn the wall gradually to the west as it slowly makes its way up towards the north-east corner of the citadel. From south to north, these jogs project *c*.1.50 m, *c*.1.40–1.45 m, and *c*.1.80 m, and accordingly yield four different, but generally short, lengths of curtain.

OVERALL DEFENSIVE PLANNING

It has already been stated that the compact circuit, small intramural area, and its position on the summit of a defensible hill point to the fact that the Theisoan fortifications are an example of the acropolis type of circuit. Although technically true, the point does warrant some clarification, as the Theisoan circuit is not as easily categorized. It is true that the choice of site on an easily defendable hill, with the trace and composite parts of the circuit reflecting the natural topography and serving as a safe refuge for inhabitants, is a defensive strategy commonly employed; and in this regard the system at Theisoa is no different from other acropolis type of fortifications in Arkadia. Still, the acropolis of Theisoa differed from these other sites (for example, Halous, Paos, or Nestane) and what often constitutes an acropolis in the traditional sense, in that the intramural area appears to have been largely occupied by houses, temple(s), and an agora.[43] In other words, while as an acropolis it had the same overall defensive function, it had a different day-to-day function: it was where people lived, worked, and prayed. That being said, we see at Theisoa the usual (and now predictable) defensive considerations behind the choice of Lavda Hill as the location for the settlement.

One might reasonably ask why the Theisoans chose Lavda and not one of the four other similar hills in the area. There is no single answer, of course, but a number of reasons. Ultimately, however, it is the 'combination of a strategically located and defensible hilltop which is somewhat flat with a reasonable radius of arable land around the top [that] makes Lavda so remarkable in comparison with the other slopes in the vicinity'.[44] Even if they were unsuitable for occupation, the slopes of these rejected hills were still important features in the overall defensive strategy, as they formed a nearly continuous and rugged periphery around Lavda, severely limiting approaches to the site. In the immediate vicinity of the Lavda, the landscape was equally amenable to the defensive needs of the settlement on the summit. We have repeatedly come across the Arkadian affinity for choosing sites where waterways played an important defensive role. The situation at Theisoa is no different in this regard. Between the precipitous Alpheios River Valley running to the north, north-east, and east of the site, the Mylaon River to the west and south-west, and the Soultina flanking the southern slope, the Theisoans clearly employed the natural topography around Lavda to their defensive advantage.[45] These rivers worked in concert with the topography of the hill itself both to protect and to dictate the main approaches to the settlement on the summit.

The impracticability of a northern approach to Theisoa has been alluded to already. The steep northern slope of Lavda and the course of the Alpheios guaranteed as much. A similar argument can be made for the eastern side of the site, where, even though the slope is more negotiable, when combined with the Alpheios an approach would also be difficult. In fact, the most practical approach to the summit of Lavda was from the south-east. This side not only enjoys the most moderate incline of the whole hill—facilitating the ascent to the summit—but, further down at its base, the terrain is especially suitable for directing an approach. Here a natural and narrow bottleneck is produced, framed by the eastern terminus of the Soultina River Valley to the south-west and on the north by the increasingly steep terrain as it begins its decent towards the Alpheios. Adding weight to the notion that 'the northern side of

[43] Goester (2005: 326); Goester et al. (2009: 193). The existence of an agora is suggested by the remains of a stoa. The architectural remains in the intramural area are too scattered to be of any use in reconstructing a plausible street plan (Goester 2010).
[44] Feije (1994: 57).
[45] The same waterways and the springs on the hill observed by Boblaye (1836: 160) and Feije (1994: 73) would have ensured the site was more than adequately watered.

Lavda [was] also its protective back side',[46] and that 'Lavda was clearly oriented towards the south',[47] is the location of the city's main—and perhaps only—gateway in the middle of the south stretch of the fortification circuit.[48]

The placement of the main gate opposite the only practical approach afforded by the terrain of the hill is not the only way in which the topography of the hill worked to shape the form of the Theisoan fortification system. Most obvious are the course and dimensions of the trace. On the west, south, and south-east side, for example, minor deviations aside, the enceinte follows almost exactly the *c.*720 m contour line of the hill.[49] This ensured that the flattest and habitable terrain was included in the intramural area. Rising to meet the slopes of the elevated knoll comprising the summit, the course of the northern and north-eastern stretches of the circuit can also be seen as being dictated by the terrain. Furthermore, as parts of the northern trace were actually comprised of (or at least built atop) a shelf cut from the natural bedrock, we see more directly how the topography of the hill shaped the form of the circuit. The same attributes hold true for the separately fortified citadel.

The form of the citadel and its placement on top of the knoll instead of encircling its base was an intricate decision dictated by both the terrain and larger defensive strategies. Indeed, if this enclosure did cover the whole circumference of this elevated rise, not only would a third of the larger intramural area have been consumed, but the approach to the citadel—this last refuge and line of defence—would have been facilitated by the relatively flat terrain. Instead, building it on top of the knoll ensured that anyone approaching would first have to ascend its southern slope under the watchful eye of the defenders above. This scenario guaranteed the additional tactical advantage of reserving the highest point of the entire site for the south-west citadel tower.

The defensive strategy of choosing a defendable hilltop surrounded by rivers and erecting a circuit that echoed its inherent topography was complemented by a series of tactical measures ultimately aimed at making the system stronger and the city safer. First and foremost in this regard is the use of towers. The vast majority of the towers were placed along the southern side of the circuit (see Fig. C19.5). While this is certainly a reflection of the fact that the southern section is the longest in the circuit, more importantly, it also reflects a concern for protecting the main approach to the city. Although this approach was from the south-east, the regular tower spacing demonstrates a concern for unwelcome approaches from the south in general. The placement

---

[46] Feije (1994: 57).   [47] Feije (1994: 83).

[48] Indeed, the location of the main gate was one of the factors that led Frazer (1898: iv. 387) logically to suppose that the main approach was from the south side of the hill, 'on the side away from the [Alpheios] river'.

[49] Feije (1994: 60); Jost (1999: 196).

of the towers framing the southern stretch, on the east and westernmost end (Towers 7 and 1), as well as those in the extreme south (Towers 4 and 5), also made sure that there were no blind spots in the system and that approaches from the south, east, and west were attended to. The general elliptical shape of the trace also meant that Towers 1 and 7 were well positioned to command approaches from the north-west and north-east respectively. As suggested by the paucity of towers, it appears that the military architects were less concerned with the defence of the north. Only two towers were inserted into this side of the circuit, one of which does not even face north, but was set at an oblique angle to face the north-west (Tower 9). While the steep north slope of Lavda below the circuit must have been deemed an effective enough deterrent, an additional tower was cautiously placed about halfway between the north-west corner and the citadel. This appropriately semicircular-shaped tower (Tower 8) ensured a 180° view in front of and along the flanking sides of the northern curtain.

Besides constructing towers at regularly spaced intervals, Theisoan military architects took great care to place the largest of these towers at both the most vulnerable spots and those commanding the greatest tactical advantage. As already mentioned, the south-west tower of the citadel was built on the highest point in the city, while Towers 1, 4, and 7 were placed at the westernmost, southernmost, and easternmost part of the circuit respectively, where they could best oversee the main approach to the city as well as approach from the north-east and north-west. Taken together, these four towers, corresponding to the four cardinal points, provided a 360° view of and around the city; the view from the summit is truly impressive. The hills of Alipheira and Bouphagion are clearly visible to the west and north, as is the confluence of the Lousios and Alpheios to the east; Mt Lykaion dominates the landscape to the south. It should not be surprising, therefore, that these towers are also the largest (and presumably the tallest) in the circuit.

At 12.50 m long by 9.60 m wide, Tower 1 is the largest tower at Theisoa and certainly an example of Ober's second-generation artillery towers.[50] The necessity of such a large tower and its associated firepower here, at the westernmost point in the circuit, was imposed by the terrain in front of it. Indeed, although the south-east possessed the easiest approach from the base, the western side of the upper half of Lavda (that is, between the 620 m and the 660 m contours) comprised the gentlest sloping part of the entire hill. As such, it was easily an area from which siege engines could be brought against the city—assuming they could be brought up the hill at all.[51] The same pattern of placing larger towers to confront areas of negotiable terrain immediately adjacent to the circuit is observable in Towers 4 and 7. Furthermore, this

---

[50] Ober (1987: 572).
[51] Or, at the very least, it represented a suitable place for enemies to muster.

need to cover the rolling terrain probably explains the unusual orientation of Tower 9 (see Fig. C19.5). Although it is set obliquely between the west and northern stretches of the wall, it is aligned exactly to face the gently sloping terrain in front of it to the north-west.

The size of the largest towers, especially Towers 1 and 4, and the south-east citadel tower, may also reflect the fact that, since they all flank openings in the curtain, they were, in effect, perceived as the weakest spots of the circuit. The placing of the openings themselves suggests that the architects wisely entertained the possibility that the considerable firepower of the flanking towers may not have been sufficient to keep an enemy at a distance from the walls. Accordingly, the openings beside Tower 1 and the south-east citadel tower were placed to the right of the towers, which meant that an enemy would have had to advance with its unshielded right side exposed in any attempt to access these openings.[52] Interestingly, this precaution was not taken for the opening beside Tower 7.[53] As an overlap type, the monumental South Gate and its passage were also well protected. Although oriented such than an enemy's vulnerable side did not face Tower 4, the overlapping north stretch of the curtain and Tower 5 to the south could have provided the necessary offensive enfilading to both the unshielded side and/or the rear.

The final tactical component of the Theisoan fortifications is the indented trace. Comprising the section between Tower 7 and the north-east corner of the citadel, the north-east wall is the only section without towers and the only stretch that does not run in a straight line. Although near the northern terminus of the indented trace there is a 'steep northern edge which makes further defensive measures superfluous',[54] we are left to wonder why the indented trace was constructed instead of a straight curtain with towers. The answer may, once again, lie in the topography. The north-east section of the circuit is the only stretch of wall set at an oblique angle to the prevailing contours of the hill. The north wall, for example, follows a course perpendicular to the slope of the summit, while, as mentioned, the walls on the west, south, and south-east side of the circuit run roughly parallel to the $c.720$ m contour. On the other hand, as the north-east stretch runs at a $c.45°$ angle to the slope of the hill, perhaps it was thought that a series of smaller stretches of straight walling could better negotiate the terrain than a long straight line. This situation accords well with Winter's observation from other sites, where he found that, when circuits contain 'fairly substantial stretches of indented trace unbroken by towers . . . we shall find that such traces were . . . generally confined

---

[52] The postern in Tower 9 is similarly placed on its right side.

[53] Perhaps the southernmost jog of the indented trace (only $c.40$ m away) was thought sufficient protection for the right side of this opening.

[54] Feije (1994: 74).

to areas where the wall either descended, or traversed the upper reaches of, a long and difficult slope'.[55]

Even if the curving, indented trace was not imposed by the terrain, it did have practical advantages. Choosing a convex course instead of a straight one not only incorporated more land into the intramural area, but ensured that the citadel remained largely independent from the rest of the circuit. In other words, in such a hypothetical scenario, with the north-east wall extending in a straight line from Tower 7 to the citadel's south-east corner, the north and west walls of the citadel would also be the main circuit walls. Obviously, the more walls the citadel shared with the main circuit, the more the walls could be breached, which ultimately would have defeated their purpose as a last line of defence. As the remains stand, even without towers, the indented trace followed the 'curved trace imposed by the terrain while maintaining its defensive character by allowing for flanking fire along the wall'.[56] In other words, although its curved nature was probably dictated by the terrain, this stretch could have incorporated towers. The construction of an indented trace instead, therefore, was a conscious decision introduced purely for purposes of enfilading.

CHRONOLOGICAL SUMMARY

From a combination of historical probability, external evidence, and architectural affinities, it would seem that the fortification circuit of Theisoa on Lavda Hill was constructed in *c.*325–275 BC.

CHRONOLOGICAL ARGUMENTS

Owing to the comprehensive research campaigns carried out since the 1980s under the auspices of the Netherlands Archaeological Institute in Athens, we are fortunate to have at our disposal a considerable corpus of information concerning the archaeological history of ancient Theisoa. It is this evidence, on which this larger reconstructed history rests, that is instrumental in establishing a reliable chronology of the fortifications. Such evidence can generally be placed here into two broad categories: first, external evidence gathered from the excavations and other archaeological investigations, including, for example, the ceramic finds and various architectural surveys; and the other

[55] Winter (1971b: 515).   [56] Feije (1994: 74).

category, of course, is comprised of the walls themselves. By employing all the available evidence and appropriate comparanda in this regard, a fairly reliable chronology for the Theisoan circuit may be recommended.[57]

Ceramics collected from both surface reconnaissance and systematic excavation provide a general chronological scope and offer a good starting point for the present investigation. Broadly speaking and excluding finds from Late Antiquity, these ceramics range from the early fourth century BC to the late Hellenistic Period (second/first century BC).[58] The architectural survey of the scattered blocks found strewn around the site tell a similar chronological story. In short, building on earlier surveys, during a two-week season in the summer of 2007, Dutch researchers catalogued and photographed all 252 *ex situ* architectural blocks from the site.[59] These blocks, some of marble and some of limestone, all belong to the Doric order, and were once tentatively thought to represent the remains of two separate structures: a marble temple dated to the Classical period based on local comparanda, and a later limestone temple (or stoa) perhaps dating to the late second or first century BC.[60] More recently, however, Mattern has argued that not only do all the blocks probably belong to the same temple, but that the Doric elements are reminiscent of those in the nearby Stoa of Philip at Megalopolis, and should be no earlier than the later fourth century BC.[61] In the 2010 Annual Open Meeting of the Netherlands Institute at Athens, Mattern largely repeated these views, but conceded that the construction of this temple may also have occurred in the early third century BC.[62] In summary, therefore, both the ceramics and the architecture suggest habitation on Lavda as early as the beginning of the fourth century to as late as the second or first century BC. That the walls were constructed sometime after the initial occupation of the hill is suggested by the fact that several architectural blocks were reused in the construction of the citadel and main circuit walls.[63] Determining exactly when the fortifications were thrown around this settlement, however, requires a closer look at the constituent parts of the walls themselves.

The fortifications present a number of interesting features that can be helpful in this regard. While the limitations of stylistic dating have been mentioned previously (and frequently) and need not be repeated here, the

---

[57] At least more specific than has previously been offered. On a date for the walls, Feije (1994: 87), for example, offers only the following: 'roughly speaking, then, the subject here is the Hellenistic period.'

[58] Feije (1994: 87); Goester (2010).

[59] For a detailed description and analysis of these pieces, see Goester et al. (2009: 194–200). For an earlier and overlapping architectural survey, see Goester (2005). While the architectural blocks were discovered throughout the site, the majority were found within the citadel.

[60] Goester (2005: 326).   [61] Goester et al. (2009: 200).

[62] Mattern (2010). The perceived similarities with the Doric Temple of Athena Polias Nikephoros at Pergamon played a part in assigning this date to the temple at Theisoa.

[63] Goester (2005: 322).

coursed polygonal masonry of the Theisoan circuit—when taken together with the other evidence—is useful. Attracted especially to the 'pleasing ruggedness and irregularity of the polygonal style',[64] the architects in the Peloponnese 'enjoyed the task of exploiting it'.[65] Indeed, as the rest of Greece slowly turned away from the polygonal style in the later fifth century BC, in the Peloponnese we see the development and use of coursed polygonal masonry as late as the second half of the fourth century and the beginning of the third century BC.[66] When this is taken together with other evidence, as suggested, an early Hellenistic date for the Theisoan circuit becomes more plausible.

As the advantages of defensive artillery were realized in the second half of the fourth century BC, the form and function of fortifications changed accordingly. One of the most obvious changes appeared in the towers, since their most important function in Hellenistic systems was to house artillery.[67] With the invention of torsion artillery around the middle of the fourth century BC, towers became larger than before in order to house the larger calibre torsion machines and were also often more widely spaced. At Theisoa, the sizable Towers 1 and 4, and perhaps Tower 7 and the south-west citadel tower, appear to be examples of these second-generation types.[68] Furthermore, with a minimum distance of *c*.60 m (and just as often as much as *c*.70 m), the relatively wide spacing of the Theisoan towers also suggests that the towers held larger calibre machines. From the assumption that 'every tower should be so placed that the bolt-projectors within it could protect the towers nearest on either side and be itself protected by their bolt- and stone-projectors',[69] it is not unreasonable to suppose widely spaced towers housed the torsion machines capable of protecting them. Thus, because those smaller towers at Theisoa (Towers 2, 3, 5, 6, and 8) are widely spaced, it is conceivable that they too housed such machines. The larger towers, in order to protect the flatter gentler parts of the hill at a considerable distance from the walls, would simply have held more of them.

Further chronological clues are provided by the form and frequency of openings in the curtains—that is, the posterns and gateway. With three and probably four posterns, it is interesting to consider that, after Gortys, Theisoa contains the most posterns of all the Arkadian circuits comprising this study. While the fourth century BC saw a steady increase in the use of posterns, they became very common in Hellenistic circuits, where a large number of them were often included in the plan.[70] True, the three or four examples at Theisoa may not appear to be a 'large number', but, in relation to the overall size of the

---

[64] Winter (1971a: 87).   [65] Scranton (1941: 51).
[66] Scranton (1941: 69, 140).   [67] Winter (1971a: 167).
[68] Ober (1987: 572). These towers exceed 7 m on at least two sides, which, according to Lawrence (1979: 389), is a characteristic common to many towers unquestionably of Hellenistic date.
[69] Lawrence (1979: 386).   [70] Winter (1971a: 239).

circuit, it is a significant amount. Moreover, the fact that two were placed on the north—one in the circuit wall and one only *c.*80 m to the east in the north citadel wall—suggests they had an 'active' military function. In other words, care was taken to ensure that troops could sally forth either from the city itself, or from the separately fortified citadel—surely one northern passage would have been adequate if they were used only to access the countryside to the north. As a more or less standard overlap type, the South Gate is less chronologically informative, since, although these types become common in the Hellenistic period, they are seen already in the early fourth century BC circuits at Stymphalos and Mantineia, for example.

The construction of the curtain and even the layout of the circuit, especially the indented trace on the north-east side, are also chronologically valuable. While the use of headers, such as those at Theisoa, do appear by the fourth century BC, it is in the Hellenistic period that they become much more common, often occurring at regular intervals.[71] Furthermore, a general pattern in Hellenistic fortifications observed by Winter is the restriction of the length of circuits.[72] Indeed, compact and easily defendable sites—as exemplified by the compact circuit of Theisoa—become more common after the fourth century BC. Arguably the most conspicuous feature of the Theisoan defensive works is the indented trace. While the motivation for its construction specifically on the north-east side of the system has already been provided, it remains to determine what this feature can tell us about the chronology of the circuit as a whole.

The presence of an indented trace instead of towers was once taken as evidence of an early (probably pre-Persian Wars period) fortification circuit.[73] It was the work of Martin at ancient Gortys, however, that has demonstrated that some examples can indeed occur much later.[74] As is the case for all the chronological markers outlined, employing the indented trace to narrow down the date of the Theisoan circuit is valid only if 'we treat the device as only one among many factors to be weighed in arriving at an absolute date'.[75] In his admirable survey of examples of the indented trace in Greek fortifications, and using a number of characteristics, Winter establishes a criteria for establishing types, and, by association, approximate chronologies for this defensive feature. In short, three categories are presented: (1) systems where towers are regularly spaced but in which the occasional jog may be substituted for towers; (2) systems where towers and jogs are present, but infrequent; and (3), the rarest type, 'whole stretches of wall laid out in a series of relatively short faces separated by frequent flanks or jogs, without any intervening towers'.[76]

---

[71] Winter (1971a: 135).   [72] Winter (1971a: 58–9).
[73] e.g., this is the view held by Scranton (1941: 157).
[74] Martin (1947–8). For Gortys, see Part Two, Chapter 5, under Chronological Arguments.
[75] Winter (1971b: 413).   [76] Winter (1971b: 423).

Indeed, so rare is this type that Winter maintains that 'we shall, I believe, look in vain for a whole series of such jogs, without any intervening towers, of the type that we encountered at Gortys and Samiko'.[77] In fact, he needed to look only 60 km south-east of Samiko and 10 km south-west of Gortys to observe that the indented trace comprising the whole north-east wall at Theisoa is an example of his type 3.

Chronologically, this type of highly developed indented trace—with a succession of three or more jogs without intervening towers—stands at the end of an evolving sequence that witnessed simple, undeveloped forms (for example, Rhamnous) progress to an intermediate phase (for example, late Classical sections of the circuit at Gortys), before finally reaching its most advance form (for example, Hellenistic walls of Samiko).[78] Important for the present purposes, however, are the dates assigned to these phases. Basing his decision on comparisons with the developed examples, Winter would place this type in the Early Hellenistic period, specifically, between *c*.335 and *c*.260.[79] Because of the extreme rarity of the highly developed form of the indented trace, it cannot be a coincidence that the only three Peloponnesian examples come from sites in such close geographic proximity. It is almost certain, therefore, that some influence was passing between these sites. In which direction(s), however, is harder to say. Still, although the chronological range is too wide to be more precise, it is very possible that Theisoan military architects, familiar with this feature from nearby Gortys and/or Samiko, brought the initiative to their own creation atop Lavda Hill.

In summary, the external evidence provided by the ceramics, architecture, as well as the two inscriptions, when taken together, suggests that the hill of Lavda was inhabited perhaps as early as the early fourth century BC and that the site of Theisoa survived into the Late Hellenistic period (second/first century BC). On the other hand, the cumulative evidence provided by the walls themselves suggests that this site was not fortified until some time in the early Hellenistic period (*c*.325–275 BC).[80] Pausanias tells us that Theisoa was one of the *poleis* that participated in the synoikism of Megalopolis. This may be key to understanding this discrepancy.

If the decision to relocate to Megalopolis *c*.370 BC was implemented, then one might imagine the citizens of Theisoa leaving their homes to be redistributed among the new pan-Arkadian population there. With the failure of the

---

[77] Winter (1971b: 421). On the walls of Samiko, see Bisbee (1937).

[78] Winter (1971b: 414). Although Bisbee (1937: 535) would date the walls of Samiko to the fifth century BC, the later fourth century BC/Hellenistic period date proposed by Winter (1971a: 236–7; 1971b: 415, 424) is more plausible.

[79] Winter (1971b: 424).

[80] Jost agrees with the general opinion that the fortifications are late, probably belonging to the Hellenistic period, and she specifically suggests (1999: 196) that they were perhaps built in the third or second century BC.

great experiment and as the Arkadian Confederacy began to wane in the later part of the fourth and early third century BC, however, many of the Great City's inhabitants must have left to return to their ancestral homes. In this conceivable scenario, we might imagine the children and grandchildren of the original displaced Theisoans returning to their old home atop Lavda hill.[81] In the face of a constant Macedonian presence in the Peloponnese and perpetual Spartan aggression directed at Arkadia, the Theisoans of the late fourth and early third century BC arguably lived in more uncertain times then those who had left for Megalopolis. Accordingly, perhaps they decided it was time to keep pace with most of the other Greek *poleis* and finally construct a wall around their small city. After disassembling the derelict structures that had laid abandoned for generations, they incorporated the old architectural pieces into their new walls. Naturally the circuit was built with the features characteristic of the time, and, as such, we see in the style of coursed polygonal, large towers, a developed indented trace, and several posterns that the fortifications of Theisoa cumulatively reflect the composite architectural features attributable to the early Hellenistic period.

BIBLIOGRAPHY

Paus. 8.27.4, 8.38.9; Polyb. 16.17; Gell (1817: 87); Leake (1830: 2.18–19, 315–16); Boblaye (1836: 160); Ross (1841: 101); Curtius (1851: i. 358–9); Rangabé (1857: 79–80); Bursian (1862: ii. 234–5); Frazer (1898: iv. 386–8); Roy (1972b: 78); Goester et al. (1981, 2009); Feije et al. (1988); Feije (1989, 1993, 1994); Goester (1993, 1994, 1995, 2005); Papachatzis (1994: 349–50); Goester and van de Vrie (1998); Jost (1999: 196); Mattern (2010); Maher (2012a: 387–423).

---

[81] The idea that Theisoa must have been resettled sometime after the synoikism is discussed by Mattern (Goester et al. 2009: 200).

Appendix of Other Attested Fortified Arkadian *Poleis*

In addition to the *poleis* described in the previous chapters and catalogue, there is evidence to suggest that other fortified *poleis* existed in Arkadia during the Classical and Hellenistic periods (if not earlier). Yet the study of these communities is beset by a number of problems that lie outside the scope of the present work—for example, when fortifications are no longer visible at those sites that are known from the ancient sources (or early modern reports) to have been fortified. Personal observation is a significant element in the methodology employed in this work, and sites in which the author did not personally inspect the remains of the fortifications were excluded.[1] Similarly excluded from the main body of work were sites otherwise known from the historical record but that have not been securely identified, or whose *polis* status is unsubstantiated. In the interest of comprehensiveness, however, the excluded sites that may have been *poleis* and that were fortified, are briefly presented in this Appendix.[2]

The letter (A, B, or C) immediately following the heading for the entry indicates the reasons for its exclusion from the main body of work: A: known fortified *poleis* sites at which no remains of the fortifications were observed by the author; B: fortified sites whose *polis* status is likely, but uncertain; C: sites known to have been fortified, but whose identification/location is uncertain.

1. Bouphagion (B/C)

The site of Bouphagion is perhaps to be associated with the remains at Paliokastro, just across the Alpheios from ancient Theisoa (Lavda), where there are remains of inner and outer fortification circuit employing both rectangular and round towers. While Pausanias (5.7.1, 8.26.8, 8.27.17) mentions the river Bouphagos, there is no mention of the community Bouphagion in the ancient historical record, and it is not certain whether it was ever a *polis* or merely a fort. On the fortifications at the site, see Charneux and Ginouves (1956).

2. Brenthe (C)

Although the exact location of ancient Brenthe has not been found, Pausanias' itinerary (8.28.7) suggests that the site should be sought near modern Karitaina.

---

[1] For reasons discussed in Part Two, Chapter 9, Megalopolis is the only exception.

[2] For a detailed summary of the evidence for the *polis* status of these communities, see Nielsen (2002: 549–99). I have excluded from the Appendix the communities of Mainalos, Lykoa, and Trikolonoi, because so little is known about them, including their exact location and *polis* status. Nonakris and Helisson are excluded because there is no evidence that they were fortified. I have also excluded from consideration Lousoi and Lykosoura, which, although possibly *poleis*, were primarily concerned with the administration of their associated sanctuary.

Pausanias (8.28.7) refers to the settlement as a *polis*, but this is the only mention of it in the ancient sources. If the site stood near Karitaina, it is hard to imagine that such a strategic place would not have been fortified (Feije 1994: 57).

3. Eutaia (A)

Eutaia is situated in the southern part of the Asean plain near the modern village of Lianos. Xenophon (*Hell.* 6.5.12) tells us that the *polis* of Eutaia was fortified, although it is not clear if he is referring to the lower city or the acropolis. If he is referring to the acropolis walls, his description may be reconciled with Loring's observation (1895: 51) of an inner and outer wall atop the summit of Agios Konstantinos adjacent to the site. Despite the rough plan accompanying Loring's account, I could find no trace of either wall on this hill. For more information on Eutaia, see Leake (1830: iii. 31), Loring (1895: 50–1), Frazer (1898: iv. 304), Pikoulas (1988a: 70–6), and Nielsen (2002: 554–5).

4. Heraia (A)

The site of Heraia lies in western Arkadia on a plateau near the confluence of the Alpheios and Ladon Rivers. Although the site was certainly fortified, it is so large and overgrown that I was unable to perceive any remains of the fortifications. Remains of the fortifications were observed, however, by Curtius (1851: 365–6) and Frazer (1898: iv. 295); although by the time of Frazer's visit very few remains were visible. On the fortifications, see Bölte (1913: 414), Meyer (1939a: 106), Jost (1985: 73, 76), Pritchett (1989: 39), and Sarantakes (1993: 74).

5. Kaphyai (A)

Ancient Kaphyai was located just north-west of Orchomenos, in the plain immediately south of modern Chotoussa. The existence of city walls is implied by Polybius (4.12.13), but nothing of the walls is visible in the plain today. Traces of the fortifications were, however, observed previously by many, including Leake (1830: iii. 103), Curtius (1851: i. 226), Rangabé (1857: 112–15), Bursian (1862: ii. 206), Hiller von Gaertringen and Lattermann (1911: 21), Papandreou (1920: 114–20), Pritchett (1969: 124), Howell (1970: 81), Jost (1985: 109–13), Sarantakes (1993: 29–31), and Papachatzis (1994: 228, 266–8).

6. Kynaitha (A/C)

Although it is likely that the settlement of Kynaitha stood on or near the modern city of Kalavryta, the precise identification of its location has not been substantiated. The city's fortifications are mentioned by Polybius (4.18). It is possible that the high rocky hill east of the modern city was the ancient acropolis, and, while no remains of fortifications have been found there, they may lie buried beneath the later medieval castle. For more information on Kynaitha and the Kalavryta area, see Gell (1817: 131), Dodwell (1819: ii. 447), Leake (1830: ii. 109–12, iii. 179), Curtius (1851: i. 382–4), Bursian (1862: ii. 266), Wyse (1865: ii. 182–6), Frazer (1898: iv. 260–1), Meyer (1939a: 107–10), Howell (1970: 96), Jost (1985: 51–3), Pikoulas (1981), Papachatzis (1994: 247–9), and Nielsen (2002: 563).

7. Methydrion (A)

Methydrion lies on a flat hill, *c*.12 km due east of ancient Theisoa (Karkalou). I searched among the thick overgrowth along the edge of the entire hill and found no traces of the fortifications. While accounts provided by early travellers and later scholars confirm the site was fortified, it is uncertain whether this fortified hill was strictly an acropolis in the traditional use of the word, or whether there was any substantial intramural habitation. Without providing any evidence, Jost (1999: 195) maintains that the site is of the acropolis type and that the walls date to the early fourth century BC. Early descriptions of parts of the fortifications are provided by Leake (1830: ii. 57), Ross (1841: 116), Curtius (1851: i. 310), Rangabé (1857: 110), Bursian (1862: ii. 230), Frazer (1898: iv. 362), Hiller von Gaertringen and Lattermann (1911: 31–2), and Meyer (1932: 1388). See also Gell (1817: 126), Boblaye (1836: 150–1), Scranton (1941: 164), Leake (1846: 201), Jost (1985: 213–16; 1999: 195), Sarantakes (1993: 69–70), Papachatzis (1994: 326–9), Nielsen (2002: 576–8), and Kollias (2003).

8. Oresthasion (A/C)

The site of Oresthasion was probably located at or very near the modern village of Anemodouro, in the southern part of the Megalopolis basin. Although I could find no trace of this wall when I visited the site, Pikoulas (1988: 102 ff.) apparently observed traces of an acropolis circuit located atop the hill of Groumourou adjacent to the village. No remains of a lower city wall have been discovered. For the various accounts of the area and alternatives to Anemodouro for the location of the site, see Gell (1817: 137), Leake (1830: ii. 45, 319; 1846: 247–8), Bursian (1862: ii. 227), Loring (1895: 27–30), Frazer (1898: iv. 413), Meyer (1939c), Howell (1970: 101), Jost (1973: 245–6), Nielsen (2002: 581–2), and Frederiksen (2011: 176).

9. Pallantion (A)

The site of ancient Pallantion is centred around a modest hill near the western edge of the Tegean plain about 7 km south-west of modern Tripolis. That the small acropolis was fortified is implied by Pausanias, who tells us that 'in ancient time they used the hill above the city as a fortress' (8.44.5). Unspecified ancient ruins were noted by Gell (1817: 136), Leake (1830: i. 117–18), Boblaye (1836: 146), and Bursian (1862: ii. 224), while traces of the fortifications specifically were observed by Ross (1841: 62–3), Curtius (1851: i. 263), and Frazer (1898: iv. 420–1). For further information on Pallantion and surrounding area, see Meyer (1949), Romaios (1958), Howell (1970: 94), Jost (1985: 197–9), Sarantakes (1993: 35–6), Papachatzis (1994: 373–5), and Nielsen (2002: 583–4).

10. Tegea (A)

The site of ancient Tegea is located roughly in the centre of the southern half of Arkadia's great eastern plain. The city walls of Tegea are mentioned by Xenophon (*Hell.* 6.5–8.9) and Diodorus (12.79.3), and implied by Thucydides (5.6.2). Trial trenches excavated in the early 1890s revealed traces of the wall in four places, and the walls of Tegea were apparently of mudbrick on a stone foundation

(Bérard 1892: 548). Scholars from the Norwegian Institute at Athens continue to search for the exact line of fortifications, but note that the walls themselves, even in the light of geophysical survey, remain strangely elusive (K. Ødegård, pers. com.). For most recent scholarship on Tegea, see Garlan (1974: 25, n. 2, 26, n. 3, 78, 149), Voyatzis (1990), Sarantakes (1993: 31–5), Papachatzis (1994: 404–9), Nielsen (2002: 592–6), and Ødegård (2005).

11. Thaliades (A/B/C)

The site of Thaliades lies on the north side of the Ladon, west of ancient Halous, in the vicinity of modern Vachlia. Although Meyer (1939a: 75–8) observed traces of a fortification wall surrounding the top of a small hill at Thaliades, because the site is completely overgrown today I did not observe any remains of the circuit. For other remains in the area and alternatives to Vachlia for the location of the site, see Leake (1830: ii. 73; 1846: 228), Curtius (1851: i. 374 ff.), Rangabé (1857: 68–9), Levi (1971: 432, n. 178), Jost (1985: 45), and Nielsen (2002: 597).

12. Thelphousa (A)

Ancient Thelphousa is located on a twin-peaked hill on the east bank of the Ladon River, just west of the modern village of Melidonion and north of the hamlet of Toubitsi. The city was certainly fortified, although I was unable to distinguish any traces of the walls that were observed in the nineteenth century by Curtius (1851: i. 371), Bursian (1862: ii. 259), and Frazer (1898: iv. 286). For further descriptions and more information about the site, see Gell (1817: 120), Leake (1830: ii. 98), Meyer (1934; 1939a: 85–7), Lemerle (1939), Jost (1985: 60–70; 1986), Pritchett (1989: 38), Sarantakes (1993: 75), Papachatzis (1994: 276–80), and Nielsen (2002: 597–9).

13. Torthyneion (A/C)

It is probable, although not certain, that ancient Torthyneion is located on Kolinos Hill, about 1 km north-east of the small village of Lasta.[3] Although Pikoulas (1990–1a) apparently observed traces of two fortification walls—one around the summit, and another lower down—I could not perceive the remains of either. For descriptions of the area and alternatives to Kolinos Hill for the location of the site, see Meyer (1936b; 1939a: 35–8), Howell (1970: 99–100), and Nielsen (2002: 600).

14. Trapezous (A/C)

The exact location of ancient Trapezous within the Megalopolis Basin is uncertain. Based on Pausanias' vague description (8.29.1), several candidates have been proposed, including at or near Karitaina (Dodwell 1819: ii. 2.381; Boblaye 1836: 164) above the modern village of Mavria (Leake 1830: ii. 292–3; Bather and Yorke 1892–3: 227), and modern Kyparissia (Karapanagiotou 2005). While the site at Kyparissia is the only one of these locations known to have been fortified, I was nonetheless unable to distinguish any remains of the city wall at the site.

---

[3] On my visit to the site I met the mayor of Lasta, and, although he was aware of the ancient remains on Kolinos Hill, neither he nor the other villagers had ever heard of ancient Torthyneion.

Bibliography

Adam, J.-P. (1982). *L'Architecture militaire grecque*. Paris: Picard.

Aldenhoven, F. (1841). *Itineraire descriptif de l'Attique et du Péloponèse, avec cartes et plans topographiques*. Athens: Chez Adolphe Nast, Libraire.

Alevridis, S., and Melfi, M. (2005). 'New Archeological and Topographical Observations on the Sanctuary of Asklepios in Alipheira (Arcadia)', in E. Østby (ed.), *Ancient Arcadia. Papers from the Third International Seminar on Ancient Arcadia, Held at the Norwegian Institute at Athens, 7–10 May 2002*. Athens: Norwegian Institute at Athens, 273–84.

Anavasi (2003). Χελμός – Βουραϊκός. Mt. Chelmos – Vouraikos [map]. 1:50,000. Topo50, Peloponnese, 8.2, Anavasi Maps and Guides (Athens).

Anavasi (2007). Ορεινή Κορινθία. *Upland Corinth* [map]. 1:50,000. Topo50, Peloponnese, 8.3, Anavasi Maps and Guides (Athens).

Anavasi (2008). Μαίναλο. Mt. Menalo [map]. 1:50,000. Topo50, Peloponnese, 8.5, Anavasi Maps and Guides (Athens).

Badian, E. (1967). 'Agis III', *Hermes* 95. Bd, H. 2, pp. 170–92.

Baker-Penoyre, J. (1902). 'Pheneus and the Pheneatike', *Journal of Hellenistic Studies*, 22: 28–40.

Bakke, J. (2010). 'Den greske bystatens geohistoriske marginer: Om videreføringen av norsk landskapsarkeologi i Tegea 2008–2012', *Klassisk Forum*, 2012/1: 47–60.

Bather, A. G., and Yorke, V. W. (1892–3). 'Excavations on the Probable Sites of Basilis and Bathos', *Journal of Hellenic Studies*, 13: 227–31.

Bérard, V. (1892). 'Tégée et la Tégéatide', *Bulletin de correspondance hellénique*, 16: 529–49.

Bisbee, H. L. (1937). 'Samikon', *Hesperia*, 6: 525–38.

Blouet, G.-A. (1833). *Expédition scientifique de Morée ordonnée par le Gouvernement Français: Architecture, Sculptures, Inscriptions et Vues du Péloponèse, des Cyclades et de l'Attique, mesurées, dessinées, recueillies et publiées par* Abel Blouet, architecte, directeur de la Section d'Architecture et de Sculture de l'Expédition, ancien pensionnaire de l'Académie de France à Rome; Amable Ravoisié et Achille Poirot, architectes; Félix Trézel, peintre d'histoire, et Frédéric de Gournay, littérateur. Deuxième volume. Paris: Firmin Didot.

Blum, G., and Plassart, A. (1914). 'Orchomène d'Arcadie. Fouilles de 1913. Topographie, architecture, sculpture, menus objets', *Bulletin de correspondance hellénique*, 38: 71–88.

Boblaye, M. E. P. (1836). *Expédition scientifique de Morée. Recherches géographiques sur les ruines de la Morée*. Paris: Levrault.

Bölte, F. (1912a). 'Halus', *Realencyclopädie der Classischen Altertumswissenschaft*, 7/2: 2286.

Bölte, F. (1912b). 'Gortys', *Realencyclopädie der Classischen Altertumswissenschaft*, 7/2: 1671–3.

Bölte, F. (1913). 'Heraia', *Realencyclopädie der Classischen Altertumswissenschaft*, 8: 407–16.

Bölte, F. (1938). 'Pheneos', *Realencyclopädie der Classischen Altertumswissenschaft*, 19: 1963–80.

Borgeaud, P. (1988). *The Cult of Pan in Ancient Greece*, trans. K. Atlass and J. Redfield. Chicago: University of Chicago Press.

Borrelli, L. V. (1976). 'Orchomenos (Kalpali)', in R. Stillwell (ed.), *The Princeton Encyclopedia of Classical Sites*. Princeton: Princeton University Press, 653–4.

Bousquet, J. (1954). 'Variétés: Inscriptions de la Terrasse du Temple et de la région Nord du sanctuaire Robert Flacelière, Fouilles de Delphes, t. III (Épigraphie), fasc. 4, nos. 87 à 275', *Bulletin de correspondance hellénique*, 78: 427–37.

Bradeen, D. W. (1966). 'Inscriptions from Nemea', *Hesperia*, 35: 320–30.

Buckley, T. (1996). *Aspects of Greek History 750–323 BC: A Source-Based Approach*. London: Routledge.

Bursian, C. (1862). *Geographie von Griechenland*. Leipzig: Teubner.

Bury, J. B. (1898). 'The Double City of Megalopolis', *Journal of Hellenic Studies*, 18: 15–22.

Callmer, C. (1943). *Studien zur Geschichte Arkadiens bis zur Gründung des arkadischen Bundes*. Lund: Gleerupska.

Camp, J. M. (2000). 'Walls and the Polis', in P. Flensted-Jansen, T. H. Nielsen, and L. Rubinstein (eds), *Polis and Politics: Studies in Ancient Greek History Presented to Mogens Herman Hansen on his Sixtieth Birthday, August 20, 2000*. Copenhagen: Museum Tusculanum Press, 41–57.

Charneux, R., and Ginouves, P. (1956). 'Reconnaissance en Arcadie: Fortifications de Paliokastro, Saint-Nicolas et Helleniko', *Bulletin de correspondance hellénique*, 80: 522–46.

Clark, W. G. (1858). *Peloponnesus: Notes of Study and Travel*. London: J. W. Parker and Son.

Cooper, F. A. (1972). 'Topographical Notes from Southwest Arcadia', *Athens Annals of Archaeology*, 3: 359–67.

Cooper, F. A. (1976). 'Phigalia', in R. Stillwell (ed.), *The Princeton Encyclopedia of Classical Sites*. Princeton: Princeton University Press, 703.

Cooper, F. A. (1996). *The Temple of Apollo Bassitas* (vols 1, 3, and 4). Princeton: American School of Classical Studies at Athens.

Cooper, F. A., and Myers, J. W. (1981). 'Reconnaissance of a Greek Mountain City', *Journal of Field Archaeology*, 8: 123–34.

Corso, A. (2005). 'The Triad of Zeus Soter, Artemis Soteria and Megalopolis at Megalopolis', in E. Østby (ed.), *Ancient Arcadia: Papers from the Third International Seminar on Ancient Arcadia, Held at the Norwegian Institute at Athens, 7–10 May 2002*. Athens: Norwegian Institute at Athens, 225–34.

Coutsinas, N. (2013). *Défenses crétoises: Fortifications urbaines et défense du territoire en Crète aux époques classique et hellénistique*. Paris: Publications de la Sorbonne.

Cracolici, V. (2005). 'Pottery from the Norwegian Arcadia Survey: Preliminary Report', in E. Østby (ed.), *Ancient Arcadia: Papers from the Third International Seminar on Ancient Arcadia, Held at the Norwegian Institute at Athens, 7–10 May 2002*. Athens: Norwegian Institute at Athens, 123–30.

Cramer, J. A. (1828). *A Geographical and Historical Description of Ancient Greece: with a Map, and a Plan of Athens.* Oxford: Clarendon Press.

Curtius, E. (1851). *Peloponnesos, eine historisch-geographische Beschreibung der Halbinsel.* Berlin: Gotha Perthes.

Daux, G. (1959). 'Chronique des fouilles', *Bulletin de correspondance hellénique*, 83: 567–793.

Demand, N. H. (1990). *Urban Relocation in Archaic and Classical Greece: Flight and Consolidation.* London: University of Oklahoma Press.

Dodwell, E. (1819). *A Classical and Topographical Tour through Greece, during the Years 1801, 1805, and 1806.* London: Cambridge University Press.

Dodwell, E. (1834). *Views and Descriptions of Cyclopean or Pelasgian Remains in Greece and Italy.* London: A. Richter.

Dogan, M., and Papamarinopoulos, M. (2003). 'Geophysical Prospection of a City Wall by Multi-Electrode Resistivity Image Survey at Asea (Southern Greece)', *Archaeological Prospection*, 10: 241–8.

Ducrey, P. (1995). 'La Muraille est-elle un élément constitutive d'une cité', in M. H. Hansen (ed.), *Sources for the Ancient Greek City-State*. Acts of the Copenhagen Polis Centre 2. Det Kongelige Danske Videnskabernes Selskab, Historisk-filosofiske Meddelelser 72. Copenhagen: Munksgaard, 245–56.

Erath, G. (1999). 'Archäologische Funde im Becken von Pheneos', in K. Tausend (ed.), *Pheneos und Lousoi: Untersuchungen zu Geschichte und Topographie Nordostarkadiens*, Grazer Altertumskundische Studien 5. Frankfurt am Main: P. Lang, 199–237.

Feije, J.J. (1989). 'Lavda: The 1988 Campaign', *Newsletter Netherlands School of Archaeology at Athens*, 2: 7–15.

Feije, J. J. (1993). 'Lavda: History of the Site', *Pharos*. 1: 183–99.

Feije, J. J. (1994). 'Lavda: The Site, the Walls', *Pharos*, 2: 49–89.

Feije, J. J, Goester, Y. C., and te Riele , G. J. M. J. (1988). 'The Research of an Ancient Settlement on Lavda-Hill', *Newsletter Netherlands School of Archaeology at Athens*, 1: 28–38.

Fields, N. (2006). *Ancient Greek Fortifications, 500–300 BC.* Oxford: Osprey.

Forsén, B. (2003). 'Chapter VIIc: The Archaic–Hellenistic Periods-Conclusions', in *The Asea Valley Survey: An Arcadian Mountain Valley from the Paleolithic Period until Modern Times*. Sävedalen: Paul Åströms Förlag, 247–71.

Forsén, J., and Forsén, B. (1997). 'The *Polis* of Asea: A Case Study of How Archaeology Can Expand our Knowledge of the History of a *Polis*', in T. H. Nielsen (ed.), *Yet More Studies in the Ancient Greek Polis*. Papers from the Copenhagen Polis Centre 4. *Historia* Einzelschriften 117. Stuttgart: Franz Steiner Verlag, 163–76.

Forsén, J., and Forsén, B. (2003). *The Asea Valley Survey: An Arcadian Mountain Valley from the Paleolithic Period until Modern Times*. Sävedalen: Paul Åströms Förlag.

Forsén, J., Forsén, B., and Karlsson, L. (2005). 'Recent Research Concerning the Walls at Asea', in E. Østby (ed.), *Ancient Arcadia: Papers from the Third International Seminar on Ancient Arcadia, Held at the Norwegian Institute at Athens, 7–10 May 2002.* Athens: Norwegian Institute at Athens, 307–20.

Forsén, J., Forsén, B., and Østby, E. (1999). 'The Sanctuary of Agios Elias—its Significance, and its Relations to Surrounding Sanctuaries and Settlement Sites', in T. H. Nielsen and J. Roy (eds), *Defining Ancient Arkadia*. Acts of the Copenhagen

Polis Centre 6. Det Kongelige Danske Videnskabernes Selskab, Historisk-filosofiske Meddelelser 78. Copenhagen: Munksgaard, 169–91.

Fougères, G. (1890). 'Fouilles de Manitnée. I. L'Enceinte et ses environs', *Bulletin de correspondance hellénique*, 14: 65–90.

Fougères, G. (1898). *Mantinée et L'Arcadie Orientale*. Paris: A. Fontemoing.

Frazer, J. G. (1898). *Pausanias' Description of Greece*. 6 vols. London: W. Heinemann.

Frederiksen, R. (2011). *Greek City Walls of the Archaic Period*. Oxford Monographs on Classical Archaeology. Oxford: Oxford University Press.

Gardner, P. (1963). *Catalogue of Greek Coins in the British Museum: Peloponnesus (Excluding Corinth)*, ed. R. S. Poole. Bologna: A Forni.

Garlan, Y. (1974). *Recherches de Poliorcétique Grecque*. Athens: École française d'Athènes.

Gauthier, P. (1993). 'Les Cités hellénistiques', in M. H. Hansen (ed.), *The Ancient Greek City-State*. Acts of the Copenhagen Polis Centre 1. Det Kongelige Danske Videnskabernes Selskab, Historisk-filosofiske Meddelelser 67. Copenhagen: Det Kongelige Danske Videnskabernes Selskab, 197–210.

Gavrili, M. (1976). 'Alipheira', in R. Stillwell (ed.), *The Princeton Encyclopedia of Classical Sites*. Princeton: Princeton University Press, 41.

Gehrke, H. J. (1986). *Jenseits von Athen und Sparta: Das Dritte Griechenland und seine Staatenwelt*. Munich: Beck.

Gell, W. (1817). *Itinerary of the Morea: Being a Description of the Routes of that Peninsula*. London: Rodwell and Martin.

Gell, W. (1823). *Narrative of a Journey in the Morea*. London: Longman, Hurst, Rees, Orme, and Brown.

Gell, W. (1831). *Probestücke von Städten mauern des alten Griechenlands*. Berlin: J. G. Cotta.

Giannakopoulos, G., Kissas, K., Lehner, M., Scherrer, P., Spyranti, Z., and Tausand, K. (2012). 'Pheneos 2011: Bericht zur ersten Grabungs- und Surveykampagne', *Jahreshefte Des Österreichischen Archäologischen Institutes*, 81: 51–65.

Ginouvés, R. (1955). 'Chronique des fouilles en Grèce en 1954: Gortys (Arcadie), l'établissement thermal', *Bulletin de correspondance hellénique*, 79: 331–4.

Ginouvés, R. (1956). 'Chronique des fouilles en Grèce en 1955: Gortys (Arcadie), la terrasse du temple (sanctuaire du bas)', *Bulletin de correspondance hellénique*, 80: 399–401.

Goester, Y. C. (1993). 'The Landscape of Lavda', *Pharos*, 1: 201–7.

Goester, Y. C. (1994). 'Lavda: Outside the Circuit Walls', *Pharos* 2: 39–48.

Goester, Y. C. (1995). 'Lavda: The Coins', *Pharos*, 3: 131–9.

Goester, Y. C. (2005). 'Lavda: The Architectural Remains', in E. Østby (ed.), *Ancient Arcadia: Papers from the Third International Seminar on Ancient Arcadia, Held at the Norwegian Institute at Athens, 7–10 May 2002*. Athens: Norwegian Institute at Athens, 321–7.

Goester, Y. C. (2010). 'Theisoa in Arcadia: Investigations by the Netherlands Institute at Athens 1985–2007', delivered at the Annual Open Meeting of the Netherlands Institute at Athens, 18 March.

Goester, Y. C., Grieb, V., and Mattern, T. (2009). 'Theisoa (Lavda): Vorbericht über die Kampagne 2007', *Pharos*, 15: 193–203.

Goester, Y. C., te Riele, G. J. M. J., and Vermeulen Windsant, C. (1981). 'Lavda 1978', *Bulletin de correspondance hellénique*, 105: 651–5.

Goester, Y. C., and van de Vrie, D. M. (1998). 'Lavda: The Excavations 1986–1988', *Pharos*, 6: 119–78.

Gourley, B., and Williams, H. (2005). 'The Fortifications of Ancient Stymphalos', *Mouseion*, 5: 213–59.

Guettel Cole, S. (1995). 'Coins, Mints, and the *Polis*', in M. H. Hansen (ed.), *Sources for the Ancient Greek City-State*. Acts of the Copenhagen Polis Centre 2. Det Kongelige Danske Videnskabernes Selskab, Historisk-filosofiske Meddelelser 72. Copenhagen: Munksgaard, 292–325.

Hansen, M. H. (1993). 'The *Polis* as a Citizen-State', in M. H. Hansen (ed.), *The Ancient Greek City-State*. Acts of the Copenhagen Polis Centre 1. Det Kongelige Danske Videnskabernes Selskab, Historisk-filosofiske Meddelelser 67. Copenhagen: Munksgaard, 7–29.

Hansen, M. H. (1994). '*Poleis* and City-States, 600–323 B.C.: A Comprehensive Research Programme', in D. Whitehead (ed.), *From Political Architecture to Stephanus Byzantius: Sources for the Ancient Greek Polis*. Papers from the Copenhagen Polis Centre 1. *Historia* Einzelschriften 87. Stuttgart: Franz Steiner Verlag, 9–17.

Hansen, M. H. (1995). '*Kome*. A Study in How the Greeks Designated and Classified Settlements Which Were not *Poleis*', in M. H. Hansen and K. Raaflaub (eds), *Studies in the Ancient Greek Polis*. Papers from the Copenhagen Polis Centre 2. Historia Einzelschriften 95. Stuttgart: Franz Steiner Verlag, 45–81.

Hansen, M. H. (2000). 'The Concepts of City-State and City-State Culture', in M. H. Hansen (ed.), *A Comparative Study of Thirty City-State Cultures: An Investigation conducted by the Copenhagen Polis Centre*, The Royal Danish Academy of Sciences and Letters, Historisk-filosofiske Skrifter 21. Copenhagen: Kongelige Danske Videnskabernes Selskab, 11–34.

Hansen, M. H., and Fischer-Hansen, T. (1994). 'Monumental Political Architecture in Archaic and Classical Greek *Poleis*: Evidence and Historical Significance', in D. Whitehead (ed.), *From Political Architecture to Stephanus Byzantius: Sources for the Ancient Greek Polis*. Papers from the Copenhagen Polis Centre 1. Historia Einzelschriften 87. Stuttgart: Franz Steiner Verlag, 23–90.

Head, B. V. (1963). *Historia Numorum: A Manual of Greek Numismatics. Second Edition*. Oxford: Clarendon Press.

Hellenic Ministry of Culture (2007a). 'Alipheira' <http://odysseus.culture.gr/h/3/eh352.jsp?obj_id=2634> (accessed 18 January 2010).

Hellenic Ministry of Culture (2007b). 'Orchomenos at Arcadia' <http://odysseus.culture.gr/h/3/eh352.jsp?obj_id=2634> (accessed 12 February 2010).

Hiller von Gaertringen, F. F. (1915). 'Stymphalos', *Mitteilungen des deutschen Archäologischen Instituts Athenische Abteilung*, 40: 72–91.

Hiller von Gaertringen, F. F., and Lattermann, H. (1911). *Arkadische Forschungen*. Berlin: K. Akademie der Wissenschaften.

Hodkinson, H., and Hodkinson, S. (1981). 'Mantineia and the Mantinike: Settlement and Society in a Greek Polis', *Annual of the British School at Athens*, 76: 239–96.

Holmberg, E. J. (1944). *The Swedish Excavations at Asea in Arcadia*. Lund: C. W. K. Gleerup.

Hope Simpson, R., and Dickinson, O. (1979). *A Gazetteer of Aegean Civilisation in the Bronze Age*. Göteborg: Paul Åströms Förlag.

Hornblower, S. (1990). 'When Was Megalopolis Founded?', *Annual of the British School at Athens*, 85: 70–7.

Howell, R. (1970). 'A Survey of Eastern Arcadia in Prehistory', *Annual of the British School at Athens*, 65: 79–127.

Hunt, P. (1998). *Slaves, Warfare, and Ideology in the Greek Historians*. Cambridge: Cambridge University Press.

Jeffery, L. H. (1976). *Archaic Greece: The City-States c.700–500*. New York: St Martin's Press.

Jost, M. (1973). 'Pausanias en Mégalopolitide', *Revue des études anciennes*, 75: 241–67.

Jost, M. (1985). *Sanctuaires et cultes d'Arcadie*, Études Péloponnésiennes 9. Paris: J. Vrin.

Jost, M. (1986). 'Thelpousa de l'Arcadie en 1938–1939', *Bulletin de correspondance hellénique*, 110: 633–45.

Jost, M. (1994). 'The Distribution of Sanctuaries in Civic Space in Arkadia', in S. E. Alcock and R. Osborne (eds), *Placing the Gods: Sanctuaries and Sacred Space in Ancient Greece*. Oxford: Oxford University Press, 217–30.

Jost, M. (1999). 'Les Schemas de peuplement de l'Arcadie aux époques archaïque et classique', in T. H. Nielsen and J. Roy (eds), *Defining Ancient Arkadia*. Acts of the Copenhagen Polis Centre 6. Det Kongelige Danske Videnskabernes Selskab, Historisk-filosofiske Meddelelser 78. Copenhagen: Munksgaard, 192–247.

Kagan, D. (2003). *The Peloponnesian War*. New York: Viking.

Karapanagiotou, A. V. (2005). 'Preliminary Notices on the Discovery of a Planned, Classical Town near Kyparissia, Gortynia', in E. Østby (ed.), *Ancient Arcadia: Papers from the Third International Seminar on Ancient Arcadia, Held at the Norwegian Institute at Athens, 7–10 May 2002*. Athens: Norwegian Institute at Athens, 331–50.

Kirsten, E., and Kraiker, W. (1967). *Griechenlandkunde*. Heidelberg: C. Winter Universitätsverlag.

Kissas, K. (2011). 'Neue Forschungen in der antiken Stadt Pheneos/Pelopponnes', *Jahreshefte des Österreichischen Archäologischen Institutes*, 80: 155–6.

Kissas, K. (2013). 'Pheneos', in K. Kissas (ed.), *Ancient Corinthia: From Prehistoric to the End of Antiquity*. AthensL Foinakas Publications, 139–45.

Kissas, K., Lehner, M., and Scherrer, P. (2014). 'Pheneos 2012 und 2013: Bericht über die zweite und dritte Grabungs- und Surveykampagne', *Jahreshefte des Österreichischen Archäologischen Institutes*, 83: 133–56.

Kollias, A. N. (2003). *Methydrion: The History of an Ancient City of Arcadia*. Athens: Athena Press.

Lattermann, H. (1913). 'Nestane und das Argon Pedion', *Archäologischer Anzeiger*, 28: 395–428.

Lattermann, H. (1914). 'Sitzung vom 9. Juni 1914', *Archäologischer Anzeiger*, 29: 100–10.

Lauter, H. (2005). 'Megalopolis: Ausgrabungen auf der Agora 1991-2002', in E. Østby (ed.), *Ancient Arcadia: Papers from the Third International Seminar on Ancient Arcadia, Held at the Norwegian Institute at Athens, 7–10 May 2002*. Athens: Norwegian Institute at Athens, 235–48.

Lawrence, A. W. (1979). *Greek Aims in Fortification*. Oxford: Clarendon Press.

Le Bas, P., and Reinach, S. (1888). *Voyage Archéologique en Gréce et en Asie Mineure*. Paris: Firmin-Didot et Cie.

Leake, W. M. (1830). *Travels in the Morea: With a Map and Plans*. Amsterdam: J. Murray.

Leake, W. M. (1846). *Peloponnesiaca: A Supplement to Travels in the Moréa*. Amsterdam: A. M. Hakkert.

Lemerle, P. (1939). 'Chronique des fouilles et découvertes archéologiques en Grèce en 1939: Thelpousa', *Bulletin de correspondance hellénique*, 39: 301.

Levi, P. (1971). *Pausanias' Guide to Greece*, ii. *Southern Greece*. Translation and Commentary. London: Penguin.

Lolos, Y. A. (2011). *Land of Sikyon: Archaeology and History of a Greek City-State*. Hesperia supplements 39. Princeton: American School of Classical Studies at Athens.

Loring, W. (1892). 'The Walls and Internal Topography', in *Excavations at Megalopolis 1890–91*. The Society for the Promotion of Hellenic Studies: Supplementary Papers, No. 1. London: Macmillan, 106–21.

Loring, W. (1895). 'Some Ancient Routes in the Peloponnese', *Journal of Hellenic Studies*, 15: 25–89.

McAlister, M. H. (1976). 'Psophis', in R. Stillwell (ed.), *The Princeton Encyclopedia of Classical Sites*. Princeton: Princeton University Press, 741.

McNicoll, A. W. (1997). *Hellenistic Fortifications: From the Aegean to the Euphrates*. Oxford: Clarendon Press.

Maher, M. (2012a). 'The Fortifications of Arcadian Poleis in the Classical and Hellenistic Periods', Ph.D. dissertation, University of British Columbia Vancouver.

Maher, M. (2012b). 'From Pausanias to Dodwell: A Grand Tour of Ancient Stymphalos', in L. Mulvin (ed.), *Orientalism and Anglo-Irish Scholarship 1740—1810 in the Gennadius Library, Athens. Symposium 4th June, 2010, Held at Irish Institute of Hellenic Studies, Athens*. In collaboration with School of Art History, UCD, Gennadius Library, Athens and the Irish Institute of Hellenic Studies, Athens.

Maher, M. (2014). 'A New Look at the Fortifications of Arkadian Gortys', *Mediations on the Diversity of the Built Environment in the Aegean Basin: A Colloquium in Honor of Frederick E. Winter*. Hosted by the Canadian Institute in Greece, Athens, Greece, 29–30 June 2012. Publications of the Canadian Institute in Greece, Publications de l'Institut canadien en Grèce No. 8. Athens, 265–84.

Maher, M. (2015a). 'In Defense of Arkadia: The City as a Fortress', in A. Kemezi (ed.), *Urban Dreams and Realities in Antiquity: Remains and Representations of the Ancient City*. Leiden: Brill, 15–45.

Maher, M. (2015b). 'Mapping Mistakes: The Cartographic Confusion of Ancient Kleitor', *Studies in Art and Civilization*, 19: 85–106.

Maher, M. (forthcoming). 'Archaeology of the Arkadian League', *Internationales Symposium: Arkadien im Altertum Geschichte und Kultur einer antiken Gebirgslandschaft. Ancient Arcadia—History and Culture of a Mountainous Region. University of Graz, Graz, Austria, 11–13 February 2016*.

Maher, M., and Mowat, A. (forthcoming). 'The Defense Network in the *Chora* of Mantineia', *Hesperia*.

Marsden, E. W. (1969). *Greek and Roman Artillery. Historical Development*. Oxford: Clarendon Press.

Martin, R. (1944). 'Sur deux enceintes d'Arcadie', *Revue archeologique*, 21: 97–114.

Martin, R. (1947–8). 'Les Enceintes de Gortys d'Arcadie', *Bulletin de correspondance hellénique*, 71–2: 81–147.

Martin, R., and Metzger, H. (1940–1). 'Chronique des fouilles et découvertes archéologiques en Grèce en 1940 et 1941: Gortys (Arcadie)', *Bulletin de correspondance hellénique*, 64–5: 274–86.

Martin, R., and Metzger, H. (1942–3). 'Chronique des fouilles et découvertes archéologiques en Grèce en 1942: Gortys (Arcadie)', *Bulletin de correspondance hellénique*, 66–7: 334–9.

Mattern, T. (2010). 'Theisoa. New Research and the Consequences for the History of the Alpheios Valley', delivered at the Annual Open Meeting of the Netherlands Institute at Athens, 18 March.

Mee, C., and Spawforth, A. (2001). *Greece: Oxford Archaeological Guides*. Oxford: Oxford University Press.

Metzger, H. (1951). 'Chronique des fouilles et découvertes archéologiques en Grèce en 1950: Gortys (Arcadie)', *Bulletin de correspondance hellénique*, 75: 130–3.

Meyer, E. (1932). 'Methydreion', *Realencyclopädie der Classischen Altertumswissenschaft*, 15: 1387–91.

Meyer, E. (1934). 'Thelphusa', *Realencyclopädie der Classischen Altertumswissenschaft*, 5A: 1618–20.

Meyer, E. (1936a). 'Theisoa', *Realencyclopädie der Classischen Altertumswissenschaft* 6A/1: 292–3.

Meyer, E. (1936b). 'Torthyneion', *Realencyclopädie der Classischen Altertumswissenschaft*, 5: 1806.

Meyer, E. (1938). 'Phigaleia', *Realencyclopädie der Classischen Altertumswissenschaft*, 19: 2065–85.

Meyer, E. (1939a). *Peloponnesische Wanderungen: Reisen und Forschungen zur antiken und mittelalterlichen Topographie von Arkadia und Achaia*. Zurich and Leipzig: M. Niehans.

Meyer, E. (1939b). 'Orchomenos 4', *Realencyclopädie der Classischen Altertumswissenschaft*, 17: 887–905.

Meyer, E. (1939c). 'Oresthasion', *Realencyclopädie der Classischen Altertumswissenschaft*, 18: 1014–16.

Meyer, E. (1942). 'Paion', *Realencyclopädie der Classischen Altertumswissenschaft*, 18: 2398–400.

Meyer, E. (1949). 'Pallantion', *Realencyclopädie der Classischen Altertumswissenschaft*, 18: 231–4.

Meyer, E. (1959). 'Psophis', *Realencyclopädie der Classischen Altertumswissenschaft*, 23: 1421–8.

Miller, S. G. (1995). 'Architecture as Evidence for the Identity of the Early *Polis*', in M. H. Hansen (ed.), *Sources for the Ancient Greek City-State*. Acts of the Copenhagen Polis Centre 2. Det Kongelige Danske Videnskabernes Selskab, Historisk-filosofiske Meddelelser 72. Copenhagen: Munksgaard, 201–44.

Moggi, M. (1974). 'Il sinescismo di Megalopoli', *Annali della Scuola Normale Superiore di Pisa*, 3/4: 71–107.

Morgan, C. (1999). 'Cultural Subzones in Early Iron Age and Archaic Arkadia?', in T. H. Nielsen and J. Roy (eds), *Defining Ancient Arkadia*. Acts of the Copenhagen Polis Centre 6. Det Kongelige Danske Videnskabernes Selskab, Historisk-filosofiske Meddelelser 78. Copenhagen: Munksgaard, 382–456.

Nielsen, T. H. (1996a). 'Arkadia. City-Ethnics and Tribalism', in M. H. Hansen (ed.), *Introduction to an Inventory of Poleis*. Acts of the Copenhagen Polis Centre 3. Det Kongelige Danske Videnskabernes Selskab, Historisk-filosofiske Meddelelser 74. Copenhagen: Munksgaard, 117–63.

Nielsen, T. H. (1996b). 'A Survey of Dependent *Poleis* in Classical Arkadia', in M. H. Hansen and K. Raaflaub (eds), *More Studies in the Ancient Greek Polis*. Papers from the Copenhagen Polis Centre 3. Historia Einzelschriften 108. Stuttgart: Franz Steiner Verlag, 63–105.

Nielsen, T. H. (1996c). 'Was There an Arkadian Confederacy in the Fifth Century?', in M. H. Hansen and K. Raaflaub (eds), *More Studies in the Ancient Greek Polis*. Papers from the Copenhagen Polis Centre 3. Historia Einzelschriften 108. Stuttgart: Franz Steiner Verlag, 39–62.

Nielsen, T. H. (1997). 'Triphylia. An Experiment in Ethnic Construction and Political Organization', in T. H. Nielsen (ed.), *Yet More Studies in the Ancient Greek Polis*. Papers from the Copenhagen Polis Centre 4. Historia Einzelschriften 117. Stuttgart: Franz Steiner Verlag, 129–62.

Nielsen, T. H. (1999). 'The Concept of Arkadia: The People, their Land, and their Organization', in T. H. Nielsen and J. Roy (eds), *Defining Ancient Arkadia*. Acts of the Copenhagen Polis Centre 6. Det Kongelige Danske Videnskabernes Selskab, Historisk-filosofiske Meddelelser 78. Copenhagen: Munksgaard, 16–88.

Nielsen, T. H. (2002). *Arkadia and its Poleis in the Archaic and Classical Periods*. Hypomnemata 140. Göttingen: Vandenhoeck und Ruprecht.

Nielsen, T. H., and Roy, J. (1998). 'The Azanians of Northern Arkadia', *Classica et mediaevalia: Revue danoise de philologie et d'histoire*, 49: 5–44.

Nielsen, T. H., and Roy, J. (1999). 'Introduction: Progress in Arkadia', in T. H. Nielsen and J. Roy (eds), *Defining Ancient Arkadia*. Acts of the Copenhagen Polis Centre 6. Det Kongelige Danske Videnskabernes Selskab, Historisk-filosofiske Meddelelser 78. Copenhagen: Munksgaard, 7–15.

Noack, F. (1927). *Eleusis*. Berlin: von Walther de Gruyter.

Norlin, G. (1980). *Isocrates: Isocrates with an English Translation in Three Volumes*. Cambridge: G. P. Putnam's Sons.

Norman, N. J. (1984). 'The Temple of Athena Alea at Tegea', *American Journal of Archaeology*, 88/2: 169–94.

Ober, J. (1985). *Fortress Attica: Defense of the Attic Land Frontier, 404–322 B.C.* Leiden: Brill.

Ober, J. (1987). 'Early Artillery Towers: Messenia, Boiotia, Attica, Megarid', *American Jounral of Archaeology*, 91/4: 569–604.

Ødegård, K. (2005). 'The Topography of Ancient Tegea: New Discoveries and Old Problems', in E. Østby (ed.), *Ancient Arcadia: Papers from the Third International*

Seminar on Ancient Arcadia, Held at the Norwegian Institute at Athens, 7–10 May 2002. Athens: Norwegian Institute at Athens, 209–24.

Ødegård, K. (forthcoming). 'State Formation and Urbanization at Tegea', in K. Tausand (ed.), *Arkadien im Altertum Geschichte und Kultur einer antiken Gebirgslandschaft. Ancient Arcadia—History and Culture of a Mountainous Region. University of Graz, Graz, Austria, 11–13 February 2016*.

Oikonomos, G. P. (1910–11). 'Anaskaphai en Thisoas', *Praktika*, 243–4.

Orlandos, A. (1924). 'Anaskaphai en Stymphalo', *Praktika*, 117–23.

Orlandos, A. (1925). 'Anaskaphai en Stymphalo', *Praktika*, 51–5.

Orlandos, A. (1926). 'Anaskaphai en Stymphalo', *Praktika*, 131–6.

Orlandos, A. (1927). 'Anaskaphai en Stymphalo', *Praktika*, 53–6.

Orlandos, A. (1928). 'Anaskaphai en Stymphalo', *Praktika*, 120–3.

Orlandos, A. (1929). 'Anaskaphai en Stymphalo', *Praktika*, 92.

Orlandos, A. (1930). 'Anaskaphai en Stymphalo', *Praktika*, 88–91.

Orlandos, A. K. (1967–8). *Η αρκαδική Αλίφειρα και τα μνημεία της*. Athens.

Østby, E. (1994). 'Recent Excavations in the Sanctuary of Athena Alea at Tegea (1990–93)', in K. A. Sheedy (ed.), *Archaeology in the Peloponnese: New Excavations and Research*. The Australian Archaeological Institute at Athens. Oxbow Monograph 48. Oxford: Oxbow Books, 39–63.

Østby, E. (2014a) (ed.). *Tegea I: Investigations in the Sanctuary of Athena Alea 1991–94*. Papers and Monographs from the Norwegian Institute at Athens. Athens: Norwegian Institute at Athens, iii.

Østby, E. (2014b) (ed.). *Tegea II: Investigations in the Sanctuary of Athena Alea 1990–94 and 2004*. Papers and Monographs from the Norwegian Institute at Athens. Athens: Norwegian Institute at Athens, iv.

Pakkanen, J. (1998). *The Temple of Athena Alea at Tegea: A Reconstruction of the Peristyle Column*. Publications by the Department of Art History at the University of Helsinki, vol. 18, Department of Art History and the Foundation of the Finnish Institute in Athens, Helsinki.

Pakkanen, J. (2005). 'The Temple of Athena Alea at Tegea: Revisiting Design-Unit Derivation from Building Measurements', in E. Østby (ed.), *Ancient Arcadia: Papers from the Third International Seminar on Ancient Arcadia, Held at the Norwegian Institute at Athens, 7–10 May 2002*. Athens: Norwegian Institute at Athens, 167–84.

Papachatzis, N. D. (1994). *ΠΑΥΣΑΝΙΟΥ ΕΛΛΑΔΟΣ ΠΕΡΙΗΓΗΣΙΣ. ΒΙΒΛΙΑ 7 καί 8. ΑΧΑΪΚΑ καί ΑΡΚΑΔΙΑ*. Athens: *Εκδοτική Αθηνών*.

Papandreou, G. (1920). '*Αρχαιολογικαι και τοπογραφικαι ερευναι εν τη επαρχια Καλαβρυτων*', *PAE* 95–146.

Parke, H. W. (1933). *Greek Mercenaries Soldiers: From the Earliest Times to the Battle of Ipsos*. Oxford: Clarendon Press.

Perlman, P. (1995). '*ΘΕΩΡΟΔΟΚΟΥΝΤΕΣ ΕΝ ΤΑΙΣ ΠΟΛΕΣΙΝ*: Panhellenic *Epangelia* and Political Status', in M. H. Hansen (ed.), *Sources for the Ancient Greek City-State*. Acts of the Copenhagen Polis Centre 2. Det Kongelige Danske Videnskabernes Selskab, Historisk-filosofiske Meddelelser 72. Copenhagen: Munksgaard, 113–64.

Petritaki, M. (1987). 'Chronika', *Arch. Delt*. 42: 164.

Petritaki, M. (1988). 'Chronika', *Arch. Delt*. 43: 163–44.

Petritaki, M. (1989). 'Chronika', *Arch. Delt.* 44: 137.

Petritaki, M. (1991). 'Chronika', *Arch. Delt.* 46: 152.

Petritaki, M. (1992). 'Chronika', *Arch. Delt.* 47: 144–6.

Petritaki, M. (1993). 'Chronika', *Arch. Delt.* 48: 128–30.

Petritaki, M. (1996). 'Κλειτωρ, μια πολη της Αρκαδικης Αζανιας', *Αρχαιολογια και Τεχνες*, 61: 81–8.

Petritaki, M. (2005). 'Κλειτωρ. Η πολη υπο το φως των ανασκαφων Γενικηθεωρηση ανασκαφικων δεδομενων', in E. Østby (ed.), *Ancient Arcadia. Papers from the Third International Seminar on Ancient Arcadia, Held at the Norwegian Institute at Athens, 7–10 May 2002.* Athens: Norwegian Institute at Athens, 351–62.

Petropoulos, M. (2005). 'Ερευνες για την αρχαια Ψωφιδα', in E. Østby (ed.), *Ancient Arcadia. Papers from the Third International Seminar on Ancient Arcadia, Held at the Norwegian Institute at Athens, 7–10 May 2002.* Athens: Norwegian Institute at Athens, 363–76.

Philippson, A. (1903). 'Dipaia', *Realencyclopädie der Classischen Altertumswissenschaft*, 5/1: 1151.

Pikoulas, Y. A. (1981). 'Τοπογραφικα Περιοχης Καλαβρυτων. Συμβολη Προτη', *Επετηριδα των Καλαβρυτων, τομ. ΙΒ '- ΙΓ'*. Athens, 3–38.

Pikoulas, Y. A. (1983). 'Αλιφειρα, το προαστειον της αχρας', *Horos*, 1: 45–55.

Pikoulas, Y. A. (1984). 'Μαντινειακά', *Horos*, 2: 205–7.

Pikoulas, Y. A. (1986). 'Ο αρχαιος οικισμος της Δημητσανας', *Horos*, 4: 99–123.

Pikoulas, Y. A. (1988). 'Η Νοτια Μεγαλοπολιτικη χωρα, απο τον 8ο π.Χ. ως τον 4ο μ.Χ. αιωνα', Ph.D. dissertation, University of Ioannina, Athens.

Pikoulas, Y. A. (1990–1a). 'Το Τορθυνειον της Αρκαδιας', *Horos*, 8–9: 135–52.

Pikoulas, Y. A. (1990–1b). 'Πυργοι: Δικτυο, χρηση, απορ…ες και ερωτηματα', *Horos*, 8–9: 247–57.

Pikoulas, Y. (1990–1c). 'Κλιμαξ (Παυσ. 8.6.4)', *Horos*, 8–9: 279–83.

Pikoulas, Y. A. (1991). 'ΤΟ ΟΧΥΠΟ ΣΤΗΝ ΚΕΡΤΕΖΗ ΚΑΛΑΒΡΥΤΩΝ', in *Achaia und Elis in der Antike. ΜΕΛΕΤΗΜΑΤΑ 13.* Athens, 265–8.

Pikoulas, Y. A. (1992–3). "Το οδικο δικτυο της κεντρικης Αρκαδιας', in *Διεθνούς Συνεδρίου Πελοποννησιακών Σπουδών, Κόρινθος, 9–16 Σεπτεμβρίου 1990*, 2: 201–6, Athens.

Pikoulas, Y. A. (1995). *Οδικό δίκτυο καί άμυνα. Από τήν Κόρινθο στό 'Αργος καί τήν Αρκαδία.* Athens: Horos.

Pikoulas, Y. A. (1999a). 'The Road-Network of Arkadia', in T. H. Nielsen and J. Roy (eds), *Defining Ancient Arkadia.* Acts of the Copenhagen Polis Centre 6. Det Kongelige Danske Videnskabernes Selskab, Historisk-filosofiske Meddelelser 78. Copenhagen: Munksgaard, 248–319.

Pikoulas, Y. A. (1999b). 'Ο ανω ρους του Ελλισσοοντος. Οδικο δικτυο και οικιστικο πλεγμα', *Horos*, 13: 97–132.

Pikoulas, Y. A. (1999c). 'Κλειτορια. Διαβασεις και αμυνα', *Horos*, 13: 137–54.

Pikoulas, Y. A. (2001). *Λεξικό των οικισμών της Πελοποννήσου: παλαιά και νέα τοπωνύμια.* Athens: Horos.

Pikoulas, Y. A. (forthcoming). 'The "Twins" of Arkadia: The Homonym Settlements', in K. Tausand (ed.), *Arkadien im Altertum Geschichte und Kultur einer antiken Gebirgslandschaft. Ancient Arcadia—History and Culture of a Mountainous Region. University of Graz, Graz, Austria, 11–13 February 2016.*

Plassart, A. (1921). 'Inscriptions de Delphes, la liste des Théorodoques', *Bulletin de correspondance hellénique*, 45: 1–85.

Pretzler, M. (forthcoming). 'Arkadians and Peloponnesians: Collaboration and Conflict with Sparta in the Sixth and Fifth Century BC', in K. Tausand (ed.), *Arkadien im Altertum Geschichte und Kultur einer antiken Gebirgslandschaft. Ancient Arcadia—History and Culture of a Mountainous Region. University of Graz, Graz, Austria, 11–13 February 2016.*

Pritchett, W. K. (1969). *Studies in Ancient Greek Topography. Part II.* Berkeley and Los Angeles: University of California Press.

Pritchett, W. K. (1989). *Studies in Ancient Greek Topography. Part VI.* Berkeley and Los Angeles: University of California Press.

Protonotariou-Deilaki, E. (1961–2). 'Chronika', *Arch. Delt.* 17: 57.

Protonotariou-Deilaki, E. (1965). 'Chronika', *Arch. Delt.* 20: 158.

Rangabé, M. (1857). *Souvenirs d'une Excursion d'Athènes en Arcadie.* Mémoires présentés par divers savants à l'Académie des inscriptions et belles-lettres de l'Institut de France. Première série, Sujets divers d'érudition. Paris.

Ray, F. E. (2011). *Land Battles in 5th Century B.C. Greece: A History and Analysis of 173 Engagements.* London: McFarland.

Reekmans, T. (1955.) 'Chronique des fouilles en Grèce en 1954: Gortys (Arcadie), Les plateaux au S.-E. du sanctuaire', *Bulletin de correspondance hellénique*, 79: 335–40.

Reekmans, T. (1956). 'Chronique des fouilles en Grèce en 1955: Gortys (Arcadie), Les plateaux située au S.-E. du sanctuaire du bas', *Bulletin de correspondance hellénique*, 80: 401–6.

Rhodes, P. J. (1995). 'Epigraphical Evidence: Laws and Decrees', in M. H. Hansen (ed.), *Sources for the Ancient Greek City-State.* Acts of the Copenhagen Polis Centre 2. Det Kongelige Danske Videnskabernes Selskab, Historisk-filosofiske Meddelelser 72. Copenhagen: Munksgaard, 91–112.

Richards, G. C. (1892). 'The Agora', in *Excavations at Megalopolis 1890–91: The Society for the Promotion of Hellenic Studies: Supplementary Papers, No. 1.* London: Macmillan, 101–5.

Rochas d'Aiglun, A. de (1881). *Principes de la fortification antique.* Revue générale de l'architecture et des travaux publics 37. Paris: Ducher & Cie.

Romaios, K. A. (1957). Ἱερὸν Ἀθηνας Σωτειρας και Ποσειδωνος κατα την Ἀρκαδικην Ἀσεαν', *Archaiologike Ephemeris*, 114–63.

Romaios, K. A. (1958). Ἀνασκαφαι εν Παλλαντιω και Ιασω', *Praktika*, 165–6.

Ross, L. (1841). *Reisen und Reiserouten durch Griechenland. Erster Theil: Reisen im Peloponnes. Mit zwei Karten und mehreren* Holzschnitten *und Inschriften.* Berlin: G. Reimer.

Roy, J. (1968). 'Studies in the History of Arcadia in the Classical and Hellenistic Periods', Ph.D. dissertation, Cambridge University.

Roy, J. (1972a). 'An Arkadian League in the Earlier Fifth Century?', *Phoenix*, 26: 129–36.

Roy, J. (1972b). 'Orchomenus and Clitor', *Classical Quarterly*, 22: 78–80.

Roy, J. (1996). '*Polis* and Tribe in Classical Arkadia', in M. H. Hansen and K. Raaflaub (eds), *More Studies in the Ancient Greek Polis.* Papers from the Copenhagen Polis Centre 3. Historia Einzelschriften 108. Stuttgart: Franz Steiner Verlag, 107–12.

Roy, J. (1999). 'The Economies of Arkadia', in T. H. Nielsen and J. Roy (eds), *Defining Ancient Arkadia*. Acts of the Copenhagen Polis Centre 6. Det Kongelige Danske Videnskabernes Selskab, Historisk-filosofiske Meddelelser 78. Copenhagen: Munksgaard, 320–81.

Roy, J. (2000). 'The Frontier between Arkadia and Elis in Classical Antiquity', in P. Flensted-Jansen, T. H. Nielsen, and L. Rubinstein (eds), *Polis and Politics: Studies in Ancient Greek History Presented to Mogens Herman Hansen on his Sixtieth Birthday, August 20, 2000*. Copenhagen: Museum Tusculanum Press, 133–56.

Roy, J. (2005). 'Synoikizing Megalopolis: The Scope of the Synoikism and the Interests of Local Arkadian Communities', in E. Østby (ed.), *Ancient Arcadia: Papers from the Third International Seminar on Ancient Arcadia, Held at the Norwegian Institute at Athens, 7–10 May 2002*. Athens: Norwegian Institute at Athens, 261–70.

Roy, J. (2007). 'The Urban Layout of Megalopolis in its Civic and Confederate Context', in R. Westgate, N. Fisher, and J. Whitley (eds), *Building Communities: House, Settlement, and Society in the Aegean and Beyond: Proceedings of a Conference Held at Cardiff University, 17–21 April 2001*. British School at Athens Studies 15. London: British School at Athens, 289–96.

Roy, J., Lloyd, J. A., and Owen, E. J. (1988). 'Tribe and Polis in the Chora at Megalopolis: Changes in Settlement Pattern in Relation to Synoikism', in Διεθνούς Συνεδρίου Πελοποννησιακών Σπουδών, Αθήνα, 4–10 Σεπτεμβρίου 1983. Athens. 12: 179–82.

Sarantakes, P. (1993). Αρκαδία. Οι Ακροπόλεις, τα Κάστρα καί οι Πύργοι τής, σιωπηλά ερείπια μιας δοξασμένης γης. Athens: Οιάτης Εκδόσεις.

Scranton, R. (1941). *Greek Walls*. Cambridge, MA: Harvard University Press.

Schaus, G. (2014). *Stymphalos: The Acropolis Sanctuary, Volume 1*. Toronto: University of Toronto Press.

Schultz, R. W. (1892). 'Architectural Description and Analysis', in *Excavations at Megalopolis 1890–91*. The Society for the Promotion of Hellenic Studies: Supplementary Papers, No. 1. London: Macmillan, 15–68.

Smith, W. (1873a). 'Arcadia', in W. Smith (ed.), *Dictionary of Greek and Roman Geography*. London: Little, Brown & Co., 189–93.

Smith, W. (1873b). 'Teuthis', in W. Smith (ed.), *Dictionary of Greek and Roman Geography*. London: Little, Brown & Co., 1133.

Snodgrass, A. (1982). 'The Historical Significance of Fortification in Archaic Greece', in H. Tréziny and P. Leriche (eds), *La Fortification dans l'histoire du monde Grec. CNRS Colloque International 614, December 1982*. Paris: Éditions du Centre national de la recherche scientifique, 125–31.

Snodgrass, A. M. (1980). *Archaic Greece: The Age of Experiment*. London: J. M. Dent.

Tarditi, C. (2005). 'The Sanctuary of Athena Alea at Tegea: Recent Excavations in the Northern Area. Results and Problems', in E. Østby (ed.), *Ancient Arcadia. Papers from the Third International Seminar on Ancient Arcadia, Held at the Norwegian Institute at Athens, 7–10 May 2002*. Athens: Norwegian Institute at Athens, 197–208.

Tausend, K. (1998a). 'Ein Rundturm in der Pheneatike und die Pyramiden der Argolis', *ÖJh* 67: 37–50.

Tausend, K. (1998b). 'Der Arkadienfeldzug Kleomenes III. Im jahre 225', *RSA* 28: 51–7.

Tausend, K. (1998c). 'Der antike Weg von Pheneos nach Orchomenos', *Jahreshefte des Österreichischen Archäologischen Instituts*, 67: 109–16.

Tausend, K. (1999a) (ed.). *Pheneos und Lousi. Untersuchungen zu Geschichte und Topographie Nordostarkadiens*, Grazer Altertumskundliche Studien 5. Frankfurt am Main: P. Lang.

Tausend, K. (1999b). 'Fortifikatorische Anlagen in den Gebieten von Lousi und Pheneos', in K. Tausend (ed.), *Pheneos und Lousoi. Untersuchungen zu Geschichte und Topographie Nordostarkadiens*, Grazer Altertumskundlische Studien 5. Frankfurt am Main: P. Lang, 306–20.

Tausend, K. (forthcoming). 'Möglichkeiten der Poliorketik in Arkadien', in K. Tausand (ed.), *Arkadien im Altertum Geschichte und Kultur einer antiken Gebirgslandschaft. Ancient Arcadia—History and Culture of a Mountainous Region. University of Graz, Graz, Austria, 11–13 February 2016.*

Tausend, K., and Tausend, S. (2014). 'Die Mauren von Pheneos und der Mäusekrieg', in K. Freitag and C. Michels (eds), *Athen und/oder Alexandria? Aspekte von Identität und Ethnizität im hellenistischen Griechenland.* Cologne: Böhlau Verlag, 19–49.

Tomlinson, R. A. (1961). 'Emplekton Masonry and "Greek Structura"', *Journal of Hellenic Studies*, 81: 133–40.

Topouzi, S., Sarris, A., Pikoulas, Y., Mertikas, S., Frantzis, X., and Giourou, A. (2002). 'Ancient Mantineia's Defence Network Reconsidered through a GIS Approach', in G. Burenhult and J. Arvidsson (eds), *Archaeological Informatics: Pushing the Envelope. CAA2001. Computer Applications and Quantitative Methods in Archaeology. Proceedings of the 29th Conference, Gotland, April 2001.* Oxford: Archaeopress, 559–66.

Topouzi, S., Soetens, S., Gkiourou, G., and Sarris, A. (2000). 'The Application of Viewshed Analysis in Greek Archaeological Landscape', *6th Annual Meeting of the European Association of Archaeologists, Lisbon, Portugal, 10–17 September 2000*, 1–15.

Tsiogas, A. (2013). 'Stymphalia', in K. Kissas (ed.), *Ancient Corinthia: From Prehistoric to the End of Antiquity.* Athens: Foinikas Publications, 135–7.

Typaldou-Fakiris, C. (2004). *Villes fortifiées de Phocide: Et la 3ᵉ guerre sacrée (356–346 J.C.)* Provence: Publications de l'Université de Provence.

Voyatzis, M. E. (1990). *The Early Sanctuary of Athena Alea and Other Archaic Santuaries in Arcadia.* Studies in Mediterranean Archaeology and Literature 97. Göteborg: Paul Åströms Förlag.

Voyatzis, M. E. (2005). 'Pottery at the Crossroads: Ceramic Trends in South-East Arcadia', in E. Østby (ed.), *Ancient Arcadia. Papers from the Third International Seminar on Ancient Arcadia, Held at the Norwegian Institute at Athens, 7–10 May 2002.* Athens: Norwegian Institute at Athens, 467–82.

Welcker, F. G. (1865). *Tagebuch einer griechischen Reise.* Berlin: Verlag von Wilhelm Hertz.

Williams, H. (1983). 'Stymphalos: A Planned City of Ancient Arkadia', *Echos du Monde Classique/Classical Views*, 27: 194–205.

Williams, H. (1984). 'Investigations at Mytilene and Stymphalos', *Echos du Monde Classique/Classical Views*, 28: 174–86.

Williams, H. (1985). 'Investigations at Stymphalos, 1984', *Echos du Monde Classique/ Classical Views*, 29: 215–24.

Williams, H. (1996). 'Excavations at Ancient Stymphalos, 1995', *Echos du Monde Classique/Classical Views*, 15: 75–98.

Williams, H., and Cronkite-Price, S. M. (1995). 'Excavations at Ancient Stymphalos, 1994', *Echos du Monde Classique/Classical Views*, 14: 1–22.

Williams, H., Schaus, G., Cronkite-Price, S. M., Gourley, B., and Hagerman, C. (1998). 'Excavations at Ancient Stymphalos, 1997', *Echos du Monde Classique/Classical Views*, 17: 261–319.

Williams, H., Schaus, G., Cronkite-Price, S. M., Gourley, B., and Lutomsky, H. (1997). 'Excavations at Ancient Stymphalos, 1996', *Echos du Monde Classique/Classical Views*, 16: 23–73.

Williams, H., Schaus, G., Gourley, B., Cronkite-Price, S. M., Donahue-Sherwood, K., and Lolos, Y. (2002). 'Excavations at Ancient Stymphalos, 1999–2002', *Mouseion*, 3: 135–87.

Winter, F. E. (1971a). *Greek Fortifications*. Toronto: University of Toronto Press.

Winter, F. E. (1971b). 'The Indented Trace in Later Greek Fortifications', *American Journal of Archaeology*, 75/4: 413–26.

Winter, F. E. (1982). 'A Summary of Recent Work on Greek Fortifications in Greece and Asia Minor', in H. Tréziny and P. Leriche (eds), *La Fortification dans l'histoire du monde Grec. CNRS Colloque International 614, Decembre 1982*. Paris: Éditions du Centre national de la Recherche scientifique, 23–9.

Winter, F. E. (1989). 'Arkadian Notes, II: The Walls of Mantinea, Orchomenos, and Kleitor', *Echos du Monde Classique/Classical Views*, 33: 189–200.

Winter, F. E. (1997). 'Use of Artillery in Fourth-Century and Hellenistic Towers', *Echos du Monde Classique/Classical Views*, 41: 247–92.

Winter, F. E. (2005). 'Arkadian Temple Designs', in E. Østby (ed.), *Ancient Arcadia. Papers from the Third International Seminar on Ancient Arcadia, Held at the Norwegian Institute at Athens, 7–10 May 2002*. Athens: Norwegian Institute at Athens, 483–93.

Woodhouse, W. J. (1892). 'Historical Sketch', in *Excavations at Megalopolis 1890–91. The Society for the Promotion of Hellenic Studies: Supplementary Papers, No. 1.* London: Macmillan, 1–5.

Wrede, W. (1933). *Attische Mauern*. Athens: Deutsche Archäologische Institut.

Wycherley, R. E. (1962). *How the Greeks Built Cities*. London: Macmillan.

Wyse, T. (1865). *An Excursion in the Peloponnesus in the Year 1858*, ed. W. M. Wyse. London: Day.

Index